S0-AJC-067

Praise for

HARRY S. TRUMAN AND THE WAR SCARE OF 1948

"This book is indispensable for those who are concerned about the Cold War's origins—and how those origins continue to shape the post-Cold War 1990s. . . . It provides a badly needed balance (and substance) in our view of Truman's policies. Overwhelmingly researched, written with clarity and considerable passion, highly provocative, Kofsky's volume is one of those small number of books that are at the center of arguments over the Cold War's causes and present consequences."

Professor Walter LaFeber
Cornell University

"This book is nothing if not controversial, provocative, irreverent and fun to read. Thanks to the author's good humor and zestful style, this is the first I have caught myself laughing out loud while reading a serious historical study."

Professor G. William Domhoff
University of California, Santa Cruz

"An intriguing, richly researched revelation of how big industry, government, and the military consciously stoked the Cold War fires and conspired to deceive the American public in order to serve their own interests."

Dr. Michael Parenti

"Frank Kofsky has done an extraordinary job of research into one of the critical moments of American foreign policy after World War II. His book has powerful implications for American society today."

Professor Howard Zinn
Boston University (Emeritus)

"A provocative, irreverent effort to demystify the foreign policy of Harry S. Truman. Superbly researched, it offers both new evidence and a fresh perspective on the origins of the military-industrial complex and the Cold War that spawned it."

Professor Thomas J. McCormick
University of Wisconsin, Madison

"Scrupulously researched and boldly narrated, Frank Kofsky's book develops a startling thesis that can't easily be dismissed: that in 1948 the Truman Administration purposely hoodwinked Congress into believing that Stalin was prepared to initiate war in Western Europe. This landmark study cannot be ignored by any serious student of the Cold War."

Professor Douglas Brinkley
University of New Orleans

By the same author

Black Nationalism and the Revolution in Music

Lenny Bruce: The Comedian as Social Critic and Secular Moralist

HARRY S. TRUMAN AND THE WAR SCARE OF 1948

A Successful Campaign to Deceive the Nation

Frank Kofsky

St. Martin's Press
New York

HARRY S. TRUMAN AND THE WAR SCARE OF 1948

St. Martin's Press, 175 Fifth Avenue,
New York, N.Y. 10010

The author acknowledges with gratitude that material from the papers of James V. Forrestal, Ferdinand Eberstadt, Arthur Krock and David E. Lilienthal is published by permission of Princeton University Libraries, and that material from the papers of Winthrop W. Aldrich is published by permission of the Baker Library, Harvard University Graduate School of Business Administration.

ISBN 0-312-12329-9 (paperback)

Library of Congress Cataloging-in-Publication Data

Kofsky, Frank.
Harry S. Truman and the war scare of 1948 : a successful campaign to deceive the nation / Frank Kofsky. — [Rev. ed.]
p. cm.
Originally published: 1993. Contains new foreword and minor corrections.
Includes bibliographical references (p.) and index.
ISBN 0-312-12329-9 (paperback)
1. United States—Foreign relations—Soviet Union. 2. Soviet Union—Foreign relations—United States. 3. United States—Foreign relations—1945-1953. 4. Truman, Harry S., 1884-1972. 5. Aircraft industry—Military aspects—United States. I. Title.
E183.8.S65K63 1995
327.73047'09'044—dc20 94-33637
CIP

First published in hardcover in the United States of America 1993.
First Paperback Edition February 1995:
10 9 8 7 6 5 4 3 2 1

To my loving wife Bonnie

CONTENTS

PREFACE AND ACKNOWLEDGMENTS

I cannot praise too highly the directors of the Harry S. Truman Library Institute for their commitment to disinterested scholarship, let the chips fall where they may. Knowing full well that my findings were unlikely to be flattering to the Truman administration, the directors nonetheless chose to confer on me the Institute's Senior Scholar Award for 1991. Without this fellowship, which enabled me to extend my sabbatical leave to twice its original length, there is no telling how many years more I would have needed to complete the research that has gone into this book. For that reason, I am profoundly grateful to the Institute, and to Dr. Benedict K. Zobrist, its secretary, for esteeming truth above hagiography.

It has also been very gratifying to me that, both at the beginning and at the end, my colleagues on the Research Committee at California State University (CSU), Sacramento, have thought highly enough of this project to allot me the maximum amounts of time at their disposal in order to pursue it. At the outset, during the mid-1980s, a series of partial leaves for the purpose of research enabled me to start delving into the sources; at the finish, a one-semester leave—the sole one available on our campus during the 1991–1992 academic year—made it possible for me to put my manuscript in final form. In addition, I am indebted to the American Council of Learned Societies for a grant that helped defray the expenses of visiting libraries and depositories on the East Coast, and to the staff of the Office of Research and Sponsored Projects at CSU, Sacramento, for helping me over the hurdles in applying for this and other awards.

Tina Bird, Tracey Louper and Deborah Kearney were my first research assistants, and they set a high standard that was difficult to match; subsequently, Scott Graves, Barbara Aitken and Chris Rush also aided me in the pursuit of elusive documents. Fred Simonelli's exploration of the papers of Winthrop W. Aldrich, former chairman of the Chase National Bank, supplied valuable information on that institution's involvement in the aircraft industry.

Anyone who has ever made use of a manuscript library knows that it is the archivists who are the true, if unsung, heroes and heroines of historical scholarship. Authors may have their names on the spines of books—but it is the archivists on whom they depend to put the all-important documents in their hands. At the National Archives in Washington, D.C., Wil Mahoney and Ed Reese initiated my wife, Bonnie, and me into the mysteries of the records of the Armed Services and the Department of Defense. Dr. Glenn Cook, archivist-librarian at the George C. Marshall Library at the Virginia Military Institute in Lexington, combined professional assistance with generous hospitality. Mike Klein at the Library of Congress gave us a warm welcome on our first full day in Washington and was the source of several fruitful leads in the bargain. Jean Holliday took great pains to see that we were well cared for both inside and outside of the Seeley G. Mudd Manuscript Library of Princeton University; and Dr. Ben Primer, the library's director, was most accommodating in securing permission to cite a vast number of items from the collections he supervises. Ever since we first had the pleasure of making their acquaintance, Elizabeth Safly and Dennis Bilger at the Harry S. Truman Library in Independence, Missouri, have been unfailingly kind and gracious, going far beyond the call of duty in answering our questions, pointing us in the proper direction and calling our attention to items that we otherwise might have overlooked. Our obligation to them is not one we will soon discharge. Being able to count Dr. Cary Conn, the Freedom of Information officer at the National Archives facility in Suitland, Maryland, as a new-found friend is one of the fringe benefits of work such as this. Without his intercession, we might still be awaiting the declassification of innumerable boxes of records from the late 1940s; and without his companionship, our visit to Washington, D.C., would have been inestimably less rewarding in every way.

I hope this book will gladden the heart of Esther Carash, who involved herself in my upbringing exactly as a protective aunt should (even if her headstrong nephew was not always sufficiently appreciative at the time). I am obliged to Ingrid Andenaes for her suggestions about the cover design and to Lora Schactili for her inspired ideas on how to bring this book to the attention of the reading public. Besides tenaciously defending the interests of the writers she represents, Deborah Kitchin, the guiding spirit behind Calibre Literary Services, tolerates their idiosyncrasies, incessant questions and endless importunings with good grace and unfailing equanimity. Working with her has been an education in the ways and mores of the book-publishing trade, and I sleep better knowing I can rely upon her vigilance. I am sure this book has been much improved by the efforts of Simon Winder, the senior editor of the Scholarly and Reference Division at St. Martin's Press, and the members of his staff who have tried valiantly, if not always successfully, to wean the author from his own folly.

I am very fortunate to have had the support of a number of scholars—none of whom, of course, deserves the least blame for the contents of these pages. The probing questions of Richard Kirkendall and William S. Borden forced me to sharpen both my thinking and, I would like to believe, my prose; firm but insistent prodding from Bill Domhoff, whose friendship extends back over three decades, also inspired me to dig deeper into the sources and to clarify various aspects of my thesis. Melvyn Leffler generously wrote on my behalf on several occasions. William E. Pemberton supplied welcome encouragement, as did Richard C. Lower and Margaret Goodart, two close colleagues in the Department of History at California State University, Sacramento. I doubt I will ever be able to offer adequate thanks to Walter LaFeber, who saw promise in this project when it was still in its infancy and interceded right from the first to open doors for me that otherwise might have remained tightly closed.

For more than a quarter of a century, Thomas and Geri McCormick have been the most loving of friends, sharing the good times and standing by me in the bad. The knowledge that their confidence in me has never wavered sustained me in those moments when my own did.

It is customary for an author's acknowledgments to close with a lavish tribute to the long-suffering spouse who made it all possible—but Bonnie Kofsky's indispensable role in the writing of this book has enormously exceeded the customary. (Indeed, if I had my way, she would be listed as a co-author; but Bonnie's unceremonious veto of my proposal to this effect was not couched in a tone that invited further discussion.) Suffice it to say that my amazing wife not only accompanied me on each of our several research trips, not only took charge of making all the preparations and arrangements for those trips, not only kept track of the interminable receipts, but actually did half of all the research as well. (She may, in fact, have done *more* than half, because sometimes I was able to sneak away to interrogate an archivist while she remained inundated in the sources). At every library and depository we visited, Bonnie sat directly alongside of me, opening carton upon dusty carton of letters or federal records, attacking one obscure, mind-numbing document after another. Thus, although it would be unjust to saddle her with any of the responsibility for the interpretation that this book advances, she certainly deserves full credit for unearthing many of the most revealing items I have cited (see the correspondence between W. Stuart Symington and Winthrop W. Aldrich for one example, and that between James V. Forrestal and Kenneth G. Reynolds for another). If it is absurd even to think about being able to repay a debt of such monumental proportions, I can at least enjoy the satisfaction of giving this wonderful woman a portion of her due. Let me, therefore, make it explicit: without the benefit of Bonnie's hard work, devotion, genius for organization and unfailing good humor, it is highly doubtful that this book would ever have managed to make its way into the world.

—F. K.

FOREWORD TO THE PAPERBACK EDITION

> **If there were no Devil, it would be necessary to invent him.**
>
> —François M. A. Voltaire, as revised in practice by the Truman administration[1]

THE WAR SCARE OF 1948 IN EUROPE

Ordinarily, few things give an author greater satisfaction than to be able to say that all the evidence come to light since the publication of his book has served only to confirm his initial conclusions. In this particular case, however, although recently discovered information does indeed support the portrait of the Truman administration that I drew in this book, whatever pleasure I might otherwise take from this fact is much diminished by the sordid nature of the fresh revelations.

Some of the new material concerns the European dimensions of the war scare of 1948. Already, in the cloth edition, I demonstrated that Truman and his chief officials—notably Secretary of State George C. Marshall and Secretary of Defense James V. Forrestal—contrived the scare in order to terrify Congress and the electorate into acquiescing in the administration's expensive and unpopular programs for foreign aid and a military buildup unprecedented in peacetime. But there was a European component to the scare as well: the Truman administration sought to use it to panic otherwise reluctant countries, especially (but not necessarily only) in Scandinavia, into joining the North Atlantic Treaty Organization (NATO). In reality, as now seems clear, Washington most likely intended certain aspects of the war-scare melodrama for European rather than U.S. audiences. This is especially true with respect to the Finnish phase of the production: of decidedly minor significance domestically, it had the most profound consequences for Denmark and Norway.

I learned of this aspect of the war scare from Poul Villaume, a colleague at the Institute of History at the University of Copenhagen. After reading the cloth edition of this work, Professor Villaume, whose book on the history of Denmark, NATO and the Cold War, *Cement of Fear: The Cold War and NATO Until 1961,* is due imminently,[2] wrote to me to recount "a true war scare" in the Scandinavian countries in March and early April of 1948. The scare, which began with "unidentified and ominous *rumors* coming out of . . . Western diplomatic circles in Moscow, Warsaw and Helsinki during the first week or ten days of March, 1948," became known as "the 'Easter Crisis,' since it took place during the Easter holidays of that year."[3] Previously, Scandinavian public opinion had favored neutrality in the Cold War. But, according to what Professor Villaume considers "the most detailed . . . account in the English language" of the decisions of the governments of Denmark and Norway to enter NATO, a study by the Norwegian scholar Magne Skodvin, the events comprising the war scare of 1948 "broke the deadlock."[4] Just as the scare successfully overwhelmed the opposition to the Truman administration's grandiose foreign-aid and military programs in the United States, so, too, did it demolish Danish and Norwegian resistance to enlisting in an explicitly anti-Soviet military alliance.

The curtain on Act I of the war scare in Scandinavia rose, as Professor Villaume notes, on rumors about "alleged imminent Soviet plans for pressuring Norway to conclude a bilateral security treaty along the lines of the bilateral Soviet-Finnish treaty which was actually being negotiated at that time"—hence the Truman administration's emphasis on Soviet-Finnish developments. "After careful reading of Skodvin's text and footnotes," he adds,

> you will conclude along with me: there is not the slightest *substantial* evidence here that warrants the . . . fear . . . in early March 1948 that the Soviets were actually about to put pressure upon the Oslo government to conclude a bilateral treaty with Moscow.
>
> Of course, this is not to say that (someone in) Moscow did not . . . harbour certain wishes of making a security treaty with Norway. The crucial point, however, that—to my best knowledge—*no evidence whatsoever on this has been produced until this moment* [emphasis added], neither from Western archives nor from the recently opened Soviet and East European archives of the late 1940s. And even more important: Western decision makers in March, 1948, did *not* have such information available. Yet they acted as if they did![5]

Professor Villaume's last point reinforces one I make later in this volume:

> the foreign policies of the Soviet Union as depicted by the top officials of the Truman administration were one thing; those policies as they existed in reality were quite another.

It was only rarely and by happenstance that the two coincided. What mattered, then, was not what the Soviets actually *did,* but rather what the ideologues of the Truman administration could convince others—at home or abroad—of what they had done or were about to do.

In Act II of the drama, the scare became more acute as it spread from Norway to Denmark: "The Danes were heavily influenced by the Norwegian (non)-events in early March . . . [and a] virtual War Scare engulfed Denmark, including the Prime Minister, during the latter part of March." Further ratcheting up the level of fear, "rumors of a Soviet attack on Denmark—or a partial Soviet aggression against some Danish strategic islands in the Baltic or the Kattegat coastal waters—[grew] ubiquitous," as a result of which, "the Danish Government immediately took several security and defense measures and introduced a degree of national emergency."

The scare reached its climax in Act III, when

> rumors of Soviet aggression towards Denmark and/or Scandinavia were intensified in Government circles by a very alarmist report delivered by a Danish diplomat at the Danish Embassy in Washington, Mr. Povl Bang-Jensen, who—after talks with State Department officials in Washington during the first two weeks in March—flew to Copenhagen to report personally to his Government about the feelings in the U.S. that war was imminent, etc. There is no doubt whatsoever that this experience and these rumors—although essentially unsubstantiated, as it soon turned out—contributed essentially to Denmark's and Norway's joining the Atlantic Pact (NATO) in April 1949.[6]

Of particular interest is the role played by the Truman administration in pouring oil on the fire of the war scare in Denmark:

> Certain intelligence information received in Copenhagen appeared to justify the fear of an immediate Soviet attack on Denmark; according to an extremely interesting and frank anonymous article one year later (April 18, 1949, i.e., two weeks *after* Denmark's joining the Atlantic

> Pact) in *Information,* a very pro-NATO, serious and well-informed Copenhagen newspaper (with close ties to the Danish defense and intelligence community), the intelligence service of the U.S. Air Force in Germany around mid-March, 1948, reported that Soviet troops were being concentrated in East Prussia under circumstances that appeared to indicate imminent aggressive operations towards [the] west (western Germany) or [the] north west (Denmark). However, according to the *Information* article, the U.S. Government very quickly established—via the CIA [Central Intelligence Agency]—that the reports of an imminent Soviet attack were a fraud; at the time, however, Washington did *not* inform the alarmed Danish Government about this. . . . The April, 1949, *Information* article concludes by stating that the reason why the disproof of the Soviet aggressive intentions towards Denmark in March, 1948, was not conveyed by Washington to the Danish Government until much later "will probably always remain a mystery."[7]

That U.S. intelligence "reports of an imminent Soviet attack were a fraud" will scarcely surprise anyone who has even a passing acquaintance with the thesis of this book, nor for that matter will the reason why the Truman administration "did *not* [so] inform the alarmed Danish Government" pose much of "a mystery."* Of greater significance is the discovery that, besides wielding the war scare of 1948 to overpower its opponents within the United States, the Truman administration also invoked it to intimidate European nations into entering the North Atlantic pact. It is readily apparent from State Department records that Washington put tremendous importance on having all the countries of Western Europe become members of NATO, but heretofore we have not known the extent to which the administration resorted to chicanery and deceit to accomplish this goal. Now that Poul Villaume has alerted us to the way in which the administration exploited the war scare of 1948 to manipulate Scandinavian governments, however, it will be fascinating to discover the extent to which it stooped to similar tactics elsewhere in Europe.

* Professor Villaume remarks in this connection that "available (apparently fragmentary) Danish intelligence archives from the first part of 1948 do not throw any light upon these events (I and some of my colleagues have, of course, checked). Personally, I would not be surprised if crucial Danish intelligence and other archival documentation on these events were destroyed shortly afterwards (i.e., in 1948-1949); this, of course, is only speculation." Poul Villaume letter to the author, July 15, 1994.

A BETRAYAL OF TRUST

In the Conclusions to this book, I am sharply critical of the Truman administration both for its "fouling of the political environment"—to be seen, for example, in its McCarthy-like eagerness to vilify political opponents as disloyal, if not downright subversive—and for its unscrupulous indifference to "considerations of ordinary decency" in making common cause with such repulsive allies as Mafia narcotics peddlers and Nazi war criminals so as to strike "at anything and anyone remotely connected to the Soviet Union." As scathing as this condemnation of Truman and the top figures in his administration may have been, it was not, in light of material that has emerged since this work's original appearance, nearly harsh enough.

It is now quite undeniable that the Truman administration's indifference to "considerations of ordinary decency" by no means stopped at the water's edge. On the contrary, the administration was just as willing to infect, maim and poison citizens within the United States as it was to cast morality to the winds overseas. One by one, the stories have begun making their way into newspapers, magazines and radio and television broadcasts. Beginning in the late 1940s, under programs authorized by Truman,

> the U.S. government deliberately dropped radioactive material from planes or released it on the ground in a dozen experiments after World War II. . . . Eight of the tests occurred in Tennessee and Utah in an effort to create a battlefield radiation weapon. In four other tests, radiation was released into the air in New Mexico so that pilots could chase the cloud of fallout to plot its movements. In at least four of these 12 experiments, radiation spread beyond the planned boundaries of the test. . . . At Dugway Proving Grounds in Utah, radiation bombs dropped at an Army site spread 50 percent farther than expected.

And then the telling fact: "All the tests were conducted between 1948 and 1952."[8] The implication is clear: so vile were these "experiments" that even the Eisenhower administration could not stomach their continuation.

That was among the first indications of the way in which the Truman administration had mocked the faith the public placed in it; it was not to be the last. Less than two weeks later came a second astounding disclosure: "Nineteen mentally retarded boys who thought they were participating in a science club in the 1940s and 1950s were actually fed radioactive milk by scientists who wanted to learn about the digestive system, the *Boston Sunday Globe* reported." The "scientists" in question were affiliated with such ruling-class institutions as Harvard University and the Massachusetts Institute of Technology; their too-trusting subjects came from the Fernald State School—David versus Goliath revisited, only this time with Goliath the victor. Obtaining permission to subject retarded children to these "experiments" meant just one more exercise in official duplicity: the school sent the boys' parents a letter that read, in part, "We are considering the selection of a group of our brighter patients, including your son, to receive a special diet."[9]

Nor was this the worst of it. While the public was still trying to come to grips with the news that the Truman administration had allowed the use of mentally retarded boys as laboratory animals, it learned that pregnant women, too, were grist for this particular mill: no fewer than 23 such women, according to the earliest reports, "were injected with radioactive iron in the 1950s as part of a controversial U.S. government medical research program whose scope is only now becoming known. . . . The *Boston Globe* said that at the height of the Cold War, doctors at the city's Lying-In Hospital shot a radioactive form of iron into 23 pregnant women to learn about the blood of the subject and their fetuses. It said the research . . . was paid for by the U.S. Atomic Energy Commission and the Office of Naval Research."[10]

The figures in the *Boston Globe*'s initial stories, however, proved to be far short of the mark, for the number of expectant women actually dosed with radioactive materials during these "experiments" probably numbered in the thousands. One such "study" alone, for example, "involved 829 pregnant women at Vanderbilt University's prenatal clinic from 1945 to 1949"—the Truman administration's fingerprints at the scene of the crime once more—"[who] say that they were fed radioactive iron drinks and that several of the children exposed to the radioactive iron during their mother's pregnancy died." And note well, please, the year when this program began: not, as the *Boston Globe* had originally stated, in the 1950s, but in 1945—before the Truman Doctrine, before the Marshall Plan, before the war scare of 1948, before the Korean War. If only the worthy gentlemen of the Truman administration might be resurrected long enough to explain what "crisis" it was that in 1945 required measures of such repugnance, such heartless cruelty.[11]

No doubt because it was not yet enough merely to irradiate retarded boys and pregnant women, Truman's "Fair Deal" administration also chose to reward military veterans for risking their lives on the battlefield by subjecting them to the same scourge. The Veterans Administration made its humble contribution to this inspired scientific effort by "set[ting] up a secret program in 1947 to complement the Atomic Energy Commission's fledgling research exposing humans to radiation, according to agency documents."[12]

As horrifying as are the foregoing revelations, we can be certain that they merely skim the surface. For one thing, we have not had anything like a full accounting of all the various programs that, with the blessings of the Truman administration, irradiated uninformed and unconsenting human subjects. By the time we have, I am willing to wager, the number of casualties, already in the thousands, may well stand tens or even hundreds of times higher.

For another, the Truman administration's infliction of radiation damage on the very citizens it was pledged to protect was only one component of a broad-based, indiscriminate assault on the populace. In addition to investigating the effect of radiation on humans—so reminiscent of Nazi and Japanese wartime injections of lethal agents into concentration-camp inmates and prisoners of war—the administration also sponsored related "research" as part of the development of weapons based on chemical, biological, psychoactive or psychotropic substances. From "hearings held by the Senate Subcommittee on Health and Scientific Research of the Committee on Human Resources in 1977," for instance, came information about the "awesome scope" of an earlier bacteriological warfare testing program:

> Army spokesmen acknowledged that 239 populated areas from coast to coast had been blanketed with bacteria *between 1949* [emphasis added] and 1969. Tests involved covering areas of Alaska and Hawaii and the cities of San Francisco, Washington, D.C., Key West, and Panama City in Florida. Some tests were more focused, such as those in which bacteria were sprayed onto the Pennsylvania Turnpike or into the New York City subway system.[13]

"Distinguished scientists," writes Leonard A. Cole, "testified at the hearings that the tests were inappropriate and dangerous." And indeed, it also emerged "that the incidence of illnesses suddenly increased in some areas near the tests." Nonetheless, the army did not so much as lift a finger to investigate how many people became ill or died due to the masses of bacteria it released. From the "fact that in 1986 [alone] the Reagan administration's budget for chemical and biological warfare exceeded $1 billion, up [more than six-fold] from $160 million in 1980," moreover, it appears clear that this particular form of state-sponsored pestilence will be with us for some time to come—another delightful legacy of those public benefactors who occupied the highest positions in the Truman administration.[14]

All in all, bearing in mind that we have probably seen no more than a few grains of sand from what promises to be a massive mountain of exceedingly ugly evidence, it seems a safe conclusion that the total number of those unknowingly victimized by one or another of these Truman administration programs could easily reach into the millions. What a sad commentary on a nation that purports to be a democracy!

Even at this late date, therefore, we are still entitled to ask whose actions, in the final analysis, posed the greater direct peril to the physical well-being and the political ideas of the people of the United States: those of Stalin and his minions—or those of Harry Truman and his? Ever since Truman entered the White House in 1945, one administration after another has relentlessly insisted that the most pressing dangers to this country stem from without—from Moscow, from Beijing, from Havana or Hanoi—when in reality, as is now becoming increasingly apparent, these dangers have been emanating from Washington all along. Thus, the Truman administration, displaying its customary disdain for the truth, set out to develop aggressive weapons with which to threaten the Soviet Union, then disguised its real intent with the pretense that its purpose was merely to defend the United States against the Red Menace. In point of fact, however, although few seem to have realized it at the time, it was this unscrupulous administration itself—with its radiation "experiments," bacteriological "tests," chemical and psychoactive "research"—from which the nation most sorely needed defending. If the covert war without mercy that Truman and his subordinates waged against the citizens they had sworn to serve does not constitute an immense and unforgivable betrayal of the public trust, nothing ever will. The buck stops here.

Frank Kofsky
July 1994

NOTES

1. François M. A. Voltaire, *Epitre à l'Auteur du Livre des Trois Impostellurs,* cited in Kathleen Sproul, ed., *The Shorter Bartlett's Familiar Quotations* (New York: Pocket Books, 1964), p. 412.
2. Poul Villaume, *Cement of Fear: The Cold War and NATO Until 1961* (Boulder, Colo.: Westview Press, 1995).
3. Poul Villaume letter to the author, February 19, 1994.
4. Poul Villaume letter to the author, July 15, 1994. The words "broke the deadlock" are from Magne Skodvin, *Nordic or North Atlantic Alliance: The Postwar Scandinavian Security Debate* (Oslo: Institutt for Forsvarsstudier,

1990), p. 37. I am grateful to Professor Villaume for calling this work to my attention.

5. Poul Villaume letter to the author, July 15, 1994.
6. Ibid., and Poul Villaume letter to the author, February 19, 1994.
7. Poul Villaume letter to the author, July 15, 1994.
8. Melissa Healy, "U.S. Deliberately Released Radiation: Deadly materials were tested in 3 states in 1940s and '50s," *San Francisco Chronicle,* December 16, 1993, p. A2.
9. "19 Mentally Retarded Boys Were Used in Radiation Study," *San Francisco Chronicle,* December 27, 1993, p. A3.
10. "Radiation Test Used Pregnant Women," *San Francisco Chronicle,* January 1, 1994, p. A3.
11. Jennifer Bjorhus, "Class-Action Status OKd in Human Radiation Suit," *San Francisco Chronicle,* July 16, 1994, p. A21.
12. "VA Participated in Secret Human Radiation Tests," *San Francisco Chronicle,* January 11, 1993, p. A2.
13. Leonard A. Cole, *Clouds of Secrecy: The Army's Germ Warfare Tests over Populated Areas* (Totowa, N.J.: Rowman & Littlefield, 1988), pp. 5-6.
14. Ibid., p. 4.

LIST OF ABBREVIATIONS

AAF	Army Air Force
ACC	Air Coordinating Committee
AIA	Aircraft Industries Association of America, Incorporated
CAPB	Congressional Air Policy Board
CAT	Civil Air Transport
CIA	Central Intelligence Agency
CNO	Chief of Naval Operations (Naval Chief of Staff)
ERP	European Recovery Program (Marshall Plan)
FRUS	*Foreign Relations of the United States*
FY	Fiscal year
GCML	George C. Marshall Library, Virginia Military Institute, Lexington, Virginia
HSTL	Harry S. Truman Library, Independence, Missouri
NYT	*New York Times*
OF	Official File
ONI	Office of Naval Intelligence
OSS	Office of Strategic Services
PAPC	President's Air Policy Commission (Finletter Commission)
PPS	State Department Policy Planning Staff
PSF	President's Secretary's File
RFC	Reconstruction Finance Corporation
RG	National Archive Record Group
UMT	Universal Military Training
SGMML	Seeley G. Mudd Manuscript Library, Princeton University, Princeton, New Jersey
UMT	Universal Military Training
WP	Washington Post

1.

Introduction: The Truth Was Expendable

As soon as there is a war scare, there is a lot of money available.

—Statement of Lawrence D. Bell, President, Bell Aircraft Corporation, to the President's Air Policy Commission (Finletter Commission), September 29, 1947[1]

POSING THE QUESTIONS

How convenient!

Those words, or something very like them, leaped into my head the moment it dawned on me—more years ago than I care to recall—that the war scare of 1948 had come along just in time to prevent the aircraft manufacturing industry from plunging into bankruptcy. The scare had begun early in March 1948, reached its zenith during the last week of the month, steadily crumbled beneath the weight of its own contradictions thereafter and expired completely by the end of April. Although brief, the scare was no less potent for that. By exploiting the pervasive atmosphere of panic and hysteria that it produced, the Truman administration was able to administer an eleventh-hour resuscitation to the aircraft industry. Within the remarkably short space of two months, the administration succeeded in boosting spending on procurement of military airplanes by an astounding *57 percent,* as the total Pentagon budget shot up by some 30 percent. No President since—not even Ronald Reagan at his most influential—has ever even come close to expanding military expenditures so spectacularly in time of peace.

Business magazines and newspapers of the period made it quite unmistakable that the aircraft industry would have collapsed had it not been for the big procurement orders that came in the wake of the war scare of 1948. As *Business Week* informed its readers in January 1948, "the aircraft builders, even with tax carrybacks, are near disaster. . . . Right now the government is their only possible savior—with orders, subsidies, or loans."[2] In pondering the eagerness with which the Truman administration stepped into the breach as the "only possible savior" and delivered the aircraft industry from "disaster," I could not help wondering whether more than mere coincidence might have been involved—wondering, that is, if the administration's decision to mount the war scare had been in any way connected with its evident desire to save the airplane makers from their inability to survive under the rules of the capitalist marketplace.

The question struck me then, as it strikes me now, as one of extraordinary significance. If research were to show that the Truman administration had fabricated the war scare in whole or in part as a means of keeping the aircraft industry from "disaster," this finding could change our perception of the early history of the Cold War—especially the way we assign responsibility for perpetuating and expanding that conflict during its formative years, from 1945 to 1950. For our understanding of U.S.-Soviet relations in that period has by and large been shaped by the interpretation that the Truman administration itself put on events at the time. Suppose it were to emerge that the administration, in creating the war scare of 1948, simply lied about Soviet intentions with respect to the West. Would not this finding furnish strong grounds for suspecting that it might have lied about those same intentions on other occasions as well? Granted that the war scare of 1948 was only one "piece of a jigsaw puzzle," conceivably it could "illuminate a whole section of the board" nonetheless.[3]

While thus intoxicated with the possibility of being able to shed new light on old but still-crucial issues, I made a rash promise to myself that if an opportunity to do so ever materialized, I would seek to get to the bottom of the relationship between the desperate straits of the aircraft industry and the war scare of 1948. Hence when, during the mid-1980s, the State University System of California began making small parcels of time available to members of the faculty wishing to do research, I leaped at the chance to launch an investigation.

From the outset it seemed to me that if my research were to be fruitful, I would have to pursue a number of different lines of inquiry. First, there was the industry itself: besides tracing the trajectory of its decline—something I could do through the general business press as well as through more narrow publications devoted exclusively to aviation—what I especially needed to learn was the extent to which aircraft company executives during the late 1940s had turned to the federal government for their salvation. Following this path in due time led me to the Air Coordinating Committee (ACC), an interagency body in the executive branch of the federal government whose function was to reconcile the policies of the various military and civilian departments that dealt with aviation matters. If there were some sort of aircraft industry subcommittee of the ACC, I thought, it would have been logical for the airplane makers to focus any efforts to influence the ACC, and through it the Truman administration, on that body.

This intuition, it developed, was sound, although several years would elapse before I was able to verify the fact from the documents. The ACC had ceased to exist in the early 1950s, and in the decades since, its records had become so obscure that it took some time merely to discover their whereabouts in the bowels of the National Archives. ACC records amount to several hundred cartons, they were then still classified and—worst of all—had never been cataloged in any detailed way. Ultimately, it took two visits to Washington, D.C., to have the National Archives declassify and make available the ACC documents I wanted to examine. It was a stroke of good fortune that in that same city the manuscript division of the Library of Congress holds the papers of Robert E. Gross, then president of the Lockheed Aircraft Corporation. These, I was to delighted to discover, provided a sprightly counterpoint to the more staid records of the ACC, for Gross, an indefatigable and colorful letter writer, was engagingly candid about the industry's campaign to manipulate the Truman administration.

The ACC was a relatively low-ranking body, several levels removed from the highest echelons of the administration. In addition to aircraft industry pressures exerted on the administration from the bottom up, it was possible that there also might have been efforts to start at the top, so to speak, by direct appeals to the president, the members of his cabinet or their immediate subordinates. This line of attack, too, subsequently proved to be productive. The papers of the secretary of the air force, W. Stuart Symington, and the secretary of defense, James V. Forrestal, revealed that industry representatives had indeed made a coordinated approach to these two officials during the summer of 1947. Then, at the beginning of 1948, the president of the Aircraft Industries Association of America, the industry's trade association, renewed the offensive more obliquely, taking a roundabout route via Forrestal's best friend and most trusted confidante, the investment banker Ferdinand Eberstadt. (Forrestal and Eberstadt, who already knew each other during their undergraduate years at Princeton, had grown close during the 1920s when both worked at the investment house of Dillon, Read and Company.) Aircraft's entree to the administration reached its peak simultaneously with the war scare of 1948, at which time, among other things, Donald Douglas, the head of the Douglas Aircraft Company, visited Washington to plead the industry's case directly to Truman himself.

A second and related topic to explore was that of big-business backing for a federal rescue of the aircraft companies. Both published and unpublished sources made it apparent that several of the aircraft manufacturers were heavily indebted to the nation's largest banks; furthermore, such giant corporations as General Motors also owned sizable blocks of their stock. In addition to these narrow concerns, managers of Fortune 500 firms were also likely to have been apprehensive about the consequences for the economy as a whole should the aircraft industry fail, for memories of the worst depression in U.S. history were still vivid in the late 1940s. Evidence from the business press as well as from private papers—in particular those of Winthrop W. Aldrich, then president of the Chase National Bank—indicated that this reasoning was substantially correct: big business did indeed support—and benefit from—the administration's decision to stave off the industry's collapse with a cornucopia of new procurement contracts.

Still, accumulating documents on the subject of attempts by big business and the aircraft industry to prod the Truman administration into throwing a life-preserver to the airplane makers was one thing; being able to determine whether the war scare of 1948 had in any way been staged for that purpose was quite another. Clearly, to arrive at a defensible answer to this question meant that one would have to discover whether the highest-ranking members of the Truman administration in March and April of 1948 had genuinely believed that the Soviets were about to embark upon World War III—or had merely *proclaimed* such a belief as a means of accomplishing certain otherwise unattainable ends.

Defining the problem had been easy enough—now was I to go about solving it? Even if administration stalwarts were completely convinced that the Soviets were not about to invade Western Europe (or Iran, Japan, etc.), they were unlikely to have been so indiscreet as to commit such thoughts to paper, especially while they were simultaneously trumpeting exactly the opposite message to Congress and the public. After no small amount of reflection, I finally decided that intelligence estimates of Soviet intentions offered the most powerful tool with which to crack this particular nut. Every government, in formulating its own policies and plans, necessarily depends on intelligence estimates regarding the intentions of other countries. If official evaluations of Moscow's intentions generally reported that the U.S.S.R. showed no sign of marshaling its forces for an immediate attack on the West, we have every reason to believe that Truman and his closest assistants would have accepted those appraisals and based their own tactics and strategies upon them.

Accordingly, I set out to read as many estimates of Soviet intentions dating from the weeks before, during and after the war scare as I could unearth. For good measure, I thought it might also be instructive, as a way of establishing the context in which the war scare erupted, to examine such estimates for two other periods—from the end of the World War II in 1945 to the start of 1948, and from the demise of the war scare in May of 1948 to the end of that year. To avoid burdening the narrative with such a formidable mass of information, however, I have chosen to reproduce representative excerpts from these latter documents in appendix A, "Estimating Soviet Intentions and Capabilities, 1947-1948." I should further explain that I have thought it better to run the risk of casting my net too widely than the reverse. Hence in addition to formal intelligence estimates by the Armed Services, the State Department and the Central Intelligence Agency, I have also made use of more casual observations contained in letters and memoranda, in minutes of meetings, in the flow of correspondence between the State Department and U.S. embassies in Eastern and Western Europe, and so on. The two types of sources reinforce rather than contradict each other, but the less formal evaluations are often particularly informative because they tend to be couched in language that is more lively and revealing. Consider, by way of illustration, what appear to have been the impromptu remarks of the United States ambassador to Moscow, Walter Bedell Smith, on September 28, 1948, at a meeting of the State Department Policy Planning Staff. At that moment, a Soviet blockade of land routes to Berlin from the west had been in place for three months, during which time the United States had supplied occupants of the three western zones via an airlift. Although tensions between the two nations, naturally, had mounted, Smith remained sanguine about Soviet intentions:

> I believe that the Russians do not themselves wish now to face war deliberately . . . [and] I feel so confident they would not now undertake a deliberate military attack on, say, one of our concentrations of aircraft at Wiesbaden, that I would not hesitate to go there and sit on the field myself.[4]

As the last word on this topic—for now, at least—let me note that instead of extending the summary of estimates of Soviet intentions in appendix A back to August 1945, I decided to break it off at the middle of 1946. I did so because, beyond a certain point, there was nothing to be gained by heaping one mountain of documents atop another. Intelligence estimates written before July 1946 in no way conflict with their predecessors; many of the later documents are, in fact, thinly revised versions of earlier ones. That being the case, I have—not without great reluctance—allowed rationality to prevail over obsession by recognizing that, even when it comes to historical evidence, there are times when one must recognize that enough is truly enough.

DECIPHERING THE ANSWERS

Hoping to assist the reader, I have, in the foregoing passages, explained what questions I felt it was necessary to ask, and therefore what sorts of documents it was necessary to consult, in order to unravel the tangled relationship between the aircraft industry and the war scare of 1948. Perhaps it may also be helpful if I expend a few more lines discussing the structure of the book that ultimately emerged from this wealth of evidence.

By now, the reader is likely to have surmised that in order to do justice to his subject, the author must tell two tales: one involving the aircraft industry or, to be more specific, the biggest companies that it comprised; and one focused on the war scare of 1948, the behind-the-scenes preparations for it and the consequences that flowed from it. Ideally, I would have preferred to weave these two themes into one seamless fabric. But one does not always get what one prefers. Just as a sculptor finds himself obliged to respect those properties of a block of marble that he cannot change, so, too, is one who strives to recount a given set of events forced to operate within the limits that the events themselves impose. The historian, in other words, never enjoys the pleasure of beginning to write on a *tabula* that is completely *rasa.*

What all such high-flown abstractions boil down to in the present instance is this: it has not at every point been possible (or I, at any rate, have not discovered a way) to intertwine developments in the aircraft industry with the developments within the Truman administration that culminated in the war scare of 1948. As a result, I must beg the reader's forgiveness, for I have found no alternative but to treat the two main themes that this history comprises separately and in sequence, rather than as the "seamless fabric" I would have liked to produce. The reason, in essence, is one of chronology. The aircraft industry plummeted into a steep decline almost the moment that the shooting stopped in World War II, and the descent continued unabated until the war scare in 1948 brought relief in the form of a lavish assortment of new procurement contracts. The movers and shakers of the aircraft industry were hardly the type to wait passively while catastrophe overtook them; and so, as their predicament steadily worsened, they waged a furious crusade to wrest more profits from the one market they knew best—the federal trough. These efforts, which went into high gear toward the close of 1946, climaxed during the second half of 1947, when the industry began to enjoy the results of its labors: in July, Truman agreed to the creation of an ad hoc President's Air Policy Commission (PAPC) under the direction of Thomas K. Finletter, a New York corporate attorney by whose name the commission is often known; then, from September through the remainder of the year, the commission heard headline-making testimony—frequently from industry executives themselves—about the ugly situation confronting the aircraft companies and the threat it allegedly posed to the nation's security.

So much of the story I present in chapter 2, which relates the saga of the industry's postwar woes, and chapter 3, which shows its executives toiling diligently to reverse through political influence their dismal failure in the marketplace. The third chapter concludes as the Finletter Commission winds up its affairs during the final days of 1947.

At this juncture, the aircraft industry temporarily vanishes from the narrative, to return in chapter 6. (I emphasize again that this arrangement stems from the nature of the material itself, not from any arbitrary decision on the part of the author.) From January 1948 through the end of the war scare, industry representatives, having shot their bolt, withdrew from the limelight and remained silent. This was a calculated strategy on their part: their fear was that by agitating too visibly for increased spending on aircraft procurement, they would discredit their cause by appearing to be—as, of course, they were—"merchants of death." The airplane makers believed that once the Finletter Commission had completed its hearings and disbanded, they had done everything in their power; from a political standpoint, the wisest strategy thereafter was to allow others—especially others in the Truman administration—to take the logical next steps. Industry figures were, accordingly, more than happy to have the administration continue the noble endeavor they had commenced. In the interim, they would conceal themselves in the wings—out of sight, to be sure, but certainly not out of mind.

It follows that if we are to understand how and why the war scare was set in motion, we must shift our scrutiny away from the aircraft industry to the Truman administration. Chapter 4 analyzes the three ostensible reasons that the administration gave for declaring, as it did in March 1948, that the Soviets were about to inflict World War III on the West: the taking of power by the Communist Party in Czechoslovakia in February 1948, Soviet pressures on Finland to conclude a treaty of mutual nonaggression and—in many respects the centerpiece of the entire extravaganza—the telegram that General Lucius D. Clay dispatched from Berlin to Washington on March 5, 1948. An introduction is not the place to go into the details; here it will suffice to say that I draw upon the administration's own intelligence reports, as well as other internal documents, to determine whether what Truman and his top officials told Congress and the public was at all consistent with the information that regularly and routinely came across their desks. In each of these three cases—Czechoslovakia, Finland and the Clay telegram—the evidence demonstrates that the Truman administration employed deceit and duplicity to convey the deliberately misleading impression that the U.S.S.R. was poised to invade Western Europe at a moment's notice.

Chapter 5 conducts us on an inch-by-inch excursion through the month of March 1948, during which time we observe Truman, Secretary of State George Marshall and Secretary of Defense James Forrestal pouring successively larger quantities of oil on the flames of the war scare. By the last week of the month, it was obvious that these valiant exertions were achieving their goals: in the new atmosphere of "crisis" that the war scare so efficiently produced, congressional opposition to the administration's foreign policy and military buildup was starting to come apart at the seams. Now that victory was in sight, however, something quite surprising occurred: Truman's war-scare coalition itself abruptly split in two: having attained their ends, Marshall and the State Department wished to let the scare sputter out of existence; Forrestal and the Pentagon, in contrast, sought to prolong it until they had achieved every last appropriation on their agenda. But keeping the scare robust and thriving was becoming increasingly difficult as one intelligence report after another arrived in Washington bearing the same message: the Soviets were *not* girding their loins for war. Faced with this fact and the necessity of choosing between the two battling factions of his administration, Truman finally intervened to impose a compromise: the military would get almost all it desired, but in return would have to permit the war scare to be put in its coffin and interred.

The airplane manufacturers rejoin us in chapter 6. (By now the reader may understand why it would have done violence to the material had I attempted to intrude them by force into the preceding two chapters.) The chapter opens by presenting evidence that the scare was a rousing success in terrifying the populace with the prospect of imminent war. The main emphasis, however, is on the gains reaped by the aircraft industry as a direct result of the war scare. We see that, practically down to the last crossed *t* and dotted *i,* the industry was able to extract exactly the rewards it wished from the administration and, through it, from Congress. In the final section of chapter 6, I show how the administration, by cunningly exploiting Republican antipathy to universal military training (UMT), trapped its political foes into supporting those military and foreign policy programs—including, of course, an enormous expansion of the budget for aircraft procurement—that it was hell-bent on obtaining.

Originally, when beginning my research, I thought that the end of chapter 6 would also mark the finish of the narrative—thereby illustrating how foolhardy it is to assume one knows the answers without first having posed the questions. Contrary to what I had expected, though, the documents made it plain that the war scare had produced an immediate effect, as significant as it was short-lived, that had to be included in any complete account. By analogy with the earlier war scare, I term this brief episode, which chapter 7 relates, the "peace scare" of May 1948. In the middle of that month, the Soviets gave ample indication that they were alarmed by the rapid arms buildup the Truman administration began during the war scare, and were therefore eager for what later generations would call a summit conference aimed at settling all the outstanding issues dividing the two governments. Such negotiations were not to be, however, because the administration, for reasons I discuss in chapter 7, lost no time in spurning the Soviet overture. But the peace scare, itself a sequel to the war scare, had a momentous sequel of its own—one that profoundly increased the already great bitterness between Washington and Moscow. So massive was the deterioration in U.S.-Soviet relations brought about by the war and peace scares that it took more than a generation for the wound to heal even partially.

In chapter 8, "Conclusions," I explore the main ramifications of the war scare of 1948 and also point to why I believe we are still very much afflicted by the actions that Truman took during and after it. The first section suggests that, because they led directly to the enormous worsening in relations between the United States and the U.S.S.R. that I recounted in chapter 7, Truman's initiatives amounted to a reckless and dangerous intensification of the Cold War. Next, I propose that we can employ the war scare of 1948 as a kind of test case to establish whether the Truman administration's defense of its Cold War policies and programs as a response to Soviet aggression can survive detailed, analytical scrutiny. (At the opening of this chapter, as the reader may recall, I stated that the idea of using the war scare as a means of re-evaluating the question of responsibility for perpetuating the Cold War was one of the things that initially inspired me to undertake this book.) Third and last, I explain why Truman deserves our condemnation for foisting upon the nation a permanent war economy that now serves primarily to accelerate the rate at which the quality of life in the United States declines.

Two appendices follow the seven chapters I have summarized above. The first of these, appendix A, "Estimating Soviet Intentions and Capabilities, 1947–1948," I outlined earlier in this introduction. The second, appendix B, "On 'Conspiracy Theories' in Fact and Fancy," is designed to minimize, if it cannot entirely eliminate, baseless attempts to discredit this book's interpretation on the grounds that it reflects a "conspiracy theory of history." I fully recognize that anyone with the audacity to write a work such as this, which flies in the face of received dogma and conventional wisdom about the U.S. role in the Cold War, is at the minimum doomed to be branded a "conspiracy theorist" for his pains; and I am prepared to take my punishment—no matter how inappropriate—accordingly. Nonetheless, thanks to two new works on James Forrestal that saw publication after I completed my manuscript (and which therefore do not appear in my bibliography), I now perceive that my discussion of the conspiratorial aspects of the war scare of 1948 suffers—for once!—from an excess of caution. The portrait of Forrestal that emerges from the pages of *Driven Patriot* by Townsend Hoopes and Douglas Brinkley is of a man who could no more resist conspiracies than a moth can resist the lure of light. Forrestal's infatuation with conspiratorial plotting was of truly addictive proportions. Not only that, but the more vile the conspiracy—and it is hard to know how else to describe the alliances that the Truman administration struck with the Mafia, with Corsican heroin-smuggling syndicates of France and with Nazi war criminals fleeing justice—the greater the likelihood that Forrestal was at, or near, the center.[5]

As if Forrestal's conspiratorial tendencies were not enough, on the last page of his study, *Eberstadt and Forrestal,* Jeffery M. Dorwart quotes a comment made by Ferdinand Eberstadt, Forrestal's most intimate comrade, to an assistant: "Mr. Eberstadt said that the country was always run by crises, [and] if one was not evident it had to be created to get things done." Throughout Forrestal's nine years as a federal bureaucrat, he and Eberstadt were in virtually constant contact; it was not unusual for them to have one or more telephone conversations a day when both men were in the country. If this notion—that the way "to get things done" in Washington is by creating a crisis—actually originated with Eberstadt, one can be perfectly certain that sooner or later he shared it with Forrestal. Knowing the latter, however, I would be willing to wager that Eberstadt's remark actually echoed a typically cynical observation passed on to him by his good friend in the Pentagon. In any case, regardless of who first uttered it, the idea of governing through crisis concoction could not have been more characteristic of Forrestal's thinking had Eberstadt's words been tattooed on his right arm. It was just such logic that, as we shall witness shortly, unleashed the war scare of 1948 upon an unsuspecting nation.[6]

2.

Crash Landing

The situation in the aircraft industry today, six months later, is pretty grim. The companies have no idea where any real business is coming from. The commercial market has proved to be far less than one would have thought, and everybody of any standing is fiercely competing to get what orders are offering. We have cut some 6,000 people out of the place in the last few weeks and are about to take at least as big a cut again.

Broadly speaking, aircraft executives are confronted with the decisions as to whether to go on tearing at one another in the fiercest competition, whether to merge to make less mouths to feed, or finally whether to liquidate.

—Robert E. Gross, president, Lockheed Aircraft Corporation, letter to James Addams, February 26, 1946[1]

I was quite touched to receive your letter of September 14th . . . and to learn of your desire to buy some Lockheed stock.

Much as I appreciate the confidence and loyalty which your intention indicates, I feel out of the deepest friendship for your good self that I should point out how really speculative all aircraft ventures, including Lockheed, appear. . . . I would be guilty of insincerity if I did not tell you that the immediate short range views are full of conjecture and risk. The industry has been left with a huge amount of plants and equipment and with orders that are only a fraction of what they were in the war. In spite of this reduction in income, it is impossible for us to shed ourselves of many of our expenses and we are hard put to it to make any profit whatsoever. . . .

—Robert E. Gross to George McManus, September 17, 1946[2]

[We have had] to take a very realistic view of our organization and we are cutting it to the very bone. Much as it hurts to admit it, we are letting people out of our organization who have been with us as long as ten years, and I do not mean merely production workers, but administrative and sales executives.

—Robert E. Gross to Clayton Crane, November 1, 1946[3]

If we can liquidate our inventory we wind up '47 with 50 million *cash.*
If we *can't* sell our inventory we are through.

—"Lockheed," December 31, 1946[4]

It might interest you to know that while the problems of the war were great and the pressure upon airplane manufacturers to produce was incessant, I feel that the hazards experienced then were never comparable to the ones we have had to face up to since. We had one underlying element of comfort and reassurance in the war—we knew we would get paid for whatever we built. Today we are almost entirely on our own, the business is extremely speculative and with a narrowed market, the competition is very keen.

—Robert E. Gross to former Secretary of State
Edward R. Stettinius, Jr., March 14, 1947[5]

I am writing you pursuant to the suggestion of Mr. Stuart Symington to outline an acute situation existing in our Company about which I talked with Mr. Symington this morning.

. . . As is customary with commercial projects, we have financed ourselves by means of commercial bank loans, and at the present time, these loans amount to approximately $35,000,000, much of which is invested in work in process or nearly completed Constellation airplanes. Financial difficulty on the part of one of our major customers accounted for the cancellation of a large number of airplanes at a time when the airplanes were nearly completed, and large sums of money were

> consequently tied up. It is imperative that these airplanes and work in process be turned into cash in order that our bank loans may be paid off. . . .
>
> . . . [W]e feel the problem must be approached from both sides on an equitable and realistic basis, and that we should ask for no more than the minimum which we feel will accomplish the result we are trying to achieve. This appears to us to be the generation in one way or another[,] out of work in process or airplanes on hand, of approximately ten or twelve million dollars on the sale of, let us say, ten or twelve airplanes of the Constellation model. We will appreciate your serious consideration of our problem, and any opportunity which you may be able to give us to discuss it in further detail.
>
> —Robert E. Gross to General Carl A. Spaatz, chief of staff, U.S. Air Force, September 17, 1947[6]

THE ASCENT

The men who directed the nation's largest aircraft companies were neither fools, idiots nor lunatics.

World War II had brought to these manufacturers sales, income and, especially, profits that were orders of magnitude higher than anything they had ever seen before. The experiences of six of the largest firms—Boeing, Curtiss-Wright, Douglas, Lockheed, Glenn L. Martin Company and United Aircraft—are typical. Between 1939 and 1944, the six "could point to a rise of 140% in their combined . . . earnings" as their profits leaped from "$21,400,000 in 1939 . . . to $52,300,000 in 1944"—an astronomical increase of 244 percent. By way of comparison, "earnings of 380 representative industrial companies . . . gained but 31% after taxes and reserves" during the same years. Overall, as *Business Week* observed, "no other business came near the aircraft makers' wartime performance." From $250 million in 1939, sales increased more than 60-fold to $16.7 billion in 1944, as the industry shot up in size from 41st to 1st place. What makes such figures even more remarkable is that 1939 was already a comparatively favorable year for the industry, as war orders poured in from France and England.[7]

So much is well known. What is not so widely realized, however, is that very little of the money that paid for the industry's expansion came from the aircraft companies themselves. Of the $3.721 billion invested in expansion of the aircraft industry from the middle of 1940 to the end of 1944, "$293 million represented private funds, while Federal funds so invested amount to $3,428 million," or 92 percent of the total.[8] "A lot of the peak [production] was in Government-owned facilities," the vice president-comptroller of the Douglas Aircraft Company testified before the President's Air Policy Commission (PAPC) in September 1947.* "We had six plants, one and a half of which were Douglas-owned, perhaps." Similarly, *Fortune* related that "the Navy poured $23 million into additions to Grumman's plant and equipment that increased the company's floor space more than fifteen times," thus devoting as much money to one company's expansion as the entire industry invested in increasing its own manufacturing capacity. But even that was not the end of the matter: "In addition, the Navy spent $6 million more on three other nearby plants that Grumman used for subassembly work." And although 1945 brought an end to the fighting, such benevolence often continued thereafter. In 1946, the Navy permitted Grumman to buy "$9 million worth of these government-owned plants and $4,400,000 worth of government-owned tools for $3,500,000—or for roughly 30 cents on the dollar." Even as late as the middle of 1947—almost two full years after the end of the war—42.6 percent of the floor space used by the "fifteen leading aircraft manufacturing companies" was still being leased from the federal government. And for some companies, the figure was much greater. Asked by a member of the aforementioned commission, "How much of your plant is company-owned and how much is leased from the Government?" the president of the Republic Aircraft Corporation answered, "I would say about 10 percent is company owned, and the balance is leased from the Government with an option to purchase."[9]

What this situation meant for the profitability of the aircraft companies is illustrated by the phenomenal financial history of one of the air force's favorite firms, the Boeing Airplane Company. At no time in the six years prior to U.S. entry into World War II did this corporation's profits rise so high as 5 percent of the book value of its stock; in 1940, the last prewar year, profits amounted to 3.9 percent, and they had been zero for the two years before that. In 1941, however, Boeing's profits jumped eightfold over those of the previous year to 31.6 percent of book value; and for that and the four following years, profits averaged 17.5 percent. Earnings per share of Boeing's stock went up almost as dramatically, from an average of $1.18 for the period from 1935 to 1940 to an average of $5.10 over the five years from 1941 to 1945.[10]

Such an astounding record reflected the fact that almost all of the money for the industry's expansion during World War II had come from the taxpayers,

* I will explain the origins of this body in the next chapter.

enabling the owners of the aircraft companies to reap fantastic profits with minimal investment on their part. For reasons that will shortly become obvious (if they are not already), aircraft industry executives stoutly resisted drawing such conclusions, insisting instead that profits should be calculated strictly in relation to sales. Boeing's president, William M. Allen, for example, told the under secretary of the air force that he "strongly disagree[d] with the premise that the rate of profit should be related to the invested capital of the company."[11] And certainly it was true that profits of the airplane makers were not particularly impressive when viewed as a percentage of sales. But before we allow ourselves to be misled by such arguments, we would do well to consider information obtained from Boeing's own ledgers for the World War II years.

From 1941 through 1945, according to air force documents, "Boeing averaged around $500,000,000 a year of gross business with a 6% profit margin before taxes, or annual earnings of about $30,000,000." For the aircraft industry as a whole, air force "surveys that have been made for the last war" showed that "after renegotiation and taxes" were taken into account, "the average net profit of all contractors was 2.4%" of gross sales, a figure that would give Boeing average *annual* after-tax profits of some $12 million, or $60 million for the entire five-year period. It is most instructive to compare Boeing's wartime profitability with the amount of money invested in the company. From its founding in 1934 through 1947, investments in Boeing totalled $25.6 million. Prior to 1941, sales of Boeing's stock raised $9.7 million, and the company's net worth at the beginning of that year stood at $9.6 million. To ensure that any errors in this analysis will be on the conservative side (that is, favorable to Boeing), we will postulate that all of the remaining investment of $15.9 million occurred between 1941 and 1945. If we now divide total profits by total investment for the years in question, we see that Boeing's profit of $60 million during World War II was *at a minimum 3.77 times larger* than the figure of $15.9 million we have assumed to be its investment. In other words, even with every assumption skewed to give Boeing the benefit of the doubt, it nonetheless turns out that for each dollar the company sank into production during the war years, it received back at least $3.77 in *net* profit (and $9.43 in gross profit). Boeing's growth in net worth, from $9.6 million in 1940 to $49.2 million in 1945, was equally spectacular: for every dollar invested, the corporation's net worth increased by $3.09 ($39.6 million ÷ $15.9 million = 3.09). These are indeed breathtaking numbers; no wonder William Allen and his ilk were reluctant to have them discussed. In ordinary times, investors would be ecstatic to receive returns on their money one-tenth that large for five consecutive years. But that, of course, is just the point: World War II was anything but an ordinary time for the aircraft industry.[12]

What was true of Boeing was no less true of the other large aircraft firms. In the first installment of its two-part series on the industry in 1948, *Fortune* reported that "the big manufacturers of airframes [airplane bodies without engines, propellers or landing gear], engines, propellers, et al., made a net-net profit of $585 million during the years of 1940–45, inclusive." Although this figure comprised only "2.1 percent of [these companies'] colossal sales," it was enough to boost "the net worth of the industry from $186 million to $696 million"—growth by a factor of almost four (3.74) in the short space of six years. During the same interval, these "six concerns [that] account for about two-thirds of all U.S. airframe production" invested about $200 million in plants and manufacturing facilities. Dividing their increase in net worth ($696 million – $186 million = $510 million) by the amount invested in them ($200 million) demonstrates that, on the average, every dollar put into these six companies was repaid by an increase in their net worth more than two and one-half times as great (510 ÷ 200 = 2.55). Such lucrative rewards are difficult to imagine, much less duplicate, in times of peace.[13]

ALL GOOD THINGS . . .

. . . must, as the proverb goes, come to an end—and so it was for the airplane builders. As I hinted in this chapter's opening sentence, the executives of the dozen or so companies that dominated the industry were well aware that sooner or later they would have to contend with peace, and they began their preparations for the day of reckoning long before it dawned. Their efforts, put in the most abstract terms, fell broadly into two separate categories, the economic and the political, although the two necessarily intersected and overlapped. Perhaps it goes without saying that the aircraft companies pursued a variety of economic strategies; in any event, one gets an almost subliminal impression that the industry's most influential figures all along harbored the belief that political maneuvering would be required to achieve the industry's ultimate salvation. But that story I will hold in abeyance for the next chapter. Here I wish to concentrate on the economic steps that the aircraft companies took in hopes of being able, if the reader will permit the author an occasional conceit, to remain aloft.

"As a matter of principle, the prospect of building weapons never appealed to me sufficiently to make me want to earn my living from such a source[,] and the only reason that we have built military airplanes at all is because I feel that in time of emergency we must do everything we can to support our Government and preserve the American way of living." Thus wrote Robert E. Gross, the president of Lockheed Aircraft Corporation, in July of 1946 to a woman who had known him since boyhood. Given the staggering profits he and his fellow aircraft executives harvested from wartime production, one is entitled to view such saintly sentiments with a certain degree of skepticism. Especially so in light of his response the previous year when asked by a different correspondent about his vision of the company's future:

> Personally I feel it is encouraging, but I must point out that much of this depends on the kind of peace we achieve. If we have a true and lasting peace, obviously the demand for military airplanes will be limited. On the other hand, if we have an armed truce, and it begins to look as though this may be the case, the demand for military airplanes might be very considerable.

These words do not sound like those of someone whose scruples incline him to reject production for the military.[14]

Nevertheless, Gross did not shrink from proclaiming, in the first of these two letters, that, "from a business standpoint, . . . we believe in commercial business and would only build military airplanes as an adjunct to commercial ones" if given the opportunity. The early postwar years would put the sincerity of these protestations to the test. By the summer of 1947, as the last of the quotations at the head of this chapter demonstrates, Gross, notwithstanding his supposed belief in "commercial business," would be a humble supplicant at the throne of the United States Air Force.[15]

Airlines and Transports

"The commercial business," as it was customarily called within the industry, fell into three broad classifications: transport airplanes for the airlines, small "personal" or "private" craft purchased by individuals or companies and diversification into unrelated fields. Some aircraft firms concentrated on one of these areas; others attempted to compete in two or more of them; in the end, however, all failed.

None more dramatically than those who, like Robert Gross at Lockheed, Donald Douglas and Glenn L. Martin, wagered on the airlines. After almost two years of peacetime efforts, *Aviation Week* was forced to concede, "The scramble for commercial business has been very costly for the aircraft builders. Lockheed, Douglas, Boeing, Convair and Martin have all had a very difficult time in developing new commercial transports and attempting to show a profit on their production. . . . No builder has as yet showed a profit on his commercial model."[16]

Reasons for this situation were not far to seek. As a report to the Congressional Air Policy Board at the end of 1947 explained, "With few exceptions[,] all of the domestic carriers have incurred operating losses during 1946–47. The net operating loss of the certificated domestic carriers was 10 million dollars in 1946, and may exceed 20 million dollars for 1947." The airlines, it seemed, had been "geared, psychologically and economically, to a program of large scale expansion, based on an expectation of continuing sharp increases in the annual rate of traffic growth." In consequence, their "investment in flying equipment has increased more than ten times; [their] labor force has more than doubled; and [their] route mileage has increased some 75%." Meanwhile, however, airborne traffic barely increased. Although the airlines "had expected 1947 traffic to be 25 to 35% above 1946, actually the 1946 volume will be exceeded by only 4 to 5%, and in the case of a number of carriers, 1947 traffic will be below 1946 volume." The conclusion was unavoidable: "The expected rapid growth of traffic, on which the [airlines'] expansion program was based, failed to materialize."[17]

Fortune, as was its wont, treated the question in language as colorful as that of the foregoing report was bloodlessly bureaucratic. "The U.S. airlines have stumbled upon an extraordinarily unprofitable equation," the magazine declared. "Last year [1946] they carried more passengers and more empty seats—and more overhead on both—than ever before." What this meant concretely was that in a single year the airlines had gone from operating 400 airplanes with a total of 7,500 seats to operating 675 airplanes containing 19,000 seats. Unhappily for them, at the same time that airline seating capacity had shot up by 153 percent, passenger traffic increased a mere 69 percent—less than half as much as the expansion in capacity. Nor were matters any better when it came to the airlines' hauling freight rather than passengers. Donald Douglas's pessimistic analysis in this regard was undoubtedly correct: "I am afraid that to develop air cargo some form of subsidy has to be given to the air cargo carrier. That is, if you give him the airplane for nothing today, he still cannot show a break-even basis, a cost per ton-mile that would really generate a great deal of business."[18]

We have already had some intimation of what this state of affairs implied for the financial health of the aircraft companies. Aircraft executives were anything but shy about pointing the moral whenever the opportunity presented itself. In his comments on this subject before the PAPC, for example, Ralph Hunt, the vice president-comptroller of Douglas Aircraft, was characteristically blunt:

> A DC-6 or Constellation will carry as many people between Chicago and Los Angeles as the Super Chief. When you begin to think of 100 Super Chiefs between Los Angeles and Chicago, it is a lot of

> airplanes, and yet 100 planes or several times that number does not support the aircraft company. Furthermore, the airplanes we believe have a considerable life; the DC-6 and Constellation we think have not less than seven years useful life and probably ten. Therefore, there are not going to be large repetitive orders for those planes.

Hunt's statement provoked the commission's chairman, Thomas K. Finletter, to ask, "In other words, there is not enough procurement visible in the future of commercial airplanes to sustain the industry?" "Yes, or even play any too large part," was the response. "It looks unlikely that commercial production is going to support any broad base for . . . expansion."[19]

It was bad enough that the ability of the airlines to buy new transports was speedily evaporating; it was still worse that several of the airlines had placed orders for such airplanes, only to cancel them after the manufacturer had already spent millions of dollars in their production. The most conspicuous casualty of this phenomenon was the Glenn L. Martin Company. "Immediately after V-J day," Martin himself told the Senate Banking and Currency Committee, "we departed from our previous tradition of concentrating exclusively on military business" to begin work on a pair of twin-engine transports, the 2-0-2 and the 3-0-3. "For a substantial time, our judgment in embarking on this commercial program appeared to be abundantly confirmed by the enthusiasm for the airplanes expressed by our potential customers among the airlines. We received contracts and expressions of intention to buy covering 152 2-0-2s and 159 3-0-3s; and at the peak, our backlog of commercial business appeared to be as high as $83,000,000." Because Martin's "customers were pressing us for early deliveries" and the company itself was "anxious to reach the market ahead of the competition," its response to "this enthusiasm on the part of the airlines" was to make "a substantially greater investment in our commercial program than would otherwise have been necessary." Hence by March 31, 1947, the firm had sunk a total of $42 million into these two airplanes—$34 million for "design, engineering, tooling and manufacturing, plus about $8,500,000 spent for materials and parts."

Then reality intruded. Even as his company was investing hand over fist in the 2-0-2 and the 3-0-3, Martin explained, "the airlines generally were encountering unexpected and serious difficulties. During the last quarter of 1946 the domestic airlines showed a net operating loss of more than $9,000,000 and in the first quarter of 1947 a net operating loss of more than $18,000,000. This had the effect of substantially undermining the reliability of our airline commitments"—Martin evidently believed in the value of understatement—"and in fact resulted ultimately in the cancellation of all but one of them." Such cancellations left Martin without even enough operating capital to continue production—the assembly line for the 3-0-3 had to be halted with only one airplane completed—and when the company called on its bankers for help, their response was that it was "impossible for them to supply us with a commercial loan in the amount which we required in order to go forward with our commercial program." The most the banks were willing to do was provide "temporary financing for us in the amount of $3,000,000" while Martin applied to the Reconstruction Finance Corporation, a federal agency established during the Great Depression to keep ailing businesses from going under, for a loan of $27 million. By the time 1947 came to a close, Martin's company "showed a net operating loss of $39,888,758," although a variety of tax credits from the World War II years reduced the loss to a mere $19 million.[20]

Martin's suffering from cancellations of orders by the airlines may have been the greatest, but it was hardly unique. Such orders were barely worth the paper they were written on, in any event; people in the industry, according to *Fortune,* derisively described them as "walkie-talkie" documents: airline executives found it easy to talk themselves into placing transport orders when prospects looked good, and equally easy to walk away from those orders the moment conditions changed for the worse. The case of Lockheed Aircraft is instructive in this regard. Its entry in the transport field was the Constellation, about which Lockheed's president, Robert Gross, would write in February of 1946, "I must say we made a gallant try to get going; but if we had known then what we know now, . . . I feel certain that we would not have attempted this Constellation program." When, later that year, the company failed to deliver its first batch of Constellation airplanes on schedule, Trans World Airlines took advantage of the fact to cancel its order, as a result of which, Lockheed "accounted for over one-half of the industry's loss after tax credits" in 1946. With an enormous unsold inventory now on its hands, the company's position was a desperate one, a point vividly conveyed by the notes Robert Gross made on the last day of the year: "If we can liquidate our inventory we wind up '47 with 50 million *cash.* If we *can't* sell our inventory we are through."[21]

It was in this frame of mind, one imagines, that the following September Gross beseeched the air force to come to Lockheed's rescue through "the generation in one way or another[,] out of work in process or airplanes on hand, of approximately ten or twelve million dollars on the sale of, let us say, ten or twelve airplanes of the Constellation model." But even though the air force agreed to step into the breach, Lockheed nonetheless was forced to report "an operating loss of $9,322,796 for the year ended Dec. 31, 1947." Still, thanks to his successful plea to the air force, Gross was able to inform his audience at the annual meeting of Lockheed shareholders in May 1948 that "the purchase of ten airplanes by the Air Force . . . aided us in the reduction of our inventories and was the first sale of Constellations as cargo carriers. . . . [B]uilding this cargo version of the Constellation for the air force may be the first step in developing a new field for subsequent Constellation sales." By this time, if anything remained of the distaste "as a matter of principle" for "the prospect of building weapons" that Gross had once claimed to feel, there was little of it in evidence. Long before, it appears, he had succumbed to nostalgia for the Good Old Days just past: "We had one underlying element of comfort and reassurance in the war—we knew we would get paid for whatever we built."[22]

Like Robert Gross and Glenn Martin, Donald Douglas entered the peacetime era with hopes that orders from the airlines would keep him solvent; and he, unlike them, did not have to endure the indignity of even a single cancellation. For all of that, however, by July of 1947 *Aviation Week* was holding up Douglas Aircraft as an object lesson in "what happens to a company heavily engaged in the production of commercial transports." Since the end of the war, the company had poured over $13 million into developing the 55-seat DC-6, even obtaining bank loans of $10 million when that step was necessary to complete the project. The assumption governing production of the DC-6 was that Douglas would break even once 200 had been sold; but as of the beginning of 1948, the firm had not managed to sell even 140; and because of that, roughly three-quarters of its working capital remained tied up in inventory and work in progress. This situation was in stark contrast with that prevailing in 1945, when, as *Aviation Week* pointedly observed, Douglas had recorded sales of $440 million in a six-month period with an inventory totalling no more than $8 million; whereas in 1947, "two years later, sales of about one-tenth that amount required an inventory position four times as large." The upshot of Douglas's endeavors in the transport field was that the company incurred "an operating loss of $14,780,579 for the year ended November 30, 1947." In light of such a dismal performance, it was hard to take issue with *Aviation Week*'s conclusion: "The Douglas experience has confirmed the view of many . . . that without the government footing the bills, most aircraft companies are incapable of operating profitably on commercial business alone."[23]

Light Airplanes

If the idea that airline orders for transports might preserve the aircraft industry contained an element of wishful thinking, the notion that the market for small airplanes could do so smacked of outright fantasy—self-delusion on the grand scale.

Sales of new light airplanes (those carrying from 2 to 12 people, including the pilot) in 1946 did, to be sure, soar from about 1,200 per month early in the year to more than 4,000 by that summer; but in November they began to slacken, falling to about 2,000 per month in December. By 1947, average monthly sales of light airplanes had plunged to about 1,400, and the total for the year was less than half that of its predecessor. In retrospect, it was clear that the rush on small airplanes in mid-1946 had been only a flash in the pan, the effect of a combination of deferred orders that could not be filled during the war and flying schools' need for new airplanes to accommodate the crowds of veterans taking advantage of the GI Bill of Rights to enroll in them. And even in the peak year of 1946, the sales of "personal aircraft" accounted for about $100 million out of an industry total of almost $1.1 billion. For the price of 100 or so large transports—Lockheed Constellations, say—one could have walked away with title to all 35,000 of the light planes purchased in 1946.[24]

Most of the largest aircraft manufacturers either merely dabbled in the light-airplane market or, as was usually the case, avoided it altogether. A few firms, however, were more daring—or, conceivably, more foolhardy. North American, for example, introduced its four-seat Navion shortly after the end of the war; by the spring of 1947, it had made a total of 1,110—and, at $7,750 each, sold 841. The company shut down the Navion production line in May 1947. Later, a manufacturer specializing in small aircraft bought the rights, tooling and unsold inventory from the company, which absorbed an $8-million loss from this venture. "North American now will concentrate on military orders," *Business Week* noted in June 1947—an accurate omen, as it happens, of things to come.[25]

A similar tale, with a similar outcome, could be told for Republic Aircraft, another of the big manufacturers that wagered heavily on small aircraft. The form Republic's gamble took was an attempt to apply mass-production methods to the making of a light airplane, the Seabee, in the belief that "the private-aircraft market is now ready to be exploited in the same way the automobile market was exploited forty years ago. On this thesis Republic has staked three years and several million dollars." The bet was a losing one in every respect, because, among other things, the company was never able to achieve its targeted costs of production. Thus, although Republic originally announced that the Seabee would sell for $3,500, by the end of 1946 it carried a price tag of $6,000. The increased costs of production, furthermore, sucked Republic dry: its working capital dropped from $11 million at the close of the war to less than $4 million slightly more than a year later. In consequence, the firm was forced to lay off 40 percent of its workers and cut back the rate of production—which, of course, simply made prices rise that much faster—while it went in search of bank loans. It came as little surprise, therefore—by this time the handwriting on the wall had become too blatant to miss—when Republic halted production of the Seabee entirely in the summer of the following year.[26]

It was "very difficult to make a profit on commercial business," recounted Mundy I. Peale, Republic's president, around the time his company was administering last rites to the Seabee. "We had a private airplane which we thought might be of some help to us, and the market which we had anticipated was not there. As a result we suffered considerable loss, trying to keep the plant and operation going." In actuality, the market for light airplanes was always a chimera at best. The grandiose vision that so enchanted some industry figures was one in which hordes of small airplanes—each, presumably, occupied by the family that owned it—darkened the sky. But for this vision to materialize, there had to be a system of adequate airports and other facilities to accommodate the airborne masses, which certainly was not the case at the time. Even had such a system existed, however, the idea that every automobile-owning family could equally well be sold a light airplane was a thoroughly loony one, for it willfully disregarded an absolutely fundamental consideration: the existing distribution of income. The nation entered its first postwar recession during the second half of 1948, when the sales of new cars suddenly slowed. Automobiles were, on the average, much cheaper than small airplanes—none of the most popular cars of the late 1940s sold for more than $5,000, whereas none of the light airplanes made by the big aircraft companies sold for less. And not only were small airplanes more costly, but many would-be owners of small airplanes "often found operating costs of $5 to $10 per mile too expensive"; the outlays required to own such an airplane were thus "still high enough" to restrict ownership "pretty much [to] the . . . luxury class." If the public's ability to buy new autos was already flagging by 1948—if a mere three years' production was enough to satisfy the enormous pent-up demand for cars existing at the end of the war—what rational basis was there for believing that millions of consumers might have the money to purchase, and then insure, fly, store and maintain, an airplane whose price was twice or more that of a typical family's automobile? The question answers itself.[27]

Diversification

The third approach to surviving in a time of peace did not involve the manufacture of airplanes at all. By 1948, nearly all of the major aircraft corporations had, according to *Aviation Week*, "attempted ventures into non-aviation fields." Curtiss-Wright, a manufacturer of engines and propellers, bought one company that made parts for electric razors and another that made motion-picture projectors. Consolidated-Vultee (Convair) tried its hand at producing kitchen ranges, frozen-food lockers and parts for buses. Bell Aircraft, which specialized in helicopters, had "an arrangement to produce 100,000 electric dish washers for the Kitchen Kraft

Corp. of Chicago," in addition to making motors for farm equipment. The Glenn L. Martin Company entered the plastics business with a factory turning out polyvinylchloride coverings. Fairchild Engine and Airplane Corporation created a Duramold division that manufactured radio cabinets. Northrop established one subsidiary to produce aluminum castings and acquired a second to produce motor scooters. Both Grumman and Douglas marketed aluminum rowboats, and the former also made aluminum dinghies, truck bodies and trailers. For wandering far afield, however, Ryan Aeronautical may have taken the prize with its line of stainless-steel caskets.[28]

But as *Aviation Week* noted, "Almost without exception, this diversification has been a most unsatisfactory experience entailing substantial losses." Fairchild's record in this regard is representative. At the end of the war, its president, J. Carlton Ward, told the PAPC, "Our company, as did many other aircraft companies, found itself with orders cancelled in divisions of our plants. We immediately sought commercial work. I can report to this committee that every one of those ventures has been financially unsuccessful." Less than a month later, *Aviation Week* informed its readers that Fairchild's "Duramold division is now in liquidation"; that Northrop had announced "the dissolution . . . of its non-aircraft foundry subsidiary, Northrop Foundry, Inc., and the initiation of bankruptcy proceedings by its wholly-owned subsidiary organization[,] Salisbury Motors, Inc."; and that Ryan Aeronautical, in "a classic example of an aircraft manufacturer's abandonment of a non-aircraft project," had sold "its stainless steel burial casket business."[29]

The experiences of Fairchild, Northrop and Ryan in seeking to diversify were all too typical. By the close of 1947, virtually every attempt of an aircraft company to conquer new business terrain had come to an inglorious end. The lessons such forays taught, moreover, were often as expensive as they were painful to absorb. The "non-aviation investments" of Consolidated-Vultee, for example, "grew to more than $19 million out of . . . current total assets [of] more than $81 million." By November of 1947, after Convair had "sustained a substantial loss" from these ventures, the company finally announced that it was "in the process of divesting itself completely from these non-aviation activities." Similarly, Salisbury Motors, Inc., a Northrop subsidiary, in a single year lost almost $1 million for the parent firm before going bankrupt. "Diversification into foreign fields is no assurance that profitable operations will ensue," Selig Altschul, *Aviation Week*'s financial analyst, concluded. "In fact, on balance, wherever attempted, heavy deficits have been incurred." Leon A. Swirbul, the president of Grumman Aircraft Engineering Company—a corporation whose performance in this regard was better than most, incidentally—was considerably more outspoken. Asked by a member of the PAPC, "Are you going to continue your non-aeronautical lines?" Swirbul made no effort to soften his language: "We cannot continue them for long, because we cannot stay in business that way."[30]

At first glance, it is by no means obvious why companies such as Bell, Convair, Douglas, Fairchild, Grumman, Northrop, Ryan and the others did not succeed in penetrating the consumer marketplace. It was one thing that these firms could not prosper on the basis of making large transports and small airplanes, because the demand for either of these species or both combined was not sufficient to keep 15 or so airframe, motor and propeller companies in robust financial health. So much is readily understandable. But after four wartime years, during which time new consumer goods had been almost entirely unavailable, there was clearly a massive backlog of demand for the radio cabinets, electric razor parts, stoves, dishwashers, aluminum castings, and so on, that the aircraft corporations chose to manufacture. Why, then, was the aircraft industry so utterly unable to take advantage of this situation?

J. Carlton Ward, the president of Fairchild, thought he had the answer:

> We in the aircraft industry are spending time . . . on the fundamentals of our industry—not on the fundamentals of the other industries where we sought to go out and compete with other established groups. It is not possible to be a past master of everything. . . . There is not time enough to compete with people whose sole job is work in these [other] fields and be good in aircraft at the same time."[31]

There may have been a morsel of truth in such remarks—but only a morsel. To get to the heart of the issue, we would do better to focus on the usual modus operandi of the aircraft industry, which could hardly be more succinctly conveyed than in this single phrase from *Fortune*'s discussion of what it grandiosely termed the "philosophy" of Republic Aircraft: "To hell with the costs when national security is at stake."[32] For a nation's armed services in wartime, there is a certain undeniable logic in ignoring the cost of a given weapon in order to guarantee that it has the desired performance characteristics. But as Mary Kaldor has shown in *The Baroque Arsenal*, a ground-breaking study of the contemporary armaments industry on an international scale, the habit of regarding the performance of a product (which in this case happens to be a weapon) as the be-all and end-all and "to hell with the costs" is a hard one to break. Developed during time of war, it has an almost insurmountable tendency to live on, as habits will, when the fighting has ceased (witness the fact that even Republic's commercial transport, the Rainbow, was "as handmade as a house by Frank Lloyd Wright"). Just because of this obsession with performance at the expense of containing costs, however, companies that specialize in manufacturing for the military find it almost impossible to compete in the making of consumer goods, a realm in which the "philosophy" of "to hell with the costs" is a sure recipe for failure. And, just as Mary Kaldor's analysis would predict, so matters worked out for the airplane makers in the years directly after World War II. Incapable of overcoming their fixation on producing to exacting specifications, and, therefore, equally incapable of bringing costs under control, the aircraft companies never managed to discover the key to success in the competitive field of consumer products. (In the international realm, Kaldor demonstrates, the same outcome awaits any nation whose largest and wealthiest corporations devote themselves to the production of "advanced" weaponry—a point yet to be grasped in the United States, however.)[33]

Compelling testimony to the validity of Kaldor's analysis comes directly from the arms makers themselves. According to an executive with one of the largest firms in that industry, studies conducted for his company

> showed an economic failure rate of 80% for acquisitions outside of defense by defense contractors. This isn't surprising. Defense industry management teams generally have little commercial experience and "market savvy." Most have been "cost plus" and "mil spec" [military specifications] trained. In short, most don't bring a competitive advantage to non-defense business. *Frankly, sword makers don't make good and affordable plowshares* [emphasis added].

Here we have it from the horse's mouth: the words are those of William A. Anders, chairman and chief executive officer, General Dynamics Corporation, delivering the keynote address to the *Defense Week* twelfth annual conference in October of 1991.[34]

The importance of this point is that diversification offered the sole remaining glimmer of hope that the aircraft industry might be able to emancipate itself from dependence on military procurement. When it, too, proved illusory, it became apparent even to casual observers that the future of the industry would henceforth revolve almost entirely about production of weaponry for the U.S. government. This is a crucial theme, and I shall return to it later in this chapter.

TIME RUNNING OUT

As 1946 wore on, aircraft company executives such as Donald Douglas, Glenn Martin, Robert Gross, Mundy Peale and Leon Swirbul surely recognized the seriousness of their predicament; by 1947, they must have been wondering if it was a fatal one. To understand why, we will need an overview of the industry as it appeared at that time.

In the early postwar period, money flowed out of the aircraft industry at a torrential pace. During 1946, the first full year of peace, "Eight of the twelve principal manufacturers of aircraft reported net losses from . . . operations. The other four showed profits only because of tax credits." A report compiled by the Aircraft Industries Association of America, the industry's largest trade association, furnished additional details: "Net sales of the 12 leading companies fell . . . to 519 million dollars. . . . The sales drop from the 1944 peak is 91.5%." ("Douglas' sales alone in 1945," its vice president-comptroller commented, "were larger than the industry total" in 1946.) Growing out of this abrupt downturn were "operating losses of the 12 companies [amounting] to 43.5 million dollars." In like fashion, the working capital "of the average major airframe manufacturer shrank" by roughly 15 percent, "liquid funds" decreased by almost half (44 percent), from $27.2 million to $14.8 million , and the "average contingency reserve of the 12 major airframe manufacturers declined from 7.2 million dollars to 3.0 million dollars" (58 percent). This drastic slide in sales, working capital and reserve funds was accompanied by a rise in inventories, which "almost doubled from 10.9 million dollars to nearly 20 million dollars per company. Inventory turnover shrank from 30.3 times in 1945 to 2.2 times in 1946—compared with prewar rates varying from 3.0 to 5.4 times."[35]

No less alarming was a new development: the increasing inability of the industry to profit on the basis of sales revenues that would have furnished handsome margins in the immediate prewar years. In 1946, the 15 largest firms in the industry had "combined sales of . . . $711,000,000 compared with $244,000,000 in 1939." Yet even though gross income had expanded by almost a factor of three (2.91) during this seven-year interval, "a net loss of over $13,000,000 occurred in 1946 despite the use of nearly $72,000,000 in tax credits, while a net profit of over $30,000,000 resulted in 1939." Their sales had jumped close to threefold since before the war, but instead of being able to record a corresponding growth in profits, the biggest aircraft companies in 1946 had managed only to continue hemorrhaging cash at a dizzying rate.[36]

Nineteen forty-six had been a terrible year for the aircraft business—and 1947 would be worse yet. In this respect, the airplane builders achieved a dubious distinction: theirs was "the only major manufacturing industry losing any money at all" in what *Fortune* magazine, with characteristic hyperbole, termed "these roaring, booming, heedless years." *The Magazine of Wall Street* called attention to the same contradiction: while "other forms of enterprise" had enjoyed "record breaking prosperity during 1947, makers of airplanes for the most part ran heavily into the red, some sustaining losses even more severe than in 1946. . . . The leading aircraft manufacturers were forced to shoulder operating losses aggregating about $100 million, although tax carryback credits of close to $60 million may substantially reduce the figure." When all of the annual reports for 1947 had been compiled, the industry emerged with a loss after taxes of $33 million, with only two of the largest companies, Grumman and North American, managing to show net profits—"and North American's net was made possible by a tax carryback of $11,700,000 plus $4,400,000 transferred from postwar reserves." What accounted for Grumman's singular good fortune? The company's "talisman," *Fortune* gushed, "is its high favor with the U.S. Navy, which has annually bought anywhere from four-fifths to all of Grumman's planes. Grumman's sustained financial health thus heavily underscores the fact that the government is still the aircraft industry's only really profitable customer." This was a point that, as we shall observe shortly, would not be lost on Grumman's competitors.[37]

"With a few exceptions . . . the aircraft builders, even with tax carrybacks, are near disaster." That was the judgment of *Business Week* in January 1948. "Aircraft manufacturing today is a sick industry," agreed *Steel* magazine in the same month. "Almost without exception the industry cannot project its plans beyond the end of this year, since by that time it will have completed deliveries of the bulk of orders for new transport planes; and it will have been wrung out by three years of heavy losses which will make it difficult if not impossible to maintain further the design and production teams built over the last 10 to 20 years." Because of "all these problems," *The Magazine of Wall Street* explained, the airplane builders were in danger of "laps[ing] into bankruptcy before long." Referring to "a crisis in U.S. aviation," *Automotive Industries* chimed in that "the aircraft manufacturing industry is in severe financial straits." And, in its most portentous tone, *Fortune* proclaimed, "It is not too much to say that the present state of the aircraft industry represents as grave an industrio-economic problem as exists in the U.S. today."[38]

The fact that so many business publications were focusing on the situation of the aircraft industry as 1948 approached was not coincidental, for a consensus had emerged in both big-business and aviation circles: time was running out. In the short space of less than three years, the industry had tumbled from first to forty-fourth in size—a lower ranking than it had occupied in 1939—and it was evident that if such a steep descent continued, very few firms would emerge from the wreckage alive. After Douglas Aircraft's vice president-comptroller Ralph Hunt told the PAPC in September 1947 that he could "see no reason to expect that the industry will do anything but lose money for the years in sight," that "certainly, in 1947 . . . it is indicated that there will be another large loss," and that he could "see no reason to expect there will not be a loss in 1948," commission chairman Thomas Finletter finally asked him the obvious question: "How long can you go on losing money?" "Not too long" was the no-less-obvious reply.[39]

Hunt's pessimism was understandable. "I think that an industry that has a capitol [*sic*] of $500,000,000 or $600,000,000, you can see you can't run an operating loss of $80,000,000 a year very long—not very many years," explained retired Major General Oliver P. Echols to a group of his former colleagues. During World War II, Echols had been in charge of army air force procurement; after leaving the army in 1946, he assumed the presidency of the dominant aircraft trade association, the Aircraft Industries Association of America. It was in this capacity that, in June 1947, he addressed the Air Board—in essence a steering committee of the highest-ranking air force officers—about conditions in aircraft manufacturing. In view of the fact that "75 percent of them [aircraft firms] lost business, lost altogether $80,000,000, on the amount of business that they had last year," Echols argued, "the prospects are not very bright. . . . The question of their getting outside [nonmilitary] business is particularly black at this time."

Even if the management and board of directors in the aircraft companies were willing to continue losing money, the general went on, there was still another problem to bear in mind:

> The stockholders don't like it. Now, we just had the example of [Lawrence D.] Bell up here, in which his stockholders [in the Bell Aircraft Corporation] wanted to divide the money, shut the door and go home. They say, "You have some $10,000,000 or $11,000,000. You are losing a million dollars a year. Can you prove to us that you are going to make any money from any business on hand, or in sight? Where is it coming from? It isn't apparent." They want to shut the shop, take the $11,000,000 and go home. Now, I sight [*sic*] that as an example, because it has happened. There are any number of the others who have stockholders who are thinking and talking the same way.[40]

In reality, however, the problems of the big aircraft manufacturers went much deeper than stockholder discontent or even a year or two of heavy losses. During 1946 and 1947, the "carryback" provision of the U.S. tax code had allowed the airplane builders to obtain refunds of their wartime tax payments that cancelled out, on the average, upwards of 60 percent of their postwar losses. But after the end of the 1947 fiscal year on June 30, 1947, this form of relief would be exhausted. From that point on, the industry would have to take its losses unadorned; there would be no more federal cushion to soften the blow.[41]

The prospect of being denied tax refunds to offset operating losses would have been less unnerving if the market for new aircraft appeared to be improving; exactly the opposite was the case, however, as both federal and private purchasing of airplanes promised only to decline further. In this connection, a report of the Air Coordinating Committee (ACC), an interagency body in the executive branch of the federal government that I treat in detail in the next chapter, emphasized "the seriousness of the position facing the aircraft industry during the last quarter of 1948." Even if the funds for aircraft procurement in the Truman administration's budget for the 1948 fiscal year were "appropriated in full," they would "sustain the industry for barely a six-month period. . . . The lead time required for production of aircraft is such that Fiscal Year 1949 funds when available will not permit an orderly continuation of this level. Of more serious impact to the industry . . . will be the drastic lay-off of trained workers during the last quarter of 1948." Nor would orders from the airlines be enough to take up the slack. Although "future orders of commercial transports are difficult to predict, . . . the available facts indicate that a saturation point in the domestic market will be reached prior to the end of 1948," and export sales would alleviate this problem "only to a small degree." This report's conclusion was that "commercial transport production . . . cannot be counted on to supplement adequately a low production rate of military aircraft." The ACC's forecast was an accurate one. Just short of one year later, *Barron's* reaffirmed these earlier findings, reporting that "additional production orders must be given some manufacturers soon if there is not to be a bad lag in 1949. It takes a year to 15 months to get into production in new aircraft types, and already it is too late to prevent a dead spot in early 1949 for some manufacturers." "By the end of 1948," added *The Magazine of Wall Street,* "producers of commercial transports will face the approach of a saturated market with close to 1000 planes in service, although a year later there may be room for another 100." The latter possibility, clearly an afterthought, was hardly enough of a silver lining to overcome the dark, ominous clouds menacing the airplane builders. Sales of an additional 100 transports might enable one or, at the most, two manufacturers to turn a profit in 1949; under no circumstance could it preserve an entire industry.[42]

If the loss of tax refunds was one face of a vise squeezing the industry and a continuing drop in demand was another, rising costs was an unmistakable third. A certain amount of these increased costs stemmed from a steep drop in output that was not accompanied by a corresponding decline in either the number of workers employed in the industry or the amount of floor space in use. As of January 1947, the output of the industry, measured in terms of the production of pounds of airframe or engine horsepower, had fallen from its World War II

TABLE 2.1:
COMPARISON OF OUTPUT IN JANUARY 1947 TO WARTIME PEAK

	Peak Month	**January 1947**	**January 1947 as percent of peak**
Airframe, millions of pounds (excluding spare parts)	89.6 (May 1944)	2.6	2.9
Engine horsepower (excluding spare parts)	35.2 (August 1944)	0.91	2.6
Number of workers employed	1,273,600	158,000	12.4
Floor space, millions of square feet	115	62*	53.9

Source: Aircraft Coordinating Committee Report 22/7.1, March 24, 1947, p. 5; Industrial Plans Section, Air Matériel Command, Industrial Preparedness in the Aircraft Industry, May 1, 1947, p. 6, RG 107 (Office of the Secretary of War), Entry 260, Office of the Under Secretary of War, Security-Classified Correspondence, 400.17 to 461, Folder 461 Pamphlets.

*Includes floor space used for non-aeronautical production.

peak by more than 97 percent. But although output tumbled to less than 3 percent of its wartime maximum—the report of the Air Coordinating Committee cited above described this as a "starvation level"—the corresponding percentages for employment and floor space, as Table 2.1 shows, remained much higher.

A second reason why costs tended to spiral out of control was that airplanes in the postwar period were much larger, heavier, more powerful and, above all, more complex than their prewar progenitors. "It is true that increased labor and material costs have added to . . . expenditures" for the development of new airplanes, Glenn Martin conceded. But, he hastened to point out, "that is only a small part of the many factors that go towards increased development costs. It is the increased requirements and complexity of present day aircraft that have so tremendously increased costs." Among the "increased requirements and complexity" that Martin enumerated were those arising out of "going to and beyond the speed of sound, . . . [which] brings many new problems to be solved"; "continually operating at higher altitudes . . . accessory equipment that operated successfully at the low altitudes fails to function in the higher atmosphere"; "new aircraft installations, such as jet power, radar, radar countermeasure, radar remote and automatically controlled gunfire equipment and a wide variety of special bombs and rockets"; and "complex navigation equipment." These were "just a few of the many items . . . in which advances must be made in order to function in the higher altitudes and higher speed ranges."[43]

Because of the proclivity for modern airplanes to grow ever-more complicated, the cost of developing them leaped astronomically between the early 1930s and 1948; *Fortune,* for example, estimated a 12-fold increase over this interval. Even in the few short years between the end of the war and 1948, for that matter, one can see this tendency at work. Early in 1947, the publications that reported on the aircraft industry generally stated the cost of developing "a new type plane" as "more than $25 million," "$25 million and up," and so on; by July, the figure had risen to "as high as $30 million"; and later that summer, readers of at least one business magazine learned that "the original cost of developing a new model aircraft of immense size and efficiency now runs between $30 million and $40 million." A 20- to 60-percent jump in little more than the blinking of an eyelid—not exactly the kind of performance that would induce the airlines, themselves already strapped to stay in business, to place new orders for transports.[44]

Burgeoning costs, falling sales and a fast-growing inventory of unsold airplanes combined to create still another pressure on the aircraft companies: the requirement for new funds in order to continue production and development. Working capital in the industry, as I pointed out above, dropped from $27.2 million to $14.8 million—a loss of 46 percent—during 1946, and this erosion continued apace the following year. Ideally, companies seek new capital by selling stock—but conditions among the aircraft firms in these years were hardly ideal. "The industry is still held too erratic by Wall Street analysts to merit long-term investment consideration," *Automotive and Aviation Industries* reported in 1946. It is not difficult to understand how "Wall Street analysts" arrived at this judgment. "Since July, 1945[,] the Aircraft group [of stocks] has declined 16 percent while the 304 common stock index has advanced 14 percent," *The Magazine of Wall Street* stated in March 1947. "Moreover," it continued, "Aircraft Manufacturing stocks on an annual basis are about 40 percent below their level at the close of 1939 while average industrial shares are selling 30 percent above 1939." At the end of 1946, as cases in point, Boeing stock had fallen 37 percent from its peak value for the year; Convair, 53 percent; Curtiss-Wright, 50 percent; Douglas, 34 percent; Fairchild, 63 percent; Grumman, 55 percent; Lockheed, 58 percent; North American, 41 percent; and

United, 51 percent. Nineteen forty-seven saw more of the same, as "consistent selling of aircraft shares" that spring "sent Standard & Poor's aircraft manufacturing stock index to the lowest level since March 1938."[45]

At the same time as aircraft stocks continued to shed their value, many aircraft corporations also started either to cut dividend payments or else eliminate them entirely. In 1946, for example, Fairchild Engine and Aviation Company failed to issue a dividend for the first time in four years; and among the biggest firms, Lockheed, Republic and United Aircraft all reduced theirs. Lockheed's dividend of $1 in that year "contrasted to $2 in each of the five preceding years"; United, which had "the longest sustained dividend record among the aircraft builders," dropped its dividend to "a current new low"; in 1946, Republic, like Lockheed, sliced its previous year's dividend in half. The situation deteriorated in 1947. As of midsummer, out of a group of "22 aircraft concerns" that the editors of *The Magazine of Wall Street* considered most important, some 40 percent had "paid no dividends in the past 12 months"; and those companies that had paid them did so by distributing "a very liberal proportion of [current] net earnings, or . . . earnings accumulated in past years." Even at that, however, several of the corporations that did disburse dividends simply lacked the money to keep them at earlier levels. In every year between 1943 and 1946, dividends to stockholders of the Glenn L. Martin Company had been $3 per share. In 1947, the most Martin could manage was 75 cents—one-quarter of the previous amount. Under these circumstances, the aircraft companies could scarcely hope to obtain much-needed financing from fresh stock offerings: the "profit possibilities of the industry are not such that equity capital can be attracted," Roger F. Murray, a vice president at Bankers Trust Company of New York, told the PAPC, and this state of affairs was one that could be expected to "deter the development of new enterprises in the industry." Aircraft manufacturers viewed the issue in identical terms. "Because of the large postwar deficits and mounting costs," Ralph V. Hunt, the vice president-comptroller of Douglas Aircraft, lamented, "the industry's need for additional funds is growing at the same time as its ability to raise new capital is measurably and constantly deteriorating."[46]

For lack of any other alternative, airplane makers were compelled to turn to the banks in order to stay in business. Thus, after "Republic's working capital had slipped from around $11 million to around $4 million," the company in December 1946 borrowed $5.7 million from the Chase National Bank (now the Chase Manhattan Bank). Similarly, the Guaranty Trust Company of New York in the fall of 1946 approved a loan of $10 million to $15 million to Martin, "and, to facilitate a close working relationship," a vice president of Guaranty became a member of Martin's board of directors. To finance their operations,

Douglas, Convair and Lockheed likewise took out bank loans of $5, $25 and $35 million, respectively. But as often as not the tremendous thirst of the aircraft firms for new capital outstripped the ability of the banks to satisfy it. Within a few weeks of obtaining its loan from the Chase Bank, Republic asked the air force to support its "application to the Reconstruction Finance Corporation for a loan of $15,000,000." So, too, with Glenn Martin. After securing the above-mentioned loan from Guaranty Trust, his company then "approached the RFC on May 7, 1947[,] with a request for a $25,000,000 loan. . . . Subsequently, this loan authorization [was] increased to a total of $26,775,000."[47]

Even the expedient of appealing to the RFC was at best a stopgap measure, however, for while that agency might provide emergency financing for a handful of manufacturers, neither its authority nor its budget were sufficient to prevent the entire industry from hurling itself over the edge into bankruptcy. By 1947 if not before, in short, it had become unmistakably clear that to pull the airplane builders back from the brink would take more than the kind of scattershot, improvised expedients that individual companies had managed to patch together to date. If the industry were to be kept among the living, it would obviously require a much larger and more systematic effort than anything yet attempted.

BIDDING FAREWELL TO "FREE ENTERPRISE"

If aircraft executives had no difficulty agreeing that their situation was desperate and that heroic exertions were the order of the day, initially there was much less unanimity on the question of just what the nature of those exertions should be. Such differences of opinion were only to be expected from an industry still largely led by its highly individualistic founding designers and engineers, rather than by the polished graduates of business schools. "Your industry is the choicest collection of cutthroat competitors in the country," Secretary of the Navy James Forrestal had lectured two of these men in 1943. "Maybe it's because pioneers still manage it."[48] To succeed, such "pioneers" of necessity had to be determined to the point of willfulness, eager to persevere in the face of obstacles that would have daunted more prudent souls. Understandably, the ability to see things eye-to-eye with their fellows was not exactly ubiquitous in this crowd.

Accordingly, airplane builders tended to advocate a variety of roads to salvation. To Lockheed's president Robert E. Gross—one of the few heads of an aircraft corporation, incidentally, whose background was neither in flying nor engineering design—the solution to the industry's woes lay in "mergers and consolidations, rather than cut-throat competition." This was a theme Gross sounded on virtually every available occasion. Writing to a professor at the Harvard Graduate School of Business Administration (Gross was a Harvard alumnus), he contended that, "As one who is out on the firing line, so to speak, I have not seen any indication that the army air forces were going to be able to support 15 separate aircraft companies in anything like their present state. . . . It is my feeling that, unless the industry can be grouped into about ten strong units, some units will not be able to command the tremendous amounts of capital that are now required for development and will eventually be forced out of business." His handwritten notes for a meeting of Lockheed foremen in July 1946 contain an even more pessimistic forecast: "Not enough biz for 14[.] . . . It all probably leads to settling down to 3 or 4 big companies (25 yr ?)."[49]

Seeking to practice what he preached, in September of 1946 Gross entered into negotiations with Consolidated-Vultee aimed at merging the latter company into Lockheed. Much to his "amazement and disappointment," however, the Justice Department opposed "the proposed merger on the grounds that it was in restraint of trade and tended toward a monopoly." Although Gross was quite bitter at this turn of events, the truth is that, as *Aviation Week*'s financial correspondent noted, "under the law, where a combine of such two companies would have such a concentrated position in the industry, the Attorney General had no alternative but to rule against this proposal." In any case, the effect of this incident was to end all talk of mergers at Lockheed; notwithstanding Gross's strong beliefs on this subject, the company thereafter looked elsewhere to assure its survival.[50]

Other leading figures in the industry had ideas of their own—all of them revolving around the principle that, in the words of *Business Week,* "the government is their only possible savior." Nor was Robert Gross, for all his enthusiasm over mergers, any exception to this rule when push came to shove. At the close of World War II, Gross, according to *Fortune,* "had hoped, and others in his industry had hoped with him, that the aircraft industry . . . would develop such strong commercial markets as to make it at least partially independent of U.S. Government orders." Perhaps; but if so, Gross had a curious way of expressing it. On May 3, 1945, for example, he had written to Eugene E. Wilson, the President of the Aeronautical Chamber of Commerce of America (the forerunner of the Aircraft Industries Association of America), to recount a conversation he had held with General Oliver P. Echols, then presiding over procurement for the army air force. The executive had to

> confess that some of the things he [Echols] told me with respect to the military and naval programs frightened me. I am sure that there is no firmer believer in the aircraft industry and no stauncher friend

> of it than O. P. . . . I was somewhat shocked to have him express the personal view that there was little if any real ground work being laid in the congress [*sic*] by the Army for a strong program. Don't you think we ought to get after Mr. Woodrum and Senator George and key a good lusty program to them.

Clifton A. Woodrum was then the chairman of the House Committee on Postwar Military Policy; the conservative Democratic senator Walter F. George headed the Senate Finance Committee; and Gross' motives in suggesting that the aircraft-manufacturing trade association "key a good lusty program to them" are hardly in need of further explication.[51]

Similarly, on September 17, 1945, with the fighting in the Pacific barely concluded, Gross had engaged in "a discussion of the post-war situation of the aircraft industry . . . concerning what he thought the Government's post-war aviation program ought to be." The army air force officer who prepared an account of this conversation for his superior duly reported the executive's belief that, "In view of the cost of developing a new type of large transport . . . the aircraft companies will generally not have the financial resources to develop models of this kind on their own initiative without Governmental orders for related or similar models for transport purposes." The syntax may have been tortured, but the point was clear. Gross's statements on other occasions, moreover, show that his comments in September 1945 had not been taken out of context; even his promotion of mergers was based on the premise that there was no "indication the Army Air Forces were going to be able to support 15 separate aircraft companies in anything like their present state." Hence regardless of what may have been his "personal feelings on the subject," he was to write in July 1946, "the aircraft industry needs substantial Government support." "Partially independent," the expression that *Fortune* used in describing the ostensible hopes of Robert Gross and his fellow executives that it claimed to be able to detect, was good enough for purposes of journalism and public relations, in which context no one of significance would take it seriously in any case. What truly mattered was that such lofty declarations not be allowed to interfere with the practical business at hand: securing a federal life preserver for an industry in acute distress.[52]

The issue that vexed aircraft leaders, then, was not at all one of whether there should be governmental aid; none of their number disputed *Fortune*'s conclusion that "the aircraft industry today cannot satisfactorily exist in a pure, competitive, unsubsidized, 'free-enterprise' economy." What preoccupied such businessmen was rather how they could most readily obtain such aid and what form it would be best for it to take. As I devote the entire next chapter to an exploration of the first of these two topics, I will set it aside for the moment in order to examine the second. Although the aircraft companies could not have been more eager to tap the U.S. treasury, their executives were also enormously concerned that any federal funds they might receive not even resemble—much less be called—a subsidy. Their reasoning was the same that impelled William Allen, the president of the Boeing Airplane Company, to insist that any computation of the airplane makers' wartime profits be on the basis of sales, not investments. If the taxpayers were ever to realize how much the creation, expansion and current well-being of the aircraft industry depended on money they had provided, Allen and his counterparts feared, their outrage might result in a demand for nationalization. Advocates of such a measure might plausibly argue that as long as the public was expected to continue footing the bill to keep the airplane builders in operation, it might as well own that for which it was being forced to pay.[53]

Thus, however else federal funds for the aircraft might be described, they must not bear the label of subsidy. Although it was "no secret that manufacturers have been disturbed about the tendency toward a socialized aircraft industry," *Aviation Week* editorialized, the fact was that "for every new subsidy there is a further dependency on the government." The industry could not "perpetually expect more millions" in subsidies "without some sacrifices" in return. The danger, of course, was that one of these "sacrifices" might involve nothing less than ownership of the industry. *Fortune* magazine, with its customary flair for the elegant phrase, drew the connection this way: "The men of the aircraft industry have regarded the word 'subsidy' the way a cigar maker regards the word 'spit'—and both government and industry have been desperately afraid that someone will come out in open meeting with the word 'nationalization.'" Such apprehensions were well founded: in 1948, as I will show in Chapter 8, "Conclusions," at least one prominent critic of an accelerating arms race made the same connection as *Fortune* and advanced just such a proposal for nationalization as big business in general and the aircraft industry in specific had dreaded—a nightmare come true for the likes of William Allen and Robert Gross, one imagines.[54]

The trick, therefore, was for the industry to achieve the beneficial *effect* of a subsidy without the *appearance* of having taken one. Donald Douglas's approach to the problem was ingenious: "Some form of subsidy has to be given to the air cargo carrier," he urged the PAPC. "What kind of subsidy?" the commission's chairman wanted to know. "Some form of subsidy that will pay him something per mile, that will give him a chance to enter a field which now on account of his costs he cannot get into," came the reply. Again, the chairman: "Some definite operating subsidy?" And again, the reply: "Yes. That is even more important in my viewpoint than to aid [the airplane makers] in the cost of development of an airplane." How clever! The airlines would, if Douglas's scheme were adopted, be the ones to accept both the subsidy and any political liabilities that might accompany it—let *someone else* be regulated or nationalized, in other words—while the aircraft companies would ultimately pocket the profits by supplying the airlines with the new airplanes they would soon be needing.[55]

Two other aircraft corporation presidents, Harry Woodhead of Convair and Glenn L. Martin, had similarly inspired concepts of how to retain the rewards while avoiding the risks. Of the two, Woodhead's was the more direct. Under it, the federal government would pay all costs for developing and producing new transport airplanes, acquire title to them, then allow the airlines to lease them at favorable rates. Martin's idea was a variation on that of his colleague: a new federally-financed corporation would provide 80 percent of the funds for any new transports that an airline wished to order, private investors would supply the balance—and, once more, everyone would live happily ever after. The fatal flaw in all such proposals was that the chance of any of them being enacted was about the same as that of the proverbial snowball in hell. A coalition of surface carriers, led by the railroads and the steamship companies, was adamantly opposed to any legislation that threatened to confer even the hint of an advantage to the airlines that competed with them for the freight-hauling dollar; and this coalition was easily able to muster enough support in Congress to defeat the ideas for subsidizing the airlines put forward by Douglas, Woodhead, Martin, et al. Most of these notions, in fact, never went far enough beyond the talking stage even to be introduced in Congress.[56]

With direct subsidies to the aircraft firms undesirable and indirect subsidies to them through the airlines unattainable, only one course of action remained. The editors of *Aviation News* and its successor, *Aviation Week,* were not in the least bashful about proclaiming what this should be. Under a headline reading, "Need for Military Production Contracts Shown by Industry Losses," for example, the former emphasized the "urgent necessity of more and larger Army and Navy production contracts to keep alive aircraft companies"; "the industry's background and very nature of operation today place it squarely on the mercies of military procurement," echoed the latter.[57]

And in reality, for all of *Fortune*'s elevated rhetoric on the subject of becoming "partially independent of U.S. Government orders," at no time between the end of World War II and the outbreak of the Korean War were the airplane makers ever able to secure more than 20 percent of their income from sources other than the military, so that by the beginning of 1950, about "one-half of the major companies" had become "100 per cent military aircraft producers and many of those still doing commercial business [had] backlogs made up of as high as 92 percent Government business." Although companies turned away from the civilian marketplace increasingly throughout the period, 1947 was in many respects the decisive year. We saw earlier that in the spring of that year North American, to cite one illustration, announced that it would discontinue producing its Navion small airplane and "now . . . concentrate on military orders." Likewise for Northrop, which indicated, shortly after North American's abandonment of the Navion, that it, too, would be giving up any attempt to diversify into "ventures outside its original field of endeavor" in order to focus instead on military procurement. Simultaneously, Lockheed's Robert Gross was interpreting his successful appeal to the air force for an emergency transfusion "of approximately ten or twelve million dollars on the sale of, let us say, ten or twelve airplanes of the Constellation model" as "the first step in developing a new field for subsequent Constellation sales." As late as 1939, 42.5 percent of the industry's orders had been nonmilitary in nature; but after 1942, nothing like that would ever again be true.[58]

Two firms in particular illustrate the unanimity with which industry executives converged on military procurement as the most certain way of keeping their firms from bankruptcy. From 1945 until mid-1947, Republic had sought to generate a profit from sales of its "commercial" aircraft, primarily the Seabee light airplane and, to a lesser extent, the Rainbow transport. The principal rewards Republic reaped from these efforts, were, as I brought out previously, the loss of $7 million of its $11 million in working capital, the laying off of 40 percent of its workforce, and the necessity of borrowing a total of $21 million from the Chase National Bank and the Reconstruction Finance Company as the price of staying in business. While Republic was sinking ever deeper into debt, Grumman Aircraft, in contrast, could boast that it was one of a tiny handful of companies to show operating profits and pay dividends in both 1946 and 1947—just as it had in every one of its 18 years of its existence—and its stock came "closer to blue-chip status than anything else in the speculative aircraft line." The secret to such atypical success for an aircraft corporation was simple: "the U.S. Navy . . . has annually bought anywhere from four-fifths to all of Grumman's planes." Thus, although Grumman did make a few feeble gestures in the direction of manufacturing small airplanes and consumer products, its "present and prospective military business [was] so good that [Chairman of the Board] Roy Grumman and [President] Jake Swirbul [were] not much concerned about the company's commercial ventures."[59]

It is surely significant that the presidents of these two corporations, as their testimony before the PAPC reveals, arrived at identical conclusions from diametrically opposed directions. Asked by a member of the commission if he anticipated that "commercial" work would be profitable in the future,

Republic's president Mundy Peale replied, "It will be very difficult to make a profit on commercial business. I think it will be done to a certain extent, but it will be very difficult." Leon Swirbul, Peale's counterpart at Grumman, was even more categorical. Did he believe "civilian business" to be of any importance "in the maintenance of aircraft production capacity?" a Commissioner inquired. Swirbul's answer was terse and unequivocal: "I do not."[60]

It remained for Oliver P. Echols, the president of the Aircraft Industries Association of America, to give this point its most evocative presentation before the same commission. "What percentage of the present aircraft industry floor space could be utilized in the foreseeable future for purely commercial orders?" one member asked Echols. "In other words, if the millennium arrived and there were no military planes, how big would the industry be?" After a certain amount of circumlocution, the general came to the point: "I just think it would collapse. . . . If you take the companies that today are building transports and military airplanes, very few of them would even be in existence in 18 months."[61]

Echols's testimony summed up the situation in crystalline fashion. Without a substantial increase in military orders in the very near future, the survival of the aircraft industry was anything but assured.

LEADING FROM WEAKNESS

Paradoxically enough, the very vulnerability of the aircraft industry conferred on it a kind of advantage with respect to securing support from the dominant business groups for its goal of winning massive new military orders. To move from the general to the specific, the ruling class—that is, the class that owns the overwhelming bulk of the nation's industrial and financial wealth and generally controls its political agenda[62]—must have entertained considerable anxieties about the consequences of allowing such an important industry to perish. With the worst depression in the country's history still vivid in people's memory, there was a widespread and persistent fear that a breakdown of the economy could recur at any time. Granted that the aircraft industry after 1945 had contracted enormously in comparison to its peak size during World War II, its failure might nevertheless set in motion a "ripple effect." Where such an effect might stop, how many businesses would be pulled into its undertow—these things no one could predict. Such thinking, no doubt, was the underlying reason why, in the words of *Barron's* magazine, the "invalid aircraft manufacturing industry . . . has probably received more sympathetic attention in Washington during 1947 than any other single business group," why *Fortune* in January 1948 declared that "the present state of the aircraft industry represents as grave an industrio-economic problem as exists in the U.S. today."[63]

This concern was most acute, naturally, among those business groups closest to the airplane producers. Aircraft's chief suppliers were a notable case in point. The making of airplanes swallowed prodigious quantities of steel and other nonferrous metals, especially aluminum and magnesium. Predictably, therefore, trade journals in the metalworking field demanded that the federal government "make aircraft industry and air lines strong; appropriate adequate funds; start building planes now." "We need," one such publication blared, "35,041 [war] planes" by the "deadline" of January 1, 1953. To put in perspective this proposal for procuring some 35,000 airplanes in a five-year period, one must realize that the U.S. military purchased an average of about 1600 airplanes in the 1947 and 1948 fiscal years (1,400 airplanes in the former and 1,800 in the latter). The program this journal was urging, in other words, would have boosted annual aircraft procurement more than fourfold (from 1600 airplanes per year to 7,008)—and this at a time when expenditures for the Pentagon already accounted for 30 cents or more of every dollar spent by the federal government. In addition to metals, aircraft companies also consumed enormous amounts of chemicals, glass and—not least—machine tools. Given that "at least 30 machine tool companies [had] passed out of the picture either through liquidation or through mergers" during the first three years of peace, the importance of this connection was not about to be overlooked by members of that industry. "What form the national aviation policy takes, of course, is of interest to thousands of metalworking companies," the trade journal *Steel* noted, "because the net effect will be to determine how much of a market the aviation industry is to be in the future." So far as the machine-tool industry was concerned, the "difficult question to be decided" was only that of "*how much* subsidy from the federal government will be necessary to support an adequate program" (emphasis added).[64]

A second kind of connection to the aircraft industry was that of economically and politically powerful corporations of the magnitude of General Motors, General Electric and Westinghouse Electric. Such companies, although not usually thought of as aircraft manufacturers, enjoyed sizeable aircraft-related procurement contracts nonetheless. At the start of the 1949 fiscal year, in fact, General Electric led all other firms—including the largest *aircraft* firms—in this regard, while General Motors was in fifth place, with Westinghouse in eighth.[65]

Ownership and investment established a connection of a third type. As General Motors was "for many years . . . the largest stockholder of North American Aviation, owning 1,000,061 shares or 29 per cent of the capital stock," control of the latter operation was in essence exercised by the Du Ponts, one of the paramount ruling-class families in the United States, through its ownership of General Motors ("remaining stock" in North American was dispersed among "28,200 holders"). Laurance Rockefeller, a representative of an equally wealthy family, owned one-fifth of both McDonnell Aircraft and Marquardt Aircraft, and similar percentages of a number of smaller aircraft companies; he also was one-third owner of a consortium—the other two members were C. Douglas Dillon and A. Felix Du Pont—that had purchased Piasecki Helicopter, an operation that would thrive mightily during the Korean War.[66]

But the individual aircraft holdings of Laurance Rockefeller—and virtually everyone else—were dwarfed in comparison to those of the Rockefeller family as a whole. Rockefeller investment in the aircraft industry was channeled through the Chase National Bank (later the Chase Manhattan Bank)—at the time, the largest such institution in the world—which John D. Rockefeller, Jr., had acquired in 1930. So great did Chase's participation in the industry become that the continued reverses of the airplane builders after World War II threatened to deal the bank a genuinely devastating blow. Both during and after the war, Chase was far and away the single largest lender to the aircraft companies. The bank's involvement took four forms.

1. In August of 1945, Chase had deposits from aircraft corporations totalling $85.4 million; two years later, these had shrunk by more than 80 percent to less than $16 million.
2. At their peak in 1944, Chase's industrial loans—most of which went for the production of airplanes—amounted to $276 million; by the next year, they had fallen by 82 percent to a value of $49.7 million.
3. Collateral loans to aircraft manufacturers—short-term loans for operating capital, secured by some asset such as a purchase order—stood at $320.4 million as of mid-1944 and made up anywhere from 30 to 40 percent of all such loans made by the bank; in addition, to obtain an accurate picture of the Chase's balance sheet, one would also have to include the numerous and sizeable collateral loans to other corporations (such as Chrysler, Westinghouse, B. F. Goodrich, et cetera) that manufactured a variety of aircraft-related items during the war.
4. Finally, Chase made Regulation "V" Revolving Credit loans to the aircraft companies. These loans were partially—but not entirely—guaranteed by the federal government. In March 1944, for example, the month that the aircraft industry achieved its maximum output, the bank had on its books outstanding Regulation "V" Revolving Credit loans of $852 million, of which $81.2 million were unguaranteed and unsecured

> by any asset; the bank at the same time also carried another $31 million of largely unguaranteed collateral loans.[67]

The Chase Bank's heavy commitment to financing military production generated huge profits in World War II, but, conversely, left the bank poorly positioned for peacetime. In concentrating on aircraft and related fields, it had neglected industry of a nonmilitary nature; and the bank, under Rockefeller control, turned up its corporate nose at the field of consumer credit. Thus, hardly had the war came to a close when Chase's new loans to the durable goods industries dropped by more than 75 percent, while quarterly profits correspondingly declined by more than a third (37.7 percent). To add to the bank's woes, early in 1947, the federal government closed its War Loan account at Chase, which suddenly found itself poorer by $1.15 *billion* in vanished deposits. Indeed, during the first three peacetime years, deposits at Chase shrank by 29 percent, from $5.7 billion at the end of 1945 to $4.2 billion at the end of 1948. Not surprisingly, in view of these reverses, the author of the standard study of the bank's history describes its "earnings performance in the postwar years" as "not distinguished." This was, if anything, an understatement. Both net earnings and profits "fell off rather sharply" after 1945, "reaching a low point . . . in 1948," a year that also "marked the postwar low in total assets as well as earnings." (Even the National City Bank, although it had "less capital than Chase," was able to report "greater assets and larger profits" in 1948.) Taken together, these developments meant that the bank could hardly afford to be indifferent about its investments in industries, such as aircraft, that manufactured for the Pentagon.[68]

All forms of the bank's involvement in the aircraft industry—loans, investments, deposits—were increasingly jeopardized by the failing health of the airplane builders, however. By January 1947, this deterioration had already proceeded to the point that the national bank examiner felt it necessary to emphasize the perilous nature of Chase's loans to Republic ($5.7 million) and Lockheed ($3.65 million). The next examiner's report, in July 1947, expanded on earlier warnings, emphasizing that "the airplane industry—carriers and manufacturers alike—is confronted with significant problems in methods of operation, products, markets and finances." (One doubts that such information came as much of a revelation to Chase management.) Making use of a four-step scale ranging from "secure" at the top to "default" at the bottom, this report lowered the status of the Lockheed loan from "especially mentioned" to the second-worst category, "classified" (the loan to Republic remained "especially mentioned").[69]

Then as now, members of the ruling class such as Winthrop W. Aldrich, the chairman of the Chase National Bank and the brother-in-law of John D.

Rockefeller, Jr., were not in the habit of sitting by idly while the value of their assets steadily dwindled into nothingness. Quite the contrary: Aldrich was aggressively singled-minded when it came to defending the interests of Chase National and the Rockefellers. Observe, for example, his response in December 1948 upon discovering that the air force procurement contracts awarded Republic and Northrop, each of which had loans from the Chase Bank, contained a provision that put claims of the federal government for taxes ahead of those of the bank for debt repayment. Picking up the telephone, he called his friend James V. Forrestal, the secretary of defense, and, prior to joining the Roosevelt administration in 1940, the president of one of the country's largest investment-banking houses, Dillon, Read and Company. "We just can't finance on that basis," Aldrich instructed the Secretary. Forrestal, seeking to mollify his one-time colleague, requested Aldrich to "have your man call my office and speak to [Forrestal's assistant] Mr. [Marx] Leva. . . . Give him all of the facts, he will look into it." Clearly, Aldrich knew exactly what he wanted and was not in the least reluctant to go after it directly.[70]

And, as this incident suggests, Aldrich, with the Rockefeller fortune and the Rockefeller bank both at his disposal, had copious political connections to exploit when the occasion demanded. Prominent in the Republican party, he took a leading role in raising money for the presidential candidacy of Wendell Willkie in 1940, the gubernatorial and presidential efforts of Thomas E. Dewey later that decade and the Eisenhower campaigns of 1952 and 1956; as a reward for the last of these, he was named ambassador to Great Britain. But his formidable influence also extended to the Democrats—the foregoing excerpts from his telephone conversation with James Forrestal certainly attest to that—if only because no ambitious politician cared to have an institution as powerful as the Chase Bank as an enemy. Thus it was that in July 1946 Harry Truman—no great lover of Republicans in general nor Winthrop Aldrich in particular—selected Aldrich to be the chairman of the President's Committee for Financing Foreign Trade.[71]

Perhaps because of this and other, similar appointments, Aldrich's political interests are usually thought to have focused on foreign affairs. In actuality, however, he was also deeply concerned about matters military—as witness the fact that on December 13, 1948, he wrote to James Forrestal with a proposal "that the top members of the Military Establishment [the original name of the Department of Defense] get together with a group of leading industrialists and bankers for a two day conference." In light of the deep immersion of the Chase National Bank in the aircraft industry, one can be sure that Aldrich's reasons for calling for such a gathering were neither abstract nor academic.[72]

There is solid evidence, moreover, that, earlier in the year, when the question of aircraft procurement took center stage in the Washington, D.C., political arena, Aldrich himself had been in the thick of things. At that time, Secretary of the Air Force W. Stuart Symington had dispatched a pair of air force colonels to carry an urgent letter appealing to Aldrich for help: "the problem is how to get the money to get what we want," Symington explained, "and any advice you could give us to that end would be very much appreciated." Four days later, Symington wrote again: "Thank you very much for seeing my friends. The client they discussed is getting in touch with you shortly."[73]

For Symington and the air force "to get the money to get what we want" meant, of course, that the aircraft industry would be pulled out of danger and ruling-class creditors and investors would be able to exhale heartfelt sighs of relief. A full narration of such a long and complicated story, however, will have to await chapter 6. In the meantime, I intend to examine how that industry, its plans in the economic realm all having failed ignominiously, moved into the political realm to accomplish its goals. It is to that topic that we must now turn our attention.

3.

Takeoff Aborted

It looks as if our airplane industry is in trouble and it would seem to be the obligation of our little shop to do the best we can to help. . . . [I] assure you that because of my respect for your judgment and belief in the future of air power, it would be a pleasure to cooperate anywhere in the administration, or with the Congress[,] that you considered it advisable. I am quite sure General [Carl A.] Spaatz feels the same way about it.

—W. Stuart Symington, Assistant Secretary of War for Air, letter to Oliver P. Echols, President, Aircraft Industries Association of America, May 30, 1947[1]

One of the first things I want to do when I get back is sit down with General Echols on this and see how the [aircraft] manufacturers think we can be of the most help.

—Memorandum for Mr. [Eugene M.] Zuckert from W. Stuart Symington, June 25, 1947[2]

Mr. Norton [Assistant Secretary of State Garrison Norton] feels that the real heart of the question is the survival of the U.S. aircraft manufacturing industry, particularly in the next six months to a year. It raises the question as to how much of a subsidy must be forthcoming. . . . Emergency legislation may be necessary in order to maintain minimum production levels.

—Air Coordinating Committee Minutes of Meeting of February 27, 1947[3]

It was agreed that the President of the U.S. should be notified that the condition of the aircraft manufacturing industry is serious, . . . and that it would probably be necessary for the Government to subsidize industry by Government contracts to some extent in order to tide industry over its present serious situation.

—Col[onel] [Carlton J.] Martin, Informal Minutes of Air Coordinating Committee Meeting of April 3, 1947[4]

It seems to me that government must recognize this situation and do something to meet it, namely, that the tremendous high cost of the development and first production of large transports from this period forward just cannot be done within the aircraft industry and will stop unless there is substantial government relief. . . . There should be no reason whatever for considering this kind of assistance by government as coming within the scope of subsidy.

—Letter of Frederick B. Rentschler, Chairman of the Board, United Aircraft Corporation, to The Honorable Thomas K. Finletter, Chairman, President's Air Policy Commission, December 9, 1947[5]

. . . [T]he men of the [aircraft] industry have regarded the word "subsidy" the way a cigar maker regards the word "spit"—and both government and industry have been desperately afraid that someone will come out in open meeting with the word "nationalization."

—"The Wildest Blue Yonder Yet," *Fortune,* March 1948[6]

MR. SYMINGTON: . . . The word to talk was not "subsidy"; the word to talk was "security."

—Secretary of the Air Force Symington, January 21, 1948[7]

NATIONALIZATION AND OTHER UNSPEAKABLES

For all their diverse attempts at penetrating the "commercial" market, executives at the leading aircraft companies were never so delirious as to put all of their eggs into such an unpromising basket. Instead, at the same time they worked to sell transports, airliners, light airplanes and a curious jumble of other products, they also sought to apply as much political-economic pressure as they (and, in due course, their allies in the ruling class) could muster, in an effort to have the federal government keep their plants alive and thriving. Slow and inconspicuous at first, this masterful campaign reached a crescendo in the last half of 1947 and the first half of 1948. So successful was it to prove that never again would the industry be forced to face the rigors of "free enterprise" without benefit of a government-furnished safety net to break whatever falls fate might have in store for it.

The origins of this strategy can be traced back to a meeting in 1943, at which E. E. Wilson, the president and chief executive officer of United Aircraft and the source of this account, and Frederick B. Rentschler, chairman of United's board of directors, asked Under Secretary of the Navy James V. Forrestal for his help in staving off the collapse of their industry once the war was over. The secretary and Rentschler were already well acquainted, for the latter's brother, Gordon, had become fast friends with Forrestal on Wall Street during the 1920s and 1930s, as each was rising to the head of a powerful bank (the investment house of Dillon, Read and Company in the case of Forrestal, the National City Bank in the case of Gordon Rentschler); and their friendship was no doubt further cemented by the tendency of both to gravitate toward other alumni of their alma mater, Princeton University. On this occasion in 1943, as soon as Eugene Wilson and Frederick Rentschler had finished their appeal, Forrestal's first response was to warn them, "If you ever repeat what I've said, I'll deny having said it." After that histrionic opening, he told his visitors, "Your industry is the choicest collection of cutthroat competitors in the country. . . . But," he added, "if you . . . expect to survive, the industry must unite and do battle for its existence. Frankly, I doubt if anyone can unite the aircraft industry, but someone has got to try it." Then, according to Wilson, Forrestal placed "a strong forefinger on my knee, and holding me with his gaze, he concluded simply, 'If anyone can do it, Gene Wilson, you can.'"[8]

What animated men such as Wilson and Rentschler no less than Forrestal was both a broad horror of socialism and a specific fear that the aircraft industry might be vulnerable to nationalization. At one point in their 1943 conversation, for instance, Forrestal had instructed the two executives that it was up to "private industry" to "avert a Marxist takeover." Although such concerns, from the perspective of decades later, may appear ludicrous, business executives of the Rentschler-Wilson-Forrestal stripe took "threats" of this nature with the utmost seriousness. "Unless we can speed up the means by which money flows into new enterprises," Forrestal told a correspondent in 1947, "we shall drift into state socialism without knowing it. . . . The control of credit in Washington, commercial banks, insurance companies, and the channeling of savings in general . . . It is unquestionably the beginning of socialism and socialism is the beginning of communism." In a second letter dated the very next day—thereby underlining his preoccupation with the matter—Forrestal returned to the attack, denouncing the U.S. occupation government in Japan for "writing up laws . . . which, in certain respects, impose state socialism on that country—which is a fine way to keep them permanently busted, and would ultimately lead to economic anarchy."[9]

So far as the aircraft executives were concerned, the offensive against private ownership was already under way, launched by the provision of the Vinson-Trammel Act of 1934 that required the navy to "build at least 10 per cent of its aircraft and engines in its own plant." Seeing in it the entering wedge for socialism, communism and other assorted evils, airplane makers never reconciled themselves to this legislation. Thus, the 1936 edition of the *Aircraft Yearbook* railed that "among the disturbing factors in American aviation is an increased tendency in some official circles to consider seriously government manufacture of aircraft and engines." Eleven years later, executives such as United Aircraft's Frederick Rentschler were still holding forth in the same vein. "It is of prime importance," Rentschler wrote to James Forrestal—in what was truly an example of preaching to the converted—"that government look to industry to both develop and produce all types of airplanes." No government competition with private ownership, in other words, and above all no insolent attempt of federal functionaries to show just how cheaply and efficiently an airplane might be assembled.[10]

Aircraft executives were constantly vigilant for conspiracies aimed at undermining private ownership—and, of course, experienced no difficulty in finding what they sought. When, for example, the U.S. postmaster general in 1934 cancelled all existing contracts for the carrying of air mail, Eugene Wilson was convinced that this action "constituted a renewal of the drive to nationalize the aircraft industry." Given this outlook, it is no wonder that Wilson and Rentschler, as their meeting with James Forrestal in 1943 shows, regarded the approach of peace with something akin to dread, for with the end of the war might come, in Wilson's phrase, "the postwar depression everywhere deemed inevitable." If such a depression were to materialize, the aircraft firms would have no choice but to appeal to the federal government in order to remain in business; and that, in turn, would most likely provoke renewed and more vociferous demands for their nationalization. Forrestal, as we have seen from his letters, fully shared these fears. Hoping to avert what all three regarded as an impending catastrophe, Forrestal advised Rentschler and Wilson that the last should resign the presidency of United Aircraft and concentrate on organizing the airplane builders so that they could agitate the federal government for "the formulation of a postwar American air policy designed to conserve private enterprise."[11]

Wilson was sufficiently impressed with Forrestal's advice to leave his position at United Aircraft and embark on reviving the airplane makers' trade association, the Aircraft Industries Association of America (AIA), which had fallen into somnolence during the war. Unifying and mobilizing the manufacturers was the first step in Wilson's grand plan. Once it had been completed, he believed, the industry could then direct its energies to obtaining a federal program that would keep it sound and solvent. Despite James Forrestal's characterization of aircraft executives as "the choicest collection of cutthroat competitors in the country," Wilson must have found them a receptive audience, for already by the spring of 1945—while World War II was still raging—he had successfully resurrected the AIA, become its president, reestablished the association's office in Washington, D.C., and, as he reported to Lockheed's Robert Gross, sallied forth "to work on . . . our number one priority project"—the pursuit of military contracts for the companies he represented.[12]

So much had been comparatively easy. The next step would take much more patience, skill and hard work. The approach favored by "many aircraft manufacturers, under the leadership of F. B. Rentschler of United Aircraft Co.," stated an Army Air Force memorandum of June 1945, was that of "stimulating a Presidential appointment of a 'Morrow Board' to recommend a U.S. Air Policy" that would provide the industry with the federal support it sought.[13] Proposals for "a new Morrow Board," "a second Morrow Board," "another Morrow Board," and the like, crop up ubiquitously, as this memorandum illustrates, in the discourse of aircraft industrialists during the last year of the war and the first years of peace; and as these executives were only too happy to expound on what such proposals entailed, we may as well turn to them for enlightenment. It was in 1925, Robert Gross explained to a Los Angeles audience in June 1945, that President Calvin Coolidge had "appointed a board under the chairmanship of Dwight [Whitney] Morrow to study all phases of aviation and to make recommendations for a national policy." Out of the report of this Morrow Board, Eugene Wilson told *his* audience in Chicago at about the same time, came "constructive suggestions that a strong air force was essential to our national defense." These, in turn, "led to the passing of the Air

Corps Act of 1926 and the Air Commerce Act of the same year. Within five years our American aircraft was the best in the world. Everything went smoothly even through the depression."

It was clear, then, what men such as Rentschler, Gross, Wilson and their counterparts at other aircraft corporations had in mind. If they could prevail upon the Truman administration to create "another Morrow Board," if they could persuade Congress and the administration to adopt the "constructive suggestions" that such a board would be sure to formulate, they could relax, secure in the knowledge that "everything [would go] smoothly even through" what Wilson termed "the postwar depression everywhere deemed inevitable."[14]

THE INDUSTRY TAKES CHARGE

Despite all the speechifying in mid-1945, the AIA made little progress towards its goal of a latter-day Morrow Board during the remainder of the year and the first two-thirds of 1946. For one thing, the association does not appear to have begun pushing forcefully for such a board until the end of 1946. Throughout most of the year, the airplane manufacturers were still flush with wartime profits, and the realities of the postwar period—the minute size of the market for airliners, transports and light planes, the inability of aircraft firms to compete with nonmilitary producers—had not yet extinguished the optimistic glow in which they basked. What is more, the armed services, whose support would be essential if the AIA were to attain its ends, were completely consumed with working out the details of their impending "unification" in a single department of defense and the separation of the air force from the army. In particular, Assistant Secretary of War for Air Robert A. Lovett, without whose backing the industry could not even think of proceeding, was determined that air force autonomy would take precedence over all other issues. And the fact that the navy—that arch foe of air force independence—favored the idea of a presidential commission on aviation made Lovett and the army air force high command just that much more inclined to look askance at it. Hence even if the industry had mounted an all-out effort during 1946, the services would have been too preoccupied with devising their new arrangements to supply much more than an occasional cheer from the sidelines. Given the complexity and the difficulty of the task the AIA had set itself, such feeble assistance would hardly suffice.[15]

All this began to change in the final months of 1946, however, starting in September with the reorganization of the Air Coordinating Committee (ACC), an interagency body in the executive branch and the fulcrum around which the AIA would apply the force required to move the Truman administration. Nominally created by an interdepartmental memorandum of March 27, 1945, signed by Acting Secretary of State Joseph C. Grew, Secretary of War Henry L. Stimson, Secretary of the Navy James V. Forrestal and Secretary of Commerce Henry A. Wallace, this committee, in its first incarnation, actually came into being primarily through the labors of Assistant Secretary of Air for War Robert Lovett. Lovett's conviction was that all aspects of "air power" would become increasingly important in the postwar years, hence the federal government would be in need of a body that could coordinate policies in the various fields of civil, military, national and international aviation. As originally constituted, the ACC included representatives (at the level of assistant secretary or its equivalent) from the foregoing four departments and the office of the Civil Aeronautics Administrator; subsequently, the chairman of the Civil Aeronautics Board elected to participate; still later, the post office gained representation; and finally, after obtaining its independence in 1947, the air force replaced the War Department.[16]

The reorganization of the ACC in September of 1946 by Presidential Executive Order 9781 not only strengthened the committee and gave it more authority, but it also furnished the AIA with an opportunity to remedy what Eugene Wilson regarded as its most outstanding defect—the absence of industry representation. "It was important that the views of the aircraft manufacturing and air transport industries . . . should be made known to the Government through a recognized channel," testified Assistant Secretary of State Garrison Norton, who in April 1947 had become chairman of the reorganized ACC, to the President's Air Policy Commission (PAPC). "Accordingly, the new committee organized an Industry Advisory Panel" with representatives of the AIA and various other aviation trade associations, as well as token members from the American Federation of Labor and the Congress of Industrial Organizations. "The Industry Panel," Norton continued,

> was asked to serve in an advisory capacity with respect to all matters of joint interest except those in which, for security reasons, participation was not possible. The Panel members were invited to submit their problems directly to the Committee and to attend the meetings of ACC and its subcommittees at which these and all other problems affecting their interests were to be discussed.

At least insofar as issues that affected the airplane builders are concerned, it was here that capture of the ACC by the Aircraft Industries Association commenced.[17]

Thanks to the labors of Eugene Wilson, the airplane manufacturers now had two direct avenues through which they could make certain that the Truman administration would give their problems a sympathetic hearing (see Figure 3.1, Chart of Organization of the Air Coordinating Committee). If they wished to start at the top, an Industry Advisory Panel—presided over by one Eugene E. Wilson—allowed them direct access to the full ACC. If, instead, aircraft executives thought it more desirable to operate from the bottom up, they could make use of the Industrial Division's Working Committee on the Aircraft Industry (or a variety of other ad hoc committees in this division) to bring measures they favored to the full committee for its endorsement. All in all, a considerable achievement for the Aircraft Industries Association under Wilson's leadership.

Later in 1946, Wilson matched the triumph he had achieved in securing industry representation on the ACC by recruiting recently retired Major General Oliver P. Echols to the presidency of the AIA (thus permitting Wilson to assume a less visible role as chairman of the association's board of directors). Rarely has a person been more thoroughly deserving of his salary. Not only did Echols, who had directed aircraft procurement for the army air force in World War II, have the respect and, apparently, the trust of aircraft executives and government bureaucrats alike, but his tirelessness, his zeal, were little short of astounding. There were endless ruminations about the aircraft industry in Washington during 1947. Whether these discussions took place within the administration, Congress or the military, however, one feature was common to them all: sooner or later—and probably sooner at that—Oliver Echols could be expected to put in an appearance to make the case for the companies that employed him.[18] George Brownell, Robert Lovett's wartime executive officer and a former War Department representative on the ACC, later related, "As 1946 passed and 1947 began the situation of the aircraft manufacturers became more and more critical. The industry pressed the Air Coordinating Committee to take the subject up again in the light of the changed conditions. The Committee did so, and has during the past several months given it continuous attention." Indeed, after becoming aware of "the critical condition of the aircraft manufacturing industry," the committee, according to its co-chairman, at once began working toward the industry's goal of having the president "appoint a board of nationally prominent disinterested citizens competent to make a thorough investigation" of aviation-related issues. That the ACC complied so rapidly with the wishes of the aircraft firms was in no small part a tribute to the assiduousness with which Oliver Echols proselytized on their behalf.[19]

To say that Echols lost not a moment in plunging into action would be a pale approximation of the truth. Hardly ensconced behind his new desk, already he was writing to William L. Clayton, under secretary of state for economic affairs and

FIGURE 3.1:
ORGANIZATION CHART OF THE AIRCRAFT COORDINATING COMMITTEE

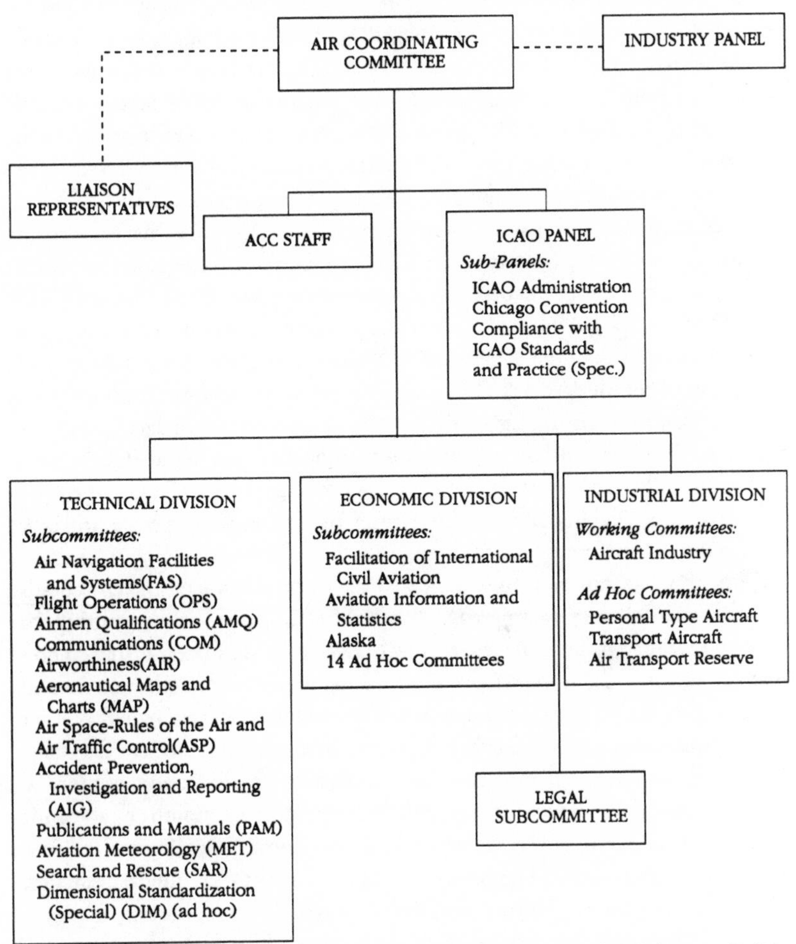

Source: *Report of the Air Coordinating Committee for the Calendar Year 1947* (Washington, D.C.: Government Printing Office, 1948), p. 17.

Garrison Norton's predecessor as chairman of the ACC, with a request that the committee revise its 1945 report on the demobilization of the aircraft industry. This report had called for annual production of about 3,000 military airplanes, or 30 million pounds of airframe, as the amount necessary to maintain the industry in peacetime; but, Echols contended, it had become out of date and failed to reflect "new developments and changed conditions."[20] Next, on February 27, Echols—still in office less than two months—followed up this initial salvo by attending his first ACC meeting, where he introduced two new proposals for that committee's consideration. One of these, adopted by the ACC's Industry Advisory Panel in its meeting of February 6, would have enabled the industry—acting through the ACC and the aforementioned panel—to recommend "to the President the names of qualified personnel to be appointed to key aviation positions in the Federal government." The ACC duly approved this idea, its chairman in mid-March dispatched a letter to the president, and on March 21, 1947, the latter replied that he saw "no reason why a program of that sort could not be worked out."[21]

Much more audacious was Echols's second proposal—that the AIA, again proceeding through the Industry Advisory Panel, be granted the power to review all "Federal agency budget requests affecting aviation in their relation to the over-all needs of the industry, and make appropriate recommendations regarding such requests." After hearing this suggestion, J. Weldon Jones, the assistant director of the Bureau of the Budget, felt obliged to remind the former major general that "direct presentation of industry views to the Bureau of the Budget is without precedent." The compromise outcome was that the members of the ACC "agreed that it is inappropriate for the ACC to furnish the Panel with member agencies' budget requests . . . , but that in the preparation of such requests, agencies will bear in mind the industry requirements."[22]

All of this was, however, preliminary to the main purpose of Oliver Echols's appearance on February 27. Immediately following the debate over permitting the Industry Advisory Panel to review agency budgets, the ACC heard from Echols what one member described as "a very interesting presentation of the current and projected position of the aircraft manufacturing industry." These remarks set off a lengthy discussion, which Garrison Norton, soon to become the ACC's chairman, summarized by declaring that what was at stake was "the survival of the U.S. aircraft manufacturing industry, particularly in the next six months to a year. It raises the question as to how much of a subsidy must be forthcoming and . . . how much the Government will provide through its orders for military aircraft. Emergency legislation," Norton concluded, might "be necessary in order to maintain minimum production levels." On that note, the committee assigned the Industrial Division to reevaluate "the minimum requirements of the aircraft manufacturers['] industry," and make "recommendations as to how best to meet any present or projected deficiency indicated from the [previous] determinations." Eugene Wilson's choice for the new president of the AIA had been a wiser one than perhaps even he knew: one meeting and already the members of the ACC were marching to the beat of Oliver Echols's drum.[23]

But the ever-busy General Echols did not confine his evangelism to the ACC. Indeed, even prior to appearing before that committee, he had made the same presentation for the edification of Assistant Secretary of War for Air W. Stuart Symington, Army Air Force Commanding General Carl A. Spaatz and the various aides and deputies of each. Echols's performance must have been, as usual, a moving one, for by the time of the next meeting of the ACC, on April 3, 1947, it was evident that the top ranks of the War Department bureaucracy had been converted to his cause. At the April 3 meeting was no less a personage than Under Secretary of War Kenneth C. Royall, substituting for Assistant Secretary of War for Air Symington, who was recuperating from surgery. Royall's reason for attending the meeting, according to informal minutes taken by the War Department's liaison representative, was to discuss item 22/7.3, "Demobilization of the Aircraft Industry—Present Condition of the Aircraft Industry—Interim Report by the Industrial Division." These minutes contain an overview of the proceedings sufficiently pithy to merit quoting virtually in full. "It was agreed," the War Department's liaison wrote,

> that the President of the U.S. should be notified that the condition of the aircraft manufacturing industry is serious, that the minimums set up to maintain a healthy industry in the ACC report of 1945 were not being met and that it would probably be necessary for the Government to subsidize industry by Government contracts to some extent in order to tide industry over its present serious situation.
>
> To accomplish this, it was agreed that the Industrial Division would prepare a letter to the President covering the following:
>
> a. The serious situation of the aircraft industry.
>
> b. How the 1945 ACC report on Demobilization of the Aircraft Industry is not being fulfilled.
>
> c. The amount of additional funds which should be appropriated to the Army and Navy to be spent in an attempt to tide industry over the present situation.
>
> d. The method of utilization of these funds to accomplish the above purpose.[24]

As this account reveals, by April of 1947, the ACC had already accepted in principle the notion that it was the responsibility of the federal government, by one means or another, to preserve those stalwart exponents of "free enterprise," the owners of the largest aircraft manufacturing concerns. These minutes are refreshingly straightforward, refusing to cloak the decision to wet-nurse the industry in spurious rationalizations about "national security." The ACC's own minutes, in contrast, were notably less candid; they insisted on concealing the committee's actions beneath an acceptable fig leaf. At the outset of the discussion, Kenneth Royall had immediately made the point that considerations of "national security" were separate and distinct from those of saving the aircraft industry from ruination. In his view, "based on a non-technical consideration of the subject," there were

> two criteria for determining the approach to the problem. The first is: What is actually needed in numbers of aircraft for military purposes, and the second is the volume of business necessary to assure the maintenance of a sound and healthy aircraft industry. Mr. Royall expressed the feeling that with regard to the first criterion we may not need 3,000 aircraft for military purposes. . . . It appears to him that the projected annual procurement of approximately 800 aircraft for the Army and approximately 500 for the Navy may be sufficient from the standpoint of tactical requirements.

Assistant Secretary of the Navy for Air John N. Brown then followed suit by proclaiming "that his concern, on behalf of the Navy, is almost exactly the same as that expressed so clearly by Mr. Royall."

Nonetheless, despite Royall's explicit statement that the procurement of 3,000 airplanes a year espoused by the ACC's 1945 report was probably not required "for military purposes," the committee ended this discussion by agreeing to "call to the attention of the President the validity of the original report on demobilization of the aircraft industry prepared by the Committee in 1945." Although the committee claimed to recognize "that the present budget estimates" had been "based on a sound judgment made in the light of existing conditions," it argued that now there were "additional factors, all unfavorable, which make it imperative that additional funds be requested *in the interest of national security* using as a basis the levels of production recommended in the [1945 ACC] demobilization report" (emphasis added). Thus did the committee go about preparing to satisfy the need of the aircraft industry (and its champions in the ruling class) for a subsidy that would not be called a subsidy.[25]

The extent to which the ACC had fallen under the dominance of the Aircraft Industries Association and Oliver Echols became clear at the next meeting of the committee on May 1, 1947, when it developed that in the interim the War and Navy Departments had "reconsidered their original position" regarding a request to the president for more money for aircraft procurement, and were now urging "that the Committee . . . table the matter with a view toward further consideration at the next meeting." The State Department's Garrison Norton, the ACC's new chairman, "said that he was personally disappointed with the War and Navy suggestion," and delivered a stirring plea for immediate action on the grounds that "the current condition of the aircraft manufacturing industry is probably one of the most crucial problems facing the United States." What had brought about such an abrupt reversal on the part of the two armed services? The answer emerged soon enough. "On the basis of his conversation with Under Secretary [of War Kenneth] Royall, Mr. Norton understands that General Echols, President of the Aircraft Industries Association, has modified his previous statements made to the ACC to the extent that the problem is primarily one falling in the fiscal year 1949 and that it is unnecessary at this time to request a deficiency appropriation" for additional military airplanes. Oliver Echols had spoken, in short, and that settled the matter, at least for the moment. So powerful had his influence over the ACC become that he did not even have to bother attending the committee's meetings in order to exert it; merely making his wishes known via Kenneth Royall apparently sufficed.[26]

Six weeks elapsed before the next ACC meeting, on June 13, 1947, at which time the battle over the nature of a letter from the committee to the president resumed. Under Secretary of War Kenneth Royall, still substituting for the convalescing Stuart Symington, again argued the position of the aircraft industry, urging that the final paragraph of such a letter "recommend that the President appoint a Board of nationally prominent citizens to determine the size of an aircraft manufacturing industry necessary to meet minimum national security requirements . . . and make recommendations as to steps necessary to maintain the required nucleous [*sic*]." John Sherman, the ACC's executive secretary, suggested that the letter instead offer the president three alternatives, one of which would be to appoint the type of commission that the AIA and Royall were demanding. William C. Foster, representing the Commerce Department, supported Royall's position, but maintained that the "inclusion of Congressional representation on the proposed Board will unquestionably further favorable consideration by the Congress of a request for additional money to sustain a given level of production in the aircraft industry." Livingston C. Merchant, the alternate for Garrison Norton, reiterated the State Department's view that the ACC's letter "should call for a supplemental appropriation which would permit the War and Navy Departments to support the aircraft programs originally requested by them." After further discussion, Royall put his proposal in the form of a motion, which was defeated when the representative from the Civil Aeronautics Board sided with the State and Commerce Departments. The ACC resolved the impasse by turning over the drafting of the letter to an ad hoc committee of four headed by Brackley Shaw, an aide to Stuart Symington.[27]

The committee finished work on the letter the next day, June 14; two days after that, the Air Coordinating Committee met again and adopted the new draft with only slight and insignificant modifications. As sent to the President on the following day, June 17, the much-debated final paragraph read, in its entirety:

> The Committee therefore recommends:
>
> (a) That you appoint a board of nationally prominent and disinterested citizens competent to make a thorough investigation of the relation of the aircraft industry to the national defense and to our air transportation requirements;
>
> (b) That this board be authorized to use any data which it may consider pertinent and to conduct such public hearings as it determines, in its discretion, to be desirable; and
>
> (c) That the board be directed to make recommendation by November 1, 1947, as to what economically feasible steps and procedures are required to maintain an aircraft industry of the size necessary for preservation of national security and to meet the needs of our air transportation system.[28]

In the end, as this letter demonstrates, the aircraft industry had gotten its way on every point. The letter did not ask for an immediate supplemental appropriation for airplane procurement, as the State Department wished; it did not set forth three alternatives, as the ACC's own executive secretary wished; it did not mention including members of Congress on the proposed aviation board, as the Commerce Department wished. What the chain of events culminating in the ACC's letter to the president of June 17 establishes beyond dispute is that in any conflict between federal bureaucrats and the aircraft industry, despite some momentary resistance on the part of the former, it would be the latter that would ultimately carry the day. If some of the civilian members of the ACC had the temerity to attempt replacing the industry's agenda with one of their own, they learned soon enough who was in the pilot's seat.

THE ARMY AIR FORCE ENTERS THE FRAY

Well before 1947, a symbiotic relationship between the aircraft industry and the Army air force had crystallized. Just as the air force depended on the industry to manufacture the latest, largest, fastest, most powerful and highest-flying airplanes, the industry depended on the air force to manufacture the ideology that would serve as a suitable pretext for the procurement of those weapons. In consequence, although aircraft executives, uniformed officers and civilian administrators did not always see eye to eye, on most questions the three groups presented a common front. And on those rare occasions when disagreements did arise, they were usually resolved—as we have witnessed in the matter of a presidential aviation commission, and as we shall shortly witness again in the matter of the distribution of procurement contracts—in ways favored by the manufacturers. Increasingly, moreover, air force officers tended to believe that what was good for the industry was good for the service. "As you know," Lieutenant General Nathan F. Twining told Major General Hugh J. Knerr in May 1947, "throughout the war we encouraged the aircraft manufacturers to develop air transports of larger and larger size. We did this knowing full well that with many of them their interests were principally in the prospects for commercial sales in a post-war period. It was, in fact, a Government subsidy..., and I believe it was money well spent, from which the military forces should reap high dividends."[29]

This was hardly the only case of the army air force arranging matters to benefit the aircraft companies. Disposal of surplus airplanes, for instance, touched a particularly sensitive nerve among the manufacturers, who were apprehensive that the airlines might prefer cheaper surplus models to the more expensive new ones. Taking this into account, the author of a June 1945 army air force study of the industry obligingly advocated that "after the war, . . . when new and improved equipment becomes available, the distribution of surplus aircraft and components should cease, in order to encourage experimentation and new production and relieve the aircraft manufacturers of the fear of the dumping of surpluses over an unlimited period of time." The solicitousness of the air force on behalf of the industry extended down to the level of the individual firm, moreover, as an example involving Douglas Aircraft illustrates. When, during the war, Douglas wanted to commence production of the C-117 for the "commercial" market in the same plant where it was already turning out that airplane for the army air force, "after thorough exploration of the problem, . . . the War Department took the unusual step of making application to the Director of War Mobilization and Reconversion for authority [to allow Douglas] to manufacture a certain number of C-117's under the cost-plus-fixed-fee contract and sell them directly to airlines." Although Douglas received the permission it sought, "the war with Japan terminated . . . before the foregoing program could be put into effect." By way of consolation, the assistant secretary of war for air then secured an "emergency ruling from the Office of War Mobilization and Reconversion . . . permitting

Douglas Aircraft to immediately start using Government-owned tooling, even prior to the adoption of a regulation on that subject by the Surplus Property Board." Relations between the industry and the air force were not exactly what one would term adversarial.[30]

Thus, as conditions in the aircraft industry worsened during 1946 and 1947, the air forces top officers searched for remedies with a growing sense of alarm. In May 1947, to take one example, Commanding General Carl A. Spaatz asked the Air Matériel Command at Wright Field, Ohio, to investigate whether the industry could be sustained by "attempting to transfer some of our routine maintenance functions" to it. Even though the answer proved to be in the negative, the very fact that Spaatz would pose the question is significant. Nor was Spaatz atypical in his concern. Hugh J. Knerr, who had organized the Air Board—a kind of steering committee for the army air force—and then become its presiding secretary-general, was another upper-echelon officer who worked to devise policies to aid the manufacturers. "The aircraft industry can be carried though the crisis of the next few years[,] while attrition takes out war equipment, by military development of the air freighter," he stated in a March 1947 memorandum; and, later in the year, he returned to this idea by suggesting that "immediate active support be given to any aircraft manufacturer who is able and willing to cooperate with the Air Force in the development of a common purpose air carrier."[31]

But by all odds the most ambitious proposal came from the head of the Strategic Air Command, General George C. Kenney, who proclaimed to his colleagues at the fifth meeting of the Air Board in June 1947:

> This job has to be done by everybody that is interested in aviation. There is the Army, the Navy, the civil airlines, the manufacturers, and maybe some of the bankers that are the angels for a lot of this stuff. They have to get together and not have a Williamsburg Conference where they hear a few lectures, but get together for about 6 weeks. They have to have a subcommittee and go into all the various phases of this thing, and finally come up with a program and the legislation drafted which is necessary to put that thing in for this . . . program . . . It does require legislation to put the thing in, and somebody has to draft it, and then sell it to Congress, and then follow the thing through and carry it along.[32]

What had provoked Kenney to such vehemence was the impassioned rhetoric of none other than Oliver P. Echols, who had just finished holding forth with a lengthy soliloquy—the transcript occupies 20 pages of double-spaced typescript—

on the pitiable plight of the aircraft industry. Echols, we shall soon observe, had already enlisted the cooperation of Carl Spaatz in the effort to pluck the industry out of danger. (Spaatz, too, evidently found Echols most persuasive, for he invited the former major general, his retirement notwithstanding, to become a member of the Air Board—a turn of events that doubtless delighted those industry executives who knew about this cozy arrangement.) Now, in keeping with his practice of leaving no conceivable stone unturned and no conceivable ally un-recruited, he had returned to induct the rest of the service's leadership as well. Echols's words must have moved his listeners greatly, for, repeatedly spurred on by George Kenney, they continued to mull them over long after their author's departure early in the first day of this two-day gathering. Their discussion came to a head late in the second day, when, in the course of debating the merits of—what else?—a presidentially-appointed aviation commission, the following exchange occurred:

> *Mr. [Roy] Alexander [an editor in the Luce publishing empire and an unofficial press agent for the army air force]: If you have the bill to sell, you don't give a damn who is on the board as long as they are honest people.*
>
> *[Major] General [Follett] Bradley: What you really want is a new Morrow Board?*
>
> *Colonel [James H.] Higgs: That is exactly right.*
>
> *Mr. Alexander: That is right.*
>
> *[Lieutenant] General [George E.] Stratmeyer: I agree with Alexander.*
>
> *Major General Knerr: Well then, we can draft such a statement, and include any objections to it.*[33]

Before matters could go much further, however, in walked Carl Spaatz to break the news that the Air Board had come late to the parade. "There has been a start made on that," said the commanding general, with respect to the suggestion for a presidential commission. "Mr. Royall has had some preliminary conversations. . . . The impetus is there in that Mr. Royall is carrying the ball. He has had conversations with the White House on the matter. . . . And the air industries are all enthusiastic about it, and he is pressing the thing."[34]

From the standpoint of this narrative, Oliver Echols's appearance at the fifth meeting of the Air Board in June 1947 is noteworthy in two respects. First of all, the immediate and enthusiastic response of the Air Board points up the importance that the army air force's highest-ranking officers attached to aiding the aircraft industry in its darkest hour. Second, it underscores the dedication with which Oliver Echols served his employers, the largest corporations in that industry. In actuality, there was no real need for Echols to have attended the Air Board meeting. As we noted above in surveying the Air Coordinating Committee meetings of April, May and June, and as Carl Spaatz reaffirmed at the close of this session of the Air Board, the army air force was already thoroughly committed to the industry's plan for a presidential aviation board. That Echols chose to exhort his fellow officers nonetheless merely reminds us of his determination to explore every conceivable avenue, no matter how minor, in his quest for the prize.*

If the army air force's officer corps was eager to do battle on behalf of the aircraft industry, even a cursory examination reveals this zeal was easily matched by that of its civilian administrators. Of no one was this more true than W. Stuart Symington, who succeeded Robert Lovett as assistant secretary of war for air in 1946, then became the first secretary of the air force when the service achieved autonomy the following year. "It now appears as if the Air Forces must face the problem of what is going to happen to the aviation industry," he advised Carl Spaatz early in February 1947. To Oliver Echols, who was particularly close to Symington, he wrote later that spring, "It looks as if *our* airplane industry is in trouble and it would seem to be the obligation of our little shop to do the best we can to help where such assistance is right and proper [emphasis added]. . . . I am quite sure General Spaatz feels the same way about it," he stated by way of further reassurance. But alas, even though the airplane builders

---

* Nor would this be the last time that Oliver Echols would take advantage of his membership in the Air Board to further the goals of the airplane builders. Both the aircraft industry and the air force high command were hostile to the Truman administration's proposed program for universal military training (UMT), because it would, if implemented, absorb Pentagon money that otherwise could go for the purchase of new airplanes. The air force, however, was reluctant to state its position openly, for fear of incurring the wrath of the president. Oliver Echols, I show in chapter 6, devised the solution; when the issue of UMT came up for discussion at the seventh meeting of the Air Board early in 1948, it was he who furnished the rationalization that allowed the air force to oppose UMT while still claiming to be loyal to the administration.

were "in terrible shape," the assistant secretary lamented to General K. B. Wolfe, there was "nothing to do about it if we haven't got the money which we tried hard to get." Nevertheless, Symington could not restrain himself from reverting to the topic two paragraphs later:

> As mentioned, the aviation industry is in really serious shape, because there is so little business and because the airlines themselves are now in such bad shape. The TWA reorganization took a terrific sock at Lockheed. . . . I understand only three aircraft companies made money last year; and that Douglas is heavily in the red this year. It is not a good situation.[35]

Certainly no one could accuse Stuart Symington of insincerity when he asserted that it was "the obligation of our little shop to do the best we can to help" the aircraft industry weather the storm. In preparing for his appearance before the President's Air Policy Commission in September of 1947, for example, he turned to Oliver Echols for assistance; Echols, it probably goes without saying, readily complied, sending the secretary a draft of some ten typewritten pages. Later that month the secretary told Echols, "If you thought it might be advisable for General Spaatz and me to meet with you and your [AIA] Directors, this to discuss the maximum utilization of all industry in the interest of air power, that of course would be a pleasure." And at year's end, in response to a request from Secretary of Defense James Forrestal for a memorandum on "Subjects to be Stressed by Representatives of the Government in Public Appearances," he made sure to include an item proclaiming, "An Air Force is of little value unless it is backed up by an adequate peacetime aircraft industry which is capable of rapid expansion in war."[36]

There can be no question that Symington's attitude toward the industry was shared by the entire War Department. "The aircraft manufacturing industry is a priority concern of the War Department," its secretary, Robert P. Patterson, stated to the director of the Bureau of the Budget in July 1947. "In addition to continuing study by government agencies, something extraordinary needs to be done in order to focus upon this problem the wide and emphatic attention it deserves."[37]

Hence it was only natural that, during the spring months of 1947, when Symington was rendered *hors de combat* by surgery, Under Secretary of War Kenneth Royall would take over "carrying the ball," to borrow General Spaatz's metaphor, for both the War Department and the aircraft industry. We have already watched Royall at work in the Air Coordinating Commission, first advancing the suggestion for a presidential aviation commission, then beating down rival proposals put forward by the State and Commerce Departments, the Civil Aeronautics Board and the ACC's own staff. To complete the saga, however, we must also glance briefly at his address to the Aircraft Industries Association Conference at Williamsburg, Virginia, on May 16, 1947. This gathering was, according to Lockheed Aircraft's president, Robert Gross, an "attempt [by] all the aircraft drummers . . . to build a case for Government support for the air industry." The apparent purpose of Royall's speech—insofar as speeches at business conventions can be said to have a purpose—was to signal to the aircraft executives the War Department's willingness to support their campaign for "another Morrow Board." Not surprisingly, given the setting, Royall focused on what could be done to ensure that the federal government would spend more on military airplanes. The conclusion of the ACC's 1945 report—that the industry needed procurement of a minimum of 30 million pounds of airframe annually to remain solvent—was unquestionably correct; still, "in spite of its merits and soundness," the ACC report had "produced few, if any, concrete results." On the contrary, pressures for "a radical curtailment of government expenditures, so that . . . there can be a reduction in our national debt and then a reduction in our national taxes," had kept its recommendations from being implemented. But "the pendulum of economy" had been allowed to "swing too far"—the time had come to "start it back in the other direction."[38]

What measures would best redress the balance? Although some had suggested an immediate request to Congress for more procurement money—Royall's none-too-subtle dig at the State Department—there was "no real possibility of getting a large increased appropriation for Army and Navy aircraft in the limited time remaining to the present session." Nor was such a step necessary in any case, for the aircraft "companies have civilian transport business which will help them over the period immediately ahead." Rather than seeking more procurement orders now, the under secretary contended, the army and the industry should instead endeavor to "impress the nation . . . as to the vital need of enough combat aircraft . . . [and] the importance of a healthy aircraft industry." Yet this approach raised another question: Who could lead the way? Clearly, neither the ACC, which was "composed entirely of representatives of government departments," nor the airplane manufacturers, who were certain to be viewed as "selfishly interested in increased aircraft production," would be acceptable in such a role. Instead, according to Royall,

> the chances of attaining our objectives would be increased, if a group of outstanding American citizens should be formed . . . to present to the people of the country a concrete and definite plan for sufficient present air power and for the maintenance of the necessary aircraft industry.

> The group would consist of men of outstanding reputation and of totally disinterested persons—not connected with any government department—and not connected in any way with the aircraft industry. They could thus consider the entire problem without the tag or the charge of either bureaucracy or selfishness.

So great was Royall's "faith in our position" that he harbored "no doubt but that the report of such a group would favor a balanced and larger schedule of military aircraft." What the administration and the military "must do," therefore, was to agree on the "minimum which we *must* have, then throw behind it the full weight of our influence, convince the people of the country of the need and practicality of our program, and get their support and the support of their representatives in Congress."[39]

"[T]otally disinterested persons—not connected with any government department—and not connected in any way with the aircraft industry." Righteous words, these. Yet as we shall see directly, when the commission urged by Royall actually came to be created, this high-flown language was honored far more in the breach than in the observance. How otherwise? Having travelled this far, the magnates of the aircraft business were not about to let a handful of pious abstractions deny them their victory at the last moment.

TWO BOARDS ARE BETTER THAN ONE?

On July 18, 1947, the Truman administration announced the appointment of a temporary President's Air Policy Commission. Thirteen days later, Congress followed suit by creating a Congressional Air Policy Board. Commenting on the sequence of events that had culminated in this result, Lockheed president Robert Gross found it an "irony that for a while we could get none and now we have two." How had such a situation come about?[40]

The answer lies in the activities of executives such as Gross, Eugene Wilson, Frederick Rentschler and the Aircraft Industries Association (AIA) that represented them. At the same time they were striving to have their position adopted by the Air Coordinating Committee, the manufacturers were also exploring every other conceivable means of securing the national aviation commission they had so long desired. Ideally, their thinking ran, if they could generate the necessary political pressure, the president would be compelled to appoint a panel of this nature. But if not, there were still other possibilities. Congress, for instance, might be persuaded to authorize an aviation policy board by statute if the president balked. During the spring of 1947, therefore, the AIA worked with friendly legislators to prod Congress into establishing such a body. This was an ingenious tactic. The election of 1946 had transferred control of Congress to the Republicans. The threat of an aviation commission dominated by his political enemies might in itself be sufficient to goad Harry Truman into action. And even if worse came to worst and the president refused to cooperate, the industry could still secure copious amounts of publicity for its cause from a series of well-staged hearings of a congressionally-chartered board.

Of the several congressional bills introduced on this topic, the most important bore the names of Representative Carl Hinshaw, a Republican from Southern California with a mere four major aircraft companies (Douglas, Lockheed, North American and Northrop) in or adjacent to his district, and Senator Owen Brewster of Maine, a prominent figure in the Republican leadership. Hinshaw's bill, in its original form, would have established a permanent National Aviation Council, headed by a presidential appointee, to replace the ACC; the Brewster bill, as Robert Gross explained, called for "the appointment of a Presidential Board to review the entire aviation industry." Ecstatic when "the Senate passed by unanimous consent, the Brewster bill," Gross told his longtime friend and banker, Frederick M. Warburg of Kuhn, Loeb:

> This is the "cause celebre" which we have been fighting for the last few months and I cannot overestimate the good effect the creation of such a board might have on our whole industry. . . . This is the 1947 version of the 1926 Morrow Board which latter, as you recall, laid the foundation for America's air power.[41]

Meanwhile, as the debates in the ACC and in Congress ground forward, the AIA continued beating the bushes for other champions. This search took the association into some curious quarters. Although "the industry is convinced that larger government appropriations for military aircraft are absolutely essential—and soon," *Business Week* stated in April 1947, "it is a little wary of pleading its case directly. It is afraid that it would then be labeled as a 'war industry,' the individual manufacturers[,] as 'war mongers.' For this reason," the magazine explained,

> the Aircraft Industry Assn. has called on the American Legion for help. The Legion responded by holding a "national aeronautics conference" in Indianapolis, financed by the A.I.A. Its keynote was the widely expressed fear that our plane-manufacturing know-how

> . . . will be lost if something isn't done quickly. Legion posts throughout the country were called on at the conference to put on a campaign for a bigger and stronger air force.

Prominent among the speakers at the Indianapolis "conference" was the aforementioned Senator Owen Brewster, who, according to *Aviation News,* in the course of his remarks "quoted an official Russian document calling for Soviet leadership in the air, cited the Russian budget which estimates [*sic*] 58 percent of the military budget for the Air Force, and referred also to the fact that Britain's new budget allows for a 370,000-man RAF as against an AAF . . . requiring only 350,000 men. 'We cannot afford to remain the world's third ranking air power,' Brewster declared." The Senator shared the rostrum with the familiar figure of Oliver P. Echols, who, by this account, "suggested a five-year production program for military aircraft." Somewhat later in the year, the Veterans of Foreign Wars were likewise tapped to do their part by conducting "an airpower [*sic*] drive" to create the illusion of "more grass roots support for the manufacturers and AAF." On this occasion, however, rather than take a public role, the AIA instead worked through the army air force; as *Aviation Week* put it, the VFW was "getting behind-the-scenes support from AAF brass."[42]

By the start of the summer, the industry's various schemes and plans had begun to converge as events moved towards a climax. On June 17, we saw in an earlier section, the ACC dispatched a letter to the president urging him to "appoint a board of nationally prominent and disinterested citizens" to investigate and report on the aircraft industry. On July 16, the Senate—to the great joy of Robert Gross and, one supposes, his counterparts at other aircraft companies—passed the Brewster bill unanimously. Although that bill then went to a conference committee to be reconciled with the Hinshaw bill passed by the House, Senator Brewster told Secretary of the Navy James Forrestal on the following day, July 17, that "the Senate and House are entirely agreed." It was at that point that the Truman administration elected to announce that the president had suddenly chosen to appoint an Air Policy Board of his own.[43]

Popular mythology has it that Truman was a president who embodied, if nothing else, the quality of accountability: "The buck stops here," and all that. Those who have actually done research on how he reached this or that decision generally know better. In all too many instances, there is an official document—a press release, say, or a speech or a letter—but nothing that reveals the actual contents of Truman's thinking. That, at any rate, is how matters stand here. Prior to the middle of July 1947, there was no indication that Truman intended to create an aviation commission; 45 years later, we know little more about what prompted him to do so than did contemporary onlookers.

Robert Gross, whose status as a major contributor to the Republican party gave him access to a certain amount of "inside" political information, believed that Truman's move was inspired by political expediency. "Things got a little bit confused in the last few days of the congressional session," he wrote Frederick Warburg. After "working originally . . . on the idea of having the President appoint a Board of private citizens," the airplane makers concluded that they should also adopt "the tactic of working through Congress to have a law passed creating a Board as opposed to a merely presidentially appointed one." Then, after both the Brewster and the Hinshaw bills had been enacted but were still in conference committee, "the President, evidently sensing that the whole idea of an Air Policy Board was gaining momentum, jumped the gun and appointed his own commission." This development presented the manufacturers with a dilemma: "For a few hours we were pretty shaky as to what course to pursue, but we finally decided to press for the legislation anyway and support the President's commission as well. As a result, we now probably have two Air Policy Boards. . . . Personally, . . . I think we can work with both Boards and I am not chastened by the creation of two."[44]

Gross's interpretation has the ring of plausibility. If the Republicans were to preempt all the many issues concerning aviation, there was no telling what manner of mischief they might do—especially with a presidential election in the offing the following year. Truman had no intention of allowing the opposition to accuse his administration of spending too much, too little or too mistakenly on "air power"; he was not the kind of politician to concede his foes such an advantage, least of all by default. Perhaps all of these thoughts went through the mind of Owen Brewster when, on July 17, he telephoned James Forrestal with a request that the secretary of the navy persuade the president to "hold things off" until Congress could complete work on its own aviation bill. The plea, of course, was futile. For a full month the ACC's letter had sat on Truman's desk while the president showed no interest in it whatsoever; as soon as it appeared that a Republican-dominated Congress was on the verge of striking out on its own, however, his administration abruptly concluded that there was not a moment more to be lost.[45]

What lends this interpretation further substance is the fact that for all the use to which Truman put the report of the Presidential Air Policy Commission (PAPC), it might as well have been the Code of Hammurabi in the original cuneiform. The commission published its report, ominously entitled *Survival in the Air Age,* on New Year's Day, 1948, and formally tendered it to the president on January 13. Thereafter, Truman scarcely ever mentioned it in public again, much less acted on its extravagant proposals for a so-called "70-group" air force, an annual procurement of 3,200 first-line airplanes (46 million pounds of airframe) and another 2,000 airplanes for the air force reserves. "Alas," *Aviation Week* moaned in April, in an outraged editorial on what it insisted was "The Betrayal of Air Power," the report had been "gathering dust . . . in some White House cubbyhole" from the moment Truman had accepted it. When, later that spring, the president finally did authorize a jump of almost 60 percent in spending for aircraft procurement (from $1.24 to $1.965 billion) as part of a 30-percent increase in the Pentagon's budget, he made no reference to the contents of the PAPC's report. So far as Truman was concerned, it was as if the air policy commission that he himself appointed had never existed.[46]

Still, it would be greatly mistaken to conclude that the commission was without significance. Granted that Truman himself refused to heed its recommendations, the PAPC nonetheless played a potent role in terrorizing the public into accepting the proposition that "survival in the air age" required a vast boost in spending for military aircraft. Day after day, week after week, for four solid months (September through December 1947) an incessant parade of high military and administration officials repeated the notion that the only hope of protecting the nation against the evil designs of the Soviet Union—which, it hardly needed saying, was merely biding its time until it could take advantage of U.S. weakness—lay in an enormous Air Force "in being" (the word "existence" was apparently unknown in those years) and a "sound and healthy" aircraft industry.

That the President's Air Policy Commission took such an approach was anything but accidental. Early in its history, the chairman, Thomas K. Finletter, met with Arthur Hays Sulzberger, publisher of the *New York Times,* to discuss how the commission should proceed. Finletter, among other things, "asked Mr. Sulzberger's advice as to whether in his opinion the work of the Commission and its report would be more effective if the views of a few important military and civilian people were secured through on-the-record hearings." It was "Mr. Sulzberger's unqualified view" that this proposal "was a good idea," and the publisher specifically suggested that the PAPC use testimony from "both civilian personnel, such as the Secretaries and Under Secretaries, and top military and naval personnel." Last and of greatest importance, "with respect to the type of information which would be most effective," Sulzberger emphatically "recommended that the witnesses go 'all out' advising the people as completely as possible of the current and future dangers to which this country is exposed in just as specific terms as possible." What is especially noteworthy about this conversation was that at the time it occurred, on October 3, 1947, the commission had been holding hearings for a single month only and, as I stated above, would continue to take testimony through the end of the year. Nevertheless, it is clear from the dialogue between Finletter and Sulzberger that already the die had been cast, the most critical conclusion reached: the commission, like its future witnesses, would "go 'all out'" in painting a gruesome picture "of the current and future dangers to which this country" allegedly was "exposed."[47]

Adding to the ability of the Finletter Report (as it was called) to pave the way for more money for the aircraft industry was its enthusiastic reception in ruling-class circles, as indicated by articles and editorials in the most prominent business publications. *Business Week,* for one, endorsed the report as "superb." *Fortune,* juxtaposing it with the earlier report of the Morrow Board in 1926, approvingly asserted, "Now, with the publication of the Finletter Report, it is likely that U.S. aviation has acquired a modern substitute for the old charter it lost." *The Wall Street Journal* likewise praised *Survival in the Air Age* as "an informative and rational document," in particular applauding its "most important recommendation bearing on the aircraft manufacturing industry," that the United States "create an 'air force in being' right away." This led the *Journal* to advocate, predictably enough, that "the armed forces should order $3,830 million of new aircraft in the next two calendar years, about $2 billion more... than at the present rate of plane procurement."[48]

The Finletter Commission is also significant in a second respect, for its composition illustrates—once more—the ability of the aircraft industry to obtain control over all aspects of what purported to be a debate over its future. (A genuine debate, one that vigorously explored all sides of the various issues, was definitely not something the manufacturers had any wish to encourage.) In his address to the Aircraft Industries Association Conference at Williamsburg the previous May, we recollect that Under Secretary of War Royall had described the future presidential aviation policy board as one that would consist of figures "of outstanding reputation and of totally disinterested persons—not connected with any government department—and not connected in any way with the aircraft industry." Thus the rhetoric; now the reality.

The Truman administration made appointments to the PAPC in such a way as to achieve what passed for "balance" in that era: five men, all white; one industrialist (Henry Ford II, replaced after his resignation by John A. McCone), one person from financial circles (Arthur Dare Whiteside, president of Dun and Bradstreet), one from the mass media (E. Palmer Hoyt, publisher of the *Denver Post*), one from academia (George P. Baker, professor of transportation at the Harvard Graduate School of Business Administration) and one (chairman Thomas K. Finletter, a New York corporate attorney) who was probably intended to symbolize "the public." Leaving aside the unrepresentative nature of this panel as too obvious to require elaboration, let us focus instead on the individual members, starting with the chairman. Even if we assume that Finletter was "not connected in any way with the aircraft industry," it is scarcely the case that he lacked ties to the administration, for he had been a special assistant to the Secretary of State from 1941 to 1944, then a consultant to the U.S. delegation to the founding conference of the United Nations in San Francisco in 1945. Given the absence, as usual, of any evidence from Truman regarding how he went about selecting members of the commission, one can only presume that Thomas Finletter was tapped for his post because he was regarded as a known quantity, a loyal Democrat who could be relied upon to see that the PAPC's final report would not be such as to supply ammunition to the administrations enemies.[49]

Vice Chairman of the Commission George P. Baker enjoyed the distinction of being the sole member to use the first-person plural pronoun—"us"—in conversing with aircraft industry executives during the hearings. By no stretch of the imagination could he be considered "not connected in any way with the aircraft industry"; in reality, short of being listed on the payroll of an airplane manufacturer, it is hard to conceive of how Baker might have had closer links to it. During World War II, he had held the rank of colonel in the army air force, had supervised its Industrial Demobilization Division, then managed the Special Projects Office of the Air Staff. Prior to entering the army in 1942, he was a member, and later vice chairman, of the Civil Aeronautics Board; immediately after the war, he worked as a special consultant to the War Department and then as director of the Office of Transport and Communications Policy of the State Department. In 1947, James E. Webb, the director of the Bureau of the Budget, hired Baker as a consultant on a "survey of aviation." Most telling of all, though, is the fact that the aviation research program administered by the George F. Baker Foundation at the Harvard Graduate School of Business Administration was not only one in which George Baker, by virtue of his "long-standing seniority in this field," occupied "the key position"—it was also one that directly depended on money from the airplane manufacturers themselves. "We feel that the Business School program is most vital to our entire industry," wrote Lockheed's Robert Gross, himself a member of the Aviation Research Advisory Committee of the school, to an assistant dean. Therefore, the executive explained, "it would be appropriate at the present time for us to make a contribution . . . of $20,000" rather than "the $10,000 to carry on the work [donated] in the early part of last year." Few people would be inclined to bite the hand that has just fed them so splendidly, and nowhere in the proceedings of the PAPC is there the slightest sign that Professor Baker was afflicted with any such unwholesome tendency.[50]

Undoubtedly the best-known member of the commission, Henry Ford II, also was the one with the shortest tenure. Following his resignation in September, Ford's place was taken by John A. McCone, who, at the suggestion of the air force, was already advising the PAPC on "national security" issues. McCone was a prominent industrialist in his own right: president of and, with Steven Bechtel, a partner in Bechtel-McCone Corporation; president of the Joshua Hendy Iron Works of Los Angeles; a major investor in the California Shipbuilding Company (Los Angeles), the Marinship Corporation (San Francisco), the Oregon Ship Building Company (Portland) and, through Bechtel-McCone, the Henry J. Kaiser shipbuilding firm (Oakland). In addition to his involvement in shipbuilding, McCone had also been active in the aircraft industry. During World War II, Bechtel-McCone operated the Willow Run aircraft modification facility near Birmingham, Alabama, for the army air force. Paid on the basis of its *estimated* (as opposed to actual) costs plus 5 percent, Bechtel-McCone supposedly was to outfit each air force airplane according to the climate in which it later would be flown, though there was considerable controversy over whether the company had ever actually carried out so much as a single modification.

In any case, had members of the Finletter Commission truly been chosen from among those "not connected in any way with the aircraft industry," McCone, who already had become very rich on the basis of wartime weapons production, would have been disqualified at the start. Recognizing that Southern California big business in general and aircraft and shipbuilding firms in particular were heavily dependent on arms spending, McCone, who viewed himself as a policymaker for the region, consistently urged high levels of military procurement. Hence, after the Finletter Commission disbanded, he issued an invitation to Secretary of the Air Force Symington to visit the area, so he could "meet and talk with a selected group of Los Angeles business leaders . . . vitally interested in your work." McCone thought it would be "constructive" for the secretary to "discuss the situation directly with some of the businessmen in Los Angeles[,] all of whom are interested in the aircraft industry because it plays such an important part in our community affairs." With his letter McCone enclosed a manifesto adopted by the Chamber of Commerce in the neighboring city of Long Beach; among its eight resolutions, naturally, was one that "urgently requested Congress to adopt . . . a National Air Policy which will assure [a] strong independent aircraft industry." Soon thereafter, McCone found a more direct way of achieving his goals: early in April he left Los Angeles for Washington in order to accept a position as an adviser on aircraft procurement to Secretary of Defense James Forrestal.[51]

Like Thomas Finletter, Arthur D. Whiteside, the president of Dun and Bradstreet, was probably selected for the PAPC because his views were acceptable to Truman and his advisers. Through Willard L. Thorp, Dun and Bradstreet's chief economist and researcher and the editor of *Dun's Newsletter,*

Whiteside's firm had established connections to both the Roosevelt and Truman administrations. Starting in 1938, Thorp occupied a variety of part-time positions in the executive branch, culminating in 1945 with his appointment as assistant secretary of state for economic affairs, a post he would hold under all four of Truman's secretaries of state. From Thorp, members of Truman's staff readily could have obtained reassurances about Whiteside's political reliability, were there any questions on this score. As for Whiteside himself, given the fact that the company he headed specialized in the collection of financial information about the nation's largest corporations, he had to have been aware that, as I showed in the previous chapter, several of these corporations stood to incur heavy or even catastrophic losses should the aircraft industry fail. It is only reasonable to suppose that this knowledge, in addition to any direct involvement in the aircraft industry he may have had, shaped his response to the information presented to the Finletter Commission. Put another way, it is simply inconceivable that such a pillar of the Establishment would do nothing more than sit on his hands and hope for the best when it was obvious to even the most benighted observer that the airplane builders would be utterly unable to survive without a large injection of federal funds in the very near future. And if their industry went bankrupt, of course, there was no telling how many other big businesses they might take down with them.

E. Palmer Hoyt—"Ep" to his friends—had connections of another sort. His was one of six names (that of George Baker was another) that Secretary of the Navy James Forrestal had proposed for membership in the President's Air Policy Commission. Hoyt and Forrestal were comrades of long standing; they subscribed to the same harsh view of the Soviet Union—as did John McCone, for that matter—and partook of the same antisocialist dogmas and other right-wing articles of faith. In Ferdinand Eberstadt they had a mutual friend who was both Forrestal's closest confidante and Hoyt's investment banker. During World War II, Hoyt had been deputy director of the Office of War Information, in which capacity he supervised the production of propaganda for the domestic market; he thus knew more than a little about how to inspire fear and hatred in the hearts of the citizenry. His great antipathy toward the U.S.S.R. virtually guaranteed that he would endorse any measure that could be made to appear sufficiently anti-Soviet in nature; more money for aircraft procurement fit the bill nicely. (Thus, Hoyt was highly critical of Truman's address to Congress of March 17, 1948: "He omitted air power and general rearmament, thereby fumbling a dramatic opportunity to present to the nation a comprehensive picture of defense necessities. For possible total war, the nation needs total defense.") Add to the foregoing the consideration that Forrestal would have had ample opportunity to convey his own anxiety about conditions in the aircraft industry to Hoyt and we have in him the perfect complement to George Baker and John McCone. With this trio of (in Kenneth Royall's phrase) "totally disinterested persons" comprising a majority on the President's Air Policy Commission, the airplane manufacturers could rest secure in the knowledge that this "second Morrow Board" would do its utmost to promote their interests. On this score, everything was working out just as Eugene Wilson, Frederick Rentschler and James Forrestal had envisioned in 1943.[52]

So much for the President's Air Policy Commission. Of the Congressional Air Policy Board (CAPB), far less need be said. In general, the congressional body was relegated to the role of tail on the Finletter Commission kite—just as the administration had intended in establishing the PAPC in the first place. Instead of holding public hearings of its own, the CAPB worked with transcripts of testimony given before the Finletter Commission; as a result, its proceedings garnered no such wave of publicity as did the presidential commission. The publication of the CAPB's report, *National Aviation Policy,* two months after the appearance of *Survival in the Air Age* came as a distinct anticlimax and, therefore, commanded correspondingly little attention. For our purposes it suffices to remark that with such stout partisans of "air power" as Senator Owen Brewster as its chairman and Representative Carl Hinshaw as vice chairman, the outcome of the congressional board's deliberations was never in doubt. As an illustration of the board's pro-industry bias, note that included on its 15-member advisory council were the presidents of the Fairchild Engine and Aircraft Company, Goodyear Aircraft, Lockheed Aircraft, North American Aviation, United Aircraft, American Airlines, and Slick Airways; the chairman of the board of the Aviation Corporation; Colonel Roscoe Turner, whose position at the Turner Aviation Corporation was not specified; and aviation writer Gil Robb Wilson, designated in one of the board's press releases as "representing the public." This arrangement left some five seats on the council to be shared by representatives of big industry (the president of Proctor and Gamble, the vice chairman of the Willis Knight Corporation), the army, the navy and organized labor. Differences between the findings of the CAPB and the Finletter Commission, not astonishingly, were minor and insignificant. Where the former panel called for spending $5.25 billion for aircraft procurement in the 1949 fiscal year, for example, the latter proposed $5.4 billion; where the former "recommended that the complete Air Force be modernized by the end of calendar year 1952," the latter "indicated that the Air Force could be modernized completely by the end of Fiscal Year 1953, or six months later than the Finletter Commission recommendation." And so forth. With the field already captured by the PAPC, the so-called Brewster Board was reduced to little more than an irrelevancy, a sideshow to the main attraction.[53]

Meanwhile, with both the Finletter Commission and the Brewster Board in operation and thoroughly under the sway of the aircraft manufacturers, industry executives were now free to expand their campaign for a government lifeline into other venues. Such efforts, as we are about to observe, took industry representatives back to where this chapter's narrative began—the office of James V. Forrestal.

GOING TO THE TOP: THE DISTRIBUTION OF CONTRACTS

Nothing shows more clearly the success of aircraft company attempts to shape policies of the Truman administration than the question of how procurement contracts should be distributed within the industry. So far as the air force high command was concerned, the awarding of contracts was definitely a matter of winner take all: in fiscal 1948, 84 percent of the money that service spent for aircraft was absorbed by three firms: Boeing, with 35 percent of the total; North American, with 26 percent; and Republic, with 23 percent. This arrangement left several large companies, including Consolidated-Vultee, Douglas and Lockheed, without a single dollar in air force contracts—and fiscal 1949 promised to bring more of the same.[54]

Such a state of affairs was simply unacceptable to leading executives in the industry, as they testified with great regularity before the President's Air Policy Commission. Nor was this merely a case of sour grapes. William M. Allen, president of the Boeing Airplane Company—the corporation that consistently engulfed the largest portion of the air force's procurement funds—told the members of the Finletter Commission that he was in favor of having those companies with "prime" contracts subcontract a portion of the work to those that did not: "I say that would be helpful and it is the only helpful solution that I see." Mundy I. Peale, the president of Republic Aircraft Corporation—another company that benefitted heavily from Air Force contracts—echoed William Allen's sentiments, even though he conceded that requiring companies with contracts to subcontract some of their work to firms without would be "a little more expensive perhaps." So, too, did Lawrence D. Bell, president of the Bell Aircraft Corporation:

> I also believe that there can be, can be [*sic*], and should be some kind of an overall plan directed by the Government to spread some of the work to subcontracting, where in a particular year one company happens to get more work than it needs or can do. I think there should be some plan to spread that throughout the valleys. . . . I think if you evaluated each individual company, as to what a normal amount of

> volume might be that is necessary to keep that company strong enough for peacetime production, . . . that if we should get a substantial amount of business more than that, I believe it would be wise to take a part of that and place it in plants that had less.

Easily the most outspoken opponent of the air force's procurement practices was Ralph V. Hunt, vice president-comptroller of Douglas Aircraft, who warned the Finletter Commission that if the current

> policy should be continued, it means that many of the units now operating will cease to exist or be seriously impaired. I do not feel that long-term strategy should be completely determined by the present fortuitous placing of models. . . . Surely, it cannot be the desire of all of us who are so interested in the defense of this country, of the Congress, of the Administration, or of the services themselves that our course be built on such chance current circumstances.[55]

That the views of Allen, Peale, Bell and Hunt were those of the industry itself became apparent when Oliver Echols testified, in his capacity as president of the Aircraft Industries Association of America, on October 14. "I do favor as a part of a policy that the Air Forces [*sic*] or Government agency who is to handle procurement should be charged with giving some consideration to the maintenance of the industry," Echols stated,

> in the sense that where you do have excellent factories working . . . and nothing in the factory, that some consideration be given to subcontracting. I would go so far as to say that under extreme cases you might advertise for bids [on subcontracting jobs] and let them [companies lacking work] bid on it. If you have a program, if you have a policy, if you have a flexible procurement law and you give the problem to the [military] services and tell them to set up the administrative procedures and have them execute the policy, I think they can do it. . . . The whole thing, as far as I can see, is a matter of setting up a program . . . , getting the business, giving it to the Government agencies, giving them a policy and telling them to set up a system to execute it.

The general went further still in the formal statement that he submitted to the Finletter Commission, calling for passage of new procurement legislation to "permit the *splitting of* [procurement] *awards* and the use of *mandatory* [emphasis added] *subcontracting*" whenever such measures were "essential to . . . preserve a nucleus" of the aircraft industry.[56]

For all the discussion the topic of subcontracting elicited during the hearings of the Finletter Commission, however, the matter was as good as settled before those hearings even began. That this is so is a tribute to the industry's ability to go directly to the highest levels of the Truman administration in order to have policies it desired put into effect—even if those policies ran counter to the wishes of the armed services themselves. As such, the way this issue was resolved offers a foretaste of things to come.

The tale properly begins on August 25 when Marx Leva, one of Secretary of Defense Forrestal's three special assistants, reminded his superior that "Mr. Donald Douglas wanted to see you on Wednesday [August 27] to discuss a procurement matter involving Navy and Air Force coordination." Forrestal, of course, had long been apprehensive about the postwar fate of the industry, as we witnessed in his meeting with Eugene Wilson and Frederick Rentschler in 1943. During 1947, he frequently reiterated his growing sense of alarm as the situation of the industry deteriorated. "Mr. Forrestal is . . . concerned over the condition, production-wise, of the aircraft industry," Marx Leva wrote Ferdinand Eberstadt, the secretary's close friend and most-valued adviser, in March of 1947. "Mr. Forrestal would like to have the benefit of your thoughts on this subject, also." In response to Donald Douglas's request, therefore, Forrestal met with the executive and arranged for him to confer with the appropriate navy officials on September 27th. Probably of greater importance, however, the two also had dinner together on the evening of Friday the 29th, thereby providing Douglas an opportunity to present his ideas on "Navy and Air Force coordination." The following day, Forrestal sent a memorandum to Secretary of the Air Force W. Stuart Symington:

> I had a talk with Don Douglas last night (Friday). I wish you would get his views on the aircraft industry. In my experience he has always been thoroughly sound and I attach great weight to the thinking of such men as he, Fred Rentschler, Swirbul, Kindleberger, etc.
>
> I came to have great confidence in Echols and [Vice Admiral John H.] Towers during the war and I suggest that you get hold of both of them for a go-around with Douglas.[57]

Symington's response is instructive, for it illustrates just how assiduously, tenaciously and skillfully industry representatives pursued their goals: "I talked to Mr. Douglas today before receiving your note, as I did also with Oliver Echols," he stated. "Echols believes the industry can run on about 36 million pounds of airframe weight—6 million was the estimate for commercial [airline and transport purchases], but that is now down—and we are making up our [procurement] figures this week and then plan to give them to the Navy, asking theirs. . . . [General Carl] Spaatz, [General Hoyt] Vandenberg and I had a conference on this before Spaatz went to Alaska." (In addition, without mentioning it to Forrestal, Symington that same day also wrote to Secretary of the Treasury John Snyder: "Oliver Echols . . . was in today talking about the condition of that [aircraft] industry . . . because of lack of funds." Noting that he had "asked Oliver to make an appointment with you at your convenience to present a few of the interesting thoughts he developed today," Symington urged Snyder, "Please see him when you can." Here we have further evidence—if such be needed—that, whatever the salary paid Echols by the AIA, it was, from the industry's standpoint, money exceedingly well spent.)[58]

Just what were the "views on the aircraft industry" of Donald Douglas that Forrestal thought so important to commend to Symington's attention? Symington's testimony before the Finletter Commission on September 9 supplies the answer. From it we learn that as early as the beginning of September 1947, when the Finletter Commission was just getting under way, top-level officials of the Truman administration had already accepted the aircraft industry's position that those companies fortunate enough to obtain large "prime" contracts should subcontract a portion of the gains to those less blessed. So much Symington's remarks made clear, for when asked whether competition should be permitted to take its toll on the aircraft industry, the Secretary replied that "competition in design and development stages does not preclude cooperation between manufacturers in cross-licensing or sub-contracting for production purposes. That, to us, would seem to be a constructive way of distributing the aircraft business." Challenged by commissioner Henry Ford II, who was dubious that such an arrangement would satisfy the industry, Symington had an immediate rejoinder: "Mr. Douglas and I were discussing it last week and I think he thought that it was a constructive idea." No doubt he did, for it was just this concept of "Navy and Air Force coordination" that Douglas and Echols, in their pilgrimage to the various stations of the Washington military-industrial circuit, had proposed to both Forrestal and Symington the preceding week.[59]

Although I treat the issue of subcontracting more fully in chapter 6, this discussion would be incomplete without at least noting the outcome of the industry's crusade, led by Donald Douglas and Oliver Echols, to compel a revision in air force procurement policies. A survey of airframe backlogs as of May 31, 1949, shows that Douglas and Echols had prevailed. Whereas in 1947, three firms had received 84 percent of all airframe orders from the air force, by mid-1949 that figure had fallen by one-fourth to 63.3 percent; and Douglas and Lockheed, both of which had been denied air force contracts in the earlier year, now each had 7 percent of the total. The distribution of orders for the navy's Bureau of Aeronautics was similar, moreover, so that the top three firms together held less than half (44.7 percent) of all airframe backlogs in 1949—a far cry from the situation in 1947. The combination of Douglas and Echols had proven to be irresistible indeed.[60]

It was one thing to arrange for the promulgation of new procurement procedures; making sure that there was enough procurement money in the federal budget to prevent the aircraft firms from expiring was another matter altogether. As 1947 drew to a close and both the President's Air Policy Commission and the Congressional Air Policy Board commenced winding up their affairs, there was still no clear indication that either the administration or Congress was prepared to do the industry's bidding. Pessimism about the prospects of the airplane makers thus began to spread. *Aviation Week,* a bellwether in this regard, noted at the end of December "the apprehension in aviation circles that the efforts of the President's Air Policy Commission and the [congressional] joint policy board may be reduced to fanfare by the refusal of the appropriations committees to implement aviation programs with funds"; and the following issue carried a similar message: "With the Republican Congress striving to lower the ceiling on Federal expenditures and cuts in pork-barrel outlays unlikely in a presidential election year, the outlook for greatly increased aviation budgets is not bright."[61] Even the onset of the war scare described in the next two chapters did not immediately dispel the gloom about the slim likelihood "of substantially increased aircraft appropriations being voted in an election year when strong influences would like to effect a cut in the size of the national budget and also reduce taxes."[62]

Had *Aviation Week* known about certain developments taking place within the Truman administration, however, its attitude might have been substantially more cheerful. On December 16, Stuart Symington dispatched a letter to James E. Webb, the director of the Bureau of the Budget, in which he protested cuts in the air force budget for the 1949 fiscal year. Symington forwarded a copy of this letter to the secretary of defense, including with it a memorandum in which he stated that the Bureau of the Budget "has allowed the Air Force but $2,904,000,000," an amount equal to only "56% of what is considered . . . the minimum essential to our security." In his letter to Webb, the air force secretary further argued that the budget did not contain enough procurement funds to assure the

> minimum rate of production required to maintain an adequate aircraft industry. . . . During the last three fiscal years, the procurement of aircraft has [also] been far below that required to maintain this minimum production rate. The budget for FY [fiscal year] 1949 in its present form . . . will not meet *the requirements of the aircraft industry* nor will it permit any reasonable degree of technical progress [emphasis added].

Although the "Air Force has consistently advocated its 70 Group Program as the minimum force adequate to the requirements imposed by the position of the United States in the modern world," even to keep that service at its current 55 groups, Symington asserted, would compel him to submit "a supplemental request [for additional funds] in conjunction with the Department of the Army."

Hoping to have Forrestal's support in opposition to the Director of the Bureau of the Budget, Symington, in his memorandum for the secretary of defense, requested "a meeting with him [Webb] and you at your earliest convenience." But that was only the beginning. Just how much importance Symington attached to this issue can readily be gleaned from a note he sent to his confidante Clark Clifford, who, besides describing Symington as "my closest friend," just happened to be the president's chief political adviser. Enclosing a copy of his letter to Webb, Symington told Clifford, "I understand this matter will be decided by Wednesday evening; and I feel more strongly about it than I have about anything since I came into Government." Unstated, but palpable nonetheless, was the secretary's presumption that Clifford would bring the question to the attention of their fellow Missourian, Harry Truman.[63]

In the meantime, as Symington was petitioning Forrestal and Clifford, pressures on the secretary of defense to aid the aircraft industry were mounting from another source. "Why hasn't the time come to tell the public about the prospects of war, specifically with Russia—with a view to getting more money for the military establishment, if necessary?" That was the first item on a list of questions that, according to a memorandum written for him by one of his aides on December 11, the Congressional Aviation Policy Board planned to ask Forrestal when he next appeared before it. Given both the infatuation of this panel with "air power" and the anti-Soviet sentiments permeating official Washington, one need not be skilled at reading between the lines to grasp what members of the board had in mind with respect to "getting more money for the military establishment" by "telling the public about the prospects of war, specifically with Russia."[64] Not that Forrestal needed much prompting; already the previous September the *Wall Street Journal* had predicted that "a Russian scare will be used to prod more Army-Navy money out of Congress." It is quite conceivable, therefore, that the proposal for a war scare—which, stripped of its euphemistic veil, was exactly what the board's memorandum contained—reinforced Forrestal's own thinking. In any case, it is incontestable that within a matter of weeks, not only Forrestal but the entire Truman administration would be translating into action the board's suggestion that it was "time to tell the public about the prospects of war, specifically with Russia."[65]

4.

War Games (I): Setting the Stage

May I just say this. I am convinced that they [the Soviets] will not take any steps which they feel would bring them into a major conflict in the foreseeable future.

—Statement of Honorable W. Averell Harriman, secretary of commerce, to the President's Air Policy Commission, September 8, 1947[1]

I am inclined to view that situation this way: We are relatively safe from attack by a foreign power for the next four or five years, and I think that with the passage of time that enough common sense will pervade the world that that danger might be lessened. I do not think any power is in a position to attack us with any prospect of success in the immediate future.

—Statement of Admiral Chester W. Nimitz, chief of naval operations, U.S. Navy, to the President's Air Policy Commission, November 12, 1947[2]

General of the Army Dwight D. Eisenhower, retiring Chief of Staff, absolved the Soviet Union of any intention of deliberately provoking war. He made the statement during . . . his valedictory public address as Chief of Staff, delivered at the National Press Club. . . .

The Soviet Union is in no position to support a global war, he added, and no other nation in the world is in a position to support one, either. . . .

He estimated that the nation's defenses were in better shape today than he thought they would be at the time of the "terrific pressure for demobilization." He considered the national defense in better condition today than at a corresponding interval after the first World War.

—Harold B. Hinton, "Eisenhower Scoffs at Fears of a War Started By Russia," *New York Times,* February 6, 1948[3]

As to war? I do not think that follows, unless we do ten or fifteen years of a Ramsay MacDonald-Baldwin-Chamberlain appeasement. A balance [with the Soviet Union] is entirely possible . . . .

—Letter from James Forrestal to Trenholm H. Marshall, Esq., February 20, 1948[4]

Full information on and explanation to our own Congress of significance [of] recent Soviet moves in Czechoslovakia and Finland may result in speeding consideration and adoption [of] universal military training and building programs for Army, Navy, and particularly Air Force.

—Walter Bedell Smith, U.S. Ambassador to the Soviet Union, to Secretary of State George C. Marshall, March 1, 1948[5]

THE ORIGINS: MARSHALL, FORRESTAL—AND TRUMAN

Perhaps the most appropriate metaphor for the war scare created by the Truman administration during the early spring months of 1948 is that of wheels within wheels. The scare was an extremely complex, convoluted phenomenon. It involved, to begin with, increasingly elaborate mechanisms of manipulation and deception. The crudest of these were aimed at the public, while more sophisticated ones were reserved for congressional leaders and those other notables who had to be alternately cudgeled and cajoled into giving the administration what it wanted. Nor did the subterfuge stop there, for even within the administration itself there were those who were denied full access to the truth. Thus, while many of its members may have suspected that the war scare of 1948 was bogus, only an elite few were in a position to be able to separate fact from fiction. And those who knew, of course, generally were not telling.

The Truman administration was divided against itself in more ways than this, however. Although at the outset the Departments of Defense and State pulled in tandem to create the war scare, their paths diverged not long thereafter. Advocates of unrestrained military spending then began to encounter opposition from the State Department, which feared that such massive expenditures could come only at the expense of the European Recovery Program (Marshall Plan), the centerpiece of the administration's costly program for sustaining prosperity at home by rebuilding Western European economies to the point where they could function as markets for exports from the United States. Worse yet, a huge arms buildup might so frighten the Soviet Union that war, not economic reconstruction, would be the outcome in Europe. In other quarters, fiscal considerations inspired apprehension about more money for the military. Both Truman himself and the subordinates upon whom he depended for counsel in this regard were convinced that inflation was the economy's most pressing problem, and such officials as the director of the Bureau of the Budget and the chairman of the Council of Economic Advisers were particularly hostile to demands of the Pentagon that, in their view, were sure to aggravate inflationary tendencies.[6] Because the public customarily laid more emphasis on domestic issues than on foreign affairs, and because 1948 was an election year, these officials had at their disposal powerful arguments they did not hesitate to use.

The internal fissures continued. If the military was united in seeking more money, unanimity broke down beyond that point. Representatives of the air force took their campaign for a bigger share of the Pentagon's allotment all the way up to the president's desk, contesting with particular vehemence what they claimed was favoritism shown to the navy. Naval spokesmen, in turn, gave as good as they got, arguing that the air force exaggerated the Soviet threat in the air while underestimating that from the seas.[7]

As a result of these conflicting forces, it is anything but easy to unravel the intricate web that the 1948 war scare comprised. That task is made even more difficult, of course, by the fact that those who scheme to mislead and delude are hardly about to leave smoking guns, much less fingerprints, for the benefit of future historians. Even in the best of cases, as James C. Thomson, Jr., has observed first hand, "a vast amount of policy making takes place behind closed doors, with no record, and a great deal is put on paper and classified so that if anything ever leaks the policy makers are protected."[8] All the more so when the policy involves systematic misrepresentation of the truth as a means of securing otherwise unattainable goals.

From the evidence that has come to light thus far, it is not clear who deserves the credit—if that be the word—for the idea of orchestrating the events of February and March 1948 in such a way as to overcome the reluctance of a hostile Republican Congress to support the administration's foreign policy and military initiatives. For that matter, it is entirely possible, as we shall see below, that the notion was conceived independently in several quarters, with coordination among them coming later.

If we are unable to identify the authors of the war-scare scheme with absolute certainty, there is no such difficulty when it comes to locating both the principal actors and the agencies that made it a reality. As the quote at the start of this chapter from Walter Bedell Smith, the U.S. ambassador in Moscow, is meant to suggest, Secretary of State George Marshall and the Department he directed played a leading role in creating a climate of hysteria during the early months of 1948. "Full information on and explanation to . . . Congress of significance [of] recent Soviet moves in Czechoslovakia and Finland," Smith cabled Marshall on March 1, "may result in speeding consideration and adoption [of] universal military training and building programs for Army, Navy, and particularly Air Force." Add passage of the European Recovery Program and one has an uncannily accurate foretaste of the course the war scare soon would take.

Evidently, Smith's words fell on fertile ground, for the following day, March 2, Secretary of Defense James V. Forrestal wrote in his diary:

> Both Secretary Marshall and Under Secretary Lovett are now ready for him, Marshall, to take the lead in renewing the drive for UMT either through the occasion of a speech in California on 19 March or before the Senate Armed Services Committee, or possibly the entire Senate. (After the manner of his, Marshall's, appearances before the entire Congress during the war.)

Coincidentally or otherwise, Marshall was already preparing to follow to the letter the prescription of his ambassador and close friend of long standing.[9]

At the luncheon meeting where Marshall, Lovett and Forrestal thrashed out these details, the trio also gave "some consideration . . . to a joint effort by Marshall and myself . . . , the thought being to capitalize on the present concern of the country over the events of the last week in Europe."[10] In point of fact, however, Forrestal had already begun laying the ground for a war scare even prior to this meeting. "I talked to the President on Sunday [February 29]," he told Walter G. ("Ham") Andrews, chairman of the House Armed Services Committee, on March 3, "and was rather hoping he might come back here [from Key West, Florida] to dramatize the immediacy and the urgency of this situation." These efforts on Forrestal's part would ultimately bear fruit on March 17, when Truman would push fears of war to their maximum with a speech to a joint session of Congress carried on nationwide radio during the day, followed by a similar address before a Democratic party organization in New York that evening.[11]

In addition to revealing that he had been at work fomenting a war scare even before March 2, the secretary's telephone conversation with Representative Andrews, like Smith's cable of March 1 to Marshall, laid out with remarkable prescience the course that the scare would take. "When the President comes back," Forrestal asserted, "I think he's got to give the most serious thought to whether we don't have to go back to Selective Service." Forrestal's expectation was quite accurate: the resumption in peacetime of a military draft was indeed one of the three measures that Truman on March 17 would call upon Congress to enact. Forrestal also mentioned that Marshall was "considering making a speech in California—in the sense of what we've been talking about." Marshall would actually make not one, but two highly publicized speeches in California over the weekend of March 19–20, in which he would argue that the Soviet Union was on the brink of emulating Nazi Germany's attempt to conquer all of Europe. Forrestal's remarks to Representative Andrews thus contain a precise blueprint of how the various constituents of the war scare would be cobbled together.[12]

Why were Forrestal and Marshall so willing to throw their weight behind a war scare? As I explore this question at length in the following two chapters, here it will suffice merely to summarize the considerations that drove each man to engage in war-scare plotting. For Marshall, the reasons are anything but obscure. The main concern of the secretary of state and the State Department as a whole was to have the European Recovery Program (Marshall Plan) adopted by a Republican-controlled Congress by April 1, 1948, with its full funding intact and with no crippling amendments attached. I will demonstrate in chapter 5, however, when I discuss this point in greater detail, that as February turned to March and the April 1 deadline loomed ever closer, the odds that Marshall and the administration would be able to attain this goal looked increasingly slim. Conceivably, however, a shrewdly designed and well-executed war scare might overwhelm Republican opposition to the administration's ambitious foreign aid legislation. If administration luminaries could hoodwink the population into swallowing the malicious fantasy that the U.S.S.R. was about to start World War III with an attack on the West, they could then create an atmosphere of "crisis," in which they would be able to contend that refusal to enact the president's program was tantamount to endangering the nation's survival.

But in order to mount a persuasive war scare, Marshall would of necessity need the cooperation of Forrestal and the Pentagon, a fact that gave the secretary of defense just the opening for which he had been searching. Already in December of 1947, he had announced that, in the coming fiscal year, he intended "to seek more funds for planes," as the *Washington Post*'s headline succinctly phrased it.[13] Thereafter, pressures on Forrestal to hurl a life preserver to the aircraft companies—pressures applied both directly through such industry figures as Donald Douglas and Oliver Echols and indirectly through the President's Air Policy Commission, the Congressional Air Policy Board and the air force—continued to grow. Forrestal's first response was to initiate a study by his staff—with the ubiquitous Oliver Echols in the role of consultant—that would give him the arguments he needed to approach Truman in the industry's behalf. By February 4, 1948, this study was in his hands, and he immediately requested an appointment at the White House. Meeting with the president two days later, Forrestal asked Truman to approve "a moderate increase of 400 million dollars" for aircraft procurement in the budget for the 1949 fiscal year. But despite bringing up the matter twice more during February, Forrestal still had received no reply from the president by the time of his luncheon with Marshall and Lovett on March 2.[14] In the interim, meanwhile, pressure of another sort was intensifying, as the army agitated the secretary for selective service legislation in order to fill its ranks. In December, we recall from the foregoing chapter, the Congressional Air Policy Board had rhetorically asked Forrestal if the time had not "come to tell the public about the prospects of war, specifically with Russia—with a view to getting more money for the military establishment." Even before this, however, there were indications that Forrestal was entertaining precisely the same idea. A "Russian scare will be used to prod more Army-Navy money out of Congress," the *Wall Street Journal* predicted as early as September 1947. In an eerie anticipation of the approach the secretary would later employ, the *Journal* asserted that "The Senate's Appropriations Committee . . . will be shown confidential intelligence reports on Red Army troop movements, its political propaganda in Germany. Forrestal wants to increase his spending rate in the occupied zones."[15]

Hence by the time Walter Bedell Smith's suggestion for a war scare arrived in Washington on March 1, the secretary of defense evidently had long since concluded that this stratagem offered him the best hope of solving his most urgent problems. A war scare, he must have felt, would create an entirely new atmosphere in Washington and the country at large, one in which any resistance to his proposals for a military buildup could summarily be thrust aside.

Once they had decided in favor of a war scare, Marshall, Lovett and Forrestal lost no time putting it into effect. On March 4, at what Forrestal in his diary insisted on calling a "Cabinet Lunch" in the office of the secretary of the interior—several members of the Cabinet, as well as two senators and a member of the House of Representatives, were in attendance, but the president himself was not—"Marshall talked over the world situation," with the result that "everyone present agreed that the public needed information and guidance on the deterioration of our relations with Russia." The scare was progressing smartly.[16]

Forrestal, in the days to come, would continue to work at top speed. A memorandum to General Carl A. Spaatz, air force chief of staff, shows his propaganda mill commencing to grind the same day as the "Cabinet Lunch." "The Secretary of Defense has inaugurated a series of informal meetings with representatives of public media to become better acquainted with them and with their problems," Spaatz was instructed, and "Mr. Forrestal's office has advised us that the Secretary of Defense would be delighted to have the Secretary of the Air Force and the Chief of Staff attend if they desire. The next such meeting will be held in Mr. Forrestal's office on the evening of 8 March."[17] Early the next week, another, similar memorandum went out to the Legislative and Liaison Division of the air force, stating that the "Secretary of Defense has asked his staff to draw up a list of members of Congress who should be included at various functions in his office. He has in mind people he should have, in addition to those who come here repeatedly[,] . . . including one or two new Congressmen each time."[18] The navy, for one, was quick to take the hint. On March 9, the chief of naval operations (navy chief of staff) "recommended . . . a program of publicity" that would "lay the groundwork for an informed American Public opinion" so as "to prepare the American people for war." Two days later, on March 11, Secretary of the Navy John L. Sullivan gave this proposal his approval.[19]

Of greater importance, perhaps, was the dinner in his home to which Forrestal invited Secretary of the Army Kenneth Royall and former Secretary of State James F. Byrnes on March 3, the day after the luncheon meeting with Marshall and Lovett. Both Forrestal and the army, as I mentioned above, were seeking to have a new selective service act passed. But, Forrestal and Royall told Byrnes, "Congress was hesitating to re-enact what its members regarded as wartime legislation," and, according to him, they suggested "it would be helpful if I made a speech urging the legislation." Byrnes agreed, and the speech was duly given on March 13 at The Citadel in South Carolina. "Forrestal and Royall furnished me information on the status of our armed forces," Byrnes wrote in his memoirs, "and I am sure Forrestal inspired the extensive publicity in newspapers and newsreels" that the speech received. The following day, March 4, "Forrestal called on Senator Walter F. George of Georgia, ranking minority member of the Finance Committee, member of the Foreign Relations Committee and one of the most powerful of the conservative Democratic Senators.

Forrestal wanted George and some of his colleagues to hear a 'presentation of the world situation by a member of the Army Staff.'" Clearly, the Secretary was more than holding up his end of the bargain, as he drove the machinery of opinion manipulation at full throttle.[20]

Thus, although the war-scare scheme had been launched only two days before, already by March 4 we can discern in embryo the form it was to take. To Marshall, the most respected member of the Truman administration, would fall the task of giving the war scare legitimacy by sounding the alarm bells that would frighten Congress and the rabble. A simple but revealing way of grasping Marshall's importance in fomenting the war scare is by comparing the number of press releases his speeches and activities generated during the period up to and including the scare with that for the remainder of his tenure as secretary of state. Prior to December 1947, the most releases published in any one month were the five issued in June 1947, at which time, of course, the Marshall Plan had been unveiled; from July through November, no other month had more than three. In December, when the European Recovery Plan was formally submitted to Congress, however, the pace accelerated. There were six press releases that month, five in January 1948, four in February, and no fewer than seven in March, as the production of war-scare panic reached its peak level. There was but a single release in April, as Marshall was in Bogotá, Colombia, at the founding meeting of the Organization of American States, for much of the month. By May, the number of releases had fallen to five (there would have been fewer had it not been for the eruption of a Soviet "peace scare," which I discuss in chapter 7). Thereafter the number declined to the usual two or three per month, save for four in October. Overall in 1948, nearly half of the State Department's press releases relating to Marshall, some 16 of 34, came during the first three months of the year—an accurate measure of the heightened profile taken on by the Secretary in the course of intensifying the fear that war loomed just around the corner.[21]

Unlike Marshall, whose performance as army chief of staff during World War II had won him a reputation that, at least until the arrival of Joseph McCarthy, kept him generally above criticism, Forrestal was a controversial figure. Several of his political stands had earned him considerable enmity in certain circles, which is no doubt why he agreed to a division of war-scare labor that put Marshall continuously in the public eye while he remained out of sight, working through others, as was the case with James Byrnes, or feeding suitably shaded snippets of misinformation about "the world situation" to influential figures such as Senator Walter George. In this way, little by little, many of those individuals whose support was necessary if the administration were to achieve its goals could be won over to the True Cause.

Meanwhile, what of Harry Truman? That Truman knew, and approved, of the war scare there can be no question.[22] Certainly, he could not have been in ignorance of it after the "Cabinet Lunch" of March 4; and neither Marshall nor Forrestal was about to go forward with such an audacious plan in the absence of presidential approval. Truman, in short, had every opportunity to nip the scheme in the bud had he cared to do so. But whose idea was it in the first place—that of the president or his advisers? And if the latter, which ones were involved and what considerations did they advance that he found persuasive? The mysteries proliferate. Why, after several months of resisting demands from the military for more money, did Truman suddenly relent and give his approval to a supplemental appropriation for the Pentagon that augmented its budget by one-third?* Why, likewise, did he permit James Forrestal to ask Congress to separate appropriations for aircraft procurement from the remainder of the federal budget for the coming fiscal year, to vote for these appropriations at once and to allow the administration to begin spending them as soon as they were approved, without waiting for the expiration of the current fiscal year? To these and similar questions, the historian would like to have concrete answers based on documentary evidence.

What one likes and what one gets, however, are frequently two very different things. Harry Truman was, we remind ourselves, an inveterate, if not especially gifted, devotee of poker. Whatever else he may have learned from that game, the one lesson he seems to have digested most thoroughly was that of playing his cards close to the vest. In any case, in seeking to discover how Truman arrived at his decisions during the war scare—to whom he talked, to what arguments he was receptive—too often, one comes up empty- handed. Hence any account of Truman's actions during the period of a scare must rely more on circumstantial evidence and plausible reasoning than most researchers would prefer. It may not be too fanciful to suggest that, as a self-styled student of history himself, Truman was all too cognizant of what kinds of documents could tarnish his reputation were they even to be created, much less left behind. The difficulty of constructing an evidential record that would account for his decisions suggests that he acted accordingly.

---

* As of August 1947, the administration was planning on a budget for the 1949 fiscal year in which "authority for new obligations for National Defense shall not be in excess of the level provided by the Congress for the fiscal year 1948." By the time eight months had elapsed, the administration had settled on a level of military spending about 35 percent higher. See Dwight D. Eisenhower, draft letter to the President, undated but after August 6, 1947, Papers of Hoyt S. Vandenberg, Subject file, Chief of Staff folder, Manuscript Division, Library of Congress.

For all of that, there is every reason to believe that the idea of a war scare was doubly welcome at the White House. That this is so is a direct reflection of the fact that Truman's popularity during these weeks was at its nadir. Polls taken by the Gallup organization, for instance, show that between April 1947 and April 1948, approval of "the way Harry Truman is handling his job as President" had fallen from 57 to 36 percent, while disapproval had exactly doubled, from 25 to 50 percent.[23] To this unpromising state of affairs, however, Clark Clifford, Truman's chief political counselor, had a solution. "There is considerable political advantage to the Administration in its battle with the Kremlin," he had written in a long memorandum for Truman the previous November. "The worse matters get, up to a fairly certain point—real danger of imminent war—the more is there a sense of crisis. In times of crisis, the American citizen tends to back up his President."[24] The war scare thus offered a chance to kill the proverbial two birds with a single stone. Not only would it enable the administration to overcome the opposition of congressional Republicans and have its diplomatic and military programs written into law, but at the same time it would serve to improve Truman's slim chances of being returned to the presidency. Marshall, with his great moral authority, could prepare the way with a series of press conferences and appearances before congressional committees; then, at the climactic moment, Truman, implementing another morsel of Clark Clifford's wisdom, could "assume before the eyes of the people the leadership on foreign policy" and thus "stay in the limelight."[25] Exactly in this manner, as we shall witness, did events play themselves out.*

A "CRISIS" CONTRIVED: CZECHOSLOVAKIA AND FINLAND

Strictly speaking, it is less than completely accurate to refer to *the* war scare of 1948. In reality, there were, if not quite two separate scares, at least two distinct versions of a single scare. The first of these, the one considered sufficient to panic the hoi polloi, revolved primarily around what was widely, but less than

---

* Although Clifford devotes some four pages to a discussion of this memorandum in what purports to be his autobiography, he nowhere so much as even hints at the ideas contained in the passages I have quoted. The implacably self-serving nature of Clifford's book, which this example well illustrates, makes it virtually worthless to anyone seeking to understand the inner workings of the Truman administration. See Clark Clifford with Richard Holbrooke, *Counsel to the President: A Memoir* (New York: Random House, 1991), pp. 191-94.

accurately, termed a Communist coup in Czechoslovakia and, to a much lesser extent, Soviet pressure on Finland for a mutual-defense treaty. The second version, devised to be administered to powerful members of Congress and prominent journalists, both of whom required additional stimuli before they could be relied upon to perform as desired, was based on the telegram sent on March 4–5 by General Lucius D. Clay, commander of U.S. military forces in Europe and military governor of the U.S. zone of occupation in Germany, to Lieutenant General Stephen J. Chamberlin, director of army intelligence. In this now-notorious message, which I will treat in detail in the following section, Clay maintained that war with the Soviets might "come with dramatic suddenness." Before considering the Clay telegram, however, it is necessary to examine the dichotomy between the administration's understanding of the events in Czechoslovakia in late February 1948 and the way it presented these events to the nation.

Walter Millis, the senior editor of *The Forrestal Diaries,* provides a succinct summation of what we may justly describe as the official view. "It was on February 24 . . . that one of the world's 'explosive points' . . . blew up with a shocking suddenness." On that date, Millis explains, "an armed and violent Communist coup d'état seized power in Czechoslovakia. . . . The Czechoslovak Republic . . . was subverted at a stroke into a satellite Communist dictatorship . . . . Throughout the West the shock was profound."[26] Here, Millis, as usual, faithfully echoes what he rather naively believes to be the thinking of Forrestal, taking the latter's public pronouncements entirely at face value. The only problem with this interpretation is that it is wholly at variance with how the administration actually perceived the situation.

The simple truth of the matter is that no one of importance in the administration believed that Czechoslovakia was "one of the world's 'explosive points,'" nor that it had been "subverted at a stroke into a satellite Communist dictatorship." Indeed, even the notion that the Czech Communist Party (CCP) had come to power as the result of a deliberately plotted plan was received with considerable skepticism. So far as Washington was concerned, by the close of 1947, Czechoslovakia was for all intents and purposes *already* in Communist hands; what happened early in 1948 simply made explicit what had long been implicit. As early as July 1947, for instance, the U.S. ambassador in Czechoslovakia, Laurence A. Steinhardt, was calling Washington's attention to the "numerous and powerful instruments of persuasion over Czechoslovakia now in possession of Soviets. Fact that these instruments have so far been outlined only for limited objectives provides no assurance . . . that similar restraint will be exercised in future." To give substance to his warning, Steinhardt itemized the power already exercised by the Czech Communists, including the "control

. . . of Interior, Finance, Agriculture, Labor, Information and Internal Trade and substantial . . . control of Ministries of Foreign Affairs and National Defence," "effective control of police," "preponderant influence in trade union organizations," "substantial control 5 out of 10 daily Praha [Prague] newspapers with nation-wide circulation," "increasing economic dependence of Czechoslovakia on Soviets," "strong Czechoslovak feeling of dependence on Soviets for future protection against a resurgent Germany," et cetera.[27]

Steinhardt also pointed out that, as he put it in a telegram to Marshall on September 29, 1947,

> Communist policy in present campaign to obtain greater dominance is still fluid and precise application in coming months will depend on world situation. If east versus west antagonism becomes deeper Communist efforts will become greater. Much will depend on course of negotiations regarding Germany at London Conference of Big Three.

The ambassador amplified on this theme the following day, noting that "Moscow is now taking a greater interest in Czechoslovakian affair than heretofore" and "may well have directed its representatives to bring the Czechoslovakian Government into complete subservience to Kremlin as rapidly as possible." Steinhardt's opinion was that the "moderate Communists who had hoped and expected to gain an absolute majority at elections next May" were being compelled by the Soviet Union "to proceed more rapidly by undemocratic means if necessary to bring Czechoslovakia into line." "In view of foregoing," he concluded,

> we must from now on reckon with probability that within a period of months, Czechoslovakian Government will become a subservient tool of Kremlin in internal as well as external affairs and that such degree of independence as Government has been able to exercise up to present time will rapidly diminish.[28]

Steinhardt's words make it rather difficult to subscribe to Walter Millis's notion that Czechoslovakia "blew up with a shocking suddenness," that it "was subverted at a stroke," or that "throughout the West the shock" in February 1948 "was profound." In point of fact, even some knowledgeable contemporary observers outside of the government understood that the war scare of 1948 was in no sense a response to events in Czechoslovakia and Finland. One of these was Hanson W. Baldwin, the well-connected military affairs editor of the *New York Times*. "In the past three months, the opinion of our leaders appears to have shifted radically," Baldwin wrote. "At the beginning of the year Washington seemed more or less unanimous that war in the near future was unlikely," whereas by the end of March 1948, the administration appeared "to feel that war in the near future is a distinct possibility and that Russia may use military force to gain her ends." Baldwin was puzzled by "this shift in opinion," the reasons for which "have not been made clear." Of one thing, however, he was certain: "Czechoslovakia and Finland are not the answers; both were discounted some time ago." The journalist's skepticism only increased with time, moreover. "Hanson Baldwin told me this morning that he is convinced that the crisis of last Spring—the Berlin business [growing out of the Clay telegram]—was wholly [a] Washington crisis," David E. Lilienthal, chairman of the Atomic Energy Commission, wrote in his journal that May.[29]

In addition to predicting that a Communist takeover in Czechoslovakia was merely a matter of time, Steinhardt also provided the State Department with a lengthy postmortem later that spring. His analysis, dispatched on the last day of April, opened with the statement that what had happened "in February 1948 was probably inherent in the situation ever since the consummation of the Czechoslovak-Soviet Treaty of Friendship and Military alliance of December 12, 1943." In his evaluation of "the extent of Soviet interference and intimidation" in the CCP's consolidation of power, he pointedly observed, "There was no evidence of any Soviet troop concentrations on the borders of Czechoslovakia," and "no direct evidence of Soviet interference." "Even the activities of Soviet Ambassador Zorin . . . cannot be placed under the heading of direct interference," Steinhardt believed. Reliable accounts of Zorin's conversations indicated that these "avoided the discussion of politics" and instead concentrated on "the grain situation." Overall, therefore, "the extent of the Soviet threats was probably less than on similar recent occasions in Finland and in Iran." But the latter two countries had "successfully resisted such threats, whereas the Czechs succumbed to them."

One of the arrows that the administration plucked from its quiver in order to depict the CCP takeover as the start of a new Soviet military offensive was the death under mysterious circumstances of Czech Foreign Minister Jan Masaryk, who either leaped or was pushed from the window of his official residence in Prague on the night of March 9–10. To this day it has not been established whether Masaryk took his own life or was murdered. Such lack of certainty, however, did not for a moment prevent representatives of the Truman administration from depicting his death as the result of a Communist assassination plot. In that light, it is interesting to observe Steinhardt's contemporaneous verdict that "there are several circumstances which would support the murder theory but the Embassy is still inclined to give credence to the suicide theory in the absence of further facts. . . . Certain unpublished statements which come from the President's immediate entourage . . . , to the effect that opened razor blades and knotted pajama cords were found in Masaryk's bedroom, give credence to the theory of premeditated suicide." Steinhardt's sources, however, "have suppressed this information because they desire the public . . . to keep on thinking it was murder." The Truman administration chose to do the same.[30]

Steinhardt, to be sure, sometimes modified his opinions about certain questions. In the summer of 1947, he saw pressure from the Soviet Union leading to a reluctant takeover by a "moderate" Communist party, whereas after the fact his analysis put greater weight on the Czech Communist party and less on the Soviets. Still, I know of nothing in any of his dispatches supporting the impression the Truman administration attempted to convey—that the conquest of power by the CCP was the first step in a Soviet grand design ultimately aimed at the subjugation of all Europe by force. What is more, far from being the exception, Steinhardt's treatment of the Czech situation was entirely consistent with Washington's other intelligence estimates. "The current political crisis in Czechoslovakia is not entirely unexpected," the army Intelligence Division reported to the chief of staff and the secretary of the army on February 24, in a memorandum that the last forwarded to James Forrestal, again undermining the notion found in the standard accounts that the CCP had startled Washington by acting with "shocking suddenness."[31]

Similarly, the CIA's reports to the president contradicted the idea that events in Prague were part of a Soviet offensive. "The timing of the coup in Czechoslovakia was forced upon the Kremlin when the non-Communists took action endangering Communist control of the police," R. N. Hillenkoetter, the agency's director, wrote Truman on March 2. "A Communist victory in the May elections would have been impossible without such control."[32] The CIA's report of March 10, based on information available "as of March 6"—that is, one day *after* the administration had begun discussions of the Clay telegram—was even more categorical than its predecessor. "We do not believe . . . that this event reflects any sudden increase in Soviet capabilities, more aggressive intentions, or any change in current Soviet policy or tactics," the CIA maintained.

> The Kremlin for some time has had the capability of consolidating its position in Czechoslovakia. The coup was precipitated by the stubborn resistance of the Czech moderates to continued Communist control of the police force. . . . The Czech coup and the demands on Finland, moreover, do not preclude the possibility of Soviet efforts to effect a rapprochement with the West as outlined in CIA 5. In fact, the Kremlin would undoubtedly consider the consolidation of its position in the border states as a necessary prerequisite to any such agreement.

> In Western Europe, the Communists continue to concentrate on legal means to gain their objectives rather than on violence and direct action. . . . The Communists could not at this time carry out a similar coup in either Italy or France, as they do not have control of the police or the armed forces.[33]

Short of reporting that the Soviets were about to renounce communism, turn over the key to the Kremlin to Harry Truman and apply for U.S. statehood, it is difficult to imagine how the CIA might have submitted a more reassuring estimate.

What was not said, as well as what was, reinforces the conclusion that the Truman administration in no way regarded the Communist accession in Czechoslovakia as a prelude to war. Thus the War Council—the name given the meeting of the three secretaries of the armed services with the Joint Chiefs of Staff—made mention neither of Czechoslovakia nor Finland in the minutes of its "Significant Actions" taken on March 2, 1948. The same was true of the meeting of the Committee of Four Secretaries (the three service secretaries plus the secretary of defense) on March 5, at which the one item of new business concerned the "Wearing of Civilian Clothes by Military Personnel while on duty at Duty Stations involving essentially Office Work." The names of both countries were also conspicuous by their absence from the agenda circulated on March 8 for the National Security Council's meeting of March 11 and from that circulated on March 10 for the War Council meeting originally scheduled for March 16, but postponed to March 23.[34]

By all odds the most consistent and unequivocal analysis of the significance of events in Czechoslovakia was that put forward—both before and after the fact—by George F. Kennan, then at the head of the State Department's Policy Planning Staff (PPS). It is, therefore, worth quoting at length his account of the paper he presented to the secretary of state on November 6, 1947. The starting point for Kennan's discussion was his "view that the containment of Communist expansionism had thus far proceeded successfully." As a result, the Communists were faced with

> the necessity of consolidating their power throughout Eastern Europe. For this reason they would soon find themselves obliged to clamp down entirely on Czechoslovakia. So long as Communist power had been advancing generally in Europe, it had been to Russian advantage to allow the Czechs the outward appearances of freedom; but now that the advance had been halted, they could no longer afford this luxury. Czechoslovakia could too easily become a path of entry for truly democratic forces into Eastern Europe

> generally. We had to expect a "sweeping away of democratic institutions and a consolidation of Communist power there."

Thus, "the discarding of the last trappings of true democracy and the establishment of an unadulterated Communist dictatorship" in Czechoslovakia, far from being an offensive maneuver on the part of the U.S.S.R., "represented a defensive reaction—and one foreseen by ourselves—to the success of the Marshall Plan initiative."[35]

While it is all well and good to cite Kennan's views, we must also inquire whether they were accepted by his superiors, especially the secretary of state. In his *Memoirs,* Kennan maintained that they were not.* His ideas, he wrote, "had made only a faint and wholly inadequate impression on official Washington. On the military establishment the impression had been practically nil. The same was true for all but one or two people in the State Department." With respect specifically to Marshall and Czechoslovakia, Kennan was still more negative: "If he [Marshall] ever read the warning I submitted to him in the autumn of 1947 to the effect that the Communists would inevitably crack down on Czechoslovakia in case the effort toward a European recovery program proceeded successfully, I am sure he had forgotten it by the end of February 1948."[36]

But Kennan was wrong. Marshall had not only read Kennan's report—he fully accepted it as well. In actuality, Kennan, for reasons on which we need not speculate, misrepresented his relationship with Marshall. While the two men were never personally close—not many of Marshall's associates ever

---

* In actuality, Kennan was not quite so unruffled at the time as he later pretended. On March 15, 1948, as a case in point, he sent a dispatch to Marshall proposing that the Italian government should "outlaw Communist Party and take strong action against it before elections [scheduled for April]. Communists would presumably reply with civil war, which would give us grounds for reoccupation [of] Foggia [air]fields or any other facilities we might wish. This would admittedly result in much violence and probably a military division of Italy; but we are getting close to the deadline and I think it might well be preferable to a bloodless election victory, unopposed by ourselves, which would give the Communists the entire peninsula at one coup and send waves of panic to all surrounding areas." One must be grateful to the editors of the collection of State Department records published in the series *Foreign Relations of the United States* (*FRUS*) for including a document that supplies a much-needed corrective to the presentation of Kennan's thinking contained in his memoirs. See U.S. Department of State, *FRUS*: 1948, vol. 3, *Western Europe* (Washington, D.C.: U.S. Government Printing Office, 1974), pp. 848–49.

achieved that particular distinction in any case—it is clear that the secretary of state, unlike his successor, Dean Acheson, had a great deal of respect for Kennan's intellect. It was, after all, Marshall himself who had the Policy Planning Staff created and who, on Forrestal's recommendation, selected Kennan to head it. A passage from one of Marshall's letters to Kennan at the beginning of 1948 well illustrates the high regard in which the secretary held his subordinate. "I just want you to know," he wrote, "how much I appreciate the splendid work you have been doing here in the Department. Your calm and analytical approach to our problems is most comforting and your judgment is a source of great confidence to me."[37] These do not strike me as words that someone of Marshall's temperament would be likely to address to a person for whose views he had as little regard as Kennan would have us believe.

The truth of the matter is that Marshall's *real* position on Czechoslovakia—as opposed to the position he espoused in public in March 1948—was for all intents and purposes identical to Kennan's. After receiving Kennan's memorandum on November 6, 1947, for example, the secretary of state that same day briefed the Cabinet, paraphrasing his assistant's words in these terms: "Moscow . . . will probably have to clamp down completely on Czechoslovakia, . . . [but] the Russians proceed to this step reluctantly. It is a purely defensive move."[38] Kennan himself could hardly have put the thought in more characteristic language.

What is of enormous significance, moreover, is that *Marshall continued to adhere to the same position even as the Communists were taking power in Prague.* He was, as he telegraphed the U.S. ambassador to France on February 24, 1948, "concerned at the probable repercussions in Western European countries of a successful Communist coup in Czechoslovakia," as there was "a real possibility that such a development in Czechoslovakia would encourage Communist action in Western European countries." But that consideration aside, the secretary of state, like the director of the CIA, saw little change of any sort coming about as a result of this development:

> In so far as international affairs are concerned, a seizure of power by the Communist Party in Czechoslovakia would not materially alter in this respect the situation which has existed in the last three years. Czechoslovakia has faithfully followed the Soviet policy in the United Nations and elsewhere and the establishment of a Communist regime would merely crystallize and confirm for the future previous Czech policy.[39]

One wonders how the ambassador in France reconciled these words with his superior's deeds in the ensuing weeks. In any case, here one looks entirely in vain for any sign that Marshall regarded the events in Czechoslovakia as an omen of war impending.

Kennan's counsel, it turns out, had been neither ignored nor forgotten. But what Kennan—whose grasp of Moscow's politics was never matched by corresponding insight into his colleagues' intrigues—either could not or would not understand was that the secretary of state was quite capable of believing something to be true while simultaneously implying just the opposite in his public utterances. We need labor under no such handicap, however. Thus, in reading the next chapter, we must make every effort to keep in mind the foregoing statements by the secretary of state, for they are a far cry from how he represented matters in his speeches and press conferences during the month of March, as he toiled assiduously to convince all and sundry that the danger of war was imminent.

Although the public version of the war scare rested primarily on the administration's distorted portrayal of the Czech "crisis," there was a simultaneous attempt to depict Soviet pressures on Finland as further evidence that the U.S.S.R. was preparing to wage an aggressive war. By and large this effort was a failure—the amount of mass-media coverage devoted to Finland was much less than that given to Czechoslovakia—and for good reason. Not only was the story inherently lacking in drama—there was no "coup," no change of government, no massive rallies, no riots in the streets, no executions—but it was slow-moving in the bargain, its resolution achieved only well after the war scare had passed its peak. In essence, what transpired was that the Soviets made it clear that they wished the Finns to enter into some kind of mutual-defense arrangement with them, negotiations ensued and both sides eventually signed and ratified the treaty that emerged. Period. Such a mundane tale was not very promising raw material for the incitement of the masses.

Nonetheless, unwilling to let pass another opportunity to create hysteria, Washington predictably sought to have the negotiations viewed as both the opening salvo in Finland's reduction to the status of Soviet vassal and as part of the U.S.S.R.'s master plan for the domination of all Europe: subjugation of a single country is but an event, whereas the subjugation of two can be made to appear as part of a pattern. My further suspicion is that in linking Czechoslovakia with Finland, the administration hoped to take advantage of the evocative power of the very words themselves. The name of each country surely carried heavy symbolic overtones for the generation that had lived through the 1930s and World War II. If "Czechoslovakia" triggered memories of one of the earliest and most poignant of the Nazi's brutal conquests, "Finland" could be expected to call to mind David-and-Goliath images of a brave little country heroically struggling, during the Winter War of 1939–1940, against a rapacious predator many times her size. (The fact that the State Department chose just this moment to publish the 1939 Molotov-Ribbentrop pact, including the secret protocols for the division of Poland between Germany and the Soviet Union, lends credence to this interpretation, for Forrestal had been agitating the department to issue these documents since the previous July.[40])

For all its troubles in this regard, however, the administration's attempt to capitalize on the Soviet-Finnish negotiations never amounted to much more than an insignificant afterthought. Yet inasmuch as these negotiations figure in the conventional accounts of the war scare, I will, for the sake of completeness, summarize Washington's appraisal of the events. Once more, as we shall witness, the public reaction of administration officials was absolutely at odds with what they were telling each other in private.

On February 23, 1948, the Finnish government received a letter from Josef Stalin in which the latter proposed that Finland and the U.S.S.R. undertake negotiations on a treaty of friendship and mutual alliance. The initial U.S. evaluation of this overture was sanguine. In the same March 1 dispatch quoted at the head of this chapter, for instance, Walter Bedell Smith wrote the secretary of state that, "As seen from Moscow, it appears there may be a chance that with firm backing from US and other western powers, Finnish Parliament might well politely, but firmly turn down request, pointing out that Finland . . . does not need mutual assistance pact." A day later, the U.S. ambassador in Finland, Avra Milvin Warren, reported in a telegram to the secretary of state that the Finnish President "estimates Communists will not attempt extra legal action although . . . government's estimate may be inaccurate."

The same day, March 2, the CIA sent a memorandum to Truman that, while gloomy about the long-term outlook for Finland, contained an optimistic short-term prognosis: "Although Finland will probably conclude a mutual assistance pact with the USSR . . . , this action will not foreshadow an imminent Communist coup in Finland." Such a coup was "unlikely at present because of the relative weakness of the Communist position" in the cabinet, the labor movement and the Finnish parliament. A virtually identical statement turned up in the intelligence summary for the secretary of state of March 8.[41] Two days after that, on March 10, the CIA again weighed in with its weekly estimate. The agency described the "demands on Finland" as a "logical step in the completion of the [Soviet Union's] defensive zone" that "had probably been under consideration for some time." The report concluded (as we observed above in the discussion of Czechoslovakia) that the "Czech coup and the demands on Finland . . . do not preclude the possibility of . . . a rapprochement with the West." These were, rather, "a necessary prerequisite to any such agreement."[42]

As the month progressed, the ambassador in Helsinki continued to be relatively hopeful about the outcome of Soviet-Finnish diplomacy. His message of March 16 noted that the Finnish "President is less nervous and depressed about situation" than originally had been the case. On March 30, Warren informed the department of a conversation with a cabinet minister, who asserted that 17,000 reserve officers loyal to the Finnish government could be expected "to prevent any Communist attempt [at] a coup through use [of] police."

After several weeks of deliberation, the Finnish government finally decided to send a delegation to Moscow to negotiate the treaty sought by the U.S.S.R., and attention now shifted to that subject. From the Soviet capital Walter Bedell Smith wrote to the secretary of state on April 1, "Although Finnish delegation has been extremely reticent with regard to their negotiations, my impression is that they are encouraged by progress so far." This judgment was supported by Ambassador Warren in Helsinki, who reported on April 7, shortly after the Soviet-Finnish treaty had been signed and its terms published,

> My French colleague convinced Finns succeeded unexpectedly well . . . ; did not expect Communist extra-legal action either at this time or during the forthcoming electoral campaign. British Minister . . . said President believed agreement [was] on terms he considers better any other perimeter countries and [was] pleased the Soviet [*sic*] not made specific demands nor taken attitude of harshness. President reiterated belief . . . election campaign may begin immediately with good prospects [for] free campaign, free elections.

An April 9 dispatch describing a conversation between a former Finnish foreign minister and the U.S. ambassador reinforced these estimates, as the Finnish diplomat related comments made to him by the president of his country, Juho Paasikivi. From this exchange Warren learned that even though Paasikivi expected the Communists to lose 15 to 20 of their 50 parliamentary seats in the forthcoming elections, he was still convinced of "Soviet unwillingness provoke Finnish incident which might result [in] civil war."[43]

Deprived of the satisfaction of having the minions of Moscow seize control of another country, the Truman administration, in an attempt to salvage as much as it could from the situation, fell back on agitating the question of whether there were secret protocols to the Soviet-Finnish treaty that might compromise the independence of the smaller nation. Thus, during the course of the foregoing conversation, Warren told the Finnish diplomat that "leading US publications like *Newsweek, Time, World Report,* and principal US news agencies like AP, UP, indicate US people consider Finland formally inducted Soviet orbit with ratification pact." One detects the fine hand of the State Department at work: if no overt Soviet takeover of another nation has occurred, merely enlist the aid of the media to proclaim that it has happened anyway. Why, after all, let mere reality stand in one's way? Finally, to lay these Washington-sponsored innuendoes to rest, the Finnish ambassador to the United States on May 10 wrote the secretary of state that he had been "instructed by my Government to assure Your Excellency that these rumours are entirely unfounded." Then, for good measure, he turned over to Marshall an extract from the transcript of a radio speech of April 9 by Juho Paasikivi, in which the Finnish president unambiguously stated, "In view of the doubts expressed abroad, it may be added that no secret articles are annexed to the Agreement." In the face of such a categorical denial, there was not much more the State Department could do, and the issue of the Soviet-Finnish treaty was at last allowed to expire.[44]

By the summer of 1948, then, the truth could no longer be gainsaid. After relaying the results of the parliamentary elections in early July, "in which Communists and their Democratic Union allies have lost considerable ground," the chargé d'affaires in Moscow went on to conclude that Finland "is still apparently far from becoming a 'people[']s democracy.'" His superior, the ambassador, the following month pointed in similar fashion to "Moscow's obvious displeasure over Communists['] complete exclusion" from the new Finnish government. And that was that.[45]

I have summarized the Truman administration's reaction to the Soviet-Finnish treaty not because of that agreement's immense historical importance, but precisely because of its almost complete lack of it. Throughout the war-scare weeks, the administration was at pains to convey the impression that Finland was simply one more domino being toppled by the Soviets in their relentless drive for world domination—the implication being, of course, that war lurked just over the horizon. Not only were the facts quite the opposite, but documents produced by the interested agencies—principally the State Department and the CIA—openly stated as much. From Walter Bedell Smith's telegram of March 1 to George Marshall through the end of April, the administration's consensus was that the Finns would probably be able to withstand whatever pressures the Soviets applied—and in any case, even if Finland ultimately was intimidated into joining the Soviet bloc, it would not be because the Soviets were bound and determined to wage war against the West. Once again, therefore, I must urge the reader to recall what we have here discussed when, in the next chapter, we turn to an examination of the administration's conduct during the month of March 1948.

THE CLAY TELEGRAM AS INTELLIGENCE

On March 5, 1948—three days *after* Forrestal and Marshall had met to plan the main details of the administration's impending war scare—Lieutenant General Stephen J. Chamberlin, director of army intelligence, received an "eyes only" telegram from General Lucius D. Clay, U.S. military governor in Germany. Pivotal as it was to the administration's war scare, Clay's message—which to date has never been published save in the version Secretary of Defense James V. Forrestal copied without comment into his diary—merits quoting in full:

> For many months, based on logical analysis, I have felt and held that war was unlikely for at least ten years. Within the last few weeks, I have felt a subtle change in Soviet attitude which I cannot define but which now gives me a feeling that it may come with dramatic suddenness. I cannot support this change in my own thinking with any data or outward evidence in relationships other than to describe it as a feeling of a new tenseness in every Soviet individual with whom we have official relations. I am unable to submit any official report in the absence of supporting data but my feeling is real. You may advise the chief of staff of this for whatever it may be worth if you feel it advisable.[46]

It was this telegram, more than anything else, that enabled the Truman administration to make its behind-the-scenes argument that urgent measures were needed if the Soviet Union was to be deterred from embarking on a new world war. Unlike the case with the Czech "crisis" and the Soviet-Finnish negotiations, for which the administration sought the widest publicity, no acknowledgment was made of the telegram at the time it was received. Paradoxically enough, however, far from lessening the telegram's effectiveness, the ultra-secrecy in which it was kept served only to heighten its power. To understand why, it is necessary to realize that information is the true currency of a political culture such as that of official Washington. To impart a morsel of highly classified intelligence with an injunction that it must never, *ever* be shared with another living soul immediately tends to enlist the allegiance of the recipient. Flattered by this confidence, the latter—a member of Congress, say, or a widely read journalist writing for a prestigious publication—now wishes to show that he or she is worthy of such great trust. Put another way, those who possess information of such ostensibly enormous value are strongly tempted to regard themselves as part of an elite; and with membership in an elite, naturally, comes *noblesse oblige.*

Armed with the Clay telegram, Forrestal was now ready to proceed with the most important part of the war scare, that which took place in camera. Before describing this aspect of the scare, however, it will be useful both to scrutinize the conventional account of the reception of the Clay telegram and to determine as much as the evidence will allow regarding the origins of this message.

According to Walter Millis, the editor of *The Forrestal Diaries,* Clay's words "fell with the force of a blockbuster bomb" on Washington.[47] One may be permitted a modicum of doubt. Even without the benefit of recent revelations regarding the Clay telegram, the notion that it caused the administration to fear that the Soviets were on the verge of launching an attack should be regarded with much greater skepticism than Millis, who repeatedly insists on swallowing the entire scare whole without benefit of salt, was able to muster. For one thing, there is the matter of the recipient of the cable and its phraseology. Clay did not even bother to send his communiqué through the chain of command to the army chief of staff, General Omar Bradley. Instead, he directed it to General Chamberlin, instructing him offhandedly, "You may advise the Chief of Staff of this *for whatever it may be worth if you feel it advisable*" (emphasis added)—scarcely the words someone in Clay's position would have used had he attached great significance to his message. Second, besides being maddeningly vague—note Clay's declaration that he cannot "support this change in my own thinking with any data or outward evidence" and that he is "unable to submit any official report"—several other aspects of the cable are dubious. Clay proposed no new tactics to deal with what was ostensibly a new situation, asked for no new instructions, and did not at any point label his message "urgent"—all inexplicable omissions in what purported to be a warning that war might break out momentarily.

What is more, it strains credulity to believe that General Bradley, Secretary of the Army Royall or James Forrestal took Clay's telegram at all seriously—except as a means of securing authorization for the Pentagon's program from Congress—when there is no indication that either the army or the Department of Defense attempted to follow up on it by seeking further clarification from its author. Anyone who has ever looked even superficially into the matter well knows that there are reams upon reams of transcripts of teleconferences between Clay and Washington dating from later in the year, when the Soviets imposed a blockade on Berlin. If any such exchanges arose out of Clay's message of March 5, however, they are so obscure that this researcher, at least, has been unable to discover them. It is also noteworthy that Millis nowhere suggests that Washington had received so much as a single corroborating report from anyone other than Clay. The point is a critical one, for professional intelligence analysts would be unlikely to give much weight to a message such as Clay's, which offered no supporting "data or outward evidence," in the absence of similar analyses from other sources.

If these considerations inspire a certain amount of suspicion regarding the sincerity of the administration's concern over the imminence of war, the extent of that suspicion can only be increased by the fact that on March 10, five days following receipt of the Clay telegram, Forrestal announced at a press conference that he and the Joint Chiefs of Staff would be departing Washington for a four-day conference in Key West, Florida (March 11–14), at which "all the wire and message-dispatch communications" facilities would be "shut off."[48] It evidently did not dawn on Millis that if there had been even the slightest threat of a Soviet attack, the secretary of defense would hardly have summoned the heads of the armed services to an isolated meeting on "roles and missions" in Florida, the latter would have been unlikely to have consented to attend and the president would have been grossly derelict in his duty had he allowed these officials to leave the capital under such circumstances. Here as elsewhere, Millis combines near-unlimited credulity regarding the administration's war scare with an incurable tendency to view events exclusively from what he believed to be Forrestal's perspective. Because his was both the first and one of the most dramatic accounts of the period, historians have long tended to accept its basic premises as correct.[49] But given the evident weaknesses of his overly uncritical approach, there is surely no need to continue following in his footsteps.

Especially is this true in light of recent scholarship. Jean Edward Smith's masterful biography of Lucius Clay makes it clear beyond a shadow of a doubt that the contents of the March 5 telegram were thoroughly and completely at odds with its author's true views. On the same day that telegram was sent, for example, Clay wrote Republican Senator Henry Cabot Lodge, Jr., of Massachusetts: "I believe American personnel are as secure here [in Berlin] as they would be at home. . . . Probably no occupation force ever lived under as secure conditions and with greater freedom from serious incidents than do the American forces living in Germany." Asked by his biographer to explain this "discrepancy between his message to Chamberlin and his many other messages to Washington at the same time," Clay replied:

> General Chamberlin came to see me in Berlin in late February [1948]... He told me that the Army was having trouble getting the draft reinstituted, and they needed a strong message from me that they could use in congressional testimony. So I wrote out this cable. I sent it directly to Chamberlin and told him to use it as he saw fit. I assumed they would use it in closed session [of various congressional committees]. I certainly had no idea they would make it public. If I had, I would not have sent it. . . . Shortly afterwards I remember that [Under Secretary of the Army] Bill Draper asked me in a teleconference to give

> him a statement he could use before the House Appropriations Committee. I told him I had already sent one to Chamberlin.[50]

There are at least two important conclusions that flow immediately from these crucial disclosures. To begin with, it is obvious that Clay's telegram could not possibly have come as a shock to those Pentagon higher-ups who were in on the plot, regardless of how much alarm they feigned for external consumption. So thoroughly did the administration base its case for the European Recovery Plan (ERP) and an arms buildup on the contents of the Clay cable, however, that even now, more than 40 years after the fact, Smith must ruefully report, "The Department of Defense declined to declassify Clay's teleconference with Draper of mid-March 1948."[51] Small wonder. It is hard to believe that an unexpurgated transcript of that conversation, in which the under secretary requested a message similar to the one Clay had already dispatched to Chamberlin, could do anything to enhance Washington's reputation for veracity during the early years of the Cold War.

Second, Chamberlin's visit to Clay came "late in February"—that is, before Forrestal's meeting with Marshall and Lovett on March 2, and *perhaps even before the onset of the Czech "crisis" on February 24–25.* In any case, the timing of Chamberlin's approach suggests that there were at least two simultaneous but independent sources for the idea of a war- scare campaign: the State Department, as evidenced by the Walter Bedell Smith's telegram from Moscow on March 1, and the Pentagon, as evidenced by the requests to Clay from Chamberlin and Draper.

Ultimately, however, Jean Edward Smith's findings about the Clay telegram raise as many questions as they answer. Who or what, for example, put the notion of soliciting a message from Clay into Chamberlin's head? Chamberlin's own papers, unfortunately, contain nothing that sheds light on this point. But the fact that he and Draper each sought a message from Clay independently of the other does lead one to believe that the thought did not simply pop into Chamberlin's mind spontaneously and unbidden. More likely, the idea was "in the air" at army general staff headquarters in Washington. It could have come up, for instance, during a meeting at which both Chamberlin and Draper were present, without any formal action necessarily having been taken ("Say, it certainly would help us in Congress if we could get a message from Clay"). For "good soldiers" eager to assist, nothing more might have been required. Just as easily, the subject might have been broached over lunch or dinner, or even during a casual conversation in an office or the halls of the Pentagon.

Or Chamberlin could have been asked specifically to take on the task of obtaining a message from Clay by someone higher in the chain of command. Who might that "someone" have been? I have not been able to find documents that provide a conclusive answer to this question; but I have seen enough circumstantial evidence to embolden me to propose a tentative one: James Forrestal and Kenneth Royall.

Note, first of all, that it was Forrestal and Royall who, on the evening of March 3, appealed to James Byrnes to make a speech urging Congress to pass a new Selective Service act. Second, it was also Royall who, in the presence of Forrestal on the day after Clay's telegram arrived, asked David E. Lilienthal, Chairman of the Atomic Energy Commission, how much time it would take to transfer atomic bombs ("eggs" in Royall-Lilienthal parlance) to the Mediterranean—an inspired tactic for giving the scare a rousing send-off within the bureaucracy.[52] And third, it was the identical pair who—starting more than one week before the Communist takeover in Czechoslovakia—sought to elicit from the commander of the U.S. forces of occupation in Japan, General Douglas MacArthur, a message similar to that sent on March 4–5 by his counterpart in Berlin. Forrestal made the initial overture, in a long letter to MacArthur whose closing lines read:

> Any call upon us to implement a United Nations decision in Palestine, or for substantial intervention in either Greece or Italy, would so far commit [the Army's] very limited reserve that in the opinion of the JCS [Joint Chiefs of Staff] we would have to call for an immediate partial mobilization.
>
> These are some general observations which I hope may be of interest to you and to which I shall be very happy to have your response.[53]

MacArthur evidently refused to take the bait; his notorious "Asia first" outlook may have led him to regard Forrestal's forebodings with a certain indifference and to dismiss the latter's veiled plea with the mental equivalent of a shrug. The indirect approach having failed, it next fell to Royall to try the direct. Writing for him to MacArthur's headquarters in Japan, the chief of staff of the army's Civil Affairs Division left no room for misunderstanding of what was desired: "Secretary of Army advised me that a cablegram from MacArthur in support of selective service would be very helpful now while matter is before the Committees of Congress. Will you please discuss this with MacArthur and see if you can arrange for such a cablegram to be sent." Regardless of MacArthur's reply to this second request, what is significant is that the appeals to him came from the same Forrestal-Royall combination that I believe to have been at the root of Chamberlin's mission to Clay in February.

Fourth and last, I encountered no record of Forrestal ever meeting alone in his office with the director of intelligence of either the air force or the navy during this period—but he had two such meetings with Chamberlin between early February and the middle of March 1948. The first was scheduled for 11:46 A.M. on February 2, and, as Forrestal's next appointment was at 12:50 at the White House, there would have been ample time both to propose a mission to Berlin and to explain why it was urgent that Chamberlin accept it. The second meeting took place at 10:10 A.M. on March 16, 1948 (Forrestal's next appointment was at 11:22 at the office of the Speaker of the House), shortly after Chamberlin had submitted to the chief of staff his "Estimate of World Situation." Elaborated out of the Clay telegram as a pearl is fashioned from a grain of sand within an oyster, this unrelievedly grim document, which we will inspect at length momentarily, was one that both Forrestal and the army chief of staff would draw upon heavily in testifying before Congress.[54]

Taken separately, none of the foregoing items is conclusive. Taken cumulatively, however, they all seem to point to the same verdict. Forrestal and Chamberlin, and probably Royall as well, were clearly up to *something*. And although that *something* may not have been solicitation of the Clay telegram, that certainly appears to be the most likely candidate for the position.

In any case, having probed the circumstances under which the Clay telegram was dispatched, we next need to try to trace its subsequent trajectory. Or, rather, *trajectories*. For after arriving in Washington, the telegram led a schizophrenic existence. On the one hand, as we shall observe directly, it was immediately subjected to intensive analysis by military and civilian intelligence professionals, all of whom overwhelmingly rejected its central theme that war "may come with dramatic suddenness." On the other, despite this repudiation, the telegram evidently was employed by top representatives of the military, Forrestal and the army staff in particular, to win congressional approval for the program that the Pentagon was seeking.

Our knowledge of the evaluation of the Clay telegram by specialists in the field of intelligence derives from what at first sight is an odd source: the Committee on the National Security Organization of the Commission on Organization of the Executive Branch of the Government, better known as the Eberstadt Committee of the Hoover Commission. Chaired by former President Herbert Hoover, the mandate of the Commission on Organization of the Executive Branch was to study that part of the federal government and make proposals for its reorganization. To a committee chaired by financier Ferdinand Eberstadt, Forrestal's closest companion since their Princeton days, the Hoover Commission assigned responsibility for investigating the coordination of intelligence by the relevant military and civilian agencies. In making its report to the Hoover Commission in November 1948, the Eberstadt Committee stated that it had found

> *disturbing inadequacies in our intelligence system.* Testimony was presented to the Committee that in the spring of 1948, a mistaken intelligence estimate, prepared by a departmental intelligence agency, stimulated recommendations—which if followed—might well have had serious consequences. Fortunately, in this instance, the Central Intelligence Agency and other intelligence groups correctly evaluated the available information in good time.[55]

The administration had no intention of publishing this portion of the Eberstadt Committee's report, but, one way or other, the mass media learned of the "mistaken intelligence estimate." Columnist Drew Pearson's explanation, offered in his December 19, 1948, radio program on the ABC network, is probably as accurate as any:

> Last week the Hoover Commission . . . revealed that the U. S. almost mobilized for war because of an irresponsible Intelligence report. This amazing revelation is something the public was entitled to know all about. However, . . . this startling fact was only made public because of the inefficiency of the Hoover Commission, which is supposed to recommend efficiency. Actually Hoover and his staff had secretly agreed to omit this reference to Military Intelligence bungling. But some one forgot to blue-pencil the report. So the people of the U.S., quite by accident, penetrated the "iron curtain" of the Pentagon and thus exploded the mystery of last spring's war scare, at a time when Congress was being asked to vote funds for the Army and Navy.[56]

Whatever the cause, there can be no dispute about the stir the release of this information created. Ferdinand Eberstadt's papers contain an impressive assortment of page-one articles about the "mistaken estimate," clipped from such newspapers as the *New York Post, Louisville Courier-Journal, St. Louis Post-Dispatch, Newark News, Washington Times-Herald, Washington Evening Star* and the *Washington Daily News.* The last of these, by way of illustration, on December 16 made the story its lead item, with a headline that proclaimed, in three lines of ultrabold type set in capital letters 1-⅛ inches high, "Military Almost Got US Into War, Says Hoover Group." Not every publication's coverage was quite this dramatic, of course; but overall, Forrestal, the Pentagon and the CIA were unlikely to have been much gladdened at receiving this unexpected gift at Christmastime.[57]

The effect of these articles, as can be imagined, was to unleash a veritable orgy of finger pointing within the Department of Defense, with each suspected culprit seeking someone else on whom to lay the blame. As a completely unintended byproduct of this whirlwind of activity, however, the release of the Eberstadt Report gave rise to a set of documents through which we can follow the response of military and civilian intelligence to the Clay telegram. For the traditional interpretation, we may once more turn to Walter Millis, who maintained that ever since receiving Clay's message on March 5,

> the intelligence services had been working at high pressure. Not until . . . Tuesday, March 16, was the CIA able to hand the President a brief combined estimate by State, Army, Navy and Air Force, saying that war was not probable within sixty days; and not for another two weeks was CIA able to extend even this tenuous forecast of peace.[58]

In one version or another, this interpretation has dominated historical accounts ever since. Interestingly enough, however, Millis's citation at this juncture is not to any entry in Forrestal's diary during March 1948, but rather the following: "Diary, 23 December 1948, which gives a summary report of the March crisis."[59] Millis never explained why Forrestal would wait until a day late in December to inscribe in his diary a narrative of events that occurred during the first part of March. Perhaps this fact did not strike Millis as sufficiently unusual to require an explanation, although, as a journalist writing on military issues for the *New York Herald Tribune* in 1948, he could not have failed to know the reasons for Forrestal's renewed interest in the Clay telegram of the previous March. Or perhaps, as I suspect to be the case, he simply chose not to reopen what he doubtless would have regarded as a can of worms.

In any case, one need not rely on deductive logic to conclude that it is the Eberstadt Report's account of a "mistaken intelligence estimate" that lies behind Forrestal's diary entry of 23 December, for so much is made clear by a set of documents relating to the extract from the Eberstadt Report that I quoted above. Carefully examined, these documents tell a story that is in complete contradiction to the conventional interpretation.

The "summary report" in Forrestal's diary to which Millis's footnote referred was taken from a memorandum stamped "Secret" and dated December 23, 1948—the same day as the diary entry—from one of Forrestal's assistants, Robert Blum. Even Blum's designation of the memorandum's subject is provocative: "The March 'Crisis'"—sardonic quotation marks most assuredly in the original. Equally so is an attached memorandum of December 20, 1948, to Forrestal, "reference your query on the 'mistaken intelligence estimate' referred to in the Eberstadt Report." Written by a second assistant, Colonel Robert J. Wood, the last sentence of this memorandum again suggests the possibility that Millis's treatment of the Clay telegram is misleading: "It appears the Army, and rather specifically General Chamberlin, is the guilty party." "Guilty party"? Guilty of *what* ?[60]

The answer begins to emerge from the chronology that Blum compiled for the secretary of defense. Even though some of Blum's dates were in error by a week—he stated the Clay telegram was sent on March 11 rather than March 4—it is his summary of the events that is important. After receiving Clay's message, Blum noted, "General Chamberlin had the telegram shown to the other agencies concerned and was himself inclined to take a pessimistic view of the situation." How else? Chamberlin had solicited the telegram specifically for the purpose of influencing Congress to adopt just such a "pessimistic view of the situation," so he certainly was not about to present it in any other light once he had it in hand. The following day, Blum's summary continues,

> a meeting was held in Army Intelligence Division at which representatives of all interested agencies were present. General Chamberlain expressed his views as to the danger of war but these views were not concurred in by the other agencies except possibly Air Force although this is not certain.

Chamberlin's "views as to the danger of war . . . were not concurred in." Here we have the first explicit acknowledgment in a contemporary document that Chamberlin's scare tactics, based on the telegram he extracted from Clay, were quickly rejected by his counterparts in other agencies. Now we begin to understand why Blum called the subject of his memorandum of December 23 "The March 'Crisis,'" why Robert Wood considered Chamberlin "the guilty party."[61]

"As a result of the meeting on the 13th" called by Chamberlin in his office, according to Blum's chronology, the CIA convened a second meeting of "all the Intelligence Chiefs and their principal advisors" two days later, March 15. From Blum's phraseology, one gathers that the intent of the CIA may have been to try and reconcile Chamberlin's "pessimistic view of the situation" with the contrary estimates of all the other intelligence agencies. In any event, the participants in the March 15 meeting "decided to prepare a brief estimate" for the president. "The agencies, including CIA, State, Army, Navy and Air Force concurred in a brief estimate sent to the President" on March 16. We will consider this document more fully in the following chapter. For now, let us simply note that, "This estimate stated that there was no likely danger of war within 60 days." On April 2, the CIA

> published an estimate which was an extension of the brief statement of 16 March. All other agencies except the Air Force concurred in

> this estimate. Air Force held that it was impossible to project any estimate beyond a 60-day period and that the danger of war should not be minimized.[62]

And there one has it. Chamberlin had not been able to persuade representatives of so much as a single other agency to subscribe to his "pessimistic view of the situation"—not that this fact in any way prevented top-ranking civilian officials and military officers from expounding views identical to Chamberlin's to congressional committees. The most the general had managed to achieve were some minor reservations by the air force about the CIA's April 2 estimate that there would be no war with the Soviet Union for the remainder of 1948. On the face of it, this was hardly much of a triumph, especially given the amount of exertion required to produce it. What is more, even this slender accomplishment becomes questionable, as I will bring out below, in light of the frivolous basis of air force intelligence's dissent from the April 2 estimate.

Before taking up that subject, however, one other key document arising out of the furor created by the Eberstadt Report demands our attention. After Forrestal's assistants had unearthed the information recounted in Robert Blum's memorandum of December 23, 1948, and its various attachments, they sought a further explanation from the army of its handling of the Clay telegram.[63] This inquiry in due course led the army chief of staff to request Major General S. LeRoy Irwin, Stephen J. Chamberlin's successor as director of intelligence (Chamberlin had been replaced, for whatever reason, during the second half of 1948), to prepare a "summary of the opening phases of the 'flurry' of March 1948 with particular reference to the intelligence estimates of the period."[64]

An examination of the memorandum of January 4, 1949, that General Irwin composed in accordance with the chief of staff's instructions gives the coup de grace once and for all to the misconception that army intelligence significantly modified its estimate of Soviet intentions on the basis of the Clay telegram. The memorandum takes the form of a chronology focused largely on the army's response to that telegram. Because it contains extensive quotations from documents written in March 1948, Irwin's chronology provides us with a more complete picture of Army intelligence's immediate reaction to the Clay telegram than does Robert Blum's account of December 23, 1948. "As a result of the Clay message," Irwin explained, "the Intelligence Division reexamined available information bearing upon possible Soviet intentions and reviewed its estimates." On March 6, the day after Clay's telegram arrived in Washington, "the results of this review were presented to Secretary Royall and top members of the General Staff by Colonel Ennis and members of the Intelligence Group *after approval of the conclusions by the Director of Intelligence*" (emphasis added).[65] I have put the preceding words in italics because they demonstrate that as of March 5, General Chamberlin, the director of army intelligence, appeared to be in full agreement with the findings reached by his staff. Given that these findings were completely antithetical to the fear-mongering estimates that Chamberlin was starting to prepare for representatives of the army to use on Capitol Hill, this fact is worth emphasizing. It also bears remarking that Forrestal's calendar places him, as well as Secretary Royall and Generals Chamberlin and Omar Bradley, in attendance at this meeting.[66]

After pointedly observing that "General Clay's uneasiness was not generally reflected in contemporary reports received from Army intelligence sources throughout Europe," Chamberlin's staff on March 6 advanced two notable conclusions with respect to the possibility of war with the U.S.S.R. First:

> It is unlikely that the Soviets will take military action either to drive us out of Berlin, or Germany, although they have the undoubted capability of initiating offensive operations in Europe and the Middle East without appreciable warning. However, we have no evidence that they intend to do so at this time.

And second:

> It remains our estimate that the Soviets will continue their expansionist policy taking care to avoid war. It is believed that this will entail a step-up in aggressive tactics through use of satellite states and Communist Parties. The possibility remains that such action might inadvertently touch off a general war.[67]

The crucial word here is *remains,* in the first sentence of the second paragraph. From the survey in appendix A of civilian and military intelligence reports written both before and after the March 1948 war scare, we know that the standard U.S. evaluation of Soviet intentions maintained that the U.S.S.R. did not want war with the West, although such a war might come about as the result of miscalculations by either side. Despite the overheated rhetoric of the Clay telegram, this report of the army's Intelligence Division continued to adhere faithfully to the same analysis. Clay's message, in short, had changed nothing of importance. So far as Chamberlin's own staff was concerned, there was no reason to subscribe to its commanding officer's "pessimistic view of the situation." It was still business as usual on March 6.

To complete our discussion of the Clay telegram as intelligence it will be instructive if we also consider the actual position of air force intelligence in the days after March 5; doing so will pound the final nail into the coffin of the no-longer-tenable interpretation that the telegram caused a drastic revision of the administration's estimate of Soviet intentions. In the autumn of 1948, as we have seen, army intelligence came under fire from the Eberstadt Committee for its alarmist mishandling of the Clay telegram (although the committee seems to have viewed this mishandling as inadvertent rather than deliberate). The army responded in the finest tradition of the bureaucratic imperative: protect your own and let all else—especially something so inconsequential as the truth—take the hindmost. In this spirit, the army charged bravely onto the field—seeking to shift the onus onto the air force. Thus, as a case in point, an article in the *Washington Star* on December 23 disclosed that "at the time the [Eberstadt] report was released last week . . . a high Government source told The Star that the estimate was made by the Air Force and referred to Russian military plans."[68]

The documents, however, give the army's arguments the lie. Blum's memorandum of December 23 to Forrestal, for example, includes summaries of interviews that the former conducted with representatives of naval intelligence, air force intelligence and the investigatory staff of the Eberstadt Committee. General Cabell, an air force intelligence officer, told Blum that "there is no evidence that the air force prepared an alarmist estimate as a result of General Clay's telegram." Even though the Air Force "had . . . been reluctant to subscribe to any estimate which discounted the possibility of war"—air force intelligence, as I shall bring out both here and in the next chapter, was mediocre at best and geared primarily to obtaining larger appropriations for that service by exaggerating Soviet air strength[69]—it nonetheless "concurred in the March 16 [CIA] estimate that saw no war for the next 60 days." Rear Admiral Thomas B. Inglis, the chief of naval intelligence, supported Cabell's position. The admiral, according to Blum's account of his comments, held that during the war scare, "one service in particular was inclined to be very pessimistic." Although Inglis had not disclosed to the Eberstadt Committee "the Service he had in mind… if he had named a Service it would have been Army, not Air Force."[70]

Robert Wood also raised this question with Ferdinand Eberstadt himself in a telephone conversation that took place on December 22. Asked by Wood if it was the Air Force "you had in mind" as being responsible for the "mistaken intelligence estimate" criticized in the Eberstadt Report, Eberstadt's reply was, "Well, they're not the ones *I* have in mind, no. . . . I, myself, was rather surprised when I heard [from the Army] that it was the Air Force. . . . Don't connect me with it in any way and I'll tell you personally, and off the record, we did not have the Air Force in mind." Later, after "thinking back over our remarks," Eberstadt qualified his previous comments: "I'm not sure that the outfit you mentioned [air force] may not also have participated. . . . I put it to you this way: that in my opinion, they were not the primary mover, but they may have been involved in it." Eberstadt rephrased the last idea in one form or another some four times during the conversation, and the clear thrust of his comments was to place the chief responsibility for the "mistaken intelligence estimate" on the army.[71]

Ultimately, even Forrestal himself exonerated the air force. The *Washington Star* article of December 23 to which I referred above also reproduced a statement released by his office: "In response to inquiries, Secretary of Defense Forrestal said today that, following an investigation, he is convinced that Air Force intelligence was not responsible for the error in intelligence estimates mentioned in the Eberstadt Report." Given that Forrestal probably did not have to be reminded of the uses to which Chamberlin and the army leadership had put the Clay telegram earlier that year, and given that Ferdinand Eberstadt was his most trusted adviser, it would been difficult for the secretary to have done otherwise.

Fortunately, there is enough documentary evidence to reveal exactly what position air force intelligence had taken during March. The basis for this position was certainly nothing to be proud of—it was, in fact, a very model of absurdity—but at least it could not be said to involve the kind of deviousness found in Chamberlin's efforts. While the CIA's intelligence estimate of April 2, 1948, was still being prepared, the director of air force intelligence, Major General George C. McDonald, went on record in an effort to have its conclusions modified. Although he was in agreement with the main point of the CIA's estimate, that "there is no reliable intelligence currently available to indicate that a Soviet-initiated war is likely within the forthcoming 60 days," he did not "concur in the conclusion that the USSR will not resort to military action before the end of 1948." And on what did McDonald base his dissent? "Lacking any additional data, an extension of this estimate to the end of 1948 is largely dependent upon the application of logic to the basic intelligence previously considered. The weakness in this process is that our Occidental approach to logic might well be diametrically opposed to that of the Oriental Russian mind."[72] And so on.

Whatever else one may think of it, the argument that General McDonald advanced was so manifestly ludicrous, so blatantly silly, that no one with an ounce of functional gray matter could possibly have taken it seriously. (Among other things, it would, if extended to its ultimate conclusion, render impossible the art of evaluating another nation's intentions.) In its very defects, however, lay its virtues. Whereas Clay's telegram and Chamberlin's report based on it had some superficial plausibility, and thus possessed the capacity to deceive and mislead, the transparent preposterousness of McDonald's formulation served as its own negation: to know it was to reject it. That being so, even if it could be shown that the Clay telegram had somehow inspired the objections of air force intelligence to the CIA's April 2 estimate of no war for the remainder of 1948, could anyone contend with a straight face that it would be possible to erect a credible war scare on the wobbly foundation these objections supplied? A child's Halloween mask would most likely have provoked greater fear.

The purpose of scrutinizing at length the response of military and civilian intelligence to the army's interpretation of the Clay telegram has been to demonstrate that the conventional account of Washington's reaction to the telegram is thoroughly, fundamentally in error. Walter Millis and successive historians to the contrary notwithstanding, Clay's assertion that war "may come with dramatic suddenness" was immediately and categorically repudiated by professionals in the field of intelligence evaluation. Nor was army intelligence in any way an exception, despite the fact that it was the director of the army's Intelligence Division who had commissioned the telegram from Clay in the first place. Even the air force—whose leadership believed that long-term estimates minimizing the likelihood of war harmed the service's continuing campaign for bigger budgets and therefore stubbornly refused to assent to them—drew the line at seconding the army's attempt to base intelligence findings on the Clay telegram. Millis described the Clay telegram as a "blockbuster bomb." So far as its effect on the evaluation of Soviet intentions is concerned, however, it is more accurate to view it as a dud. If the war scare of 1948 had depended on nothing more than an objective appraisal of Clay's message by the appropriate intelligence agencies, the scare would have been over before it started.

THE CLAY TELEGRAM AS PROPAGANDA

Resolve one riddle, confront one worse: such is the rule that seems to govern everything connected with the war scare of 1948. It has taken several decades to determine how the intelligence-gathering agencies of the Truman administration actually evaluated the Clay telegram. It may take several more before we reach a complete understanding of the ways in which top officials in that administration utilized the telegram as a propaganda weapon to accomplish their policy goals. And to say even this much supposes that the information we seek has not been so skillfully concealed or destroyed that we will never have a full accounting.

For all of that, however, we do have some evidence of how the Clay telegram was employed to impress members of key congressional committees and other influential individuals with the gravity of the situation. We know, to begin with, that no sooner did Clay's cable arrive in Washington than James Forrestal wheeled it into the fray. The first opportunity Forrestal would have had to put the telegram to the use for which it was intended was on Monday, March 8, 1948, when he, the Joint Chiefs of Staff and the three service secretaries appeared before the Senate Armed Services Committee in executive session. What did he say on that occasion? It is at this point, alas, that we sense a curtain starting to descend. Records of the Senate Armed Services Committee "do indicate that Secretary Forrestal, together with the Service Secretaries and Service Chiefs, did appear before the Committee on that date, but that the proceedings were not stenographically recorded."[73] One presumes—not being able to do much more—that Forrestal, ever wily in the techniques of bureaucratic infighting, asked to have no written record of the March 8 session kept. Not only would such a request have impressed the senators with the importance of the highly classified intelligence they were about to hear, but it also would have helped Forrestal retain maximum control of his invaluable information and, through it, the subterranean course of the war scare. If those were his aims, and I have little doubt on this score, he succeeded all too well.[74]

Yet the curtain that Forrestal sought to draw over his wielding of the Clay telegram turns out upon further examination to have been, if not exactly transparent, less than wholly opaque. From an article in *Newsweek,* for example, we discover that the secretary did not let this first chance to invoke the Clay telegram escape him: "On Monday [March 8], Defense Secretary James Forrestal told a closed meeting of the Senate Armed Services Committee that American military authorities in Germany had abandoned their belief that the world was safe from war for at least ten years." The unmistakable reference here, of course, was to the Clay telegram. But Forrestal, for reasons already set forth above, was intent on preserving secrecy about the Clay telegram, hence his only recorded comment on emerging from the meeting of the Senate Armed Services Committee was the cryptic utterance, "Events are making progress for us." Likewise, when asked at his press conference two days later "about a certain Clay letter to you in regard to a change in the evaluation of the international situation with regard to the possibility of a war," Forrestal responded with a flat denial: "I have had no such message." Nonetheless, *Newsweek*'s account was reinforced by that of *Washington Post* writer Marquis Childs, in his column of April 6. Asserting—wrongly, but understandably—that "it was Clay's report which precipitated President Truman's call for the draft and the other moves aimed at alerting this country," Childs also stated that "part of the report, with its forecast of a shadow that might mean war, was communicated to the Senate Armed Services Committee." On balance, then, we are on safe ground in concluding that Forrestal at once set out to exploit the Clay telegram to the fullest. It may have been worthless as an item of intelligence, but for the purposes of the secretary of defense, it appears to have been invaluable.[75]

And for the Army's high command as well. To see this, we need look no further than the eight-page, single-spaced memorandum "Estimate of World Situation" written by General Chamberlin for General Bradley and submitted on March 14, 1948. By this date, Chamberlin already had seen his "pessimistic view of the situation" twice debated and twice rebuffed—first by his own staff on March 6, then at a meeting of representatives from all intelligence departments that he had called in his office on Saturday, March 13. Although the CIA had scheduled a second meeting of the latter group for Monday, March 15, in order to work out the final language of its report to the president, Chamberlin must have known by the end of the meeting on the 13th that there was no chance his estimate would be adopted subsequently. To add to his difficulties, the Joint Chiefs were slated to appear before the Senate Armed Services Committee on Thursday, March 18, and one of Chamberlin's responsibilities was to prepare an intelligence summary to be incorporated into the army's presentation.

Chamberlin's solution to his predicament was to abandon any effort at having the CIA and the other intelligence organizations support his analysis and instead offer General Bradley and the general staff his own war-scare *magnum opus,* the "Estimate of World Situation" of March 14, for use before Congress. It follows that if we would understand how the army—and probably the secretary of defense as well—employed Clay's message to get Congress to do its bidding, it is to this memorandum that we must have recourse.[76]

Chamberlin's "Estimate" is the kind of tedious, tendentious document that gives historians second thoughts about their choice of career. It is an unremitting jeremiad, an ostinato of impending catastrophe, in which everything is meant to point to a single conclusion: the necessity for building up the strength of the U.S. Army. The sole exception lies buried in a long paragraph midway through the report. Here Chamberlin conceded the existence of a "substantial concurrence of opinion, shared in by all Washington intelligence agencies (except that of the Air Force), and supported by intelligence opinion in the United Kingdom, that the Soviets do not desire to go to war at the present time."[77] (Note that Chamberlin neatly managed to misrepresent the air force's position that war was not likely at the moment, but that it could not be ruled out for the remainder of 1948.) This isolated ray of hope, however, is completely submerged by a torrent of doom and gloom—even the "Estimate's" topic headings are designed to fill the stoutest of hearts with fear and trepidation. If in the following I quote at inordinate length, I apologize to the reader in advance. My rationale is that no mere paraphrase is adequate to convey the flavor of Chamberlin's report; to do it justice, it must be savored in the author's own words (although I have taken the liberty of italicizing some of the more lurid passages).

"The Soviet Army is virtually on a war footing," Chamberlin wrote under the heading "World Military Imbalance." It was, he contended, capable of expansion "to 320 line divisions within 30 days." "Intensive training . . . , provision of improved weapons, and rapid progress toward development of a long-range air force have further enhanced Soviet offensive power," and the Soviet "submarine fleet is being steadily expanded." "In offensive operations in Europe," furthermore, "Soviet forces could be supported by some 1,200,000 Satellite troops." Although the Soviets did have certain weaknesses, these "affect largely the Soviet long-range capabilities and do not appreciably effect [*sic*] the short-range capabilities of quickly overrunning great expanses of the European continent." The United States, in contrast, "has no forces in being which could prevent the Soviet overrunning of most of Eurasia. . . . There is no overall defense plan for Free Europe," and those "forces which might oppose Soviet aggression throughout the world are incapable of offering more than a weak and unorganized delaying action in any of the likely theaters."[78]

Chamberlin's discussion of "Increasing International Tension" was equally encouraging. "Since the end of the war, . . . the Soviets have been actively pursuing a policy aimed at securing world domination." Their "primary targets" included virtually every country in Western Europe save for the nations of Scandinavia and the Iberian Peninsula, and Chamberlin tossed in "Iran, China and Korea" for good measure. The formation of a Western European military alliance, then under discussion on both sides of the Atlantic, "can only have a limited usefulness . . . unless a counterpoise is provided for the overwhelming Soviet military strength." As the "Soviets advance on their objectives with little evidence of effective counter-measures," it becomes "more and more evident that the will to resist cannot be supported alone by improving the economies of countries endangered by the Communist menace but requires the development of visible armed strength to reinforce the present governments and redress the balance of power."

To paint the picture in hues still more dismal, the "Estimate" postulated, "US Armed Forces Unequal To Commitments." "U.S. armed strength has declined continuously since V-J day," Chamberlin maintained. "Our actual military commitments, on the other hand, have increased substantially and are being increased almost continuously in reaction to day by day requirements of a deteriorating situation." Neither the Marshall Plan nor the proposed NATO alliance "can block further expansion of Soviet power unless they are supported . . . out of United States military resources. The most immediate problem is created by the threat of

Communist domination of Italy. *The resultant threat to the United States . . . may require the use of United States troops in Italy"* (emphasis added). But the United States would be powerless to act if such were the case, for the country "possesses at present no reserves of troops or materiel which could be made effective in time to avert disaster. Our current readily available reserve strength . . . is inadequate to take essential effective offensive action and, *simultaneously provide for the minimum security of the Continental U.S."* (emphasis added).[79]

In the unlikely event that his second topic, "Increasing International Tension," had not made the point with sufficient force, Chamberlin resumed flogging it in his fourth, "War Increasingly Possible." "The risk of war is now greater," he began. There were, he argued, "only two probable courses of action open to the United States," either "withdraw to the Western Hemisphere or resist Communism aggressively wherever found," and, naturally, "the latter must be assumed in our contemplation of the future." From which it followed that "*war will become increasingly probable*" (emphasis added).[80]

Given these premises, Chamberlin's "Summary" and "Conclusions" were exactly what one would expect. The U.S. policy of "support[ing] a number of nations in their resistance to Soviet aggression . . . is not proving successful in stemming the Soviet advance." The strength of the nation's armed forces "*is insufficient either to protect the security of the United States* . . . , to meet existing military commitments . . . or to assure the threatened nations of sufficient support to encourage their own will to resist." Hence "it is apparent that we must strengthen our armed forces now, not only to fulfill existing and possible future tangible and moral commitments, but also *to protect the security of the nation itself*." This strengthening must begin with the army, which "is carrying the burden of military occupation duties and other overseas commitments" even though it "is the least prepared of the Services to fulfill its national defense mission." Its occupation forces, in particular, are "weak and exposed to engulfment, *along with their dependents and U.S. civilian employees,* in the event of a major war." Yet if "our foreign policy requires further support from the armed services, it is the Army which will be called upon to bear the brunt of supplying men and equipment" (emphasis added throughout).

The entire purpose of this exercise, of course, was to fashion a supposedly compelling brief for the army's wish list. It surely comes as no surprise that Chamberlin advanced just such a list in his recommendations. These included: "resorting . . . to compulsory military service" (that is, reinstating selective service); increasing "the size of the Regular Army to the degree necessary"; undertaking "industrial mobilization" (that is, channeling federal money to the near-bankrupt aircraft industry) so as to "provide for our own rearmament and to assist in rearming friendly states"; and "placing unmobilized civilian components in the highest practicable state of readiness, training and strength" through the passage of universal military training.[81]

But granted the purpose behind it, was Chamberlin's "Estimate of World Situation" actually used in the way its author envisioned? Although the evidence is fragmentary, it does suggest that the answer to this question is yes. In a closed meeting of the Senate Armed Services Committee on Wednesday, April 21, 1948, for instance, Army Chief of Staff General Omar Bradley testified, "We are not sure of that now, that there is no war right away, and we do not believe as your military advisers we can afford to sit back and not advise you that we are thinking a little differently. . . . I think that we would be neglecting our duty," Bradley informed the senators, "if we did not come up here and try to tell you that we are a little bit more afraid something will happen than we were three months ago when we were talking in terms of reserves." Then, in halting and disjointed phrases, the General got to the point: "The trouble of it is that we do not know when it is coming . . . and we have to be somewhat prepared to meet it all of the time . . . and the reason we have come up here on this Selective Service, at least so far as I am concerned, I am more worried now than I was two or three months ago, and therefore we think something ought to be provided to take care of the short-term view, and that is Selective Service."

Not only do Bradley's words follow the overall line sketched out by Chamberlin in his memorandum of March 14, but in certain places they are uncannily reminiscent of those of Lucius Clay. Where Clay on March 5 had written, "I have felt a subtle change in Soviet attitude . . . [but] I cannot support this change in my own thinking with any data or outward evidence," Bradley conveyed the same thought this way: "So many things have happened and you cannot put your finger on any one of them, but it seems to be a difference in attitude on the part of the Russians."[82] Chamberlin's efforts, in short, had not been for naught.

We have, in this chapter, witnessed the stage being set for the war scare of 1948. By the time Clay's telegram of March 5 came into the possession of James Forrestal, these preparations were complete. In the next chapter, we shall sample their results.

5.

War Games (II): Attacking the Foe

There is a joke that used to go around; the question was asked what the difference was between German National Socialism and Russian Communism. The answer was: "It's colder in Russia!" It would be dangerous to go too far along that line and . . . particularly dangerous to view Russia as a problem in military-political sense as only sort of a stream-lined version of Hitlerite Germany.

—George F. Kennan, Director, State Department Policy Planning Staff, testifying before the House Armed Services Committee, January 8, 1948[1]

The people of the United States are fundamentally and overwhelmingly opposed to the "Marshall Plan" as an implement to the "Truman Doctrine." The only reason that this is being put over is on account of the scare propaganda which is essential to its existence.

—Letter of Murray Maverick to Honorable James Forrestal, April 12, 1948[2]

At Mr. Lovett's request Mr. Kennan discussed Soviet intentions. He expressed disbelief that the Soviet leaders contemplated

launching world conflict by armed force. . . . [The Kremlin] was not operating on any fixed timetable, and parallels between Stalinism and Hitlerism were dangerous.

—Minutes of the Third Meeting of the Washington Exploratory Talks on Security, July 7, 1948[3]

WEEK ONE: MARSHALL IN THE SPOTLIGHT

With the arrival in Washington of the Clay telegram on March 5, high-ranking members of the Truman administration had the weapon they had been seeking to use on Congress. But this weapon was meant to be employed in secret in order to seduce refractory notables; the administration would have to contrive a different pretext in order to peddle its war-scare wares to the public and less prominent members of the legislature and the press, most of whom could be readily manipulated without the use of precious "insider" information. The need, moreover, was daily growing more acute. In what the *New York Times* called "the most vigorous attack . . . to date" on the European Recovery Program (ERP), Senator George W. Malone of Nevada on March 5 led half a dozen or more of his fellow Republicans in a delaying tactic that at the minimum jeopardized the administration's timetable for the passage of the program and at worst threatened it with defeat. The fact that Malone's allies appeared to include the acting majority leader of the Senate only added to the administration's discomfort.[4]

The bad news continued to accumulate as the week wore on. On March 8, the *Times* reported that it was "doubtful . . . and in some quarters held improbable" that Congress would be able to vote on ERP "by April 1, the deadline repeatedly urged by the Administration." (This deadline grew out of the determination of Truman, Marshall and the State Department to have ERP funds in hand in time to employ them in the Italian election. Washington believed that enactment of ERP by April 1 would give it a carrot and stick to use with Italian voters in the elections later that month: the promise of Marshall Plan aid if they rejected the Communist-led forces of the left—and the threat of withholding such aid if they did not.) "Speaker [of the House] Joseph W. Martin Jr. told reporters today . . . that he saw few signs pointing to final passage by April 1, and other House leaders believe the action may come around April 15."[5]

To Secretary of State Marshall and his closest associates, these accounts were like nightmares coming true. Increasingly desperate, these officials showed themselves willing to grasp at any straw, no matter how slender. Such a straw was not long in coming. On March 10, as remarked in the previous chapter, Czech foreign minister Jan Masaryk fell to his death in Prague, either a suicide or a murder victim. Here, at last, was the opportunity for which the administration, and the secretary of state in particular, had been waiting. Marshall's public reaction to the death of Masaryk is one of the most critical episodes in the entire war scare, for with it he initiated a pattern to which he would adhere until he had succeeded in pushing the fear of war to its zenith. His conduct on this occasion therefore demands the most intense scrutiny.

This scrutiny is all the more necessary because of the Aesopian, veiled language—which deliberately avoided clarity and explicitness in favor of the cryptic and enigmatic—that the secretary of state chose to employ. To understand why this was the case, why Marshall refused to speak forthrightly, we must keep in mind the situation. On the one hand, the administration he represented hoped to be able to exploit the fear of war to overcome public and congressional resistance to Truman's foreign and military policies. On the other, however, Marshall certainly could not resort to anything so direct as an unequivocal statement that war was likely to result if the administration's measures were not swiftly enacted, for to do so would be likely to produce precisely the opposite outcome from the one he desired. If, that is, the nation were to become genuinely convinced that war was at hand, support for the Marshall Plan would immediately go up in smoke. After all, what sense is there in reconstructing Europe if World War III is going to break out there tomorrow, say, or next week? Better by far to spend the money instead on increasing the nation's military might. Besides, the reaction of the U.S.S.R. also had to be taken into account. It was unlikely that the Soviets would not consider striking first if they were to conclude that the United States was preparing to make war on them. Hence Marshall's task may be thought of as the political counterpart of managing a nuclear reaction: first adding sufficient fuel to generate the panic that would ensure passage of the administration's program, then inserting cadmium rods to bring under control, both here and in the U.S.S.R., the notion that war was inevitable.

As a result, all of Marshall's most significant pronouncements during the war scare are rent by the contradiction between a facade of calm and reason that barely conceals the actual incitement of fear and hysteria at a deeper level—truly the kind of political feat that only a virtuoso would dare attempt. Marshall's use of the death of Jan Masaryk to move the war scare to center stage offers a representative illustration. No sooner had word of Masaryk's death arrived in Washington than the secretary summoned a press conference. The world situation had suddenly become "very, very serious," he told reporters on March 10, and Czechoslovakia had fallen under a "reign of terror." Immediately thereafter he added, with consummate disingenuousness, "It is regrettable that passions are aroused to the degree that has occurred." How "regrettable" could he have found these "passions," when it was Marshall himself who had taken the lead in arousing them? A remarkable performance—chutzpah raised to new heights. Nor could the contradictory character of Marshall's words be dismissed as the kind of murky syntax that sometimes results when public figures speak impromptu. After calling attention to the fact that this was "an unusual statement that he [Marshall] allowed to be quoted," The *New York Times*'s reporter furnished the following account: "Secretary Marshall replied informally and then permitted direct quotation after carefully and slowly examining in the stenographic record what he had said." Clearly, Marshall's remarks were anything but impulsive; they were, rather, the product of a man taking enormous pains to get each nuance just so and to see that each and every word was recorded exactly as he wished.[6]

Commenting in the *New York Times* on March 12, James Reston perfectly caught the dichotomous strain in Marshall's comments. "In his appeal against public agitation and excitement about 'the very, very serious' world situation yesterday," Reston wrote, Marshall had "described the state of affairs in Czechoslovakia as a 'reign of terror.'" Yet while "official reports" indicated "there is certainly an element of fear there, . . . the general feeling in Washington is that Secretary Marshall's 'reign of terror' statement neither describes the situation accurately nor contributed to the calm and deliberation that he desired." Of course—spreading panic had been the reason for calling the press conference in the first place; and the fact that Marshall's purpose may have eluded a reasonably sharp-eyed journalist is merely an indication of the skillfulness with which the secretary went about his business. In any case, Reston offered his readers an analogy on which it would be impossible to improve: "the Secretary's performance was like a man getting up in a theatre and announcing: 'I advise everybody here to be very calm because the whole block around this theatre is on fire.'" As a result, "this morning, there was more public excitement, less calm and less public understanding about the nature of the world situation than before the appeal for calm and understanding had been made."[7]

Indeed there was. The principal figures in the administration now thought they had found a way to seize the initiative, as the war scare began to gain momentum. "The atmosphere I'd say is considerably improved," James Forrestal told Robert Cutler, a sometime adviser, in a telephone conversation on March 10. Although he claimed that "the improvement derived from other events that one can't take much pleasure in," Forrestal nonetheless remarked, "I think the political aspect of it is much better."[8] Courtesy of the secretary of state, he might have added.

There were, obviously, reasons why Marshall's language on March 10 had been inflammatory—a vast departure from his usual restrained manner. Except at moments of crisis, usually involving the threat of war, public opinion in the United States has generally been more closely focused on domestic issues than on those of foreign policy. This was also the case early in 1948, when inflation was for much of the population a more pressing concern than European economic recovery. In addition, what had happened in Czechoslovakia at the end of February 1948 was not the stuff that gives rise to stirring mass-media images—no tanks and trucks rolling across borders, no wave upon wave of goose-stepping troops, no pitched street battles between brutal invaders and heroically resisting citizens. Unable to rely on the events themselves to foster a sense of alarm, therefore, the Truman administration instead chose to weave a phony "crisis" from whole cloth. The administration's leading officials, we remember from the last chapter, did *not* see events in Czechoslovakia as evidence of a Soviet decision for war. Marshall's reaction to the Czech Communist Party's takeover, for example, was to state that "in so far as international affairs are concerned, a seizure of power by the Communist Party in Czechoslovakia would not materially alter . . . the situation which has existed in the last three years." And even as he was holding his press conference on March 10, the CIA was simultaneously reporting, "The Czech coup and the demands on Finland . . . do not preclude the possibility of Soviet efforts to effect a rapprochement with the West."[9] But all that was beside the point. The administration had a job it wanted done and no instrument other than Marshall's words with which to begin it.

Marshall's press conference of March 10 was the first shot in the administration's new offensive, but it was quickly apparent that far more would be required to overpower the opposition. In the Senate the next day, "Mr. Republican," Robert Taft of Ohio, introduced an amendment cutting the appropriation for ERP's first year by nearly one-fourth, from $5.3 billion to $4 billion. In the House, the Republican leadership, ignoring a letter from Truman to Speaker Joseph W. Martin, insisted on lumping ERP together with military aid to China, Greece and Turkey—a decision that dismayed the Trumanites because it threatened to delay passage of ERP beyond the administration's self-imposed April 1 deadline.[10]

To counter these tactics, the administration worked to capitalize on the furor created by Marshall's comments on the 10th. On the following day, Truman held an afternoon press conference, during which he combined an appeal to have "the European recovery program . . . carried out promptly" with a portentous statement that his faith in world peace had been "somewhat shaken."[11] That evening at 8:00 P.M., Marshall delivered a brief address from the chancel steps of Washington Cathedral, with the president himself in attendance. The Secretary's speech pounded home the ideas he had raised the day before. "The world is in the midst of a great crisis," his opening sentence proclaimed; his penultimate sentence reminded his listeners of the "extremely serious world situation." With this beginning and ending, Marshall sought to establish the all-important *tone,* which he recognized as more important than any specific content, of his remarks. Like Truman earlier in the day, Marshall coupled his "crisis" rhetoric with an appeal for passage of ERP. And, just as he had on the previous day, he also attempted to disguise the administration's own efforts to terrify the nation by invoking the pieties—"cool judgment," "moderate terms," "a level head," et cetera—that he ritually employed for that purpose.[12]

Friday the 12th, the next day, was, by comparison with the two before, uneventful. The administration received a bit of good news when the Senate rejected by an almost two-to-one margin Senator Taft's amendment to the ERP appropriation bill that would have cut its first-year funding by $1.3 billion.

In contrast to the usual low-key Washington weekend, the pace of the scare accelerated on Saturday with former Secretary of State James F. Byrnes's speech—prompted, as we noted in the last chapter, by a request from James Forrestal and Secretary of the Army Kenneth Royall ten days earlier—at The Citadel in South Carolina. No longer a member of the administration, Byrnes, unlike Marshall, enjoyed the luxury of being able to throw any pretense of moderation to the wind. In that spirit, the *New York Times* reported, he demanded "American action, not a 'letter of protest,' should Russia threaten the independence of Greece, Turkey, France or Italy," and warned "that the United States may have to meet an international crisis 'only four or five weeks from now.'" "By action," the *Times* explained, "it was plain . . . that [Byrnes] meant the use of American troops to enforce United States policy"; and the "crisis" he envisioned was that "the Russian threat might require [U.S. armed] intervention before the elections in Italy on April 18." Nor could Byrnes bear to close without ringing certain hackneyed changes, as the *Washington Post*'s account makes clear: "[There] is no important difference in the direct methods of Hitler in 1938 and the indirect methods of Stalin in 1948." If the speaker could no longer claim the official standing of his successor, Byrnes apparently hoped to compensate for that by the complete absence of restraint in his remarks.[13]

Although historians have tended to concentrate on the most purple passages of Byrnes's speech, there was more to its significance than mere bellicosity. In the second part of his address, Byrnes foreshadowed a split that was to arise at the highest level of the Truman administration—a conflict over the nature, duration and especially control of the war scare. In that light, it is worth examining the program Byrnes proposed as a response to the alleged Soviet threat. Given that James Forrestal had both conceived the idea for the speech and then made certain that it was highly publicized, it is safe to say that the agenda Byrnes advanced at The Citadel was an accurate reflection of Forrestal's own.

Where Marshall and the State Department hoped to use the scare to compel passage of ERP, Forrestal and Byrnes had a different set of priorities. As early as the beginning of December 1947, as I indicated in the preceding chapter, the secretary of defense had announced his intention to increase spending on aircraft procurement in the approaching fiscal year.[14] Thereafter, in an effort to secure selective service for the army and more money for both the Pentagon and the airplane manufacturers, Forrestal had bombarded the president with a steady stream of memoranda, presentations, and the like, but with nothing to show for his troubles.[15] In the last of these documents, Forrestal's first interim report as secretary of defense, he had written to Truman on February 29, 1948, that the "most critical immediate problem is the serious shortage of manpower in the Army. . . . I cannot overemphasize the importance of this shortage." On this occasion he had also stressed what he claimed was the need for more military aircraft: "Our reserve . . . is none too large, as I mentioned several weeks ago.... It may, therefore, be necessary to consider some increase in expenditures for the purchase of planes."[16] Now that the war scare was going into high gear, Forrestal had the opportunity he had been seeking to convince the administration, as well as the Congress, of the Pentagon's urgent requirement for bigger budgets and more bodies. He was not about to forfeit it by default. The speech by James Byrnes would be the initial step in mobilizing opinion inside and outside of the administration in support of the measures he favored.

Byrnes's speech at The Citadel, therefore, must be understood not only as one more maneuver in Forrestal's effort to heighten the war scare, but also and more specifically as part of the secretary's attempt to ensure that by the time the scare was over, he would have attained the program he was urging on the White House. So much is clear from a close reading of Byrnes's remarks. First of all, the army's strength was "pitifully inadequate," Byrnes maintained, and a peacetime selective service should be inaugurated at once so that the country could have "an army in uniform and not on paper." Second, development of the atomic bomb had made "the air program one with highest priority," hence the air force also should have its appropriation increased. Universal military training, in contrast, might have some value in the long term, but such a measure would be useless "for the situation that may exist four or five weeks from now." As for the Marshall Plan, although Byrnes gave it a pro forma endorsement, he was quick to add that its passage would "not stop the Soviets from further expansion this spring, if they have decided upon such expansion."[17] One would love to have witnessed Marshall's reaction to Byrnes's remarks. The theft had only just begun, and already the thieves were falling out. It would take some time, however, before the full implications of the differences among the architects of the war scare would emerge.

In the meantime, by virtue of the tireless work of Marshall, Forrestal and their subordinates, a mere four days of the war scare had brought about a spectacular change in the political climate of Washington. James Reston, writing on Saturday, March 13, found the "mood of the capital this week-end . . . exceedingly somber. . . . Responsible citizens are yelling, 'Quiet, quiet!' at the top of their voices, and even the President has mentioned that awful three-letter word, war." Seeking to account for "this sudden mob-surge of apprehension," Reston noted that the "Executive branch of the Government, in an effort to gain Congressional support of its policies, has been talking a good deal about war lately." In its eagerness to manipulate Congress, the Truman administration had "acquired the habit of emphasizing and sometimes even of overemphasizing the danger" posed by the U.S.S.R. "We legislate, in short, in an atmosphere of crisis," Reston concluded.[18] True enough; but much more was still to come.

Within the administration, it was evident over the weekend of March 13–14 that the "atmosphere of crisis" described by James Reston had already started to pay dividends. From Congress came word on Sunday that early that morning the Senate had voted overwhelmingly (69 to 17) to give the administration the full $5.3 billion it had requested for ERP—with no unfriendly amendments attached. There were, to be sure, one or two flies in the ointment. The upper house had rejected the administration's appeal for a four-year continuing authorization of $17 billion, choosing instead to make funds available one year at a time. On the same day, moreover, Senator Taft, stumping Maine in pursuit of the Republican presidential nomination, made page-one headlines by taking sharp issue with James Byrnes's speech on Saturday. Taft contended there was "no reason to believe Russia was intent on any immediate 'military aggression,'" the *New York Times* stated, and the *Washington Post* added, "The Ohio Senator said Russia so far was only consolidating the sphere of influence awarded her by the Yalta agreement." The candidate also threw down a direct challenge to the administration's war-scare scheme: "If President Truman and General Marshall have any private intelligence" that war with the Soviet Union is imminent, "they ought to tell the American people about it." Otherwise, he averred, the country should proceed on "the basis of peace."[19] Yet overall, these were but minor irritants; on balance, the administration appeared to be making great strides.

And just such strides would be necessary if it were to overcome the formidable obstacles that remained. It had been relatively easy for the President to obtain a favorable vote on ERP in the Senate, because the State Department had effectively co-opted the Republican chairman of the Senate Foreign Relations Committee, Arthur H. Vandenberg of Michigan, who functioned as the floor leader for ERP in the upper chamber. In the House, in contrast, where the administration's relations with the Republican leadership were much more antagonistic, there was no counterpart to Vandenberg on whom the White House could depend for consistent support. Besides which, ERP was only one part of the administration's program, and congressional approval of its proposed military buildup in particular was anything but assured. Confronted with this situation, Truman and his advisers elected to continue their reliance on the war-scare tactics that had already proven so effective.

Monday, March 15th, therefore, saw an intensification of the Truman-Marshall double-barreled attack of the previous week. In mid-afternoon, the White House announced that the president would address a joint session of Congress on what the *New York Times* called "the grave foreign situation" the day after next, Wednesday, March 17.[20] Originally, Truman had been slated to make a St. Patrick's Day speech in New York on that date; but, according to Forrestal, "Marshall had felt that was not a proper forum"—Truman would be appearing at a Democratic party event rather than before a "bipartisan" audience—and suggested the congressional setting instead. Forrestal's brief account states, "The President said he was going to deliver a message to Congress on Wednesday going all out for Selective Service and UMT"—a curious omission of any reference to ERP. Did Forrestal neglect to mention the Marshall Plan because he considered its inclusion too obvious to state—or because of his relief at finally obtaining Truman's support for a portion of the Pentagon's own agenda after many weeks of failed attempts? (It had taken a request from the Joint Chiefs of Staff, returning on March 14 from their Key West, Florida, conference with Forrestal on "roles and missions," to win Truman's assent to a resumption of selective service. Forrestal's own appeals on this score, some of which I cited above, Truman chose to ignore. In view of the alacrity with which the president acceded to the Joint Chiefs' appeal for selective service, his unresponsiveness toward Forrestal undoubtedly reflected the coolness with which he viewed the secretary of defense rather than his position on the issue per se. I will return to this latter point below, in discussing the third week of the war scare.)[21]

Announcement of Truman's speech had just the effect for which Marshall must have been hoping. It was the subject of the lead story in the *New York Times* on Tuesday, March 16, and, as Forrestal remarked in his diary that day, "Papers this morning full of rumors and portents of war."[22] Here, truly, was a way of killing a pair of birds with a single stone. By prevailing upon Truman to address a joint session of Congress, the secretary of state had managed not only to raise the level of tension several notches, but also to wrest back control of the war scare's interpretation from the military wing of the administration headed by James Forrestal.

Also on the afternoon of the 15th, Marshall testified before the Senate Foreign Relations Committee, again exhorting Congress to grant the administration's request for more money for the Greek and Turkish military. Although the committee had supposedly met in executive session, the next day's newspapers carried a full account of his remarks. "Should we fail to continue our efforts," he warned, "the consequences would be swift and tragic *and they would not be confined to Greece*" (emphasis added). His testimony concluded on a characteristic note, as ominous as it was vague. "The hour is far more fateful now than it was one year ago," Marshall told the legislators. "Totalitarian control has been tightened in other countries of eastern Europe, and . . . other European peoples face a similar threat of being drawn against their will into the communist orbit."[23]

The fruits of the administration's efforts began to materialize at once. On Monday, while Marshall was testifying in the Senate, the House Foreign Affairs Committee had voted 13 to 7 to defeat a Democratic motion to bring ERP to an immediate vote on the floor, and by the same margin had continued to insist on combining military aid to China, Greece and Turkey in the same bill with ERP.[24] The following day, however, the tide commenced to turn. Advised by Speaker Joseph W. Martin of a "grave crisis in our international relations," the House Republican Steering Committee "advanced the timetable" for consideration of ERP and—significantly—"called for House passage of an omnibus measure Easter week." For the first time, House Republicans had gone on record in favor of the Marshall Plan. In addition, there was good news for Forrestal, the military and the aircraft industry as well, for the same steering committee had also "agreed today to speed expansion of the defense establishment to achieve supremacy on the seas and in the air."[25] In a press conference held after the steering committee had adjourned its meeting, Martin amplified on Republican intentions. "With the situation the way it is in the world," he told reporters, "we have to keep our Army and Navy strong. We want to give them everything that is needed to put them in the strongest possible defensive position. And many members believe the amounts sent in for the Air Force should be substantially increased."[26]

By the morning of March 17—the day of Truman's address to Congress and the nation—the war scare had been in existence for a single week. Already in that short time, the administration had forced a striking change in the political equation. The Senate had enacted the Marshall Plan essentially in the form sought by the administration; and in the House, Republican resistance to ERP, if not wholly vanquished, was certainly weakening. House Republicans—almost always a greater problem for the president than their senatorial colleagues—had also indicated their willingness in principle to vote more money for the Pentagon, though it was not yet clear whether this support would also extend to selective service and universal military training. Through its incessant harping on the perilous situation supposedly confronting the United States, in short, the administration had succeeded in transforming the prospects for its foreign policy and military measures from extremely bleak to most promising. It was an impressive achievement, the price of which was nothing more consequential than the truth.

We might, in that light, pause momentarily, prior to considering Truman's St. Patrick's day speech, to remind ourselves of how U.S. intelligence agencies actually perceived current world circumstances and Soviet intentions. On March 15, 1948, as a case in point, just as the White House was announcing Truman's intention to address Congress on March 17, the Joint Strategic Plans Committee submitted a report to the Joint Chiefs of Staff with the suggestion that the report be approved and forwarded to the Research and Development Board. A major premise of the report was that although the "possibility of war will increase with the passage of time, . . . a planned war with full preparation is not probable within the next five to seven years."[27] Along the same lines, one could do no better than cite the CIA's memorandum of March 16 to the president, which reported a reassessment of "Soviet intentions for the next sixty days" by the agency itself "and the intelligence organizations of the Departments of State, War [Army], Navy and Air Force." These bodies all concurred in the memorandum's three conclusions "with respect to the possibility of Soviet military action":

> a. [There is] no reliable evidence that the USSR intends to resort to military action within the next sixty days.
>
> b. The weight of logic, as well as evidence, also leads to the conclusion that the USSR will not resort to military action within the next sixty days.
>
> c. There is, nevertheless, the ever present possibility that some miscalculation or incident may result in military movements towards areas, at present unoccupied by the USSR.

This was a message rather different from the one the president was planning to deliver to the country on the following day.[28]

WEEK TWO: TRUMAN SPEAKS—MARSHALL BELLOWS

The relentless advance of the war scare reached a climax on the morning of St. Patrick's Day. "Tense Capital Awaits Truman Speech to Congress Today on State of World . . . ," blared a four-column headline in the *New York Times*'s blackest typeface; "Truman to Call Halt on Russia," readers of the *Los Angeles Herald Express* were informed; and in their *Washington Post* column "Matter of Fact," Joseph and Stewart Alsop wrote, "The atmosphere in Washington today is no longer a postwar atmosphere. It is, to put it bluntly, a prewar atmosphere."[29] In stark contrast to all this gloom and gnashing of teeth, however, Forrestal was positively ecstatic: "I feel better about the world situation than I have for 2½ years," he wrote a friend that same day. If the administration were truly fearful of war, the Secretary's words concealed the fact most skillfully.[30]

The stage was now set for Truman's moment in the spotlight. With the exception of his press conference of Friday, March 12, he had remained in the background as the war scare gathered momentum, and he would retreat back into the shadows after today. But on Wednesday, March 17, the starring role was all his.

As Truman worked on the address, a split arose within the administration over its tone and content. Because Marshall and his closest associates were constantly fearful that they would lose control of the war scare and matters would get out of hand—a fear that was not entirely without foundation, as the speech by James Byrnes had demonstrated—the State Department contingent favored a low-key, matter-of-fact presentation. The members of Truman's political coterie, notably Clark Clifford, repeatedly encouraged Truman to take precisely the opposite course. "Should the President make any recommendation with reference to strengthening this country's air power?" was, for example, the first of four questions he posed to James Forrestal in a memorandum soliciting the latter's ideas for the President's speech, and the other three questions likewise focused on military issues.[31] Even though there was no mention of "air power" in the final draft of Truman's address, Clifford's queries in this regard show the direction in which he was leaning.

We can also surmise the kind of counsel Clifford was likely to have given Truman from a very long memorandum—a monograph, actually—on election-year political tactics that this key adviser had written late in 1947. "There is considerable political advantage to the Administration in its battle with the Kremlin," he told the President. "The worse matters get, up to a fairly certain point—real danger of imminent war—the more is there a sense of crisis. In times of crisis, the American citizen tends to back up his President." Truman's own political experience no doubt led him to recognize that Clifford's instinct for the jugular was more likely to yield the desired results than the cool, cerebral approach preferred by Marshall; and as there was, after all, no "real danger of imminent war"—aside from that produced by the administration's own incendiary language—he elected to side with the former by enhancing the "sense of crisis."[32]

There are three noteworthy aspects to the speech itself. First, Truman followed Marshall's lead in dwelling on the ostensible imminence of war. Formulations such as "the critical nature of the situation in Europe" (used twice), "the world situation is too critical," "vital importance that we act now," "necessity for speedy action," "great urgency," "urgent steps," and the like, are ubiquitous. Second, the speech aimed to build tension by repeatedly invoking the phrase "one nation" as a rhetorical device: "one nation has . . . refused to cooperate," wartime agreements "have been persistently ignored and violated by one nation," "one nation . . . has persistently obstructed the work of the United Nations," and so on. Only after he was one-third of the way through his address did Truman explicitly charge "the Soviet Union and its agents" with these offenses. No doubt this specific "naming" of the Soviet Union was one of the features of the speech to which Marshall—who in his own remarks always left it to his audiences to deduce that he had in mind the U.S.S.R.—objected. Although Truman venerated his secretary of state and was usually only too willing to accept his advice, in this case Marshall was overruled.

The third aspect of the speech is that of its contents, the actual measures that Truman proposed to Congress and the country. Two of these reflect the wishes of the architects of the war scare, Marshall and Forrestal; the third, I will argue in the chapter that follows, was tactical in nature, proposed as a means of ensuring adoption of the other two. At the head of the list, of course, stood ERP, "prompt passage" of which would be "the most telling contribution we can now make toward peace." "Prompt enactment of universal training legislation"—which Marshall had been seeking ever since returning to office in 1947—was the next recommendation, although I believe Truman never expected to have such a program approved. "Temporary re-enactment of selective service legislation," the final item on the President's agenda, was a testimonial to the central role of Forrestal and the Pentagon in shaping the war scare. Top representatives of the military were quick to realize that no such scare could be credible without their active participation; initiation of a peacetime draft was a part, but only a part, of the price they would demand in exchange. Contrary to what had been rumored in the press, however, Truman did not on this occasion specify the amount by which he wished to increase appropriations for the military in order to finance the programs he was prodding Congress to pass. To have done so would have blurred the clear outline of the speech; such secondary details, which had not yet been worked out in any case, could for the moment be left to the custody of James Forrestal and other representatives of the armed services.[33]

No sooner had Truman completed his speech than Marshall went to Capitol Hill to appear before the Senate Armed Services Committee in another ardent appeal for UMT. Marshall's statement to the committee marked a new and dire step in his descent into war-scare hyperbole, as for the first time he espoused the notion that Stalin's foreign policy was identical to Hitler's: "It is said that history never repeats itself. Yet if these free people one by one are subjugated to police state control even the blind may see in that subjugation of liberty a deadly parallel." The implication was that the Soviets would soon emulate the Nazi example by undertaking the conquest of Europe. And with its army allegedly reduced to a "hollow shell"—"an amazing statement by a Secretary of State . . . when the foreign policies he is espousing require the backing of military force," the *New York Times*'s Hanson Baldwin thought—the United States would be unable to resist.[34] As the war scare evolved, it was becoming increasingly difficult to distinguish the position of the current secretary of state from that of his predecessor.

That night in New York, Truman gave the second of the day's two speeches, addressing the Friendly Sons of St. Patrick, a Democratic party organization. His remarks for the most part were a rehash of his speech to Congress earlier in the day, with the exception of a single new twist—the baiting of Henry Wallace. Secretary of agriculture from 1933 to 1941, vice president of the United States from 1941 to 1945, and thereafter secretary of commerce until Truman demanded his resignation in 1946, Wallace was the single most formidable critic of the administration's Cold War policies, and his presidential candidacy at the head of the newly-formed Progressive Party threatened to draw enough votes from Democrats disgruntled with the incumbent's harsh anti-Soviet stance to give victory to the Republicans in November. To counter the threat, Truman once more fell back on the counsel of Clark Clifford, who (with James Forrestal's encouragement) had advised Truman that "Wallace should be put under attack whenever the moment is psychologically correct" by belaboring the idea "that the core of the Wallace backing is made up of Communists and . . . fellow-travelers." This approach served a dual purpose: implying that the country was besieged by Communists both within and without intensified the atmosphere of crisis, thereby improving the chances that Truman would get Congress to approve ERP and his military programs; and identifying Wallace with the Communist party enabled the administration to deprive him of those would-be supporters who did not want to be associated with anything bearing that dreaded label. Accordingly, on the evening of March 17, Truman proceeded to put Clifford's tactics into effect by proclaiming to his Democratic audience: "I do not want and I will not accept the political support of Henry Wallace and his Communists."[35]

As was true of previous installments, this latest episode in the war scare yielded immediate returns. Six of the seven leading stories on the first page of the *New York Times* for Thursday, March 18, concerned either Truman's speeches, Marshall's congressional testimony or reactions to one or the other. One of these articles reported a development that the administration surely found gratifying: the House Foreign Affairs Committee, by an 11 to 8 vote, had sent the ERP bill to the floor with the full funding of $5.3 billion that Truman had requested. Better yet, Representative Charles A. Hallock of Indiana, the Republican floor leader, had "declared his strong 'hope' that the House would now be able to pass the European recovery bill . . . 'before April 1.'" Yet all was not as rosy as it seemed at first glance. Even if the House did manage to approve ERP before that date, its "omnibus" version of the legislation, including military aid for China, Greece and Turkey, would necessitate a conference with the Senate, threatening to delay final passage beyond April 1.[36]

There was also disquieting news with respect to the administration's military program, which, according to the *Times*'s William S. White, "faced the most formidable difficulties." Especially was this true in the House, "the more critical arena on the issue of the draft and UMT." Here it was "evident within an hour of the . . . President's address that the immediate reply from the Republican leadership was a qualified 'no' to each." In the case of UMT, moreover, it is difficult to discern in what respect the Republican "no" was the least bit "qualified." "Representative Leo Allen of Illinois, who as chairman of the Rules Committee holds the most important strategic position . . . among the House Republican leaders," told White that "there was 'no more prospect' for a vote [on UMT] than there had been before." Given that Allen had "kept immobilized in his committee a universal military training bill approved last July by the [House] Armed Services Committee," these words were scarcely grounds for optimism. Both Allen's unremitting hostility to UMT and the decisive role his committee played in blocking UMT legislation were a matter of common knowledge in Washington. As early as February 27, 1948, for example, Forrestal had written the President that "the real battleground is the House and if the [UMT] bill can be gotten out of the Rules Committee there I am confident we could muster sufficient support to begin hearings in the Senate." The existence of this state of affairs is one reason among many for suspecting that the administration could not honestly have expected to obtain UMT legislation from this particular Congress. As White revealed, "Others high in the House Republican hierarchy said privately that it could be taken for granted that UMT would not emerge from the Rules Committee." Truman would have to have been a complete political ignoramus to be unaware of this situation.[37]

As the week came to an end, evidence continued to accumulate that White's early appraisal was on the mark. On Thursday, March 18, a second *Times* reporter confirmed that "there was speculation in Congress that the President might get one of his [military] programs through, but not both." In the House, there were "signs that the draft possibly would be accepted . . . , though reluctantly," but the odds that universal training would be passed were still highly unfavorable. "[A] UMT bill has been blocked for eight months by the Rules Committee . . . and appeared to be blocked as firmly as ever, as of today." Friday the 19th brought more of the same. There was some sentiment in the Senate for the draft, but little support for UMT. The Senate Armed Services Committee, which had heard Marshall's testimony directly after Truman's speech to Congress, was clearly unpersuaded, voting to recall the secretary on Monday, March 22. In the House, UMT remained a dead letter, even though "reports from the House Armed Services Committee . . . indicated an inclination to support an outright draft."[38] And a poll taken by the Associated Press showed that "a majority of Senators remain to be convinced that Congress should write into law President Truman's proposals for universal military training and revival of the draft. . . . Many said they would support one, but not both, of the proposals." Of the 91 Senators willing to express an opinion, only 32 favored UMT, only 31 the draft.[39]

Two days after Truman's speeches and Marshall's testimony, then, the administration had recorded some gains, but was still far from certain that either its foreign policy or military buildup would be enacted by Congress soon enough or in a form the administration could accept. It was time to ratchet up the level of hysteria once again.

This time it would be Marshall, resuming his role as the leading proponent of the war scare, who would deliver the speeches. The setting would be in California—specifically, the campuses of the University of California at Berkeley on Friday, March 19, and at Los Angeles the following day. And with the administration's sense of trepidation increasing every day that its programs went unapproved, Marshall's rhetoric would be more alarmist than ever. His two appearances in California crowned a dozen days of extraordinary effort: there is no similar period during his tenure as secretary of state, either before or after March 1948, in which he was so frequently before the public. If the administration's war scare had all the bombast of grand opera at its most histrionic, Marshall's addresses in California were the climactic aria in the production.

In these two speeches (which, because they overlap so greatly, I will analyze in tandem), as in virtually all his public remarks during the war scare, Marshall attempted to camouflage his intention to inflame anxieties about war with a superficial patina of moderation and restraint. On the surface, the two speeches therefore seem to be nothing more than appeals for accelerated passage of ERP (Marshall was enough of a realist to make no mention of UMT on a college campus). On Friday, March 19, at Berkeley, for instance, he employed such phrases as: "timely action," "prompt decision" (twice), "urgently needed," "time is a critical factor," "not delay action," "the lapse of time may result in . . . a serious loss of position"; on Saturday at UCLA: "urgent action," "prompt judgment," "failure to act promptly . . . add[s] immeasurably to the cost," "every day of delay increases... the risk of failure," "if the process is unduly prolonged . . . we have lost more ground to recoup." One of Marshall's aims in these passages was to suggest that partisan debate of the issues was somehow less than legitimate. In this vein, he called for, among other things, "that unity essential to resolute action" that could be obtained only if "we keep all considerations regarding our international problem above the turmoil of a presidential campaign" (March 20, UCLA). Keeping foreign policy "above" politics—what a marvelous idea!

Far more sinister than these comments, however, was Marshall's shameless wallowing in the theme he had already unveiled earlier in the week—the Hitler-Stalin analogy. As usual, he first adopted the stance of someone who was urging calm and rationality. "It is important that we judge the situation . . . in a very sober fashion," he told his listeners in Los Angeles. "If there ever was a time for cool judgment, it is today." Presumably to encourage that "cool judgment," Marshall resorted to warning his Berkeley audience that one "aspect of the situation is the duplication in Europe of the high-handed and calculated procedure of the Nazi régime," with the result that "*never before in history has the world situation been more threatening to our ideals and interests than at the present time*" (emphasis added). To beat the point further into the ground, the secretary returned to it four paragraphs later: "I find the present situation disturbingly similar to that with which I labored as Chief of Staff. I watched the Nazi Government take control of one country after another until finally Poland was invaded in a direct military operation." The lesson was clear: a repetition of the Nazi conquest of Europe was inevitable if the United States refused to take "timely action," reach a "prompt decision," and so on. Marshall's casting the matter in these fantastic terms was methodical and deliberate, for he advanced the identical argument the next day. "Mankind is engaged once more in the age-old struggle between freedom and tyranny, between independence and subjugation," he intoned, and in this "worldwide struggle . . . , the United States cannot stand aloof and see the other free nations destroyed one by one." Ineluctably, Marshall worked his way back to the same statement, in virtually the same words, he had made the previous day: "I find the present situation very similar to that with which I labored as Chief of Staff. I watched the Nazi Government take control of one country after another," blah, blah, blah. No wonder that George

Kennan, who refused out of principle to play fast and loose with analogies of Stalin to Hitler (as witness the quotations at the beginning of this chapter), concluded that the secretary of state failed to comprehend his ideas.[40]

At one place in his speech at UCLA, Marshall remarked, "It is difficult to make plain the facts of the situation without arousing the emotions of our people to a point where anger or fear might lead us into hasty or unwise decisions." It is especially "difficult" when one strives to do just the opposite. In hammering on the notion that, as James Byrnes had put it a few days earlier, there was "no important difference in the . . . methods of Hitler in 1938 and the . . . methods of Stalin in 1948," the secretary knew exactly what he was about, exactly what effect he hoped to elicit. The page-one headline in the *New York Times* for March 20 makes it plain that he achieved his goal: "Nazi Regime Is Duplicated In Europe, Says Marshall."[41] How remarkable, then, that at the same moment Marshall was ringing the changes on the notion of Stalin as the reincarnation of Hitler, the U.S. ambassador in Belgium was sending him a telegram recounting a recent conversation with the British foreign secretary, Ernest Bevin, whose "advices were to effect she [the U.S.S.R.] [was] not ready or willing launch war. He thought Stalin [a] strong stabilizing influence against war." In private, Marshall's views were essentially similar; in public, however, he was all too ready to compromise his integrity at the altar of political expediency.[42]

However reckless his tactics, the secretary of state's spearheading of the administration's offensive accomplished its objective; by the following week, the opposition was unmistakably in retreat. On Tuesday, March 23, the *New York Times* reported that a majority of the Senate Armed Services Committee had "become convinced that quick enactment of both a . . . draft and universal military training was 'an absolute necessity' for the good of the United States." The following day's tidings were even more startling:

> House support of the $5,300,00,000 European Recovery Program was developing into a stampede for the bandwagon today following a letter from former President [Herbert] Hoover to Speaker Joseph W. Martin Jr., urging support of the measure as a "major dam against Russian aggression." Even before the letter was read in the House . . . , it was apparent that any effort to organize scattered isolationist forces had collapsed. Mr. Hoover's letter made it equally certain that attempts to cripple the bill by emasculating amendments would be overwhelmingly defeated.[43]

The corner had been turned, at least so far as the Marshall Plan was concerned. Over the weekend of March 20–21, "Republican chiefs" predicted that by

March 31 or shortly thereafter, ERP would be passed in exactly the form the administration wanted—no cuts in its appropriation, no crippling amendments. In a matter of days—less than two weeks, in all—the war scare had done the trick.[44]

Having propelled fears of impending war to the pinnacle, already by the week of March 22 Marshall could be confident that attainment of his principal goal, enactment of the administration's ERP bill without significant modifications, was a certainty. Thereafter, he embarked on a change of course as sharp as it was abrupt. Whereas the previous week his language had been alarmist and extreme, now it was subdued, almost soothing. The Secretary's public appearances after March 20 were notable for the absence of both horrific scenarios of the impending Soviet conquest of Europe and strained parallels between Hitler and Stalin (also missing, significantly, was any mention of UMT). So fast did this new trend develop and so far did it go that as early as March 22, "the State Department relaxed its note of tension . . . to announce that Secretary Marshall plans to stay in Bogotá for the expected six weeks the forthcoming Inter-American Conference will last." To anyone halfway versed in decoding the pronouncements of Washington officialdom, the point was impossible to miss: the administration had suddenly become strikingly sanguine about the international situation—so much so that, as this article noted, Marshall's "absence would extend beyond the Italian elections of next month." After all the dire forecasts the administration had made in the event of a Communist victory in the Italian voting, here was newfound serenity of a high order.[45] As the influential Republican head of the House Ways and Means Committee, Harold Knutson of Minnesota, trenchantly observed, "Things can't be very serious when Secretary of State Marshall goes to Bogotá for six weeks."[46]

This reversal of course came about not because of any new intelligence reports regarding Soviet intentions—the administration's real estimates of those intentions scarcely varied throughout the month of March, or, so far as that goes, even the year—but because of the State Department's uneasiness that incessant dwelling on the likelihood of war courted disaster. The Department was apprehensive that, as we have discussed above, if Congress became convinced war was unavoidable, it would probably choose to scuttle ERP in favor of a massive arms buildup, something that most Republicans already found more palatable than foreign-aid "giveaways." And then there were the Soviets. Under Stalin's inspired tutelage, they had left themselves pitifully vulnerable to the Nazi invasion that came in 1941; it was hardly to be expected that they would be so obliging a second time. Too much war talk, in short, could turn into a self-fulfilling prophecy. Hence Marshall's new stance during the last ten days of March.

WEEK THREE:
FORRESTAL AND THE MILITARY TAKE THE LEAD

But the secretary of state was no longer able to speak, much less act, for an undivided administration. In choosing to engage in extravagant statements about Soviet plans and the world situation, he had let the genie out of the bottle. Others were intent on seeing that it was not yet stuffed back in. Marshall was now on the verge of achieving his most important aim (or perhaps his *only* aim, if one accepts the interpretation that even such a persistent advocate as he did not truly expect a UMT program to be enacted), but the Pentagon's agenda was still hanging fire. So long as that continued to be the case, so long would representatives of the military, in uniform and out, strive to keep the war scare alive. The armed services would not be denied: the civilians had had their turn; now the military's time had come.

Secretary of Defense Forrestal, as I remarked above in connection with James Byrnes's speech of March 13, had for several weeks been importuning Truman to initiate a peacetime draft, increase the military budget and provide an injection of federal funds to heal the ailing aircraft industry. Yet not until March 10, when the Joint Chiefs of Staff themselves went on record in asking for selective service, did he make headway on any of these fronts.[47] And though Truman endorsed this measure in his St. Patrick's Day address to Congress, as late as March 20, Forrestal still had not obtained approval of either of his requests for more money. On March 11 at the Key West conference, however, the Joint Chiefs had also decided to seek Truman's support for a supplemental appropriation for the military. Armed with this ammunition, Forrestal found himself in an improved position to win Truman's support for the remainder of his program.[48]

And Forrestal, make no mistake, was definitely in need of such ammunition if he hoped to carry the day with the president. My sense is of the Forrestal-Truman relationship is that it was neither warm nor intimate. It was, to begin with, then Secretary of the Army Robert Patterson, not James Forrestal, who was Truman's first choice to serve as secretary of defense when that post was created by the National Security Act of 1947; Forrestal was offered the appointment only after Patterson declined. Second, among the president's top political aides, there was considerable mistrust of the secretary of defense—not just the incumbent, but the position itself. Clark Clifford, in his November 1947 memorandum to Truman, had suggested that for purposes of being reelected, the president should present himself to the public as "the Commander-in-Chief." But there was an obstacle, created, "ironically enough," by a "pet project of the President—Unification [of the Armed Services]. There is now a 'Super-

Cabinet Officer'—the Secretary of Defense." Clifford claimed to detect a tendency for "several of the incumbent Cabinet Officers . . . to regard themselves as the rulers of independent baronies. . . . There is serious danger—*irrespective* of . . . whomever happens to have the job at any moment—that this tendency will become really exaggerated in the Department of National Defense."[49]

Third, these doubts increased during the course of 1948, when Truman's political claque suspected that Forrestal was intriguing with the Republicans to hold on to his job after what was widely expected to be the certain defeat of the incumbent in November. (There may have been some truth in these suspicions. Forrestal had generally good relations with the opposition leadership; and, as I mentioned in chapter 2, through his friend Winthrop W. Aldrich, the head of the Chase National Bank and a major source of money for the Republican presidential candidate, he enjoyed unimpeded access to Thomas E. Dewey as well. Ferdinand Eberstadt, Forrestal's confidante and the person to whom he most frequently turned for advice, was also a politically active Republican and quite close to Dewey.[50]) Finally, the same mental instability that caused Forrestal to take his own life in May 1949 could easily have made Truman reluctant to give great weight to the secretary's ideas. In any case, it is a matter of record that Forrestal's recommendations alone seldom managed to obtain Truman's approval during 1948.

Now, however, with the Joint Chiefs backing his position, Forrestal felt sufficiently confident to tell the three service secretaries on March 18 they could testify in Congress "that a supplementary [budget] request would be forthcoming in the near future."[51] In light of this expectation, the meeting Forrestal, members of his staff and the Joint Chiefs had on March 20 with Director of the Budget James E. Webb must have given him pause. Webb, on whom Truman usually placed a great deal of reliance, was "especially eager to know whether or not it would be possible for the Military Establishment [Department of Defense] to go in with a smaller program initially, and to take another look—say in three months." Some "crisis"! While the secretary of state was in Los Angeles spinning out hair-raising tales of an impending Soviet attack on Western Europe, back in Washington the budget director was asking the secretary of defense to defer any military buildup for three months. The director's next question also speaks volumes about how utterly *un*threatening Truman's inner circle perceived the international situation to be: "What new factors have entered into the international picture which makes such a program necessary?" The war scare was fine for public consumption, in other words, but when it came down to hard questions of dollars and cents, Webb was patently skeptical that there were "new factors" making the Pentagon's ambitious and expensive program "necessary."[52]

Forrestal may have been disappointed by this response, but he was nowhere near defeat. He had, after all, some trump cards of his own to play. If the administration could use the war scare to batter Congress into doing its bidding, Forrestal could just as readily employ the same device to overcome presidential reluctance. Truman was in no position to repudiate the war scare publicly without, on the one hand, jeopardizing the passage of ERP and, on the other, impugning his own credibility in an election year. He was, in fact, now hoist with his own petard. In insinuating that the United States was on the threshold of a war with the U.S.S.R., Truman and Marshall had in effect adopted for their own purposes the same propaganda purveyed by advocates of bigger military budgets. No one could be so naive as to expect that the armed services would be too proud to exploit this new and delightful state of affairs. The political opposition, moreover, also surely had to be taken into account. Never more than lukewarm at best about foreign-aid spending, congressional Republicans, especially in the House, could be depended upon to show much greater enthusiasm for expenditures on the armed services—particularly if, in so doing, they thought they could paint the president and his party as so preoccupied with giving away taxpayers' money abroad that they failed to provide for security at home. If it took a bit of a nudge from the Republicans before Truman would support Forrestal's program, the secretary of defense was willing to see that the necessary stimulus was applied.

By the week of March 22, therefore, although Marshall may have been preparing to administer last rites to the war scare, for the secretary of defense and the Pentagon, the festivities were only getting under way. On Thursday, March 25, Forrestal testified before an open session of the Senate Armed Services Committee seeking approval for the draft and a supplemental appropriation of $3 billion, an increase of almost 30 percent over the $11 billion already in the fiscal 1949 budget for the military. In a vein reminiscent of Marshall at his most strident, he proclaimed the existence of a "deadly parallel" between Hitler's subjugation of Czechoslovakia and Poland "and the successive toppling of national governments in Europe during the last three years. . . . The record shows that despotism, whatever its form, has a remorseless compulsion to aggression. . . . Today, another power . . . seeks to spin its web over all Western Europe. . . . Today another great and despotic power threatens freedom in Europe . . . [by] its methods of subversion and infiltration (backed by armed strength in instant and obvious readiness)."*

* Interestingly enough, Forrestal was not only present when George Kennan sought to debunk the Hitler-Stalin analogy before the House Armed Services Committee on January 8, 1948, but had requested that Kennan accompany him to the meeting in order to address the committee. The secretary, who often acted as a patron to the younger man, claimed that he thought highly of Kennan's ideas. Putting them into *practice,* of course, was rather a different matter.

This "blunt talk," as the correspondent for the *New York Times* called it, "appeared to startle some members of Congress."[53] But that was only the beginning. Later in the same session, Secretary of the Navy John L. Sullivan testified that, "Recently submarines not belonging to any nation west of the 'iron curtain' have been sighted off our shore." "Although Sullivan named no names," the *Wall Street Journal*'s account obligingly explained, "Russia is the only nation behind the iron curtain known to have any submarine fleet." The secretary was "not prepared to evaluate the significance of these sightings," he said. "However, we all recall that an early step of the Germans in 1917 and 1941 was to deploy submarines off our coasts."[54] Here was the Nazi-Soviet parallel with a vengeance!

This sensational disclosure had exactly as much substance and veracity as the other claims made by the administration during the war scare. Hanson Baldwin, the military affairs editor of the *New York Times* and himself a graduate of Annapolis, promptly made inquiries of the navy, then proceeded to anoint the secretary of the navy with well-deserved scorn:

> "Off our shores," it appears, was, in at least one instance, in mid-Pacific. At least two of the alleged seven "sightings" of strange submarines were said to have been made [by the untrained crews of] merchant vessels. One ship said it saw a "periscope" in the Johnston-Palmyra Island area southwest of the Hawaiian islands. Another merchant vessel thought it saw a periscope at night 200 miles from San Francisco. Other strange submarines were supposed to have been sighted in undescribed ways in a vague area defined as "off the Aleutians," the westernmost of which lies just 440 miles from Russian Kamchatka.
>
> This is pretty flimsy evidence upon which to build a defense program. Anyone who has ever been to sea or in the air over the sea, especially in times of tension, knows that alleged "periscopes" are "sighted" nearly every time the wind riffles the surface or a bit of floating wreckage comes into view. There is nothing more difficult to sight with accuracy—and especially to verify—than the pencil-wake of a periscope; sighting a periscope at night would be very unusual, all the more so since submarines, particularly in peacetime, usually cruise on the surface at night.

"All of which," jeered Baldwin, "'is a hell of a way to run a railroad.'"[55]

The journalist's treatment was, if anything, too generous. This became clear later in the year, when the Office of Naval Intelligence (ONI), which had been made to bear the responsibility for Sullivan's oceanic fantasies, took its revenge.

"ONI men . . . are quick to deny responsibility for Secretary of the Navy John L. Sullivan's statement about the presence of 'unidentified submarines' off the California coast," Donald Robinson wrote in the November 1948 issue of the *Saturday Evening Post.* "During congressional hearings on the draft, Sullivan got headlines by intimating that Russian submarines were reconnoitering American waters. He noted that similar reconnaissance by Nazi and Jap submarines prefaced Pearl Harbor." Reports in the press of the secretary's testimony were, according to Robinson, "the first indication ONI had of the presence of those submarines." An investigation was duly launched, the outcome of which was that "ONI found that there was nothing to Mr. Sullivan's statement. No Russian submarine was then closer to the United States than 3000 miles."[56] This belated revelation was all well and good, but, of course, few of those who were panicked by Sullivan's original testimony ever became aware of the sequel. By the time the truth emerged, such dishonest claims had already achieved their ends. What had been done could not be undone.

The reality is that spokesmen for the military, in their pursuit of bigger appropriations, were simply quite oblivious to the truth—something they seem to have regarded as an inessential luxury, in any case. Were this not so, the secretary of the navy could not possibly have testified as he did, for a mere five days before, a memorandum from Army Chief of Staff General Omar Bradley's office to the Joint Chiefs of Staff had categorically stated, "The present strength of the U.S. Navy exceeds that of the combined strength of all of the other navies of the world." In view of this fact "and the capability of air power to destroy surface craft together with the Soviet's [*sic*] limited capability to develop a navy," the report concluded, "the expenditure of funds and manpower in the maintenance of major caliber conventional seacoast weapons within and outside the Continental United States is not justified." Furthermore, even if the Soviets were to "build a fleet of over 300 modern submarines, based on most recent German submarine design and capable of extended long-range actions," neither the Soviet merchant fleet nor the Soviet Navy was "likely to be able to provide continuing support for a large overseas operation *by 1957*" (emphasis added). Soviet submarines off the California coast, indeed.[57]

Besides illustrating the lack of scruple of Pentagon officials in resorting to the most blatant subterfuge, this incident also demonstrates the complexity of what might be called, with apologies to physics, the "fine structure" of the war scare. Here Sullivan and the other service secretaries were essaying several feats simultaneously: first, attempting to use the war scare to spur Congress into taking action; second, attempting to employ the ensuing congressional pressure to overwhelm resistance in the White House and the Bureau of the Budget; third, doing battle among themselves in an effort to increase their respective shares of the pie.

Only in this light can we fully understand why Sullivan lacked any demonstrable compunction not only about lying in public, but lying in such a crude way that his mendacity was almost sure to be exposed. In going before Congressional committees to appeal for funds, each of the services naturally played its strongest suit. The army, as we have had ample occasion to observe, could call upon the Clay telegram and point to its occupation duties in Germany, Japan and Korea to make its case. The air force was in the enviable position of having greater public support than either of the other two services: a Gallup poll published on March 19 in the *Los Angeles Times,* for example, showed that a larger proportion of the public favored increasing the size of, and paying more in taxes to support, the air force than was the case for either of the other two services.[58] The air force leadership was well aware of this situation and, as I will bring out below, exploited it to the maximum.[59] The navy, in contrast, had no such advantages. To compensate for what it lacked in fact, its secretary evidently chose to have recourse to fiction. In endeavoring to comprehend Sullivan's disgraceful performance on March 25, I am in no sense seeking to excuse it—nothing could be further from my intent. So far as I am concerned, Sullivan earned every bit of the contempt that dripped from Hanson Baldwin's analysis of his testimony. Rather than serving as an apologist, what I wish to do is explain something that at first sight is completely puzzling: why an official of such high station would voluntarily put himself in a position where he was virtually certain to be shown up as a fool, a knave, or both.

Meanwhile, submarines or no submarines, events were brewing that would expose the hollowness of the war scare. On March 25—as Forrestal, Sullivan and the other Service Secretaries were testifying in the Senate, and a mere eight days after his own address to Congress—Truman wrote Edwin G. Nourse, chairman of the Council of Economic Advisers, encouraging the council to continue holding the line on military spending. The previous day, Nourse had informed the president that any "additional pressures coming from the expenditures, the appropriation, or even the consideration" of an increased military budget "must inevitably aggravate . . . inflation dangers which we emphasized in the materials presented for use in your Economic Report last January." Truman's reply on the 25th was instructive: "We must be careful that the military does not overstep the bounds from an economic standpoint domestically. Most of them would like to go back to a war footing—that is not what we want."[60] Once again, the familiar dichotomy raised its head: in public, speak of war; within the confines of the administration, plan for peace. From Forrestal's standpoint, however, Truman's sentiments were not auspicious.

Even less so was another development to which the administration was forced to respond. On Tuesday, March 23, Republican Senator Homer Ferguson announced that the staff of the Special Investigating Subcommittee he headed would undertake "an immediate inquiry into the Administration export license policy," seeking "especially . . . to know about shipments of American goods to Russia and her satellites."[61] The war-scare chickens were now starting to come home to roost; and most unwelcome to the administration would be the eggs they were about to lay.

To suggest that the White House found news of this nature dismaying is to display a talent for understatement on the grand scale. Notwithstanding its mindless twaddle about war, the administration had no wish to disrupt existing patterns of trade among Eastern Europe, Western Europe and the United States (although it did attempt to prohibit the direct or indirect sale to the Soviet Union of goods that had military applications). In Washington's view, such trade served to stimulate the rebuilding of Western Europe at the same time as it smoothed the behavior of the domestic economy. "Success of ERP . . . depends upon substantial volume of trade between Western and Eastern Europe," Paul G. Hoffman, the administrator for economic cooperation, told Secretary of Commerce Averell Harriman. "Measures involving substantial reduction of this trade would raise political as well as economic difficulties in several ERP countries." Accordingly, Hoffman recommended that the administration's trade policy be "designed to assure continuance of eastern bloc exports critical to western economic recovery and defense potential, including strategic materials needed by US."[62] In addition, the ability of Western Europe to purchase crucial raw materials from its eastern neighbors, rather than the United States, would minimize the likelihood that politically disastrous inflationary pressures would arise from more dollars pursuing fewer commodities at home; and meanwhile, Eastern Europe's need for manufactured items could simultaneously accelerate the reconstruction of Western European industry. As a draft press release that Harriman circulated at the Cabinet meeting of March 26 explained, "curtailment of this trade" between Eastern and Western Europe "would mean increased demand on the United States, both in terms of money and in terms of physical supplies, much of which could not be supplied without the institution of drastic domestic controls."[63] Finally, U.S. exports to Eastern Europe might even help overcome stagnationist tendencies in the U.S. economy. For all these reasons, therefore, administration officials hoped they would be able to finesse the issue of East-West trade while the Republicans were distracted elsewhere.

Such was not to be, however. Instead, on Wednesday, March 24, while the war scare was still in full flower, a subcommittee of the House Surplus Property Investigating Committee began hearing testimony that between May 1947 and the end of the year, "Forty-six new B-24 engines 'suitable for bombers or troop-carrying planes,'" as well as "21,178 combat-type planes [sold] for scrap, at scrap prices [even though] some . . . were obviously new," had been shipped to the U.S.S.R. and Poland. "Everybody in New York knows there are boxes and cases marked for Russia lying all over the . . . waterfront," one particularly colorful witness told the committee. "They are being loaded every day. . . . They've brought in sixty Soviet-flag ships into New York harbor and loaded them with material for Russia since the first of the year. They carry everything from tractors and bulldozers to electric generators."[64] The next day, more revelations came when "a Washington aircraft dealer told the House Surplus Property Investigating Committee . . . that he sold $340,000 worth of aircraft engines and parts to Russia last year after the State Department told him that it had 'no objections.'" The opposition was not about to let such a heaven-sent opportunity pass unexploited. "Shipments of potential war materiel to Russia at a time like this were 'disgraceful and almost treasonable,'" Republican Styles Bridges of New Hampshire declared at a hearing of the Senate Armed Services Committee that same day.[65]

To no one's surprise, the administration was at once badgered by demands for an explanation of how, with a war against the Soviet Union ostensibly lurking in the wings, the government could permit such shipments to take place. When the question was put to him at his press conference of March 25—while the Senate Armed Services Committee was being harangued about the U.S.S.R.'s "remorseless compulsion to aggression" by Forrestal and treated by Secretary Sullivan to word that "submarines not belonging to any nation west of the 'iron curtain' have been sighted off our shore"—Truman attempted to downplay the matter, evidently hoping that if he were successful, existing trade relations with the Soviets could be preserved. Thus, he responded to reporters' questions with a statement that simply beggared belief: "Russia is, at the present time, a friendly nation and has been buying goods from us right along."[66]

The assembled reporters must have wondered if they were hallucinating. Only the previous week, the secretary of state had accused the Soviets of creating "the duplication in Europe of the high-handed and calculated procedure of the Nazi régime," and Truman himself had termed "the Soviet Union and its agents" a "growing menace." That very day, the secretary of defense would tell the Senate Armed Services Committee that the U.S.S.R. "seeks to spin its web over all Western Europe . . . threatens freedom in Europe . . . [by] its methods of subversion and infiltration (backed by armed strength in instant and obvious readiness)." Yet here was the president, offhandedly describing the selfsame country as "a friendly nation." Could anything have been more astounding? What had become of the Stalin-Hitler parallels? The Soviet submarines off California's coast?

Forced onto the defensive by revelations of continuing trade with the Soviets, Truman had let slip enough of the truth to make a mockery of the administration's pretense that the Soviets were intent on World War III. Not only had airplanes, engines and who knows what else been shipped to the U.S.S.R. all throughout the past year, but, as the *New York Times*'s account stated, "Authoritative sources at the State Department denied reports that the President would soon issue a proclamation banning shipment to Russia of all matériel used predominantly for war purposes. No such proclamation has been drafted or discussed with the President, a department spokesman said." Just one more piece of evidence that the war scare had been a work of fiction from start to finish.[67]

From this moment dates the onset of the war scare's fatal decline. Already it had suffered a severe (though not immediately understood) setback when, during the first part of the week of March 22, the secretary of state became confident that the European Recovery Program would be approved by Congress. For all intents and purposes, Marshall simply resigned from the war-scare coalition at that point, ending his shrill hawking of the Soviet threat and resuming his customary, much more reticent role. Without Marshall's active involvement, Forrestal and the military could look forward to a steep uphill struggle in toiling to preserve the scare intact. But Truman's characterization of the Soviet Union as a "friendly nation" dealt it a blow from which it would never fully recover. Although the scare dragged on throughout the month of April, it no longer possessed the potency it had shown during its first two weeks of life. As a result, though Pentagon officials did gain a great deal of what they desired, they were unable to secure all of the additional billions for which they were clamoring. Budgetary considerations, among other things, restrained Truman from giving the armed services everything they asked for; and the waning of the war scare meant that Congress could no longer be stampeded into enacting the military's wish list by margins sufficient to overcome a presidential veto.

By the end of the month, the *New York Times* made explicit what heretofore had been only implicit. "Truman Planning on Basis of Peace," its headline on March 31 read, "$3,000,000,000 Defense Fund Set on Assumption That War Is Not Now Imminent." The article that followed recounted a meeting of the president, the secretary of defense, the service secretaries and the Joint Chiefs on March 24—the day *before* the inflammatory senatorial testimony of Forrestal and Sullivan, incidentally—in which Truman, acting "on the assumption that war was neither imminent nor inevitable," had "scaled down [military spending] from 'war' to 'peace' proportions." In response to a presentation by Forrestal and the armed services that envisioned plans for Pentagon budgets "ranging into astronomical money brackets, President Truman said: 'I want a peace program, not a war program.'" Thus, although still an indispensable tool for the manipulation of public and congressional opinion, within the counsels of the administration the war scare had been formally consigned to oblivion a mere two weeks after its debut.[68]

THE COMING OF APRIL AND THE BEGINNING OF THE END

For all of that, Forrestal and the military were nowhere near ready to concede that the war scare—their last, best hope—had been merely a short-term tactic, not a permanent fixture. From the last week of March until well into May, therefore, they did their utmost to prevent the scare from succumbing. (This determination to maintain the momentum of the war scare probably explains why an account of "a highly secret report sent some weeks ago by Gen. Lucius D. Clay" turned up in the column of *Washington Post* columnist Marquis Childs on April 6. The most likely source of the leak was James Forrestal, who made it a practice to cultivate prominent journalists for just such exigencies.[69]) Unlike the case earlier, however, they could no longer count on the secretary of state to agitate Congress and the public. Their task was made even more difficult by the fact that, in addition to fighting on one front to keep Congress in a state of maximum anxiety, they also had to battle on another against the resistance of Truman and his advisers to fueling the fires of inflation by expanding the military budget.

In their testimonies before the Senate Armed Services Committee on March 25, Forrestal and Secretary of the Navy Sullivan had pointed the way. It remained only for representatives of the other two branches to follow. Secretary of the Air Force W. Stuart Symington, taking a stance at least as aggressive as that of Sullivan, was more than equal to the challenge. Owing to a certain distaste on the part of the public for being subjected to atomic bombardment or fighting in long, bloody land wars, the air force, as I commented above, was well positioned to capitalize on the war scare. Its advantage extended to Congress, whose members were convinced (no doubt correctly) that in voting money for airplanes and bombs one ran a much smaller risk of being turned out of office than one did in conscripting the sons of one's constituents, to say nothing of sending those sons into mortal combat on foreign soil. Whether he was speaking to the public or addressing a congressional committee, in short, Secretary Symington knew he was preaching to a congregation composed largely of the converted. "The press, the Congress, and the people are sold on this Air

Force program," he told Forrestal on March 31, and repeated these words almost verbatim in testifying before the Senate Armed Forces Committee one week later.[70]

Nonetheless, in his appearances outside of Washington, Symington's creativity easily rivalled that of Secretary Sullivan. Speaking to a meeting of the Denver Rotarians on April 8, for example, he baldly asserted that "we are not at peace." He "pointed out," according to the United Press account of his speech, that although "actual shooting between the United States and another nation was not taking place, . . . there was still no peace." Symington left his listeners in no uncertainty about what nation he held responsible for this situation, stating that the "threat of the Red army and the Red air force hangs like a cloud on the horizon." Overall, in his view, "America's position today could be compared to that of Britain when Prime Minister Chamberlain went to Munich."[71]

Or again, consider some of the preposterous nonsense the secretary propounded in an article that appeared, with near-perfect timing, in the February 1948 issue of the *American Magazine.* "No longer are we the leading air power of the world," he argued, for "in quantity, we have slipped behind the Soviet Union. . . . There is no doubt that Russia is going all-out for air power. The Russians are reported to be producing aircraft at the rate of 75,000 to 100,000 a year."[72] One wonders what would have ensued had Symington been forced to answer such questions as by *whom* were these figures "reported" and what *kinds* of aircraft were supposedly being produced in such great number?

In any case, Symington could not proceed with quite the same abandon in Washington, where his listeners were likely to be better informed and less impressionable. For congressional committees and the media, therefore, the air force devised a less rabid presentation, but one that still adhered to what might be called the standard air force line, at the heart of which, as we have already seen, lay a simple, easily digested proposition: the Soviets are ahead of us. This argument, long since worn threadbare by repetition,[73] Symington tried to dramatize by casting it in numerical terms, albeit somewhat less absurd ones than he had employed in his *American Magazine* article. In mid-April, for instance, he told the House Armed Services Committee that "the Russians are building as fast as they can the greatest air force in the world, . . . about 12 times the number of planes that we are. It would seem . . . if they want to reach a decision with this country, that they want to reach it in the air. If that is true, what we ought to do is build an adequate air force ourselves." The line was reiterated later in the month by Air Force General Hoyt S. Vandenberg, who would take office as the chief of staff in May. Speaking on April 24 to the Executives Club of Chicago, Vandenberg asserted that "Russia is manufacturing many times as many airplanes as we are. We do not have to choose whether or not we will meet the issue in the air. That choice has already been made for us."[74] Why the Soviets would choose to forgo the advantages on land that their large army gave them in order to take on the vastly superior aerial forces of the United States was evidently another query that no one ever thought to put to either Symington or Vandenberg.

A transcript of the hearings before the Senate Armed Services Committee on April 7, 1948, presents us with an incomparable opportunity to observe Symington in action, effortlessly flummoxing the legislators despite intermittent efforts by Secretary Forrestal to pull him back to earth. The senators hoped to pin down Symington about Soviet aircraft production and the composition of the Soviet Air Force, but, as this exchange shows, he was far too adroit to be so easily trapped:

> *Secretary Symington: . . . . We have had figures on Russian aviation production which run from 8,000 a month, which we think is too high [a revelation Symington withheld from the readers of his article in* American Magazine*], to 1,000 a month, which we think is much too low. We believe they are building more than that.*
>
> *Secretary Forrestal: That is not all military airplanes.*
>
> *Secretary Symington: I do not think that affects these figures because . . . on the worst basis from the standpoint of the Russians and the best basis from the standpoint of ourselves, they are building 12 times the number of airplanes that we are building. . . .*
>
> *Senator Byrd: You spoke of the Russians making 12 airplanes to our one. How does that compare in heavy bombers?*
>
> *Secretary Symington: We do not know that.*
>
> *Secretary Forrestal: I might say that the last intelligence report that I examined was 1,000 planes a month, 350 were war planes, 300 were trainers and commercial.*
>
> *Senator Robertson: Mr. Symington, could you give us information on that? . . .*
>
> *Senator Symington: . . . I can tell you all we know about the Russian Air Force very quickly. We know they have jet fighters in the air . . . which are better than any jet fighter we have in*

> *production yet. We know that they have four engine jet bombers that we photographed as long ago as last August. Last August we know that they had 14 airplanes of the B-29 type. In October we saw 47 of them in one mission and recently we have seen over 100 of the B-29 type. . . . We know they have jets directly across from Alaska because our B-29s have seen them in quantity. 14 were seen at one time over the Bering Straits. They were fast enough to circle the B-29 at full speed.*[75]

Just as Symington was fast enough to circle the senators, also presumably operating at full speed. Disentangling fact from propagandistic invention is never easy where the secretary was concerned, but we may at least make a stab at it. First, neither the United States nor the U.S.S.R. had a jet warplane in production at this time. Second, although each country's air force depended on an airplane derived from the B-29 for long-range bombing missions, the U.S. version of this bomber had been so improved by 1948 that the air force gave it a new designation, the B-50, whereas the version employed by the Soviets—derisively dismissed as a "Chinese copy" by Symington later in the year, as we shall soon see—was much closer to the original.[76] Third, even if the Soviets actually did have "over 100 of the B-29 type" bombers, this number was still dwarfed by the size of the U.S. air force's B-29 fleet—"2,300 plus in storage and 580 that are actually in use," Symington himself stated subsequently in the hearings.[77] His performance before the Senate Armed Services Committee thus shed little light on issues such as the Soviet Union's actual aircraft manufacturing capacity, the makeup of its existing bomber squadrons or the status of its jet airplanes vis-à-vis those of the United States. But shedding light, of course, was never the secretary's intent.

Symington's pronouncements ultimately proved to be a bit much even for Forrestal, who, though he shared the air force's aim of getting White House approval for fatter Pentagon budgets, intended to distribute the money in (to use the vogue word of the period) a "balanced" fashion—not to consign the lion's share to one of the services alone. Thus, once the effects of Symington's testimony began to reverberate around Washington, Forrestal asked one of his assistants to determine "upon what evidence are the statements based that Russia is producing 1,000 combat aircraft a month." His intention patently was to call a halt to Symington's hyperbole, because one month earlier he had requested the same information from the CIA; and, in a telephone conversation on April 9 with Representative Clarence Cannon, during which both men concurred in deploring Symington's lurid exaggerations, Forrestal told the legislator the same thing he had said two days earlier before the Senate Armed Services Committee: "I asked [the CIA] for the breakdown of that thousand planes—and its components were 300 commercial planes, 350 trainers and 350 combat planes." Besides, Forrestal added, "the production figures on anything in Russia, whether they are optimistic or pessimistic, I place very little reliance upon, because I do not believe that there is sufficiently solid foundation at least for me to place a judgement on."[78] None of which counted for much with Stuart Symington, however. When pressed by Forrestal on the point, Symington simply turned the matter over to a gentleman whom we have already had the pleasure of meeting—the Director of Air Force Intelligence, Major General George C. McDonald. It was the selfsame General McDonald who, as I brought out in the last chapter, distinguished himself by seeking to have the conclusions of the CIA's April 2, 1948, estimate of Soviet intentions modified because "our Occidental approach to logic might well be diametrically opposed to that of the Oriental Russian mind."

Once again, McDonald showed the quality of his "Occidental approach to logic." To describe as insubstantial the memorandum that he composed at Symington's behest is an act of charity. The document is, to begin with, utterly devoid of quantitative data. Rather, McDonald merely listed 17 different sources for the figure of 1,000 Soviet (military?) airplanes manufactured per month, with no indication of what production figure each source reported, what weight Air Force intelligence assigned to each source, and so forth. On top of this, some of the sources upon which McDonald claimed to have drawn were simply laughable: "n. To a limited degree, U.S. commercial activities operating outside the continental limits of the U.S.; o. Travelling businessmen of the U.S. as well as other friendly nations who have returned with valuable information of this nature; p. Material from foreign language broadcasts, commercial radio, telegraph and radio telephones; q. There is a type of braggadocio about the Soviets which in some respects is comparable to the U.S. in that some of the newspapers both small-town and large are inclined to brag about production quotas being met."[79]

Just as Secretary Sullivan could have discovered whether there were actually Soviet submarines off the coast of California merely by consulting his own intelligence service—in the unlikely event that he cared much one way or the other about the facts of the matter—Symington would not have had to go far afield to obtain a more accurate appraisal of Soviet aircraft-manufacturing capacity (which would still have left untouched the question of Soviet military *intentions*). On Thursday, April 1, 1948, Walter Bedell Smith, the U.S. ambassador in Moscow, submitted to the State Department a 55-page, single-spaced report entitled "Soviet Intentions," prepared, Smith explained, "with the assistance of specialists in the various sections of the Embassy, including consultation with the Military, Naval and Air Attachés, who concur in its findings." There was no chance that the air force high command was unaware of this report, moreover, for Smith stated that the "Military [Army], Naval and Air Attachés are transmitting copies . . . to their respective departments." James Forrestal for one, believed "Soviet Intentions" sufficiently significant to record a summary of its conclusions in his diary.[80]

Were the Soviets outstripping the United States in production of the latest types of military aircraft? Were they planning to precipitate a showdown in the air with the United States? Unlike Secretary Symington and General Vandenberg, the authors of "Soviet Intentions" thought not. Among the "weaknesses" of the U.S.S.R., they noted the absence of "evidence that the Soviets have either constructed or designed a very heavy bomber of the B-36 type or any bomber with a radius of action greater than 1,500 statute miles. If this is correct, 4 to 5 years would be required before such bombers could be available to the Soviet Air Force." Even then, it appeared that the Soviets did not possess "a sufficient number of modern air bases suitable for the operation of heavy bombers and jet aircraft," "technical know-how to operate strategic long-range air forces along the lines of Anglo-American operations of World War II," nor "actual experience in conducting such operations." In consequence, the "Soviet Air Forces cannot conduct today long-range strategic air operations against the North American continent, from bases in continental Europe, England or Sptizenbergen [*sic*]." This was also the case with "Soviet strategic air operations against the US from Eastern bases, with the exception of limited scale strategic operations against Alaska" or "one-way missions" against "US industrial areas." From which it followed that "at the present time the [Soviet] Armed Forces are unable to launch an overseas or sustained airborne attack against the U.S."[81]

Nor would the Soviets fare appreciably better in a war against the United States that took place in Europe. First of all, "the USSR's lack of strategic air force in strength sufficient to sustain attacks against industry in the U.S. would leave the U.S. free to increase its own capacity while at the same time steadily weakening the Soviet's." Hence in the event such a war broke out, "within two years the U.S. should have air supremacy over Europe," which would give it time to complete "the training and equipping, with improved weapons, of a powerful army. Freedom [control] of the seas and air superiority will insure strategic mobility permitting the U.S. to select the time and place of an eventual attack with ground forces."[82]

There were other sizeable obstacles to overcome as well before the U.S.S.R. could even dream of challenging the United States. In the important area of electronics—a field on which the creation of advanced aircraft depends—the Soviets were "known to be deficient in knowledge of modern production techniques and lack sufficient numbers of well-qualified development and production personnel." "Lack of the atomic bomb," while not "the controlling factor," was also "important . . . in determining the Soviet Union's military capabilities and willingness to undertake a war." "Present inefficiency in the operation of the Soviet economy" compounded the difficulties the Soviets would face, especially as there would be no lend-lease assistance from the United States in *this* war. It was "doubtful" that the level of Soviet industrial production "has yet reached 1940 figures"; Soviet railway facilities and equipment were "inferior" ("this most important branch of Soviet transport now approximates 3⁄4 of its prewar capacity"); the number of vehicles produced annually was "small"; and transportation should therefore be "regarded as one of the weakest points in [the] economy." Such a picture of the respective capabilities of the United States and the U.S.S.R. was quite at variance with the one drawn by spokesmen for the Air Force such as Stuart Symington and General Vandenberg.[83]

(Secretary of the Navy Sullivan might also have found the contents of "Soviet Intentions" a bit of an embarrassment. The Soviet Navy was "still a long, long way from equality with either the British or the United States Navies," the writers declared, and, "moreover, even these small forces are geographically divided into four widely separated fleets," all of which were "relatively impotent compared to the American and British naval forces available for immediate deployment against them. . . . Further, Soviet naval forces are, with the exception of submarines, not considered to be strong enough to form any threat to any American or allied landing or supply activities on the [European] continent." But not even Soviet submarines would pose a serious problem for the United States should war occur. "Soviet undersea forces[,] because of the lack of operational experience and numbers[,] would present much less of a threat than the German U-boats which were successfully countered by the techniques developed during the last war." This was anything but the message that Sullivan hoped to impart in his testimony of March 25.[84])

Symington's remarks to the Armed Services Committees of the House and Senate in April, in other words, were the product not of a scarcity of information, but rather of a refusal to make use of information readily available to him. So much also emerges from between the lines, as it were, of a speech Symington gave to the Executives Club of Chicago in December of 1948—a moment when there happened to be no debate over the Pentagon's budget preoccupying Washington. During the question-and-answer period, he was asked, "How does the Russian Air Force compare to ours in size and efficiency?" It is enlightening to compare the judiciousness of his answer, which I reproduce in full, to the tendentiousness he had displayed the previous spring:

> In general, you can divide air power into three things: Fighters, bombers and lifts. That is pretty much over-simplified.
>
> In fighters, they, in our opinion, are as good as we are or thereabouts. They picked up most of the German engineering talent in their rapid move through Germany and removed them

> from the severe bombing in Western Germany from the British and ourselves.
>
> In lifts, we don't know much about that. We believe we are ahead of them in bombers, at least, *from a production standpoint. We are confident we have more bombers,* especially as their principal bomber appears to be pretty much a Chinese copy of our B-29.
>
> If I had to guess, I would say that they are ahead of us in numbers of planes, quantity, and *we are ahead of them in quality* [emphasis added].[85]

Apparently, Symington believed that a group of Chicago's leading business executives should not be misled by the terrifying accounts of Soviet superiority he and General Vandenberg had fed to the Congress, the press and the public several months earlier.* Now that the war scare had expired, the fabrications that it had comprised also could be discarded like last season's fashions.

As for the army, we have already had, in the previous chapter, some indication of how that Service employed the Clay telegram to make its case. Unlike the Navy, which held no top-secret intelligence tidbits to display before congressional committees and therefore had to gamble instead on Sullivan's desperate ploy, the army did possess just such a priceless document; it was, accordingly, allowed it to present its brief quietly behind closed doors, where its estimates and arguments would not be subjected to the small-minded

---

* The Soviets may have had more airplanes, but, as Hanson Baldwin noted at the height of the war scare, that fact was less significant than at first it seemed. Although "the Soviet maximum output during the war was 40,000 to 50,000 planes . . . [t]his figure is misleadingly large, since it cannot be compared in airframe [fuselage] weight with the United States wartime production. Practically none of the Russian wartime production represented four-engine planes; most of it represented single-engine craft." "Soviet Power—III," *New York Times,* March 23, 1948. Note also that at the end of World War II the Soviets were still making airplanes that "were of wooden, plastic-bonded, or mixed construction, with wood-fabric, duraluminum, and steel structures"; Robert A. Kilmarx, *A History of Soviet Air Power* (New York: Praeger, 1962), p. 201. *Mechanical Engineering* magazine summed up the matter both succinctly and idiomatically: "During the war, Stalin claimed aircraft production reached 40,000 airplanes a year. The U.S. turned out 96,318 in 1944, but our airplanes were heavy metal jobs, not lightweight plywood craft. In airframe weight, the U.S. outproduced the USSR by from five to ten times" (April 1949, p. 417).

scrutiny of carping journalists. Hence even though the remarks of Chief of Staff General Omar Bradley before the Senate Armed Services Committee in executive session on April 21 did become public, it is not clear that Bradley expected this result at the time he testified. The general, as I brought out in last chapter's analysis of the use of the Clay telegram, told the Senate Armed Services Committee, "Up to two or three months ago, we were thinking as you are. We are not sure of that now, that there is no war right away, and we do not believe as your military advisers we can afford to sit back and not advise you that we are thinking a little differently." In words that were all too similar to those of the Clay telegram of March 5, the General explained, "So many things have happened, and you cannot put your finger on any one of them, but it seems to be a difference in attitude on the part of the Russians." Having skillfully prepared his listeners, Bradley made his pitch: "The reason we have come up here on this Selective Service, . . . we think something ought to be provided to take care of the short-term view, and that is Selective Service."[86]

By this late date, however, it had become difficult to find anyone in Washington who could be induced to listen to such language with a straight face. Not only had the scare itself grown stale; not only had Marshall and the State Department long since ceased promoting it; not only had the president himself described "Russia" as "a friendly nation"; not only had the Soviets reacted with complete equanimity to the exclusion of the Italian Communist Party from the government in the wake of the April elections; but so many varied intelligence estimates reporting a conclusion precisely the opposite of General Bradley's had accumulated that the scare was imploding beneath the weight of its own contradictions. Although all such reports were, of course, highly classified, it takes greater credulity than I am able to muster to assume that word of their contents did not slowly but surely get into circulation among the cognoscenti. Because nothing shows more vividly how little the Truman White House must have feared that war was "at hand" by the time Bradley finally saw fit to proclaim his own reputed misgivings in the matter, a survey of those contents will be illuminating.

We might begin with the army's own intelligence staff study dated March 26, 1948. The purpose of the study was to "estimate the individual and progressively cumulative effect upon the U.S.S.R., Western Europe and the United States" of passage and implementation of ERP, enactment of selective service and/or UMT, a defeat of the Communists in the Italian elections and creation of a North Atlantic military alliance. Chief among the "Facts Bearing on the Problem," as the study was titled, was that the "U.S.S.R. does not at present have the capability of waging a prolonged global war." As a consequence, "Soviet leaders" were not about "to risk all they have gained by precipitating war with the U.S." The danger of a Soviet attack was likely to arise only if the

Soviets became convinced that the military buildup in the United States and Western Europe was intended "to prepare for an eventual attack upon the U.S.S.R.," in which case "the military occupation of Europe and the Near East by the Soviets then becomes a distinct possibility."[87]

Specifically, with respect to the first three developments listed above, the study predicted, "The Soviets will take no military action." "The formulation of the ERP," to start with, had "not provoked any Soviet military reaction, and there is no reason for believing its implementation will either." Regardless of the outcome of the Italian elections, the Soviets, "in conformity with their policy of not taking any action which will precipitate war with the U.S., will not sanction the intervention of either their own or satellite military forces in Italy." Enactment of the administration's proposals for either UMT or selective service or both would cause the Soviets to "carefully analyze U.S. intentions." On balance, however, Soviet "defensive forces are in being, and their defensive capabilities become greater with the passage of time." Such legislation would not, "therefore, provoke any military action on the part of the Soviets."[88]

In the case of the fourth development, the Soviets would be "thoroughly alarmed by the far-reaching implications" of the formation of a North Atlantic military alliance between "the U.S. and Western Europe." Again, "Soviet leaders" would "carefully re-assess the military capabilities and intentions of the U.S. . . . to attack the Soviet Union," would "increase the readiness of their armed forces" to repel an attack and would "seriously consider the immediate military occupation of Europe and the Near East." But even though the "advantages to the U.S.S.R." of such an occupation might be "many, . . . so too are the disadvantages. Indeed, the latter could prove to be catastrophic." In the final analysis, the Soviets would not be inclined "to risk everything," and thus could be expected to "decide against precipitating war with the U.S. on this point alone."[89]

The next thorn in the side of the war-scare proponents was the intelligence estimate entitled "Soviet Intentions" sent by the U.S. Embassy in Moscow on April 1. The conclusions of this document, already summarized above, were essentially the same as those of the army's March 26 study. The following day, Friday, April 2, the CIA published its report, "Possibility of Direct Soviet Military Action During 1948." Prepared "by a joint ad hoc committee representing CIA and the intelligence agencies of the Department of State, the Army, the Navy, and the Air Force," the findings of this report—with which Forrestal was also familiar[90]—echoed those of its two immediate predecessors. "Such evidence as is currently coming to hand," the agency observed, "suggests that Soviet leaders do not presently intend to exercise their military capability of overrunning Western Europe and part of the Near East." War, to be sure, might still come about. "In view of the well known suspicions inherent in the minds of Soviet leaders, and the isolation of most of these leaders from the west, it is possible that the Politburo might come to [the] conclusion . . . that the US actually has intentions of military aggression within the near future." "Even if Soviet leaders did not expect imminent US aggression," they might nonetheless believe that "an ultimate military clash with the US was inevitable and that . . . it would be to the USSR's advantage to strike . . . in 1948." Especially was this true in light of the fact that the United States and Western Europe were "now joined in a military alliance" and the this country was "increasing . . . production of atomic bombs and longer range aircraft" that would improve "US capabilities for covering strategic Soviet targets."[91]

But if these currents predisposed the U.S.S.R. toward war, opposing them were ones yet more powerful. "Soviet leaders, . . . habitually cautious and deliberate," would be "reluctant voluntarily to incur the risks inherent in a major war." Reinforcing this caution would be the fact that the "USSR suffered enormous physical damage in World War II and has probably not regained production levels of 1940 in all basic industries"; capacity was still "inadequate in a number of vital fields, including transportation, communications, and in the production of steel, oil, and machine tools." Furthermore, in order to make use of Western Europe's "economic potential, the USSR would have to supply raw materials and food to an already impoverished . . . continent cut off from the resources of . . . other parts of the world." Considerations of psychology and morale were also relevant. Overrunning Western Europe would mean that "the hostile populations of these areas and the satellites would form an enormous subversive element that would become particularly dangerous with the approach of US forces. In addition, . . . control and assimilation of the economies of Western Europe . . . would impose a tremendous strain upon Soviet administrative organs." Not least, exposing "Soviet personnel . . . to the standard of living and political ideas of Western Europe" would tend "to undermine Soviet ideology and discipline."

Thus, although war might come about through misunderstanding—the Soviet Union, that is, "might resort to direct military action in 1948, particularly if the Kremlin should interpret some US move, or series of moves, as indicating an intention to attack the USSR or its satellites"—the CIA's estimate affirmed that the "preponderance of available evidence and . . . the 'logic of the situation' supports [*sic*] the conclusion that the USSR will not resort to direct military action during 1948."[92]

Representatives of allied governments also weighed in with comparable estimates. During a meeting in Washington three days after the CIA released the above report, for example, Paul-Henri Spaak, Belgian prime minister and minister of foreign affairs, told a number of State Department officials that "he was optimistic and believed that plans should be made on the basis that war would not occur for at least three or four years." Granted that accidents were always possible, Spaak's view was that they "caused wars only if one side were seeking a pretext, which he was sure was not the case at present." The State Department's notes of Spaak's remarks also convey his belief that the U.S.S.R. was "acting on the assumption that any overt [hostile] act in Europe would mean war with the United States regardless of whether . . . the United States entered into [a] formal treaty . . . for the defense of Western Europe. The Russians," Spaak held, in language very similar to that used in the army intelligence staff's study of March 26, "were unprepared to risk losing everything by provoking war over any one country. In contrast to the pre-1939 situation, the Soviets had no desire to fight in Europe."[93]

Likewise of significance in this connection was another document of the same date (but apparently not circulated extensively until April 20), "Russian Capabilities in Undersea Warfare." This analysis, by Rear Admiral Thomas B. Inglis, the chief of naval intelligence, is informative for what it tells us about contemporary U.S. estimates of Soviet military capabilities. (In his sole reference to Soviet intentions, the admiral mentioned in passing that "Neither the U.S. nor the U.S.S.R. wants war.") The Soviet Union was hampered by "poor transportation and an under-developed industrial economy," Inglis maintained. Although "rapidly improving," its air force was "inferior, especially in long range bombers"; its geography had "prevented Russia from becoming a great sea power"; and, "for the time being at least, geography and the lack of means to control the sea prevent Russia from bringing the war to [the] continental U.S."

Conversely, Inglis was completely sanguine about the ability of the United States to "carry the offensive to Russia" and keep "the fighting away from our own shores . . . should war break out tomorrow." The Soviet Navy's "mission" was "chiefly defensive in nature." Its surface fleets amounted to "little more than small cruiser task groups," able to cause the United States "little concern" at most. "The handful of available big-gun ships" were "obsolete," while "Soviet air attacks would be no more serious than those we turned back at Okinawa." And so forth. The only "serious threat" that the Soviets could mount from the sea or the air, in short, resided in "their submarine forces." The inescapable corollary of the admiral's remarks was that, whatever the intentions of the Soviets might have been in 1948, their submarine fleet alone hardly offered a basis on which they would elect to go to war against a foe as formidable as the United States.[94]

Three days later saw the arrival of a second CIA report, "Review of the World Situation as it [*sic*] Relates to the Security of the United States." Published on Thursday, April 8, this estimate attempted to gauge Soviet intentions for the remainder of the year. Even if, in light of the implementation of ERP and an arms buildup by the United States, "the Kremlin were to . . . reconsider its current policy of aggression by means short of general war," the report contended that the Soviets would still "probably prefer to seek a general settlement unless convinced that war on Western initiative was . . . inevitable. . . . In any case," according to the agency, "the existing Soviet margin of safety is so great that the Kremlin can afford to wait upon actual developments (as distinguished from verbal expressions of intention . . .) before coming to a decision in so fateful a matter." It was "therefore unlikely" that the Soviets would make a "basic policy choice as between general settlement or preventive war . . . during 1948." From this judgment flowed the obvious conclusion: it was "still improbable... that the USSR has any intention of provoking war."[95]

The State Department received the benefit of another European perspective on the last day of April, when the diplomatic representative of Washington's closest ally, British Ambassador Lord Inverchapel, handed the secretary of state a message summarizing the thinking of Ernest Bevin. The British foreign secretary did "not himself believe that either the Russians, or still less the satellites, want war at the moment." It was widely known, in reality, "that Moscow has ordered the Communists in France and Italy to drop direct action, for fear that this might involve them in war. . . . Moreover, no signs of military preparations in Russia itself, Eastern Germany, or the satellite countries have been detected. All this goes to confirm Mr. Bevin's reading of present Russian policy," which was that the Soviets would stop well short of "pushing things to the extreme of war." Although war could still come about inadvertently—a standard disclaimer that, as we have observed, was included in virtually every contemporary estimate—that possibility did not pose the greatest peril. On the contrary, "the most dangerous phase" would occur if "Russia . . . suddenly became conciliatory."[96]

How did Marshall see fit to respond to his British counterpart? He was "grateful" for Bevin's perspective "on the current political situation with particular respect to relations with the Soviet Union." And, inasmuch as "the information available to the United States Government" tended to confirm the British "estimate that the Soviet Government does not want war at this time," the secretary of state was "in general agreement with Mr. Bevin's clear and comprehensive analysis of the situation." Marshall's real views at the close of the war scare, in other words, were exactly the same as they were at the start—and they did not in any way include the baseless notion that Stalin was merely Hitler in different garb. Once it had served its purpose, that idea Marshall quickly relegated to the appropriate receptacle.[97]

This account would not be complete without discussion of a report by the State Department Policy Planning Staff, "Factors Affecting the Nature of the U.S. Defense Arrangements in the Light of Soviet Policies." The report bears the publication date of June 23, 1948, but a note on the first (unnumbered) page states that its conclusions "were arrived at independently before the Staff had seen despatch no. 315 of April 1, 1948[,] from Moscow, . . . on the subject of 'Soviet Intentions.'" Hence it seems a reasonable surmise that the findings of the report were probably common knowledge within the administration's upper echelons during April and May. (Forrestal also included a summary of this document in his diary.)[98]

The report touches on a variety of topics, but for our purposes the most important is, naturally, its estimate of Soviet intentions in the military realm. To reach its conclusions, the authors (primarily George Kennan) attempted to evaluate the "factors" that would "militate" both against and for "the likelihood at this juncture of international, planned Soviet armed action which would involve this country." Among the former were these:

1. Unless "a European aggressor" could deliver "a decisive blow to the North American military-industrial potential" at the start of a war, that power could "never be sure of final victory." And it was axiomatic that the Soviets, "could not be sure of being able to deal such a blow in present circumstances."
2. The "physical destruction" endured by the Soviets during World War II "was far more severe than is generally realized in the west, and has not yet been by any means made good by new construction." "A huge reconstruction problem still remains and . . . important sectors of Soviet economy—. . . particularly transport—are in a state of serious backwardness and obsolescence."
3. "The war-weariness of the Soviet peoples is as great, if not greater, than in the case of any other of the major countries," a "factor" that the Soviet government could not ignore.
4. "In seeking control" over other nations, "Soviet leaders have a strong traditional preference for political means as opposed to direct military action." "Russians are traditionally cautious in planning military actions, and the Soviet leaders particularly so." Only in the war with Finland did they choose "to resort to direct military aggression," and there was "every reason to believe that they had cause to regret this experiment."
5. Military conquest also "would not assure to the Soviet Government the type of control" it sought in Western Europe—that is, "a maximum of power with a minimum of responsibility." Invading other nations and "raising the red flag" over them "would be certain . . . to produce profound antagonisms . . . which would be a burden to any permanent communist control."
6. Morale would be weakened among the Soviet occupation forces that would have to be stationed in the West in the event of a Soviet invasion.

7. Finally, the Soviets felt no urgency about achieving their aims, for "the official Russian mind is dominated by the conviction . . . that this country is bound sooner or later to suffer another economic depression" similar to that of the 1930s.

The forces favoring a Soviet decision for war were both fewer and weaker. The most important of these were that the "Soviet leaders might reckon that their military strength" would never be as great, relative to that of the United States, as it was then; and, recognizing "that their political plans have already suffered a severe set-back in Europe . . . they might prefer to resort to armed action at this juncture." Still, after "weighing these various factors" and making the obligatory observation that war had to be "regarded, if not as a probability, at least as a possibility," the Policy Planning Staff found that "the evidence points to the conclusion that the Soviet Government is not now planning any deliberate armed action . . . and is still seeking to achieve its aims predominantly by political means." So strongly, indeed, did the authors hold to this conviction that they even argued (in characteristically convoluted and verbose language) that it was "not probable that the pattern of Soviet intentions as outlined above would be appreciably altered in the direction of greater aggressiveness by the development of the atomic weapon in Russia." Were they to possess atomic weapons, in fact, the Soviets might "actually prove to be more tractable in negotiation when they . . . no longer feel that they are negotiating at so great a disadvantage."[99]

Granted the differences of nuance and approach that existed among these intelligence estimates, there was not a single one of them that hinted, much less explicitly asserted, that the Soviets were about to undertake an armed offensive against Western Europe. Sooner or later, and probably sooner at that, the cumulative weight of these analyses was bound to prevail against those who refused to let the war scare die. A conversation that Forrestal had late in May 1948 with Stanton Griffis, the U.S. ambassador to Poland, illustrates the obstacles to perpetuating the scare. Under the heading "Griffis on war," Forrestal recorded in his diary the Ambassador's views: "Doesn't believe the Russians want one. Saw no sign on his motor trip to Czechoslovakia of any great concentrations of troops. Believes domestic problems of Russia are so serious that they would think hard before starting a fight." Undoubtedly, Forrestal was not the only person with whom Griffis shared these thoughts. As word of them, and others like them, percolated through the various layers of Washington officialdom, increasingly the reaction of those in high places to assertions that the Soviets were on the verge of uncorking World War III became a mocking smile that segued ever so gradually into a half-stifled yawn.[100]

Nevertheless, despite the proliferation of formal and informal intelligence reports that the Soviets had no intention of going to war, Forrestal and the military struggled to the last to avoid being deprived of their most wicked weapon. With Ambassador Walter Bedell Smith, they shared both the fear that "Congress and public may be lulled into erroneous belief that [the] battle is won and we can relax and reap the fruits of victory" as well as the conviction that it was "more important than ever to follow through vigorously by building up our own strength." Hence the corollary: "It is vital that the public be constantly reminded."[101] Certainly the secretary of defense could not be accused of failing to do his utmost. On Wednesday, April 21, he told the Senate Armed Services Committee, "The tensions we are in are not impermanent; I think that they are permanent." "The problem," he maintained, was that "we set up a plan last year based on the assumption of no immediate danger of war," but conditions had changed and now it was necessary "to contemplate the possibility of war."[102] Such efforts to swim against the tide were, ultimately, of little avail. As Forrestal wrote in his diary, describing a May 21 meeting of top administration officials (including Marshall, Under Secretary of State Robert Lovett, Kennan, Secretary of Commerce W. Averell Harriman, National Security Council Executive Secretary Sidney W. Souers, and Clark Clifford), "I said I was concerned . . . because of the changing tempo of the Congress and in the relaxation of tension. . . . On March 17 we could have had Selective Service through both Houses in three days." Hardly had the war scare passed from the scene and already Forrestal was nostalgic for the good old days. Shortly thereafter, on May 29, he complained in a letter to Marshall that a diminution of the war scare had produced "a dangerous complacency on the part of certain elements in the country."[103]

Thus, before they would accept the fact that the scare had outlived its usefulness to the administration, both the military establishment and, especially, the secretary of defense needed to have matters painstakingly—and sometimes painfully—spelled out to them. As early as March 24, recall, Truman, acting "on the assumption that war was neither imminent nor inevitable," had "scaled down [the military budget] from 'war' to 'peace' proportions." On that occasion, he had informed Forrestal, the Joint Chiefs and the service secretaries to their faces, "I want a peace program, not a war program."[104]

But his words obviously had gone unheeded. So much is evident from what Forrestal wrote in his diary following a May 7 White House meeting attended by the secretaries of state and the treasury, the director of the Bureau of the Budget and the executive secretary of the National Security Council. "The President . . . wished to make it very clear to all present that the increases on which he had given the green light . . . were not to be construed as preparation for war—'that we are preparing for peace and not for war.'" The point then had to be reiterated for the benefit of the Joint Chiefs and service secretaries in another meeting less than a week later (by which time the peace scare discussed in chapter 7 made it imperative to end the brink-of-war sloganeering). Forrestal, apparently reluctant to deliver the sad tidings himself, had an assistant write a statement that he asked Truman to read. In it, the president declared his intention to hold military spending to $15 billion in the next fiscal year "unless world conditions *deteriorate much further* and the present period of tension *became* a period of crisis" (emphasis added). Then, just to make sure there were no misunderstandings, Truman also distributed to all participants in the meeting copies of a memorandum to Forrestal, in which the president instructed the latter that, "In implementing the increased [military-spending] program, you should emphasize to all responsible civilian and military leaders that it is not one of mobilization for war."[105]

The secretary of defense had gambled that he would be able to prevent the war scare from subsiding—and he had lost. Not only was he unable to achieve full White House support for his most ambitious goals, but, equally important, friction with Truman over prolonging the scare had frayed the relationship between the two even further. Forrestal's belated acquiescence came too late to repair the damage. "He wants to compromise with the opposition" was Truman's curt, disgruntled verdict on his subordinate.[106]

For all of his efforts, as Forrestal discovered to his sorrow, there were too many bureaucratic forces arrayed against the war scare to allow it to be perpetuated indefinitely. Unveiled for the edification of the public on March 10, the scare had burgeoned with amazing rapidity. Within the brief space of a fortnight, it had utterly reversed the outlook for the administration's programs. By the week of March 22, significant opposition to the Marshall Plan had nearly evaporated and congressional assent to the initiation of a peacetime draft and a sizeable increase in military spending seemed assured. It was, in short, time to bring down the curtain before the production took on a life of its own.

Easier said than done, however. By this point, divisions latent within the Truman administration had become manifest. On one side stood Truman and Marshall, supported by the director of the Bureau of the Budget and the Council of Economic Advisers, all seeking to call a halt to the war talk while they still had the power to do so. On the other stood Forrestal, the Joint Chiefs, and the service secretaries, striving to nurture the scare until they had obtained everything they desired. The outcome, as I discuss at greater length in the following chapter, was a bargain of sorts, in which the proponents of military expansion would come away with most of what they sought, but the war scare would be unceremoniously laid to rest. The secretary of defense soon indicated he understood what was expected of him under the terms of this agreement. "Secretary Forrestal has expressed the view that *for the time being* speakers of the National Defense Establishment who are apt to be quoted prominently in the press should avoid statement or speculation on the possibility of proximity of war with Russia or that it is inevitable," the army chief of staff instructed his subordinate officers a week after the White House meeting of May 13. "He believes a non-aggressive attitude should be displayed to the public [emphasis added]."[107]

For the aircraft industry, the administration's decision to support a higher level of military spending, even with the understanding that the war scare would henceforth be muted, meant the difference between life and death. Directly below, we shall see in detail how this eleventh-hour resuscitation of the industry was accomplished.

6.

The Fruits of Victory

So, the aircraft builders, even with tax carrybacks, are near disaster. . . . Right now the government is their only possible savior—with orders, subsidies, or loans.

—"Aviation RFC?" *Business Week,* January 31, 1948[1]

As the international scene becomes more troubled . . . , it is likely that regardless of unbalanced budgets, Congress will find it impossible to resist the pressure for increased aircraft appropriations. The Czech crisis, for example, served as a strong stimulant for an enlarged aircraft procurement program.

—Selig Altschul, "The Dynamic Aviation Scene," *The Commercial and Financial Chronicle,* March 11, 1948[2]

I think we can sell a 70 group air force to our people almost over night. I think we can sell a 100 group to the American people almost over night because the American people are looking for an escape. . . . They are looking for a miracle. They want some easy way out.

—Senator Wayne Morse (Republican, Oregon), April 7, 1948[3]

The Air Force has the sex appeal. There is no question about that and you can sell 100 groups to this country if you need it.

—Senator Leverett Saltonstall (Republican, Massachusetts), April 7, 1948[4]

As soon as there is a war scare, there is a lot of money available.

—Statement of Lawrence D. Bell, President, Bell Aircraft Corporation, to the President's Air Policy Commission (Finletter Commission), September 29, 1947[5]

AIRBORNE!

"The war scare has produced a great many disturbing rumors, one of which is the imminent transfer out of this city of a score or more of Federal agencies." Those words of Jerry Kluttz appeared in the *Washington Post* at the end of March 1948. "Frankly," Kluttz added, "no move will be made soon unless war comes much sooner than anyone in authority here expects"—a message his readers must have found enormously comforting.[6]

Evidence that the war scare made a profound impact on the public showed up in other ways as well. Auto makers, as a case in point, were being "deluged" with new car orders as a consequence of the administration's "war talk," the *Wall Street Journal* reported. "Ask any auto company sales manager and he'll tell you the pressure from would-be buyers has never been as intense as now. It shows up in an unprecedented flood of letters, telegrams and long distance calls." A sales manager for Pontiac informed the newspaper that his "orders 'zoomed upward' right after President Truman's speech to Congress on the international situation in March. He says demand is greater now than at any time since the war." *Business Week* stated much the same: "Automobile demand, which showed faint signs of tapering earlier this year, has hardened—it's stronger now than at any time since the end of the war." New cars, of course, always sold well in springtime; but this year, something different was involved—"the fear of war, and the desire to be equipped for it with a new auto." That was how things stood early in April. One month later, *Business Week* noted that not only new autos were affected—"fear of war" was also "boosting used-car prices well beyond seasonal expectations." Although the "upturn" may have been partially due to the warm weather, "it gathered headway with each front-page story of increased tension with Russia. . . . As a result, second-hand car prices today stand from 5 percent to 20 percent higher than at the beginning of April."[7]

Because the Truman administration's war scare came and went with blinding rapidity, it is difficult to measure its effect in the usual manner. Instead, to grasp its hold on the nation, we must turn to indicators—more humble and less scientific, perhaps, but not necessarily less enlightening—such as those I have just cited. In its issue of March 22, 1948, for instance, *Newsweek* published an impressionistic survey of "all this talk about war." To determine "what is the average American saying about it," the magazine turned to its correspondents in several large cities. The results were revealing. In Boston: "Loose talk of 'the next war with Russia' is sweeping New England these days," and "very few" in the region "would be surprised by war within eighteen months." In Chicago: "A cold fear is gripping people hereabouts. They don't talk much about it. But it's just as real and chilling as the current 11-degree weather. . . . Many people, perhaps the majority, are now convinced it's no longer a question of whether war will come, but when." In Atlanta: "Talk of war, and of an overt act to start it, have grown markedly here in the past month. Reserve officers are telling one another: 'Break out that old uniform. You'll be needing it.'" In Los Angeles: "To judge by letters-to-the-editor, Los Angeles residents are becoming more and more afraid of war." In Seattle: "Generally, people here have come to feel that war is on the way. They're resigned to it."[8]

No doubt most of these "average Americans" did not subject the events of March and April to close scrutiny, but, as the foregoing examples suggest, were simply carried along in the tidal wave of hysteria set in motion by the Truman administration. For these souls, the glaring inconsistencies in the administration's case—implying the Soviet Union was about to invade Western Europe one moment, terming it a "friendly nation" the next—were less important than the atmosphere of foreboding the scare so swiftly engendered.

Many members of Congress were similarly susceptible. "As the roll call went on in a seething and excited House," according to the *Washington Post*'s account of the session that saw the European Recovery Program adopted, "shouts of 'aye' came from one Republican after another who had seldom, if ever, voted for any international legislation." Being a member of the legislature guaranteed no immunity from the prevailing dementia.[9]

From the standpoint of inducing Congress and the public to panic, then, we would have to award the war scare high marks indeed. But what about its ability to yield what the administration, in fomenting it, had hoped to obtain? Did the scare accomplish what its architects intended?

The answer has to be an unambiguous yes. Going into the spring of 1948, the State Department was fearful that the European Recovery Program (ERP) either would not be enacted or would be crippled by hostile amendments; the army leadership was clamoring for the inauguration of peacetime selective service; Secretary of Defense James V. Forrestal and all three armed services wanted money for a military buildup; and aircraft manufacturing was, in the words of the editors of *Steel*, "a sick industry." By the time summer arrived, the administration had achieved passage of the Marshall Plan with its full funding intact; a military draft was in place for the army; each service had had its budget increased; and the aircraft industry, having received "the largest airplane and engine orders in peacetime history," was "now out of the oxygen tent after government ministrations."[10] These were impressive results—especially if one bears in mind that the administration achieved them in an election year from an opposition that detested Harry Truman. Due to the atmosphere created by the war scare, however, Republicans who abhorred foreign aid on principle could be stampeded into supporting the most ambitious such program to that time; and the same Republicans who only one year before had thumbed their noses at the White House by cutting the administration's proposed budget for the Pentagon by 10 percent had become so eager to lavish money on procurement for the air force's "70 group" program that during the spring of 1948 they voted $822 million more for it than Truman was willing to spend.

The first explicit sign that the administration intended to save the aircraft industry from the rigors of capitalist competition could be glimpsed as early as December 1947, when Secretary of Defense Forrestal, as recounted in previous chapters, announced that he was planning to increase the amount of aircraft procurement in the approaching fiscal year.[11] But despite pressure from the air force and the Congressional Air Policy Board (CAPB), Forrestal refused to commit himself to a specific figure until the Joint Chiefs of Staff submitted a strategic war plan and until his own staff had completed a study of the needs of the aircraft industry.[12] Forrestal had assigned this study to (Army) Lieutenant General LeRoy Lutes, the deputy chairman of the Executive Committee of the Munitions Board, a subsidiary agency in the Department of Defense. Lutes sent Forrestal a memorandum on the subject on February 3, 1948, in which he recommended that the secretary "interview the President with [a] view to determining whether or not he would approve a moderate increase in the [fiscal] 1949 budget . . . to provide additions to the aircraft procurement programs." What Lutes had in mind as a "moderate increase" was $400 million, an amount that would "bring total [aircraft] production to approximately 39 million pounds" during the next year, "which certainly should keep the industry in a reasonably healthy state."[13]

Forrestal immediately moved to put Lutes's recommendations into effect. Two days later, on February 5, he had a telephone conversation on this subject with Representative Carl Hinshaw, the Republican vice chairman of the CAPB, whose Southern California district included several large aircraft companies. In order to obtain an increase in the appropriation for aircraft procurement, Forrestal told Hinshaw, he would "have to do some talking with the White House. I'll have to do a little foot work around there, you see. . . . I'm going to try and see him [the president] today." The secretary, however, was not actually able to meet with Truman until the following day, February 6. Prior to his appointment at the White House, he composed a list of what he called "Talking Points for Conference with the President," which in the main hewed to the recommendations advanced by LeRoy Lutes in his memorandum of February 3; this document shows that Forrestal was then planning to ask for Truman's "views on . . . increasing the fiscal year 1949 budget by 400 million dollars for procurement of 9 million pounds of airframe weight." Later that day, Forrestal converted these "Talking Points" into a memorandum of his own, in which the secretary sought Truman's permission "to tell the Hinshaw-Brewster Committee [CAPB] that a program is recommended providing for a moderate increase in the fiscal year 1949 budget of 400 million dollars which will purchase 9 million pounds of aircraft." This was, so far as I have been able to discover, Forrestal's first formal request to the president for more money for the aircraft industry. It was not to be his last.[14]

As this bureaucratic process ground on, a most familiar face suddenly reappeared on the scene: Oliver Echols, the indefatigable president of the Aircraft Industries Association, was about to make his presence felt once more. On January 31, Marx Leva, one of Forrestal's three special assistants, wrote a memorandum relaying the contents of a telephone call from "Eber"—that is, Ferdinand Eberstadt, Forrestal's closest confidante and adviser. General Echols, "whom Eber regards as a very able and experienced person," had, it seems, been "in to see him recently. Echols outlined to him a proposal for aircraft production planning." Although Eberstadt told Leva that he was aware of "the natural bias which Echols has," the banker nonetheless believed that there was "a great deal of benefit" that Forrestal's department could derive "from the type of thinking of which Echols is capable. Accordingly," Leva continued, "Eber recommends that we get Echols in for a conversation." Leva also informed Eberstadt "of the work which General Lutes has been doing for you in this connection, and told him that I would recommend to you that General Lutes have a conversation with General Echols. If you approve, I will go ahead and take care of this with General Lutes." Forrestal, as will emerge soon enough, did give his approval to Leva's suggestion. Thus was the fox escorted into the henhouse.[15]

From the fact that Forrestal raised the issue of increasing the appropriation for aircraft procurement twice more with the president during the month of February, one gathers that Truman's initial response was not favorable.[16] Be that as it may, already by February 18 Forrestal felt sufficiently convinced that he would prevail to send a list of questions to the secretaries of the navy and the air force, in effect asking them to supply him with a brief he could use in justifying more money for aircraft procurement.[17] And prevail, of course, he did. By the end of March 1948, if not before, Truman had agreed that the federal government should come to the rescue of the airplane manufacturers. How he was persuaded to support this policy and how he determined the amount of money he would furnish the aircraft industry remain as much of a mystery as the way Truman reached most of his other decisions during this period. The *New York Times*'s Arthur Krock, who was summoned to the White House on April 7, 1948, has left the only account known to me of Truman's reasoning—and Krock's notes on this topic, which follow in their entirety, are anything but enlightening:

> He [Truman] discussed rearmament, and said the reason he is holding down the new air groups beyond the point Symington and the air generals want is because "we are on the verge of an aviation discovery that will make obsolete everything now being manufactured." He said, also, that his plan was to have our aviation manufacture kept flexible, as we did during the war so that we can step up production when we want to, and alter plans, too. He said that, while on many subjects he was troubled by conflicting counsel, on this one he thought he has an informed opinion.[18]

These words conceal more than they reveal.* From the evidence I presented in chapter 5, for example, it is clear that Truman, the chairman of the Council of Economic Advisers and the Bureau of the Budget were all afraid of the inflationary consequences of a massive arms buildup; and, as we shall observe below, the director of the latter agency was especially critical of air force requests for more procurement money. We also know that the State Department was anxious lest military spending deprive the European Recovery Program of

* To justify his reluctance to meet with Stalin, incidentally, Truman also told Krock that "Stalin is merely the Secretary of the Politburo and has no more final authority over agreements he makes than General Marshall has. The President can refuse to send Marshall's agreements to Congress, and the Politburo can fail to ratify Stalin's" (Private Memorandum, April 7, 1948, p. 2; Papers of Arthur Krock, Box 26, SGMML, Princeton University). Could the man really have been *that* ignorant? Or was he again merely seeking to provide Krock with a quasi-plausible rationalization to defend decisions actually made for far different reasons?

adequate funds. But Truman disingenuously omitted any mention of these considerations in explaining why he was "holding down the new air groups beyond the point Symington and the air generals want," referring instead to a mysterious "aviation discovery" that allegedly would "make obsolete everything now being manufactured." (Whatever "aviation discovery" Truman may have had in mind, after almost half a century it has yet to materialize.) In addition, the president denied that he had been burdened by "conflicting counsel," despite the fact that within his administration an intense bureaucratic contest over the size of the Pentagon's budget had already begun. Finally, he failed to tell Krock either how much money his advisers said would be needed for the aircraft industry to be "kept flexible" or how they had arrived at such a figure. Overall, bearing in mind that agitation for a "70 group" air force was already threatening the president's attempt to fasten a lid on military spending, the most reasonable interpretation of this interview is that it was merely an effort by Truman and his staff to manipulate the *New York Times,* or at least the head of its Washington bureau, into supporting the White House, rather than the "air power" partisans, in the forthcoming budgetary battles.

Something else that Truman was hardly about to discuss with Krock was the furious whirlwind of activity then whipping through Washington on behalf of the aircraft industry—a storm that would ultimately engulf even the White House. Within a single week, as a case in point, the presidents of two different aircraft companies flew from the West Coast to lobby the administration: William E. Allen, the president of Boeing, had an appointment with Forrestal on Saturday, March 20, while the following Friday, March 26, Donald Douglas saw the president; so far as I am aware, Douglas never met with Truman, nor Allen with Forrestal, at any other time during Forrestal's tenure as secretary of defense. It takes no great powers of creativity in any case to imagine the principal topic of conversation at these two encounters. By the time of Douglas's arrival, Truman, at the behest of Forrestal and the Joint Chiefs of Staff, had already approved the addition of $3 billion to the $11 billion in the military budget for fiscal 1949. Included in the new appropriation was LeRoy Lutes's "moderate increase" in the budget for aircraft procurement, now, however, grown from its original figure of $400 million to $725 million (with an additional $50 million for research and development).[19] Still, Allen and Douglas are likely to have wanted more and, therefore, may have taken this opportunity to appeal to Forrestal and the president to speed the healing flow of federal money from the Treasury to this "sick industry."

Forrestal, it turned out, was about to attempt just that. That he was alarmed about the condition of the aircraft industry is suggested by, among many other things, his correspondence with his friend Frederick B. Rentschler, the president of United Aircraft. In *The Forrestal Diaries,* Walter Millis excerpted a portion of Forrestal's letter of April 6 to Rentschler: "We have to see there is enough in the hopper to get the industry off the ground," Forrestal wrote. (Given the ultraserious nature of the secretary's disposition, the pun was most likely inadvertent.) "I talked with both the House and Senate Appropriations chairmen and I believe there is a reasonable chance that we can get made available for immediate contract authorization all the aircraft part of the 1948–49 budget, together with the aircraft part of the $3 billion supplemental [appropriation] which the President sent in [to Congress] last week." But what Millis omitted from this letter is as significant as what he saw fit to include. The next paragraph must have greatly reassured Rentschler that if Forrestal had anything to say about the matter, everything would be worked out to the complete satisfaction of the top executives in the industry: "Oliver Echols is going to be a great help and so will John McCone who reported in today to give me a hand in certain planning areas." Perhaps out of tactfulness, Forrestal did not mention that Echols and McCone would be joining an executive of the Douglas Aircraft Company, Arthur Raymond, who already had "reported to Mr. Forrestal's office on March 31 to commence the confidential work he had been asked to do." And who better, after all, to advise the secretary of defense on aircraft procurement than, on one hand, the head of the industry's trade association; on another, the man who, as we noted in chapter 3, regarded himself as the spokesmen for Los Angeles's biggest corporations in general and the aircraft manufacturers in particular; and, on a third, a high-ranking representative of one of that industry's largest firms?[20]

Indeed, on the same day he wrote Rentschler, Forrestal dispatched a letter to Echols: "Confirming our discussion, the time has come to coordinate all aircraft requirements of the Army, Navy and Air Force into one joint pattern.... I would like for you, working through the Aircraft Committee [of the Munitions Board], to take the necessary action to prepare and recommend to me a proposed plan of administration which you believe best suited to the successful operation of the contemplated program." What he hoped to do, Forrestal explained to Carl Hinshaw, the CAPB's vice chairman, was "to come back later on, after I've had time to dig into this and Echols and his crowd could give me some evaluation" of the aircraft procurement program from the industry's standpoint. In similar fashion, Forrestal told the head of the board, Senator Owen Brewster, that he was "trying to get John McCone, who worked on the Finletter report, to come down here to be of some help in the military establishment. In view of his background and his interest in aviation he could be of the greatest assistance to me." It took remarkably little time before Forrestal's dependence on Echols and McCone was virtually complete. Already by April 12, for instance, his reply to Donald Douglas, who had written the secretary on the usual subject of procurement planning, was to state: "I am asking Oliver Echols to take a look at your letter and to talk to me about it." This reliance would soon be decisive in enabling the airplane builders to shape Pentagon procurement policies entirely to their wishes.[21]

In addition to revealing his decision to enlist Oliver Echols and John McCone as advisers, Forrestal, in his letter of April 6 to Frederick Rentschler, had also told the executive that he was asking Congress to do two things to provide instantaneous relief to the aircraft manufacturers: first, appropriate at once all the money for aircraft procurement in the budget for the next fiscal year; and second, allow the administration to use those funds forthwith to award procurement contracts to the industry, even though "normally the funds made available at the beginning of the new fiscal year, July 1, would not be obligated until next October." (The federal fiscal year then ran from July 1 to the following June 30.)[22] That the secretary was willing to employ measures of such an unprecedented character is a testimony to the dire circumstances of the aircraft industry—and his concern to remedy them. On Friday, April 2, Forrestal had taken the first step by proposing the idea of immediate appropriations and contract placements to Chan Gurney, chairman of the Senate Armed Services Committee; the next day, Saturday, March 3, he discussed the idea with Representative John Taber, chairman of the House Appropriations Committee, then formally presented the idea in writing to Taber and Styles Bridges, chairman of the Senate Appropriations Committee, on Monday, April 5 (the day before his letter to Rentschler).[23]

Like Forrestal, Secretary of the Air Force W. Stuart Symington, too, was doing his part. Besides conferring with the secretary of defense regarding the problems of United Aircraft and Frederick Rentschler,[24] Symington on April 1 sent an urgent appeal for assistance to Winthrop Aldrich, chairman of the Chase National Bank—an institution that, as we witnessed in the second chapter, had a deep involvement in the aircraft industry: "I am very sorry, but things you have seen in the papers make it impossible for me to be in New York tomorrow," Symington apologized,

> and therefore I am taking the liberty of sending Colonel Forbes and Colonel Wertenbaker with a memorandum for Mr. Forrestal from the Air Force. Colonel Wertenbaker represents me and Colonel Forbes knows the subject as thoroughly as anybody in the Pentagon.
>
> As you will note, the problem is how to get the money to get what we want; and any advice you could give us to that end would be very much appreciated.

> Inasmuch as all this is top secret, I am asking these officers to deliver this memorandum to you, to be prepared to discuss it with you, and to await your written advice, this in that it cannot be discussed over the telephone.[25]

Nor was that all. In testifying before the Senate Armed Services Committee on March 25—the occasion of Secretary of the Navy Sullivan's memorable disclosure that "recently, submarines not belonging to any nation west of the 'iron curtain' have been sighted off our shore"—Symington had made a thinly veiled pitch for an increase in the air force's budget. As matters stood, that service would receive enough money merely for "continuation of our present 55 groups, . . . [and] a rate of procurement" that would provide "modern airplanes" for 34 combat groups. "Note that this is less than half [of what] General Eisenhower and General Spaatz [considered] as essential to our security, . . . long before world conditions reacted [*sic*] to their present critical stage. . . . The point we should all remember," the secretary instructed the Committee, "is that . . . , from the standpoint of our survival, unless there is world agreement between now and then, our position will be far more critical when the Russians have the [atomic] bomb; and it should be emphasized that we will not have an adequate, modern Air Force available . . . unless we start building that Air Force NOW [*sic*]."[26]

The committee was quick to take the hint. So, also, were the full Senate and House. Congress, as I discussed in the previous chapter, was easily swayed by the seductive appeal of "air power"—the agreeable notion that the air force, armed with atomic bombs, could fight all future wars in some other part of the world while providing an invulnerable shield that would protect the United States itself from aerial attack. Once it became evident that the air force was trying to capitalize on its popularity in a way that promised to penalize the other services, the result was a general free-for-all. The army and the navy, not wishing to have their own aspirations jeopardized by congressional infatuation with "air power," quickly attempted to reply in kind by making the case for bigger appropriations of their own. To keep Pentagon spending limited to what they regarded as a reasonable figure, Truman, the State Department and the Bureau of the Budget each sought, for different reasons, to repel this latest military offensive. In the middle of the melee stood James Forrestal, one moment petitioning Truman to allocate more money to the armed services, the next beseeching the military bureaucrats to refrain from sabotaging budget agreements they had previously accepted, the next trying to restrain Congress from showering all its munificence on the air force while scanting the army and navy.

A brief summary of the details will suffice. When Symington was asked, following the completion of his prepared testimony before the Senate Armed

Services Committee on March 25, how much more money a "70 group" program would require, he replied that the additional cost would be $822 million. Forrestal was then recalled for questioning, and his response was to argue that if the armed services were to remain "balanced" with respect to each other, the Air Force program would actually necessitate a supplemental appropriation of $18 billion, rather than the $3 billion the administration had just requested. This answer, predictably, caused all hell to break loose. The army immediately requested an increased appropriation, on the grounds that it would need more money in order to fulfill its supporting role if the air force were expanded; and the navy was not about to consent to being left behind. Consequently, after much wrangling and innumerable meetings, the Joint Chiefs decided to recommend to Forrestal that the administration seek a supplemental appropriation not of $3 billion, but of $9 billion. Forrestal, attempting to maintain the momentum of the war scare without falling afoul of the president, countered by asking the Joint Chiefs, "number one, their recommendation for the division of that part of the supplemental $3 billions that does not deal with aircraft procurement; number two, what they would divide, how they would divide, an increase of $5 billions." Finally, on April 19, the Chiefs were able to arrive at an agreement with Forrestal and each other on a total military budget of about $14.5 billion, which included a supplemental appropriation of approximately $3.5 billion.[27]

Although Truman two days later authorized Forrestal to propose a supplemental appropriation of this amount to Congress, he withheld his final approval pending a review by the Bureau of the Budget. The outcome of that review, as the secretary of defense learned at a meeting at the White House on May 6, was that James E. Webb, director of the Bureau of the Budget, advocated reducing the supplemental appropriation by about $1 billion to roughly $2.5 billion. Forrestal responded by asking to present his case directly to the president. The following day, he was confronted not only with Truman, but, flanking him, the secretary of state, the secretary of the treasury, the director of the National Security Council—and, of course, James Webb. At this meeting, according to the account Forrestal committed to his diary, Marshall took the initiative by asserting that "the policy of this country was based upon the assumption that there would not be war and that we should not plunge into war preparations which would bring about the very thing we were taking these steps to prevent." Truman then declared that he "approved the statement of the Secretary of State and said he wished to make it very clear to all present" that increases in military spending to which "he had given the green light . . . were not to be construed as preparation for war—'that we are preparing for peace and not for war.' " Truman next summoned the Joint Chiefs and the service secretaries to a meeting with Forrestal and himself on May 13, at which time he read and distributed a message essentially similar to that given the secretary of defense on May 7.[28]

But appearances, as I have had frequent occasion to remark, can be deceiving; and this is a case in point. Truman's bark at the meeting of May 13 was in reality considerably worse than his bite. The meeting had, in fact, been called at Forrestal's request, and we saw in the last chapter that the statement Truman read there was the work of one of the secretary's own assistants ("My statement," Forrestal called it). Beneath the sometimes gruff surface of the president's words, moreover, was the reality that the armed services had won most of what they desired. Although the Bureau of the Budget had urged him to approve supplementary military spending no greater than $2.5 billion, Truman in the end chose to submit to Congress an appropriation of $3.2 billion—an amount that, "from a budgetary viewpoint alone, . . . is greater than should be requested . . . at this time," he told his listeners on May 13. Walter Millis's interpretation of these events was that the Budget Bureau "had slashed the $3.481 billion supplemental to $3.17 billion," indicating that its director "had largely won" the bureaucratic contest. I admit to having some difficulty regarding a reduction of 2.2 percent out of a total of $14.17 billion as a "slash"; and, considering that Truman patently spurned Webb's advice to cut the supplemental appropriation by $1 billion, I do not find it any easier to understand how the latter could be said to have "largely won." For all the administration's erstwhile preoccupation with lowering the federal deficit, controlling inflation and the like, the truth of the matter is that Truman was habitually generous where the military was concerned. Expenditures on the armed services during the late 1940s comprised the largest single item in the federal budget, consistently accounting for one-third or more of all federal outlays, and in no other peacetime year after World War II was there anything remotely approaching the 30-percent leap in military spending that 1948 witnessed. Even prior to the Korean War, the Pentagon was hardly on a starvation diet, and least of all in 1948.[29]

Meanwhile, as the administration was thrashing out its position on the size of the military budget, Congress, with Stuart Symington and Air Force Chief of Staff Carl Spaatz egging it on, was having a field day with "air power." "A fast-expanding Air Force of seventy combat groups . . . would be 'better understood by Russia' than a UMT designed to train 19-year-old youths as future reserves," Symington exhorted the Senate Armed Services Committee on April 7. Symington spoke in a similar vein in front of the Armed Services Committee of the House when he testified there on April 13. Here, his cue was a question from an "air power" fanatic par excellence, Texas Democrat Lyndon B. Johnson: "Do you think that we are more likely to insure the security of this nation with a strong effective 70-group air force or with U.M.T.?" The secretary was ready and waiting with his answer: "Well, if my two boys have to go back again into the Army and the Marines, I would rather see them have a minimum air force than I would a group of younger boys trained for six months or a year." Spaatz was more blunt still: "For Uncle Joe sitting in the Kremlin, one of the blue chips in this pot at this time—and it depends on the appropriations we get whether or not it will continue in the future—is the ability of our strategic force to drop a hell of a tonnage of bombs, . . . and also the ability to drop the atomic bomb, . . . on significant parts of Russia."[30]

By this time, however, such set pieces amounted to little more than oratorical exercises in the House, for already on April 7 its Armed Services Committee had passed and sent to the secretary of defense a resolution stating "that this nation should have an Air Force with a minimum strength of 70 combat groups"—an accurate foretaste of what lay ahead. Within two days of Symington's testimony before this committee, the House voted unanimously to add to the administration's requested budget another $822 million of "contractual authority to get the seventy-group Air Force started," then approved by the lopsided margin of 343 to 3 an appropriation totalling $3.2 billion for contracts to be bestowed immediately upon the aircraft industry.[31]

The Senate, less impetuous and more worried about the impact on inflation of almost a billion dollars of additional federal spending, was not so readily stampeded. At one point toward the end of April, the administration even thought it might be able to slow the tide by persuading the Senate to accept a compromise proposal for 66 groups. In the end, though, the fixation with "air power" also swept the upper chamber. With 74 in favor and only 2 opposed, the Senate on May 7 followed the House's lead in appropriating an additional $822 million for the air force's 70-group program. A finished bill emerged from the House-Senate conference committee on May 10, and the president signed it on May 21. To judge by appearances, the "air power" contingent in Congress had triumphed over the administration by including the additional $822 million for a 70-group air force. In actuality, quite the reverse was true. The final version of the bill contained a stipulation that the money it appropriated could not be spent without a presidential "finding" that the "contracts let are necessary in the national defense." This left control of the ultimate disposition of the funds just where Truman wanted them—in his own hands.[32]

If this result was a victory for the administration over "70 group" zealotry, by no means was it a defeat for the aircraft industry. To comprehend this seeming paradox, it is necessary to understand that, second only to having its future underwritten by the federal government, the most important goal of the leading aircraft firms was to be able to enjoy smooth, predictable conditions. Speaking informally with his former air force colleagues at the fifth meeting of the Air Board in June 1947, Oliver Echols bore down on the point emphatically.

Airplane procurement, he insisted, "has to be a program on a planned basis. You have to look at it not from month-to-month, or 9 months to 9 months, or be in a hell-of-a-rush to put $600,000,000 on order here, then have nothing for the rest of the time. It has to be so many orders planned every quarter, so many orders let every quarter on a program basis."

In advocating that aircraft procurement be made "a program on a planned basis," Echols was, naturally, espousing the position that industry executives themselves favored. If the air force and the navy were to place procurement orders regularly and uniformly, Lawrence Bell, the president of Bell Aircraft Corporation, testified before the President's Air Policy Commission,

> it would help out every manufacturer, because as it is today and as it has been in the past 35 years that I have been in business, a feast has been [the] experience one day and a famine the next. There is no continuity to the program. No manufacturer of military aircraft knows what the policy of the Government will be in a couple of years, whether he should make greater investments . . . or not, because he cannot foretell the future.

Asked by a member of the Commission for "any suggestions" about how the cycle of "peaks and valleys . . . within the industry . . . might be corrected," Donald Douglas did not equivocate: "It seems a matter of administration by the Government to attempt to the best of their ability to eliminate them." James Forrestal agreed. As he put it in a letter to Douglas early in April 1948, "We have great need of orderly and not hysterical planning."[33]

Viewed in this light, an additional $822 million piled onto the $725 million already in the supplemental appropriation for aircraft procurement was a sterling example of "hysterical planning," threatening the industry with what promised to become a genuine embarrassment of riches were all of it to become available in a single year. To meet the demand generated by a procurement budget of this magnitude, the aircraft firms would have only two choices, each in its own way unpalatable. One alternative would be to expand the scale of operations. The danger here, of course, was exactly that pointed out by Lawrence Bell: a company might invest heavily one year when contracts were abundant, only to find the next year's procurement budget greatly reduced, thus necessitating another painful retrenchment. Indeed, as the *Wall Street Journal* noted in June 1948, even *without* the extra $822 million, "the aircraft manufacturers are not entirely happy about the new Air Force program. There is some feeling among the plane builders that Congress may find the cost too big for the popular taste and later on cut back the available funds." The fact that

Congress had acted on aircraft procurement in the midst of a war scare made it that much the more likely that it might wake up the next morning repenting, so to speak, its excesses of the night before. Such a situation was the very last thing that industry executives wished to confront.[34]

Alternatively, the aircraft companies could simply accept all the procurement work that came their way without expanding either their facilities or labor force, knowing at the outset that they would be unable to meet the production deadlines called for in their contracts. In its own fashion, however, this latter approach was no less risky than the former. Throughout the debate within the administration over Pentagon spending during February and March, James Webb, the director of the Bureau of the Budget, had objected to any proposal to allocate more money for aircraft procurement, on the grounds that he did "not believe any additional planes could be delivered by 1950 or 1951." So wrote Felix Larkin, Forrestal's legal counsel, on March 17, 1948, summarizing a series of meetings between various of the secretary's assistants and members of the Bureau of the Budget's staff. "In a sense," Larkin noted, "I think the Bureau of the Budget feels that the Air Force is crying 'wolf.' " The following week, Larkin, in a second memorandum on the same subject, described another such meeting on March 20, at which "the Bureau of the Budget criticized the Air Force's production schedule and the lack of coordination" in that service's procurement procedures.[35]

The credibility of the air force, in short, was at stake, as was that of the aircraft companies: the bigger the backlog of unfilled procurement orders, the more dubious appeared the argument for federal salvation of the industry. If, after all, the airplane makers were unable to keep up with their existing contracts, where was the logic in providing them with new ones? For all the tenacity with which he pursued the goal of a 70-group air force, even Stuart Symington understood how important it was that the aircraft firms not fall behind schedule. Thus, when William E. Allen, the president of the Boeing Airplane Company, called him in hopes of persuading him to help quash a strike at the company's Seattle plant, the secretary was quick to turn the conversation in the direction of his own preoccupation. First, he scolded Allen: "I don't know how you're handling it because it's none of my business. I'd like to get some airplanes." Then he asked, "How many planes are you behind now? . . . When are you going to make those planes up?" And finally, overcome by exasperation, he resorted to threats: "Well, you may get your orders cancelled if we don't get the planes."

After he had regained his composure, Symington attempted to explain the situation:

> I've sat here and taken the rap to get the money to get the planes. And as a result of that, there's a great bitterness all through the

> Government about what we've done. One of the chief criticisms is that we get more money than we need from the standpoint of what we can get in deliveries because the airplane companies are giving us promises on deliveries they can't meet. . . . I don't want to get into your business because I think you know a lot more about it and will run it a lot better than I ever could. . . . I just want to get the planes because when there's another look at the way the law was signed and . . . they see a lot of this stuff hasn't been spent, et cetera, . . . they might cancel on that basis.[36]

Under the circumstances he outlined to William Allen, even Symington himself—although he could never have afforded to acknowledge as much publicly—was probably relieved not to have the task of presiding over the distribution of yet another $822 million in contracts within a single year.* Even without this additional appropriation, the air force would procure some 33.5 million pounds of airframe during the 1949 fiscal year—an almost-threefold increase over the figure for the previous fiscal year, a fourfold increase over that for the 1947 fiscal year and a fivefold increase over that for fiscal 1946.[37] All of which led the *Wall Street Journal* to remark during the course of that spring's fracas over the "70 group" air force, "So large is the plane program now being drafted that congressional and military leaders are even beginning to worry whether the aircraft industry has the capacity to fill the proposed orders."[38] For just that reason, aircraft industry leaders gave no sign of being heartbroken when it became evident that the air force would not have its procurement budget for the next fiscal year augmented by an additional $822 million. Appearances to the contrary notwithstanding, from the industry's perspective, as Donald Douglas, Lawrence Bell and other executives had testified before the President's Air Policy Commission, it was preferable by far to have the administration provide a steady stream of contracts that could be fulfilled, rather than a deluge

* In describing the criticism of his actions within the administration, Symington, for once, did not exaggerate. Shortly before the end of 1948, he sent a memo ostensibly thanking Director of the Bureau of the Budget James Webb "for telling me you had heard the Air Force—including specifically Mr. Whitney [Assistant Secretary of the Air Force Cornelius Vanderbilt Whitney], several ranking officers, and myself—were working with big aviation companies and others to lobby for a large Air Force regardless of the position of the Administration." W. Stuart Symington letter to James E. Webb, December 13, 1948, Papers of James E. Webb, Bureau of Budget, box 8, HSTL.

now that carried with it the danger of massive cancellations or cutbacks in the near future. The industry was willing to eschew what Bell had referred to as "a feast one day" in order to purchase immunity from "a famine the next."

KEEPING FAITH: "THE SUBCONTRACTING DEAL"

Having analyzed the outcome of the budgetary battle between "air power" advocates and the administration, it will behoove us next to consider the many ways in which the administration used the money it obtained from the taxpayers to succor the industry. A logical place to begin is with James Forrestal's idea of having all funds for aircraft procurement in the budgets for fiscal years 1948 *and* 1949 made available immediately—that is, several weeks *before* the end of the current (1948) fiscal year. "Under normal procedures," *Aviation Week* noted, "new orders would not be placed until late fall," by which time "skilled workers would have been laid off and productive capacity virtually lost." Instead, however, with Forrestal and Symington "prodding the military into an unmilitary speed on this matter, . . . telegraphic letters of intent went out from Wright Field to Air Force contractors less than 24 hours after Forrestal authorized spending the funds." The official rationale for this extraordinary procedure was that it would enable the aircraft industry to identify and overcome bottlenecks in production early in the proceedings. Communications among the top Pentagon officials show rather a different motive at work. "Now that the President has signed the Appropriation Bill for military aircraft procurement," Stuart Symington instructed the under secretary of the air force the day after the signing took place, "in order to help this critically sick industry, it is important for us to submit to Mr. Forrestal at the earliest possible date, the type of plane and the quantity that we want. Mr. Forrestal has told me that he believes one of the most important things in the military establishment [Department of Defense] is the immediate placing of business to these companies." Symington expressed a similar thought in writing to Forrestal's adviser John McCone to vent his frustration at what he regarded as unnecessary delays: "For many weeks, we have all placed great importance on the placing of orders in this industry which is in such critical shape because of lack of orders," yet the aircraft procurement bill had inexplicably been allowed to languish "in the Bureau of the Budget [until] May 20 even though passed by the House May 11."[39]

The administration may have hoped to preserve the polite pretense that nothing more momentous than its concern about supposed bottlenecks in production underlay its decision to speed contracts to the aircraft firms, but the business press presented a more candid picture. *Aviation Week*'s contemporaneous account reported that "production lines were running out of orders this spring. At Lockheed the P-80 line was ready to stop. At Allison the end of jet engine production was in sight. . . . [Only an] unprecedented procurement speed has averted the serious crisis that the Air Co-ordinating Committee gloomily forecast for this summer." "The industry was facing a grim prospect in the spring of 1948," the same publication recalled the following winter. "Lack of sufficient military orders meant that many production lines would face a shutdown by early summer. More than a few companies faced exhaustion of their working capital, loss of skilled labor forces and the dissipation of their design engineering teams. Even if sizeable military orders were forthcoming at the start of the new fiscal year," they would have "come too late to avert this crisis." In similar fashion, *Business Week* displayed the headline "Aircraft Industry Rescued" over its story on the "big military orders placed last week by the Navy and the Air Force." The subheadline was no less revealing: "Action came just in time: Some companies were facing shutdowns; now they foresee profits instead." The cash infusion had arrived without a moment to spare.[40]

Noteworthy, too, in this connection is the actual amount of money for aircraft procurement that the supplemental appropriation to the fiscal 1948 budget contained. On February 3, when General LeRoy Lutes first suggested a "moderate increase" in spending for aircraft procurement, the figure he proposed to Forrestal was $400 million. The secretary, as we observed earlier in this chapter, accepted this recommendation and, two days after receiving Lutes's memorandum, discussed with Truman the idea of enlarging the budget for aircraft procurement by that amount. By the second half of March, however, the supplemental appropriation for aircraft had somehow managed to grow to $725 million, or almost twice the sum in Lutes's memorandum of February 3. What brought about the change?

Two developments seem to have been paramount. First, early in February, a memorandum for Forrestal from one of his assistants apprised the secretary that "the [aircraft] manufacturing industry is now expected to be able to turn out more of their backlog" than had previously been thought possible, meaning that Lutes's "moderate increase" would no longer be enough to keep the airplane plants open until the end of the next fiscal year. Second, in the interim since Lutes's original recommendation, both Oliver Echols and John McCone had become Forrestal's advisers on aircraft procurement, virtually guaranteeing that the Pentagon's policies in this area would be trimmed to the industry's own specifications. Thus, it was no mere happenstance that discussion within the administration was settling on a figure of $725 million dollars for the supplemental aircraft appropriation, rather than the earlier amount of $400 million, just about the time Echols and McCone were popping up at Forrestal's side, for with this addition, the total budget for military aircraft would come to around $2 billion—exactly the target at which the industry itself had long been aiming. In a memo he wrote on the last day of September 1947, H. E. Weihmiller, a special consultant to the President's Air Policy Commission, explained the reasoning: "Apparently a figure of around one billion dollars a year for the *airframe* industry is its general goal. As their [*sic*] part is approximately one-half the total airplane cost, two billion dollars a year for the whole aircraft industry is their indication." With Echols and McCone newly installed as Forrestal's specialists on aircraft procurement, there was now little likelihood that the industry would fail to achieve its ends.[41]

Administration solicitousness toward the industry demonstrated itself in countless other ways as well. Marshall Plan funds, for example, were channelled to a number of Western European nations specifically to enable them to pay for airplanes and parts from U.S. manufacturers. Likewise, Forrestal and the air force negotiated an agreement with the Canadian government whereby North American Aviation produced its newest jet fighter, the F-86A, in Canada. "This solves several problems," remarked *Automotive Industries,* and not the least of its virtues was that it required "no large U.S. dollar transfers." The Pentagon also began the practice of taking advantage of military-assistance programs to find additional money for the aircraft industry "without . . . having to ask for more from Congress." As George Thayer has explained, such programs, which were "administered by the Defense Department," required the United States government to buy "from its own Army, Navy and Air Force, war surplus that was then given free to foreign countries. The three services, therefore, not only had a lucrative means of clearing their inventories but also acquired in the process large sums of money to buy new equipment that was outside the purview of direct Congressional control."[42] If the spirit of the Constitution had to be subverted in order to make certain that the aircraft industry prospered and the National Security State remained untrammeled, the Truman administration was more than equal to the task.

Next to providing the money that prevented their demise, easily the most important service the administration performed for the aircraft companies was to structure both the awarding of contracts and the arrangements for payment in such a way that all the major firms, rather than merely the most capable few, survived. To begin with, even before any funds for procurement had been appropriated, the administration had responded to Oliver Echols's call for "a law [that would] make advertising and sealed bids the exception rather than the rule in aircraft procurement" by obtaining from Congress the Armed Services Procurement Act. Introduced under the aegis of James Forrestal during 1947, when he was still secretary of the navy, this legislation "eas[ed] the requirements for competitive bid contracting . . . and open[ed] the way for negotiation of aircraft contracts," leading one naval officer to write, "It has been said that the military departments have been given *carte blanche* authority to buy anything it desires [*sic*] by negotiation." The act, according to this author, further stipulated that "when the secretary determines that it is in the interest of national defense . . . , contracts may be awarded by negotiation for the specific purpose of maintaining the source of supply." In plain English, that meant that a service could choose to keep alive a failing firm—or even an entire industry—on the grounds that to do so would be "in the interest of national defense." This section of the act "appears to be an authority for [an] outright subsidy," the same account concluded—and in this instance, appearance and reality were in perfect accord.[43]

In addition, the Armed Services Procurement Act also contained "many new benefits for the contractor." One of these, to take a typical instance, provided contractors with reimbursement for any machine tools they had purchased "as soon as the costs are approved by the procurement officer, in bold contrast to the wartime problem of operating in the red for months or even years until tooling costs had been paid for out of production deliveries." The change in procedures meant that "the contractor will start showing a profit as soon as units begin rolling off the production line . . . regardless of the size of the contract." When the contract had been fulfilled, moreover, the contractor would have the option of buying back at a discount the machine tools used to complete it, and the federal government would pay for "its pro-rata share of their useful life." Finally, the kinds of expenses that would be "allowable as costs under the new program" were vastly increased; it took nearly three column-inches in the pages of *Automotive Industries* just to list them all.[44]

With respect to the dissemination of contracts, we learned in chapter 3 that as early as the summer of 1947, Secretaries Forrestal and Symington had tacitly committed the administration to the arrangement proposed by Donald Douglas and Oliver Echols for distributing procurement work in such a way as to ensure the survival of the largest companies that lacked large prime contracts of their own. This commitment became more explicit when Symington returned in November 1947 to testify again before the President's Air Policy Commission. Having "discussed this with just about as many people" in the aircraft companies "as were willing to discuss it," he had concluded that "the happiest possible solution would be some arrangement whereby . . . the Air Force itself would . . . not eliminate the private enterprise aspect of the industry, but which would make it possible for us to specify that those companies which had not been successful in design, but which had adequate and necessary facilities . . . , be considered for subcontracting work by the companies successful in getting the business." Asked by Commission Chairman Thomas Finletter, "Would the industry take to that?" the secretary was able to provide abundant assurance: "The suggestion was made by perhaps their leading representative," and Symington's own inquiries had demonstrated to his satisfaction that "most [aircraft executives] would be for the subcontracting deal."[45]

Aircraft appropriations had not yet even been approved in the spring of 1948 when the administration commenced to implement "the subcontracting deal." Ever since becoming secretary of defense, Forrestal had evinced a keen interest in the financial health of the aircraft industry. Indeed, one of his first acts as secretary was to assign an aide to compile "three books"—looseleaf notebooks, actually—"on the subjects of oil, air and shipping, with the fundamental facts affecting each." During the spring and early summer months of 1948, however, when the fate of the industry was hanging in the balance, his concern with the aircraft industry verged on the obsessive. At the beginning of April 1948, just as he was proposing to make all federal funds for aircraft procurement available at once, Forrestal also began putting in place measures to establish the subcontracting arrangements favored by industry spokesmen. On April 2, he drafted a memorandum for the secretary of the navy, instructing him to "proceed immediately to complete contracts on all unobligated 1948 funds and negotiate and prepare contracts at the earliest possible moment for the proposed FY [fiscal year] 1949 funds" for naval aircraft; the navy was also to "urg[e] the prime contractors to subcontract component parts and major assemblies where feasible in the interests of strengthening the industry." (At about the same time, Forrestal also requested a report on Lockheed Aircraft's negotiations with the air force for the sale of 10 Constellation airplanes. We recollect from chapter 2 the plea of Lockheed's president, Robert E. Gross, to the air force for "approximately ten or twelve million dollars on the sale of, let us say, ten or twelve airplanes of the Constellation model." Forrestal was relieved to learn that "the Air Force has purchased these 10 planes," hence the company could now be "taken off the critical list.")[46]

At the end of the following month, the secretary of defense assigned Felix Larkin, one of his aides, to prepare "a study as to how much the industry, as a whole, will benefit from the new aircraft program and to what extent the business will merely aid already solvent concerns." In mid-July he reminded Larkin, "I believe you are getting up for me an analysis of the aircraft industry—and the extent to which it has benefited, particularly in terms of diversification of business which has resulted." One week later, he wrote to Lieutenant General LeRoy Lutes at the Munitions Board, "What I am interested in this subject is: the extent to which the appropriations of 1948–49 have really broadened the base and improved the health of the aircraft industry or whether most of the business has simply gone to those companies which already were in fairly good shape such as Grumman, Boeing,

North American, Northrup [*sic*], etc." On the same day, he sent a related memorandum on the same subject to a second assistant, W. H. Mautz. At the end of August, he asked yet a third assistant, Wilfred McNeil, for a memorandum on "the types and numbers of the proposed aircraft procurement program of 1) Air Force [and] 2) Navy," suggesting that "Mr. Mautz shorten his vacation by a week" in order to work on the project. As a result of these unceasing exertions, by the end of the year the secretary was able to inform James Webb, director of the Bureau of the Budget, that "both the Air Force and the Navy are taking all possible action to increase the amount of subcontracting within the industry to the 'have not' companies." Forrestal's word to Oliver Echols and Donald Douglas in August of 1947 had not been given lightly.[47]

While Forrestal labored to redesign the Pentagon's procurement practices, Stuart Symington was toiling to make sure that the aircraft companies themselves complied with the new subcontracting arrangements. For these arrangements were not automatically self-enforcing; if they were to succeed, it would only be by dint of the administration's assistance. To see why this was so, we must keep in mind that cartel agreements to divide the market within a given industry—which is, in essence, what the largest airplane builders were demanding in these years—are notoriously porous when the agreement is not legally binding on the group's members. In such a circumstance, many companies will make secret deals that violate the terms of the cartel. Because of this fact, it has been the case historically that firms in an oligopolistic industry often turn to the federal government to do for them what they cannot do for themselves—namely, enforce obedience to the rules of their own cartel. The aircraft industry took just this approach in 1947 and 1948. "Certainly competition will supply the most economic method of purchasing anything," Ralph V. Hunt, the vice president-comptroller of Douglas Aircraft, conceded to members of the President's Air Policy Commission, but he was quick to qualify that admission in the same sentence: "It must be carefully controlled, in order not to be self-destroying."[48] That there was no legislation allowing the Truman administration to compel corporations with contracts to subcontract a portion of the work to those without was, to be sure, a problem. Even in the absence of such legislation, however, industry leaders expected that heavy pressure from the administration would oblige the aircraft companies to uphold the subcontracting procedures for which their own representatives had lobbied so arduously, thereby creating the kind of "carefully controlled" environment envisioned by Douglas executive Ralph Hunt. Thus, it became the task of Secretary of the Air Force Symington to see that any recalcitrant manufacturers toed the line.

How he went about it is well illustrated by his speech at the annual meeting of the board of directors of the Aircraft Industries Association in mid-May 1948.

The air force had done its part for the aircraft companies by "making funds available"; this, the secretary told his audience, had been "its main contribution. Industry must take it from there out." But, he warned, having sought new rules for the procurement game, it was essential that the aircraft companies abide by them: "Since the end of the war, . . . it is our opinion that at times manufacturers are thinking of themselves first and the overall picture second. . . . In regard to designs [currently in production], the aircraft industry today is divided into two groups—the have's and the have-not's. The facilities belonging to the have-not's must be put to work on the designs belonging to the have's. The Air Force must go all-out with industry in our joint effort to accomplish this aim."[49]

Chastising "the have's" for "thinking of themselves first and the overall picture second," demanding that "the facilities belonging to the have-not's . . . be put to work on the designs belonging to the have's"—these admonitions made a mockery of the notion that the administration had hurried appropriations through Congress and into the desperate hands of the airplane makers in response to a Soviet threat. For surely had any such emergency existed, this subordination of rapid, efficient production to the goal of delivering each individual firm from danger would have been inconceivable. Only if the administration's true purpose was, as I have argued, to preserve the status quo in the aircraft industry in a way that the largest firms found acceptable can we understand why it took the position it did with respect to subcontracting. A wide distribution of subcontracts throughout the industry was something that almost all of the top aircraft executives endorsed, even though, as Republic Aircraft's president, Mundy I. Peale, acknowledged before the President's Air Policy Commission, such an approach was "a little expensive perhaps." If that was what industry leaders such as Peale wished, however, the administration was more than willing to lend its support. "We would be paying more money . . . on that basis," Stuart Symington admitted to members of the Finletter Commission, "because there would be two additional costs. First, you would have a higher unit cost because of lower volume. Second, you would have to pay a profit on the subcontracted part." Yet none of that mattered to the secretary once he had determined that "most [of the industry] would be for the subcontracting deal." If efficiency and frugality had to be sacrificed in order to resuscitate the aircraft companies, in other words, that was just too bad—regrettable, perhaps, but unavoidable nonetheless. The price might be high but, so far as the Truman administration was concerned, it was one that simply had to be paid.[50]

The reasons behind the administration's decision to implement the policy on subcontracting favored by the aircraft companies were no less obvious to experienced observers of the industry than were that policy's effects. The "significant re-appearance in the industry . . . of subcontracting on an expanding scale" was occurring, *Aviation Week* reported, because the air force "particularly has indicated that it favors subcontracting as a method of keeping firms going who do not receive prime airframe or engine contracts." To what lengths this practice could extend was illustrated when "the Air Force . . . returned to a wartime practice in 'subcontracting' the entire production quantity of Northrop B-49 eight-jet Flying Wing bombers to Convair at its Fort Worth, Texas, plant" so that the latter corporation could be "provided . . . with much-needed business." Such a situation, the editors of *Business Week* remarked, was "unique in peacetime aircraft production." But it kept the largest companies in the industry from expiring, and that was all that mattered.[51]

The administration's efforts soon began to produce the desired results. "The government will pump $250,000,000 more cash into the aircraft manufacturing industry this year than last year," *Aviation Week* predicted in August 1948. Such a "record peacetime contract authorization for plane procurement" would amount to an increase by two-thirds over the previous year's total and indicated that "1950 fiscal year cash payments to the industry will top this year's by a big margin." Two weeks later, the publication had equally thrilling news:

> The aircraft industry is beginning its largest peacetime production program. Its biggest customer is the United States government. Federal expenditures for aviation have skyrocketed from $1,760,192,000 during fiscal 1948 to $4,895,386,000 approved by Congress and obligated for spending during fiscal 1949.

Not surprisingly, given such a vast upsurge in federal spending, "Airframe and engine production will soon triple its early post-war rate." Hence by the time it issued its yearly report at the close of 1948, the Aircraft Industries Association was anticipating that "most major companies" would record "at least modest profits for 1948. Total sales of the 15 major firms are expected to reach a new postwar high of $1,110,000,000[,] . . . a gain of nearly 25 percent over 1947 sales of $848,000,000 by the same companies."[52]

Such glad tidings quickly gave rise to a celebratory mood among industry executives. As late as mid-April 1948, for example, Lockheed's president, Robert E. Gross, had been apprehensive about the future of his company. "Nineteen forty-nine looks thin, unless we get one of these new air force programs," he wrote in one letter. But by the time a mere four weeks had passed, his longtime friend and associate Guy W. Vaughan, the president of the Curtiss-Wright Corporation, was willing to proclaim to a meeting of the Aviation Writers Association that, by virtue of the administration's program for increasing procurement, "for the first time, the aircraft manufacturers will be able to plan for the future with some degree of confidence. As a result the long-range outlook for the manufacturers is brighter today than ever before in its history."[53]

Within the space of three months, evidence that Vaughan was correct had become incontrovertible. "We are doing considerably better now than a year ago and I will look forward to telling you about it when you arrive at the end of the month," Robert Gross rejoiced to one correspondent early in August 1948. His disposition was equally sunny in a pair of letters at the end of the month. "We have an aircraft program, and rather a respectable one, going at the present time in the United States. We are operating on a much more sustained and even keel than we were a year or two ago," he told a friend in England. Gross displayed even greater elation a few days later in a letter to Guy Vaughan: "I am enclosing a copy of our six months statement which was just issued this morning, and because it shows such an encouraging improvement I couldn't resist seeing that you get one." This optimistic outlook persisted into 1949. "We did have a pretty good year last year," Gross wrote in April, "we look forward to a profitable 12 months." The next month brought more of the same: "It would appear that our prospects as a group of companies are fairly good by comparison with the prospects of some of the industries. . . . I do think the industry will have a respectable program for several years to come."[54]

The end-of-the-year survey of the aircraft manufacturers compiled for the January 1949 issue of *Automotive Industries* left little doubt that the changes Robert Gross was seeing at Lockheed extended to the industry as a whole. "The nation's most . . . sensitive enterprise" was finally "out of the red and operating on a firm financial basis . . . for the first time since V-J Day, 3½ years ago." As a result, profits would be "a certainty this year with some companies scheduled to wipe out their 1946 and 1947 losses. The volume of work now on the books indicates a conservative doubling of last year's output in units and a near-tripling of the dollar-value of products delivered." These predictions of better times to come in 1949 were fully borne out, *Aviation Week* disclosed the following year. Not only had "every company" in the industry "made a profit in 1949 for the first time since the war," but "aggregate profit more than tripled over 1948."[55]

Still, these gains were achieved at a price. As I noted in chapter 2, the industry had come, in the words of *Automotive Industries,* to "depend upon military procurement for 75 per cent of its business and upon government support in civil aviation for an additional 15 per cent." If this state of affairs suggests that the Truman administration's decision to increase procurement levels and hasten contracts to the aircraft companies was nothing less than a sizeable step toward enshrining a welfare state for the aircraft industry, the point is underscored by the fact that giant firms outside of it, including Allison (a division of General

Motors), General Electric and Westinghouse, "now have substantial military contracts that will run through 1950," and the latter two had even "obtained special facilities in which to expand production."[56] The permanent war economy might not attain full growth until the next decade, but already, owing to the beneficence of the Truman White House, it was thriving.

What the new federal largesse meant for the aircraft manufacturers—and their creditors and investors in the ruling class—is nowhere better demonstrated than in two of the innumerable reports that the secretary of defense requested members of his staff to prepare. The first of these, dating from early July 1948, was written by W. H. Mautz and sent as a memorandum to Felix Larkin, who transmitted it to Forrestal for inclusion in his "Aircraft Book," the looseleaf binder that the secretary consulted to stay abreast of conditions in the industry. "The strong financial position with which the industry entered the post-war period was completely reversed during 1946 and 1947," Mautz began.

> Sales declined to about $1.6 billion [from a peak of $8 billion in 1944]; net worth decreased from $700 million at the end of 1945 to $600 million at the end of 1947; working capital dropped from $623 million to $451 million, with inventories representing 88 per cent of working capital.
>
> The industry suffered a $178 million operating loss during the two years [1946 and 1947]. . . . Ten of the major companies operated at a loss, including the six larger airframe companies.[57]

Already by the time the next such report was sent to Forrestal's successor, Louis Johnson, less than ten months later, the situation had changed remarkably:

> At the end of 1948, the aircraft industry was in its best financial condition since the end of the war. Sales of the sixteen major airframe manufacturers reached a postwar high in 1948 of $1,188 million compared with $856 million in 1947 and $730 million in 1946. Only three manufacturers . . . lost money during 1948, while eleven of the sixteen manufacturers operated at a loss during 1947.[58]

For this dramatic reversal of its fortunes—an increase in sales during 1948 of 50 percent over the 1946-1947 average—the aircraft industry could thank Harry Truman and the war hysteria that he and his administration set loose. For almost three years, the airplane builders had worked, planned, plotted; now, by virtue of an atmosphere in which truth and reason alike counted for naught, their well-laid plans had come to fruition. If the war scare of 1948 was actually "a wholly Washington crisis," as Hanson Baldwin, the military affairs editor of the *New York Times,* acutely observed at the time, it accomplished one of the principal goals of its creators nonetheless: a drowning industry was plucked from a sea of red ink without a moment to spare.[59]

On every other front, moreover, the administration's war-scare scheme proved equally triumphant. Republicans suspicious of, if not downright antagonistic toward, foreign aid were blandished and bludgeoned into supporting the largest and most ambitious such program the nation had ever seen. Truman and his advisers also were successful, as I discuss immediately below, in maneuvering the Republicans into swallowing their misgivings and enacting unpopular peacetime selective service legislation. With respect to military spending, the administration, after suffering the ignominy of having its budget for the armed services cut by 10 percent in the preceding year, more than evened the score by persuading Congress to vote for an increase in funds for the Pentagon of almost 30 percent for fiscal 1949. Last, the administration was able to frustrate the designs of Congressional "air power" zealots by obtaining legislation that placed control of all expenditures for aircraft procurement in the White House, regardless of how much money the legislature chose to appropriate for this purpose. As the spring of 1948 entered its closing days, one would have been hard-pressed to imagine how the administration—or the aircraft industry—might have asked for more.

UMT: A TRIUMPH IN THE GUISE OF DEFEAT

But, some may object, didn't the Truman administration suffer a significant setback by failing to secure universal military training (UMT) from Congress? That, admittedly, is the conventional interpretation of the events of spring 1948. But it is, in my view, wholly mistaken. Among other things, it violates the first principle of historical research drummed into the head of every beginning graduate student: do not take *anything* at face value—least of all the words of the principal actors. (Or, as I prefer to formulate it: by all means listen to what they say, but never forget to keep an eye on what the bastards actually *do.*) Far from counting the rejection of UMT as a reversal, I will argue in the remainder of this chapter that Truman and his associates in fact made such a development the cornerstone of their strategy for compelling a Republican-controlled Congress to approve the military and foreign policy measures the administration held most dear.

The Truman administration, to be sure, *appeared* to be committed to the creation of a UMT program. As early as October 23, 1945, Truman had sent to

Congress the first of what would turn out to be a series of futile messages calling for passage of UMT legislation; and he reiterated this request the following December. One of the recommendations in his State of the Union address on January 14 of the next year—it ranked eighth on a list of 21—was for UMT. To bring more pressure to bear, Truman on November 20, 1946, appointed an Advisory Commission on Universal Military Training chaired by Dr. Karl Compton, president of the Massachusetts Institute of Technology. Meanwhile, he continued to prod the legislature for a UMT program in his message on the budget of January 3, 1947. When Compton's Advisory Commission on UMT completed its work, Truman forwarded its report to Congress on June 4, 1947, with still another call for the passage of a training bill. During the first three months of 1948 alone, Truman made three more such appeals, culminating in his address to a joint session of Congress on March 17, 1948, on which occasion, as we have witnessed, he asked for passage of ERP, selective service legislation and, once again, UMT.[60] In addition to these efforts by the president, Secretary of State Marshall, who had long been a frequent and vocal advocate of UMT, also repeatedly importuned Congress for its enactment, particularly during the early weeks of 1948. He testified for it in front of the Senate Armed Forces Committee on March 2, for example, did so again directly after Truman's speech on March 17 and returned for a third time on March 22.

How, in view of all this activity, is it possible to assert that the administration's inability to secure enactment of a UMT program was anything other than a defeat? It is sometimes best, as the authors of the *Talmud* understood, to answer one question with another. With that in mind, I suggest we approach this issue by posing a pair of different questions instead: In urging UMT legislation in 1948, did Truman, Marshall, Forrestal and other high-ranking members of the administration actually believe there was a reasonable chance of obtaining such a program from Congress? And if not, then what was the point of introducing it in the first place?

Answers to these two questions will, I believe, illustrate once more the high degree of political cunning attained by the administration's tacticians—as well as the dangers inherent in confusing the public professions and the private positions of the administration's foremost figures. Let us, to begin, examine how administration officials appraised their chances of inducing Congress to enact UMT legislation. "We knew full well that there was not a prayer of getting UMT passed by the 80th Congress," Army Chief of Staff General Omar Bradley wrote in his memoirs. UMT was "widely opposed by most educators, many religious organizations and by the doves and pacifists," as well as by influential members of Congress such as "the Senate's 'Mr. Republican,' Bob Taft, . . . [and] Congressman Leo Allen, Chairman of the powerful House Rules Committee." (It was Leo Allen who not only had barred the administration's UMT legislation from reaching the floor of the House during the preceding eight months, but who also told the *New York Times*'s William S. White, immediately after Truman's address to Congress on March 17, 1948, that "there was 'no more prospect' for a vote [on UMT] than there had been before.") Bradley's estimate was fully shared by his successor, General J. Lawton Collins. In his autobiography, *Lightning Joe,* Collins narrated an incident in which Dewey Short, the Republican head of the House Armed Services Committee and a legislator whom Collins "had gotten to know and respect, . . . abruptly rose from his chair and left the committee room" in the middle of the general's testimony. Later, Short apologized: "'Lightning Joe, you were about to convince me, so I *had* to walk out on you.' He and other members of Congress simply could not swallow their inherent distaste for any form of compulsory military service in peacetime," Collins thought.[61]

If the military firmly believed that Congress would never authorize a UMT program, the opinions of such prominent civilians as Clark Clifford, Truman's chief political operative, were in no wise different. "As we got into it more deeply and we checked with leaders in a number of different areas in the country," he remarked in an oral history interview, "I believe we all concluded, at that time, that it would be impossible to get the necessary legislation through the Congress."[62]

"Ah, yes," the alert reader may respond, "but these are all after-the-fact recollections—and long after the fact, at that." Point well taken. The truth, however, is that these observations two or three decades after the war scare of 1948 are essentially identical with estimates composed at the time. In mid-November 1947, by way of illustration, Captain Ira H. Nunn, the navy's legislative counsel, sent a memorandum to the secretary and under secretary of the navy (with a copy to one of Forrestal's assistants) summarizing some comments by the aforementioned Dewey Short to the House Armed Services Committee in executive session. "Mr. Short, an ardent opponent of UMT, stated that his views on UMT have not been altered by his trip to Europe," Nunn reported. Some three months later, Nunn filed a similar memorandum on a closed hearing on UMT held by the Senate Armed Services Committee. With only a single exception, "all members present were desirous of delaying action on this measure but without taking the definitive step of disapproving it." The view of the committee was that "UMT will not get out of the Rules Committee of the House," hence the reluctance of its members to consider it: "Why . . . waste the time of the Committee on hearings on a measure which is not going to succeed?"[63]

James Forrestal, too, recognized that the House Rules Committee had the decisive voice in determining the fate of UMT. From a telephone conversation with Chan Gurney, chairman of the Senate Armed Services Committee, he learned in November 1947 that the outlook was "not good for consideration of Universal Military Training in this Session. In fact," said Gurney, his colleagues had "a distinct feeling that the Senate put through the Unification Bill [National Security Act] this last year, and that the House obligated itself to handle Universal Military Training and they [the House] should go through with passing the U.M.T. Bill before the Senate takes it up." Gurney's committee, it transpired, had voted unanimously to query the House Armed Services Committee "and find out what their procedure would be" before commencing its own discussions of UMT. Three months later, the situation was unchanged. An internal memorandum circulated in the Department of Defense on February 18, 1948, noted that "the Senate Armed Services Committee in executive session yesterday considered U.M.T., took no action, but agreed to consider the matter again. . . . It was indicated that progress of the legislation in the House would have a bearing on action by the Senate Committee." Thus, by the time Forrestal wrote Truman on February 27 that "the real battleground is the House and if the [UMT] bill can be gotten out of the Rules Committee there I am confident we could muster sufficient support to begin hearings in the Senate," the secretary knew full well that this was a very large *if* indeed. On the basis of his conversations with several people "high in the House Republican hierarchy," William S. White of the *New York Times* was able to state that "it could be taken for granted that UMT would not emerge from the Rules Committee" in 1948. It defies belief to suppose that someone as well-connected to legislators and journalists alike as Forrestal—and someone who also had at his disposal information obtained by the Congressional liaison staffs of each of the three armed services—was ignorant of how matters stood until he read about it in the newspapers.[64]

Within the administration—or maybe even the nation at large—no one gave the impression of being a more ardent proponent of UMT than the secretary of state. But even he could not have helped realizing that in 1948, this cause was a lost one. Early in March, Charles E. Bohlen, the department's counselor, passed on to his superior the view of the Senate minority leader that "there was practically no chance of [UMT's] going through; . . . the sentiment in the Senate was not basically favorable to the idea for a number of reasons. . . . there was not much that could be done to change this sentiment short of some outbreak of hostilities abroad or something of that nature." And that was the *Senate,* which was, at least by comparison with the House, relatively well-disposed to UMT. Marshall received similar news from the another State Department source one week later. "The best information available to the [Policy] Planning Staff is that the prospects are poor for enactment of the UMT legislation this year, even with the weight of your prestige behind it."[65]

Truman himself, moreover, must also have been aware of the long odds against UMT's enactment. "Mr. Truman used to go up, oh, at least once a month and have lunch up on the Hill with [minority leader] Sam Rayburn and the House people, or over with the Senate. Les Biffle [secretary of the senate and the administration's liaison with Senate Democrats] had a dining room there where he invited Senators in to visit with over lunch. Those were very effective trips." The words are those of Secretary of the Treasury John Snyder, a fellow Missourian and the person closest to Truman in the administration. They make it apparent that the president was fully informed about what was taking place "up on the Hill." And in the unlikely event that he felt in need of more information about UMT's chances in the 80th Congress (or anything else), all he had to do was ask.[66]

Even before Truman delivered his two St. Patrick's Day addresses, then, he and his assistants surely understood that UMT was a doomed proposition. Contrary to what the traditional interpretation would have us believe, however, this fact inspired little mourning within the administration—even on the part of the armed services. As early as mid-March of 1948, Secretary of the Army Kenneth Royall could write to James Forrestal, "Two of the considerations which appeal to me about Selective Service are: 1. It will provide additional readiness over the next 18 month period, which UMT could not do. 2. It would utilize present installations, equipment and training personnel without necessity of a new organization and new procedure." Hence Royall's recommendation to the secretary of defense was that "both systems should be requested. I recognize, however, that there is a possibility that if this were done, Congress might enact Selective Service and reject UMT." If forced to choose, the army, it was clear, awarded pride of place to the former; universal military training it could live without.[67]

The army and the secretary of defense rationalized their abandonment of UMT by maintaining, as Forrestal did in the following colloquy with Democratic Senator Millard Tydings of Maryland, that ultimately, come the millennium, UMT would supplant the draft:

> *Secretary Forrestal: That is our proposal, that UMT is a successor to the Selective Service and avoids the continuance of it.*
>
> *Senator Tydings: You are going to have Selective Service temporarily, and UMT to absorb it when the draft goes out?*
>
> *Secretary Forrestal: Yes.*

To be interpreted correctly, however, this statement should be viewed in light of Forrestal's comment later in the same hearing of the Senate Armed Services

Committee: "I think the tensions we are in are not impermanent; I think that they are permanent." One would not have been well advised, in other words, to hold one's breath while awaiting the "absorption" of selective service by UMT.[68]

Already by March 1948 if not before, this had become the army's official position on UMT. The Department of Defense "should advocate the passage of Universal Military Training . . . as a matter of the first priority," Chief of Staff Omar Bradley wrote to the secretary of the army later in the year. But Bradley took pains to add in the very next sentence, "The legislation should provide for implementation of the UMT program, however, at such time as the world situation permits termination of Selective Service." Just as soon as the lion lies down with the lamb—such was the meaning, in the general's lexicon, of "first priority."[69] Other parts of the national security bureaucracy had a similar outlook. In attempting to persuade Marshall to support inauguration of a peacetime draft over UMT, for example, the State Department Policy Planning Staff pointed out that "the informal opinion of members of the National Security Council Staff" was that "the best way to attain . . . immediate strengthening of our military position is through measures such as Selective Service." The Joint Chiefs of Staff, for their part, agreed, damning UMT indirectly with faint praise. "Some form of *compulsory military training* is essential," they instructed the secretary of defense on March 10, and while this fact did "not exclude the desirability of Universal Military Training" per se, it was "only from the long-range point of view that initiation of such training will be useful."[70]

If, during and after the war scare, the army leadership was at least willing to feign that it still favored UMT in theory, the air force was loath to engage in even that degree of pretense. Thus, although Secretary of the Air Force W. Stuart Symington repeatedly protested that, as he wrote Truman on March 29, 1948, "the Air Force, including [Chief of Staff] General [Carl] Spaatz and myself, has not only been backing, but has been working for, your policies on Universal Military Training and Selective Service," his notion of support was an example of casuistry at its best. When pressed on the point, the air force fell back on a passage from the May 1947 report of the President's Advisory Commission on Universal Training (the Compton Report), which said, among other things, "If the introduction of universal training should have . . . an indirect effect of weakening, rather than strengthening, the other elements of our national security, then our Commission is of the firm opinion that the adoption of universal training would be a mistake and would diminish, rather than increase, our national security." From there it was a very short leap to the conclusion that funds spent on UMT were funds that could not be devoted to increasing the size of the air force. Hence it did not take much effort for Symington and the air force high command to convince themselves that adoption of such a program would indeed have the "indirect effect" mentioned by the authors of the Compton Report.[71] With friends like these "backing" and "working for" it, UMT needed no enemies.

In actuality, by taking the position on UMT that he did, Symington was simply upholding the pledge he had made to Army Air Force Commanding General Carl Spaatz on assuming office as under secretary of war for air. "Upon joining up," Symington stated in an oral history interview, "I said to Spaatz, 'There are two things I would like to do. One, give you all . . . the benefit of any business experience I've had. . . . The other: you and your staff decide what we should have from the Congress in the way of an Air Force. Then I will try to sell that to Judge Patterson [then Secretary of War Robert Patterson] and the Bureau of the Budget and the President and the Congress.'" The Air Board—a kind of air force steering committee comprised of the service's highest-ranking officers—had decided at its meeting early in January 1948 to work against UMT; Symington, if he were to be faithful to his word, had no choice but to go along.[72]

It is most enlightening to follow the discussion, captured in the verbatim minutes of the Air Board's meeting on January 6 and 7, 1948, as its members hammer out a policy on UMT. Although, by the end of the meeting, air force hostility to UMT would to a large extent revolve around cost and budgetary considerations, the first—and surely the most truculent and persistent—arguments uttered against it were based on altogether different reasons. As envisioned by its authors, the administration's UMT program would require each service to accept a cross-section of those who wished to enlist after completing a six-month course of training. At the first day of the Air Board meeting, this feature at once excited the wrath of General George C. Kenney, the chief of the Strategic Air Command, who repeatedly protested: "I don't want to spend $59,000 on training a half-wit. . . . A half-wit isn't any use to us." "Have we lowered the standards so that a half-wit can get in?" "Tell me where is the place for this moron?" "What machinery is set up in keeping a half-wit from being in the active Air Force or the Reserve?" And so forth.[73]

Before a decision could be reached, another matter intervened and the board took no action on UMT; but when the meeting later returned to that subject, General Kenney immediately resumed the offensive:

> I suggest that the Board go on record: That we are not interested in and are opposed to wasting any time on anyone who doesn't meet the intelligence standard now required to man the Air Force. Because this business of shoving them off into some miscellaneous pool is just going to result in this enlisted reserve pool . . . being composed of a lot of morons. . . . Let somebody else have these

> halfwits. . . . You don't want halfwits [in the Air Force]. . . . I would rather have 100 smart ones than a million halfwits.

Whether through sheer tenacity or because his fellow officers shared his antipathies (or both), Kenney succeeded in defining the terms in which this aspect of the issue was debated. Thus, as the members of the Air Board were drafting the final version of their recommendations to the chief of staff, Major General Muir S. Fairchild, urging support for Kenney's views, asserted that there was "no point in the Air Force training a group of morons and halfwits which we can't use, and which do not even meet our enlistment standards." Dissent from this position was minimal and perfunctory; metaphorically and otherwise, the general himself enjoyed the last word: "You know we talk about a budget where we make better systems, but any of these factors will tell you that you don't do anything with a moron (laughter)."[74]

Yet Kenney's elegant rhetoric alone might not have convinced the Air Board to reject UMT had it not also been for the fact that, if adopted, such a program would be competing with the air force for the same funds. The first person to advance this observation was Lieutenant General Jimmy Doolittle, who noted, during the second session on UMT, that "because the cost of Military Training will certainly be a part of the military budget," initiation of UMT would "undoubtedly leave less money for the Services, less money for the Air Force." "It seems to me," he told the meeting, "that this is a very sound basis for this Board to go on: That the Air Force in-being is a primary agency of national security, and that that should be adequate for the 70 Group Program . . . ; and that no other expenditure should interfere with them."

Doolittle's thesis was quickly endorsed by several of his fellow officers, including Lieutenant General John K. Cannon ("UMT will be a liability not an asset to an Air Force in-being"), Secretary-General of the Air Board Major General Hugh J. Knerr (who thought UMT "a foolish waste of time and money") and Major General Follett Bradley ("That seems to be our policy— . . . an Air Force in-being, and nothing should be permitted to interfere with that"). But before this sentiment could be translated into a statement of policy, Major General Edward P. Curtis pointed out a potential problem: "We can't take the position that just because a thing is no good for the Air Force . . . , we are opposed to Universal Training." No sooner had Curtis spoken, however, than who should spring forth but Oliver P. Echols, the president of the Aircraft Industries Association, with a timely rationalization that saved the day:

> I think the Compton Board that made the report on the UMT put the Air Force in-being ahead of the UMT. . . . When they made this

> report, they had in mind that in no way would this UMT interfere with the Air Force in-being. It seems you can use that as a basis within your Services and to the Congress as a very effective argument.

How curious that it should be General Echols who explained how the air force could prevent Pentagon funds from being diverted to UMT. One wonders whether it occurred to some members of the Air Board that if the budget of the air force were diminished by spending for UMT, there would be that much less money available for the purchase of new airplanes. Did anyone reflect that such a turn of events might be the source of some, shall we say, dismay among the general's employers? Whatever may be the answers to these questions, it was precisely Echols's "very effective argument" that, as we saw above, Stuart Symington later invoked to defend his and the air force's failure to support UMT. One more time had Oliver Echols intervened as policy was being made; one more time had he been able to shape the outcome to the needs of the aircraft industry.[75]

The army was indifferent to UMT, the National Security Council and the State Department Policy Planning Staff inveighed against the program, the navy historically had refused to support it (I furnish evidence for this assertion below) and the air force barely bothered to disguise its disdain for it—but what of the secretary of state and the president? We saw in the preceding chapter that over the weekend of March 20–21, it became clear that enactment of the European Recovery Program in the form sought by the administration was assured. Thereafter, Marshall simply let the issue drop; so far as I have been able to determine, his testimony in a closed session of the Senate Armed Services Committee on March 23 was the last time during this period that he advocated UMT in a public setting. Marshall's papers do not contain any material that would allow one to determine whether his silence after March 22 reflected a loss of interest, a conviction that the effort was a hopeless one—or the discarding of a tactic that for his purposes was no longer necessary.

With respect to Truman himself, we have the typical paucity of evidence; apart from official pronouncements, there is little from the war-scare period to indicate his position on the issue. By the beginning of the next year, however, it had become quite unmistakable that his allegiance to UMT extended no further than lip service. The election of 1948 returned control of Congress to the Democrats; had Truman been truly concerned to achieve adoption of a UMT program, he would then have been free to urge it without having to concern himself about Republican opposition. It is therefore revealing that the sole reference to the subject in his 1949 State of the Union message consisted of nothing more than a single passing mention—"Universal training is essential to the security of the United States"—near the end. "Apparently Mr. Truman likes merely to stay on the record" was Doris Fleeson's pithy comment in the *Washington Star*.[76]

Even more instructive is Truman's behavior in the following year, when his actions alone *prevented* Congress from writing a UMT program into law. This time, ironically, the situation was reversed: a Congress in the hands of the president's own party eager to pass UMT, while the president himself proceeded to concoct a series of excuses—"no new programs [should be allowed to] interfere with . . . building up manpower in the Korean crisis," "training facilities are not immediately available," and the like—aimed at rebuffing any such attempt. Finally, faced with Truman's adamant unwillingness to budge, Congress in 1950 backed down and once again defeated UMT. In criticizing the president's decision, the writer of an editorial in the *New York Times* trenchantly observed that

> the decision to shelve U.M.T. at this session was reluctantly taken by the Senate Armed Services Committee twenty-four hours after Mr. Truman had made the suggestion. While reiterating his support [!] for U.M.T., the President pointed out that the program "could not possibly be put into effect at once" because of the demands it would make on trained manpower and on installations sorely needed for the Korean war. This is, of course, true; but there was no intention to put U.M.T. into effect at the present time. It is generally accepted that establishment of a training program of this sort would have to await the conclusion of current hostilities.

The verdict is inescapable: the Truman administration no longer wanted UMT—then or at any time in the future.[77]

In August 1950, Truman declared his active, open rejection of UMT. In 1949, he had done next to nothing to encourage its passage. Why, therefore, suppose that he favored such a program the previous year? If we concede that his administration *claimed* to be crusading for UMT during the war scare of 1948, that does not mean we are under any obligation to assume that rhetoric and reality necessarily coincided. UMT, when Truman once more proposed it in March 1948, was an exceedingly dead horse—for that matter, it had been one ever since he sent UMT legislation to Congress in mid-1947, if not before—and the evidence that I set forth above suggests that everyone of consequence in the administration recognized the situation for what it was.

But if that is so, then why—to return to the second of the two questions that I posed at the outset of this section—did the Truman administration even bother to introduce UMT legislation at all? The answer is that although UMT may have been a dead horse, even dead horses sometimes have their uses. Here, newspaper accounts offer us a clue. Two days after Truman's speeches of March 17, 1948, calling for passage of the Marshall Plan, a selective service bill and UMT, the *New York Times* noted "speculation in Congress that the President might get one of his [military] programs through, but not both." Two days after that, a poll taken by the Associated Press similarly reported that "a majority of Senators remain to be convinced that Congress should write into law President Truman's proposals for universal military training and revival of the draft. . . . Many said they would support one, but not both, of the proposals."[78]

Congressional Republicans, particularly in the House, might never consent to swallow UMT. But could they afford to be seen, in an election year, as utterly unwilling to enact any of the administration's legislation when the President and the Secretary of State were loudly proclaiming that the nation stood on the brink of World War III? I contend that they could not. Those at the top of the Truman administration—Truman himself, Marshall, Forrestal, the service secretaries and certainly Clark Clifford—understood that the Republicans were vulnerable in this regard, and hastened to take advantage of that fact to make sure that Congress gave them the programs they desired. "Dear Bernie," Forrestal wrote to Bernard M. Baruch on March 31, 1948, "On our best information, here is a list of the people in the Senate who are opposed either to Universal Military Training or Selective Service. You will note that there is only one who is against both." The Republicans are unwilling to approve a UMT program? Very well, then—let them pass the Marshall Plan, a peacetime draft and an expanded budget for the military and the airplane industry instead. The administration left Republican legislators in no uncertainty whatsoever about the alternatives open to them. "They told us they must have UMT or a return of the draft," said the ranking Republican on the Senate Armed Services Committee to a reporter following a meeting with Forrestal, the Service Secretaries and the Joint Chiefs of Staff on March 8. The next month Forrestal, characteristically prolix, again spelled out the terms of the trade-off for the benefit of the same committee: "Non-enactment of U.M.T. at this time may make it necessary to maintain our regular forces, for an indefinite period, at a strength which can be reached only through Selective Service."[79]

In reality, the Republicans themselves had ensured that they would have little choice once push came to shove on this issue. In opting to reject Truman's UMT proposals—a decision that House Republicans appear to have taken almost instinctively—they found that they had adroitly marched themselves directly into the trap the administration had slyly set for them. The Republicans might be able to get away with one such rejection; but they could not possibly turn down all of the president's proposals without making themselves appear narrowly, selfishly partisan, so obstructionist and irresponsible that they would choose to jeopardize the nation's security rather than cooperate with the president in an alleged moment of crisis. For a political party seeking to regain the White House after an absence of 16 years, the risk that it might be viewed by the electorate in such a negative light was simply too great to take. So much became apparent as early as March 8, when the Senate Armed Services Committee finally voted to hold hearings on UMT. According to the *New York Times*'s account, "A factor in the decision . . . , it was said in responsible quarters," was the fear that "the whole Congress might be accused of dodging a controversial issue because a single committee (House Rules Committee) was blocking it." As it was no secret that "the whole Congress" was controlled by the Republicans, the political implications of this situation were too obvious to have to be spelled out in so many words.[80]

To grasp just how the Truman administration went about using UMT to assure adoption of the remainder of its military and diplomatic agenda, it is necessary to scrutinize the activities of Secretary of Defense Forrestal with particular care, for it was he who, more than anyone else, implemented such a strategy. At the Cabinet meeting on January 31, 1948, Forrestal learned from Truman that the president "wanted me to head up the handling of UMT for him."[81] It follows that if we wish to understand the administration's true stance on UMT, it is above all Forrestal on whom we must focus.

The first point to note in this connection is that Forrestal's initial attitude toward UMT faithfully mirrored that of the navy, which traditionally was hostile to the concept. "Before I took on this job," he told Senator Henry Cabot Lodge in November of 1947, "I was not sold on U.M.T., as from the Navy's viewpoint, it did not seem that U.M.T. was either necessary or would produce a trained Reserve Corps for the Navy." For that reason, the secretary wrote to Senator Leverett Saltonstall, he had "been very reluctant to come out as an ardent advocate of it unless there were very powerful reasons," but now "those reasons are emerging . . . out of the contemporary scene." Forrestal was more specific in his letter to Lodge. Although he "certainly [did] not feel that U.M.T. [was] the complete answer," it was "a step in the right direction" toward providing the armed services, "particularly the Army," with the enlisted personnel they desired. Having become "better acquainted with the over-all picture," he was now "convinced that U.M.T. is the best solution." "From the standpoint of the ground forces, . . . I am satisfied . . . it is absolutely necessary."[82]

The depth of this latter-day conversion, however, is open to question—especially if one keeps Forrestal's *actions,* as distinguished from his professions, clearly in sight. His support for UMT was obviously conditional in nature: if the "ground forces" could devise a more efficient means of filling their ranks, UMT would be neither "the best solution" nor "absolutely necessary." But, as I pointed out earlier, by March of 1948, it had become the army's position that selective service was preferable to UMT, and Secretary of the Army Royall therefore urged Forrestal to ask Congress for "both systems," despite the "possibility that if this were done, Congress might enact Selective Service and reject UMT." The fact that the army was willing to accept the defeat of UMT—which, I maintain, was a foregone conclusion in any case—as the price of obtaining selective service allowed Forrestal and the Truman administration a free hand to use the former as a means of extorting the latter from a decidedly unenthusiastic Congress. With the passage of selective service legislation, however, Forrestal had no further need to proclaim the virtues of UMT. His recommendations for the president's 1949 State of the Union speech, submitted in mid-November 1948—when a just-elected Truman could count on the support of a Democratic majority in Congress—tacitly conceded as much: "In view of the measures already in process," the adoption "of Universal Military Training is not an urgent requirement." Now commanding support neither from Truman nor Forrestal, the entire topic of UMT was, we have seen, relegated to a single sentence in the State of the Union message that Truman delivered the following January. Once the chances of its being passed went from nil to very good, a UMT program, it turned out, was not "absolutely necessary" after all.[83]

Like Secretary of State Marshall, who had attempted to use the specter of imminent war to frighten Congress and the public just enough to win approval of the European Recovery Plan, but not so much that the nation actually started to go to war, Forrestal sought to walk a narrow and slippery wire. On the one hand, he had to convince Republican politicians that the president was genuinely intent on obtaining a UMT program from Congress. On the other, he simultaneously had to intimate, without ever explicitly stating, that the administration was prepared to accept the defeat of UMT—but *only* on the condition that Congress enact all the other military and foreign policy legislation the administration had introduced. Here again, as with Marshall and the ERP, the talents of a master political manipulator were required. In order to have UMT serve its intended purpose, Forrestal first had to induce Congress to separate that measure from the selective service bill, then subtly encourage the Republicans to kill it. For UMT, as I have tried to make clear all along, was much more valuable to the administration dead than alive: if properly accomplished, its demise would essentially guarantee passage of the administration's remaining measures. Once the Republicans had indulged themselves by voting down UMT, they would be in need of "a justification for junking President Truman's proposed . . . program," in which case they would have no alternative but to support an "enlarged" Air Force and "a limited draft." Or such, at any rate, was the expectation and the plan.[84]

To make sure that a rejection of UMT would not also drag selective service down to defeat, Forrestal's first task was to convince Congress to debate the two measures separately. We can observe him at work on this part of his scheme during the weeks from mid-March through the end of April 1948. On March 19, he and Chan Gurney, chairman of the Senate Armed Services Committee, discussed how Congress should proceed with the UMT and selective service bills. Gurney's thinking was that his committee "might incorporate [the two] in one bill." To discourage this approach, Forrestal said that the administration's UMT proposal would be delayed by "all sorts of people who will want to have their finger in it," and that therefore, "dealing with it in two bites [that is, two bills] is going to be the thing we'll probably wind up doing." Two weeks later, he wrote to Walter G. Andrews, the chairman of the corresponding House committee, to suggest that legislation for UMT and the draft should not be taken up together: "It may be, therefore, that under the relevant circumstances the House Armed Services Committee would prefer to consider only the first Title of the attached Bill," that dealing with UMT.[85]

But in pursuing this complicated strategy, Forrestal was forced to send so many vague, contradictory and deliberately misleading signals that he ended by confusing, frustrating and, in certain instances, angering even those Republicans who were trying to cooperate with him. Thus, Senator Gurney informed the secretary on April 12, "It seems that Ham Andrews has just told Senator Saltonstall . . . that Andrews got the impression that universal military training and selective service could not be in operation simultaneously." "I can see where he may have derived that impression," Forrestal conceded. "I said that we need to put Selective Service in right now, and it would probably be a year before UMT got fully going. . . . I think . . . I'm to blame for leaving an impression, because I thought he was talking about if we planned to have UMT and Selective Service start right now, I said Selective Service was the thing we had to get immediately." But the members of Andrews's committee were not mollified by this convoluted explanation—if explanation it were—and on April 29 the chairman telephoned Forrestal in an effort to obtain some clarification. "Well, they want to know your position," he said at one point; at another, "Tell us whether you are for the bill or not, or whether you'd rather have UMT in it"; at a third, "What are you going to say about the Selective Service Bill? Are you for it or against it?"; and at a fourth, "What we want to know is what you think of this Selective Service Bill." But the essence of the administration's tactics, as Forrestal executed them, consisted of a refusal to be pinned down; that way, congressional Republicans could be kept in fear that if they rejected both UMT and selective service, Democrats would bombard them with accusations of leaving the nation's defense imperiled. Hence, to ensure that the Republicans would be unable to escape from this trap, Forrestal deftly sidestepped all attempts to commit him to an unambiguous position: "I'll say it's up to you gentlemen—you're holding the reins of legislation. . . . We must have something in order to make this military program effective and if we can't get anything but Selective Service—if we can't get anything but *your bill*—of course, we'll have to take it [emphasis added]."[86]

Members of the Senate, however, were less easily hoodwinked. At the closed hearings of the Senate Armed Services Committee on April 21 that I discussed in the final pages of chapter 4, several senators saw through Forrestal's tactics with sufficient clarity to charge him, as did Senator Richard B. Russell, with having betrayed both them and UMT:

> We hesitated as to whether we should take up the UMT ahead of the House, and finally after a great deal of prodding we did take up the UMT. . . . Some of us went out on a limb . . . and said we were for the UMT. . . . Then we get a message down here that the UMT is not enough, and we have got to have Selective Service. . . . Now we have a program . . . [for] a 66 group Air Force, and we have abandoned UMT. . . . Everyone knows that UMT is going to increase in cost, if you adopt it, to around $2 billion a year. But if you are going to hold your total budget at the figure that he has given us here and increase your airplane procurement as you go along, it is a manifest physical impossibility to get one man in UMT, it cannot be done.

Senator Russell was joined in the attack by Senator Millard Tydings of Maryland, who in response to Forrestal's statement, "We are not discarding UMT," countered, "I think that you are. I think that you gentlemen have got to come up here and fight for UMT or Congress is never going to adopt it. I think that if you come up and say, 'We would like to have it but we will settle for an Air Force or something else,' you will never get UMT or a damn thing." These accusations Forrestal made little effort to refute. Instead, he sought to sidetrack his senatorial critics by calling upon Army Chief of Staff General Omar Bradley, who (as we saw earlier) came to the secretary's aid by delivering a semi-intelligible paraphrase of Lucius Clay's telegram of March 5, 1948. (An all-purpose weapon, the Clay telegram could be pressed into service not only as a sword to vanquish one's opponents, but as a shield to deflect unwelcome inquiries as well.) In the long run, one suspects that the senators were neither placated nor fooled by such evasive maneuvers. But by then, there was little they could do. Their counterparts in the House had already taken the administration's bait and written *finis* to UMT. As a result, the administration would soon obtain exactly the program of military expansion—including more money for the aircraft industry—it had been seeking all along.[87]

But surely, some readers may be thinking, the administration could not have been *this* devious. For those who share this point of view (and perhaps also believe that it is Santa Claus who brings them presents on December 25), consider the following exchange between Secretary of the Treasury John Snyder and an oral history interviewer. The interviewer has asked Snyder—described by Margaret Truman as "one of his [Truman's] closest friends" and "his closest friend in the Cabinet"—if he favored a recommendation for reestablishing an excess-profits tax sent to Congress by the president on July 27, 1948.

> *Snyder: Well, I went on record as supporting that request. It was largely strategic and I felt that it would have a sobering influence, because we were trying to slow down an inflationary trend at that time and it would serve as at least a psychological warning to the Congress that we were in an inflationary atmosphere.*
>
> *Hess: Did you and Mr. Truman really think that you were going to get something of this nature through?*
>
> *Snyder: We were positive that we were not.*
>
> *Hess: Why was it put forward?*
>
> *Snyder: Just what I said.*
>
> *Hess: Just strategic?*
>
> *Snyder: Yes.*[88]

If the administration had few scruples about resorting to such "largely strategic" ruses on the one occasion, is there any earthly reason for thinking it had more on the other? Truman, Marshall, Forrestal and whoever else was in on the scheme easily could have told themselves that, as John Snyder might have phrased it, proposing UMT legislation would have "a sobering influence" and "serve as at least a psychological warning to the Congress that we are in a dangerous situation." The "danger," of course, was that unless the administration could outflank the Republicans, the latter might feel free to defeat the Marshall Plan, the draft, the military buildup, or any combination thereof. Brandishing UMT was the best means the administration could devise for seeing that this ghastly turn of events did not come to pass.

Interestingly enough, one contemporary observer thought he could detect the administration exploiting the sentiment against UMT in exactly this fashion. "I happen to know the U.M.T. appropriation was put on the bill at the last minute for trading purposes. I am yet, and still and always a 'Damn Yankee' and I am not for 'blind swaps,'" Representative Charles A. Plumley of Vermont wrote to Stuart Symington in February 1949, denouncing what he regarded as an attempt to use Republican aversion to UMT in order to get money for the administration's other military measures. "I see no reason why U.M.T. should have to again be given a black eye—deliberately (with the knowledge and acquiescence of the President (concealed). . .) to the possible destruction of the program for U.M.T.," he protested. His passion for universal training might overwhelm the clarity of his syntax, but no one could accuse Plumley of lacking insight into the political wiles of the administration.[89]

The hypothesis that the Truman administration introduced UMT legislation not as an end in itself, but rather as a means to obtain a peacetime draft, an across-the-board military buildup and the resuscitation of the aircraft industry, has the additional virtue of explaining an otherwise inexplicable fact. It has long been well known that if any one action destroyed what little chance there was for adoption of UMT, it was Stuart Symington's testimony before the Senate Armed Services Committee in closed session on April 7. At these hearings, we saw in the first part of this chapter, Symington argued that a "fast-expanding Air Force of seventy combat groups . . . would be 'better understood by Russia' than a UMT designed to train 18-year-old youths as future reserves," and that, "if it comes to the question of what we think is best for the country, we think it is better to have a 70 group . . . program than it is to have a Universal Military Training program."[90] The result was that Congress promptly appropriated an additional $822 million for a 70-group air force—an expenditure that, given existing budget constraints, virtually guaranteed the rejection of UMT. Yet despite this act of seemingly blatant insubordination, Truman refused to inflict on Symington anything more severe than a slight reproof.

Presidents do not usually react with equanimity at the sight of their appointees destroying with a few minutes of testimony any chance of obtaining legislation they have been seeking for years; and Truman in particular was someone who laid great emphasis on personal loyalty in those who served him. Had the president truly placed a high value on enactment of UMT, would he not have been irate at Symington's conduct? If such was the case, however, there is no sign of it in the documents I have seen (and that includes every single item in Symington's correspondence at the Harry S. Truman Library). Quite the contrary. Given Truman's penchant for blunt language, his reaction to Symington's conduct was astonishingly mild. In responding, for example, to one of the secretary's incessant complaints that the Navy was receiving too much money for airplanes and the air force too little,[91] Truman merely allowed himself to comment in passing that "the opposition of the Air contingent to universal training is an exceedingly short-sighted approach because even the aviators ought to have the fundamentals of discipline if we are going to have an effective Force."[92]

Symington's readiness to disparage the worth of UMT, even if in so doing he caused the demise of what was widely thought to be an important aspect of the administration's program, led reporters at one point to ask Truman if he planned to "spank" his air force secretary. Some members of Forrestal's staff added their voices to the chorus by proposing chastisement of a different sort—an explicit repudiation by the president of Symington's testimony in the Senate.[93] Far from acting on these suggestions, however, Truman not only refused to punish his unruly assistant, but actually appointed him to two other positions (chairman of the National Security Resources Board in 1950, administrator of the Reconstruction Finance Corporation in 1951) after Symington himself insisted on resigning his air force post. Part of the reason for Truman's indulgence of Symington, of course, may have been the friendship between the two;[94] but part may also have derived from the fact that Truman was not genuinely concerned to obtain UMT legislation from Congress in the first place. Once it became evident that the threats to the Marshall Plan had been overcome and that the Republicans would be forced to accept selective service legislation and a military buildup as the price for their rejection of UMT, the administration's purported campaign for UMT had served its purpose. Thus, when Robert B. Landry, the White House air aide, reported to the president that Symington was concerned about the furor his testimony on UMT had caused, Truman merely "laughed and said, 'You tell Stu to keep his mouth shut, and this will quiet down.'" If his poker-playing chum "Stu" hacked at UMT in order to get more money for the air force by defeating a measure that its topmost officers abhorred, Truman evidently cared so little about "his" program that his sole response was to chuckle and look the other way.[95]

Confronted with the daunting task of trying to induce a Congress controlled by the opposition to approve an expensive and inflationary set of policies that commanded little popular support—and in some instances engendered considerable hostility—Harry Truman in March 1948 was willing to use virtually any expedient that came to hand. Contriving a war scare with the Soviet Union, as we have seen repeatedly, was one; holding the threat of UMT over the head of Congress was, I believe, another. If this analysis is correct, is the notion that from the very start Stuart Symington was in on the plot to make UMT a sacrificial lamb too fanciful to be entertained? Even if Truman himself did not tell him, Symington could have learned of the administration's little secret just as easily from such mutual Missouri cronies as John Snyder or Clark Clifford, both of whom were close to the air force secretary and privy as well to many of the president's most intimate thoughts (witness Snyder's remarks above in this connection). Such an interpretation would explain not only why Symington was not penalized by Truman for encouraging Congress to spend money on military airplanes at the expense of UMT, but also why he had the audacity to pursue this tack in the first place. Granted that we do not yet have, and may never find, a document that puts the matter this baldly, we should nonetheless keep in mind the point made by James Thomson: Some of the most important presidential decisions are reached "behind closed doors, with no record."[96] In cases such as this, where absolute certitude does not appear to be a possibility, circumstantial evidence and reasonable plausibility may allow us to reach a tenable conclusion nonetheless.

7.

A Worm in the Apple: The Peace Scare of May 1948

Our success . . . will bring with it the added danger that Congress and public may be lulled into erroneous belief that battle is won and we can relax and reap the fruits of victory. . . . If Kremlin temporarily assumes defensive, it is more important than ever to follow through vigorously by building up our own strength . . . . It is vital that the public be constantly reminded.

—Walter Bedell Smith, U.S. Ambassador to the Soviet Union, to the Secretary of State, April 22, 1948[1]

I said the most dangerous spot is our own country because the people are so eager for peace and have such a distaste for war that they will grasp for any sign of a solution of a problem that has had them deeply worried. I said we should begin immediately to see to it that the country is not lulled into any illusory sense that the current [Soviet] proposal would constitute a final solution.

—James V. Forrestal, Breakfast with General [Lucius D.] Clay —The Berlin Situation, October 21, 1948[2]

> **Uncertainty over the outcome of prolonged diplomatic negotiations between Washington and Russia . . . weighs heavily as a psychological factor contributing to skepticism toward shares of airplane manufacturers. . . . It is understood that anything approaching an amicable understanding would bring concerted demands for retrenchment in armament appropriations.**
>
> —J. C. Clifford, "Confused Prospects for Aircrafts," *The Magazine of Wall Street,* July 2, 1949[3]

> **Soviet "war scare" has not been without advantages to USA as it has been factor in evoking public support for necessary defense and aid measures.**
>
> —Walter Bedell Smith, U.S. Ambassador to the Soviet Union, to the Secretary of State, December 23, 1948[4]

A TRIUMPH TARNISHED: THE PEACE SCARE OF MAY 1948

The war scare begat the peace scare.

The English language is rich in metaphors—opening Pandora's box, playing with fire, sowing the wind, fools rushing in, and the like—that describe individuals who, through their failure to ponder sufficiently the consequences of their actions, mire themselves in painful situations of their own making. All of these are apropos, to one degree or another, with respect to what might be called, by analogy with the earlier war scare, the peace scare of May 1948. When, with no warning whatsoever, a Soviet radio broadcast on May 11 announced that Moscow had accepted a U.S. proposal for "a discussion and settlement of differences existing between us," no doubt it seemed that this development had materialized out of thin air.[5] In reality, however, this peace scare was a direct outgrowth of the earlier war scare. Although it lasted but a matter of days, by the time it was over, it had succeeded in marring the succession of victories that the White House had achieved during the previous two months as well as in renewing doubts about the administration's competence at the conduct of foreign policy.

Washington's incessant attempts to create the impression, during March 1948, that the U.S.S.R. was about to plunge the world into war inspired misgivings throughout the ranks of the State Department, particularly with respect to how the Soviets would perceive—and react to—this inflammatory language. For all its fomenting of war hysteria, the administration, as I sought to demonstrate in discussing U.S.-Soviet trade relations in chapter 5, did not wish to exacerbate relations with the U.S.S.R. Doing so promised to have only unwelcome consequences. At the minimum, a worsening of relations threatened to disrupt East-West commerce, which in turn jeopardized the success of the Marshall Plan by slowing Western European economic recovery. If, moreover, the Soviets were to conclude from all the administration's bellicose blather that war was indeed in the offing, the Marshall Plan would be an early casualty of the fighting—Congress would certainly compel the abandonment of foreign aid programs to concentrate on military measures. It was essential, therefore, that one way or another, Washington provide the Soviets with reassurances about U.S. intentions.

In his memoirs, George Kennan, the director of the State Department Policy Planning Staff, claimed that he and Charles Bohlen, the department's counselor, initiated the idea "for some conciliatory gesture on the part of this government—some gesture making it clear that our purpose was not to humiliate the Soviet government or to press it against a closed door—that we were entirely willing to talk over our problems at any time." Accordingly, the two of them "recommended to General Marshall that a statement along these lines be made to the Soviet government," and Marshall accepted the suggestion. Kennan's account notwithstanding, the first mention of this idea that I have discovered came from neither him nor Bohlen, but from John Paton Davies, a member of the Policy Planning Staff. In a memorandum of March 19, 1948—written at a moment when the war scare was still hurtling down the tracks at full throttle—Davies proposed the essence of the ostensibly "conciliatory gesture" that the department would later deliver to the Soviet leadership. The first part of such a message, he said, should "convey directly to Stalin the gravity with which we view present Soviet policy and our determination to prevent further Soviet expansion in Europe and the Near East." Once this point had been established, Stalin then could be told "that the door is always open; that if he or Molotov wishes to talk with the President, they will be received in Washington and that if either he or Molotov do not wish to leave Moscow that the American Ambassador is always available as a channel of communications with the President."[6]

Questions of authorship aside, there was little chance that such a proposal such as Davies's would, or could, be put into effect so long as the war scare was raging unchecked. Once the administration began winding down the scare, however, the notion of sending a soothing message to the Soviets again came to the fore, gradually working its way through the bureaucracy until, late in April, it reached the secretary of state and the president. By prior arrangement with Truman, Under Secretary of State Robert A. Lovett (the acting secretary in the absence of Marshall) presented the idea at the Cabinet meeting of April 23, 1948. In his diary, James Forrestal recorded Lovett's view that Soviet policy with respect to the U.S. was "of a dual nature as of this moment: (1) constant probing to find out the solidity of our intent; and (2) a reflection of their own fear of a preventive or aggressive war on our part." Lovett's surmise was that the Soviets were responding to "the overexcitable statements, some by military people, on a preventive war, and the activities of Henry Wallace and his proposal that the President sit down with Stalin and make a world agreement." A similar explanation came from the pen of *New York Times* journalist James Reston once the peace scare had erupted. The secretary of state, Reston stated, was "said to have felt—and certainly his advisers have felt—that the post-Czechoslovak crisis was being carried too far here and that it was time to settle down a bit." It would brand one a churl lacking all refinement and decorum, I suppose, to remark that it was precisely the repeated efforts of the president, the secretary of state and the secretary of defense during March that ensured the "crisis" would be "carried too far"; that it was their speeches, press conferences and congressional testimony that had thrown open the gate to "overexcitable statements . . . by military people on a preventive war," giving this crackpot notion a legitimacy it had lacked hitherto.[7]

In any event, on April 23 Lovett read to the Cabinet a telegram that the State Department planned to send to Ambassador Smith in Moscow for his comments. It advanced much the same points as John Paton Davies's memorandum of mid-March—namely, an assertion of "the determination of this country to insist on its rights in Berlin and elsewhere and to resist further aggression against free states," coupled with "an assurance to the Soviet Union that this country has no imperialistic or expansionistic programs or plans; that it seeks peace with the Soviet Union and does not want war or disturbances which might lead to war."[8]

In its final form, as delivered by Ambassador Smith to Soviet Foreign Minister Vyacheslav M. Molotov on May 4, this second portion of the U.S. note stated that Washington hoped "to make it unmistakably clear that the United States has no hostile or aggressive designs whatever with respect to the Soviet Union," and that "assertions to the contrary are falsehoods" arising from "complete misunderstanding or malicious motives." Furthermore, although the "present state of United States–Soviet relations is a source of grievous disappointment to the American people and to the United States Government"—the responsibility for which, naturally, lay entirely with "the pressure of Soviet and world Communist policy"—nevertheless, the United States still did "not despair . . . of a turn of events which will permit us to find the road to a decent and reasonable relationship between our two countries, with a fundamental relaxation of . . . tensions." Immediately thereafter came the phrase around which the entire peace scare would soon revolve: "As far as the United States is concerned, the door is always wide open for full discussion and the composing of our differences."[9]

In Walter Bedell Smith's opinion, the U.S. note was "a statement for the record." The Soviets, however, seem to have believed otherwise—or at least acted as though they did. Their response had two parts—one sent formally through diplomatic channels, one made publicly through the media. The former consisted of a reply to the U.S. note of May 4, handed to Smith by Molotov on May 9. Prior to receiving it, the U.S. ambassador had thought that the Soviet rejoinder "might lead up to a suggestion for another CFM [meeting of the Council of Foreign Ministers]," but it did not. "They are not ready to talk yet," he concluded.[10]

But perhaps they were. The opening paragraph of the formal Soviet note could certainly be so construed: "The Soviet Government shares the desire, expressed in this statement by the Government of the USA, to better these relations, *and is in agreement with the proposal to proceed with this aim towards a discussion and settlement of the difference existing between us* [emphasis added]." Although, to be sure, this sentence advocates no specific measures—the language of diplomacy being renowned neither for crystalline clarity nor the absence of ambiguity—what it seems to say is that in the interest of improving relations, the Soviets have accepted a U.S. proposal to discuss and settle outstanding differences. Be that as it may, in transmitting the Soviet reply to Washington, Smith made no mention of this sentence. Either the ambassador did not deem it worthy of comment or else its possible implications escaped his attention. To him, the Soviet message was "simply our statement in reverse."[11]

The foregoing passage from the formal Soviet reply to the U.S. note is particularly significant, however, because it figures so heavily in Moscow's second, public response. On May 10, the same day Smith dispatched an account of his conversation with Molotov to the State Department, the Soviets released to the media an edited version of the U.S. note, together with a declaration that was very nearly a verbatim restatement of their private reply: "The Soviet Government adopts a positive attitude toward the wishes of the United States Government, expressed in that statement, to improve these relations, and it is in agreement with the proposal to begin, in this connection, a discussion and settlement of the differences existing between us."[12] Coincidentally, on May 12 at New York's Madison Square Garden, Henry Wallace addressed the first large rally in his campaign for president as the candidate of the Progressive Party—

and he used the opportunity created by news of this diplomatic exchange to good effect. Proclaiming that the U.S. and Soviet notes "represent great hopes to those of us who have consistently maintained that peace is possible," Wallace read to his audience "An Open Letter to Premier Stalin" that called on both the United States and the U.S.S.R. to "take immediate action to end the cold war." Only in this way, he asserted, could humanity achieve "the Century of Peace which the Century of the Common Man demands." The Smith and Molotov notes had unlocked "the door to negotiations," but that was only a beginning. This initial step "must be followed by . . . an open, fully reported meeting of representatives of . . . the United States and the Soviet Union." The peace scare was at hand.[13]

By its reckless recourse to the language of war impending, the Truman administration had trapped itself in a position where it had little choice but to attempt to repair the damage done to relations with the U.S.S.R.; now it was about to harvest some of the unanticipated, but by no means undeserved, fruits of its tactics during March. In making public Smith's note of May 4, the Soviets put the administration in an extremely awkward position, and Wallace's speech two days later only compounded its distress. On the one hand, precisely because the administration had done so much to encourage fears of war, the possibility that peace might still be attainable kindled "the immediate, hopeful and entirely natural enthusiasm of people all over the world for any move that might conceivably lessen the tension between Moscow and Washington."[14] On the other, however, the governments of the Western European nations, France and England especially, were infuriated at the notion that the United States might be going over their heads to make a bilateral deal with the Soviets for the future of the Continent. Caught in this dilemma, the administration unhesitatingly chose to appease its closest allies by blasting any chance for a rapprochement between East and West.[15]

To counter the Soviet release of the Smith-Molotov exchange, therefore, the administration quickly fired off a series of statements to the effect that there had been no change in its policy, that Smith's note had not been intended as a proposal to discuss, much less resolve, outstanding issues, that détente was no closer than it had been before, and so on. Truman himself immediately issued one such statement on May 11; in a press conference on the following day, Marshall, in the words of James Reston, "threw more cold water . . . on the Soviet proposal for a Untied States–Russian 'peace' conference" (observe Reston's use of quotation marks around the word *peace*); and the day after that, Truman administered the coup de grace by telling reporters "that the recent exchange of views with Russia had not increased his hopes for peace." Simultaneously, Washington moved to convince the French and the British that their fears of secret U.S. negotiations with the Soviets were baseless.[16] And that, apparently, was that—no peace conference, no settlement. By the time that Stalin, on May 17, released a favorable reply to Wallace's "Open Letter" of the 12th, it was already too late to revive hopes for an amelioration of the Cold War.[17]

In moving to dispel the threat of peace, however, the administration left itself open to renewed charges that its policies with respect to the Soviet Union were inept, ill-conceived and inflexible. One of the "criticisms . . . being made here," James Reston reported in the *New York Times,* was that "the reaction of the State Department and the White House to the Soviet maneuver was too negative." Not only were "influential members of Congress . . . in touch with Under Secretary of State Robert Lovett" to press for a more affirmative response to the Soviets, but at the May 12 meeting of the Senate Foreign Relations Committee, "so great was the criticism . . . of the way in which the State Department had handled the Soviet reply that the regular order of business had to be suspended." For its decision to whip up a war scare, the administration was thus compelled to pay a substantial price: first, by providing the Soviets with raw material for an embarrassing peace scare; and then by electing, once that new scare was under way, to calm the fears of the Western Europeans through a categorical repudiation of negotiations with the U.S.S.R. Given this seemingly aimless stumbling to and fro, it was no wonder that James Reston concluded, "The last of this criticism of the State Department has not yet been heard."[18]

The war scare that began in March was astonishingly abbreviated, progressing from seed to blossom to death in a mere matter of weeks. But by comparison with the peace scare, which was over virtually in the blinking of an eye, it was as long-lived as Methuselah. What are we to make of the second scare? Why did the State Department send the Soviets a message that, as James Reston described it, "was imprecise and did invite conversations that the United States did not intend and was not prepared to meet"? Why did the Soviets choose to make the note and their reply to it public? And, last, why was the Truman administration so quick to reject the Soviet reading of the exchange as a prelude to a general "discussion and settlement of the differences existing between us"?[19]

Some of these questions are easier to answer than others. Any interpretation of the Soviet decision to publish an edited version of the Smith-Molotov exchange, for instance, can be only speculative until historians gain full access to Soviet archives. With respect to the actions of the administration, though, we are on considerably firmer ground. That Washington could hardly be candid with the Soviets about its motives for trumpeting scare stories of war earlier that spring surely requires no explanation. Merely attempting to visualize Smith having a forthright conversation with Molotov on this topic—"Say, old fellow, we trust you're not taking all this war stuff seriously. It's just something we have to do in order to get those damned Republicans to swallow our program"—taxes one's imagination beyond the breaking point. Besides which, even if the U.S. ambassador were to let the cat out of the bag in this fashion, there is no guarantee that the ever-suspicious Soviets would have known what to make of such a revelation, to say nothing of whether they would believe it.

Then, too, the truth of the matter is that Truman and Marshall wanted an improvement in U.S. relations with the U.S.S.R.—but only up to a point. The administration's goal was to calm the suspicions of the Soviets so that they would not mount a preemptive war and so that East-West trade might continue unimpeded. Beyond that, however, Washington had no wish to go, for any additional relaxation of tensions between the two nations would have denied the administration one of its most potent political weapons. On the international front, the formation of the North Atlantic Treaty Organization, through which the United States soon would exert heavy influence over the Western European political economies, would be slowed or even stopped by any presumed thaw in the Cold War. As for a conference between the United States and the U.S.S.R., Washington feared that Western European nations would be so panicked or demoralized by any such development—to the Europeans, the administration believed, it would carry overtones of the Western betrayal of Czechoslovakia at Munich—that they would be tempted to forsake their alliance with the United States drift into neutralism or, worst of all, fall into the Soviet orbit.

Domestically, an accord with the U.S.S.R. would also be little short of disastrous. For one thing, without the specter of an evil, rapacious Soviet Union menacing the peace and tranquillity of the world, selling the administration's foreign aid and military programs to a Congress controlled by sullen, resentful Republicans would be the very devil of a task. This was still a highly relevant consideration at the moment when the peace scare burst upon the scene, inasmuch as appropriations for the Marshall Plan had been voted for a single year only and the selective service bill—which was very much on the mind of Secretary of Defense Forrestal throughout May and well into June of 1948—had not even been enacted by Congress. On May 28, for example, Forrestal wrote the president that he was "seriously concerned about the legislative situation in connection with Selective Service." The entry in his diary three days later, describing a conversation the secretary had held in his home with Senator Taft the previous evening, was more detailed: "I told him [Taft] I was very much concerned about the fate of Selective Service; that it was manifest that there was a growing apathy throughout the country on this matter which reflected the conciliatory gestures of Russia, the speeches of Wallace and the general easing of tension since last March. I said that without Selective Service our defense establishment might really become a hollow shell as a result of the competitive wages offered by industry, the 'peace' campaign of Wallace and many other considerations." Forrestal's worries about the passage of selective service grew throughout June, and they were reflected in language that became increasingly extreme. "Failure to enact the Selective Service Law . . . would be widely interpreted as an indication of American indecision and vacillation—an interpretation which might have extremely far-reaching effects," he instructed the chairman of the House Armed Services Committee on June 17. "Failure on our part to provide military strength at the present juncture would be a great disservice to the nation. . . . The failure to enact *any* Selective Service Bill at this time could have the most serious consequences for the United States."[20]

To overcome legislative resistance to its military programs, as we have witnessed, the administration thus found it expedient to foster the impression that relations with the U.S.S.R. were on a steep downhill slope. The trick, of course, was to make sure that this exercise in deception did not get out of hand, as it had verged on doing in March, while at the same time keeping terror and hysteria acute enough to prevent the legislature and the electorate from concluding that the worst of the Cold War had passed. "Our success . . . will bring with it the added danger that Congress and public may be lulled into erroneous belief that battle is won and we can relax and reap the fruits of victory," Walter Bedell Smith fretted. To avert this hateful possibility, it was "vital that the public be constantly reminded." The ambassador, accordingly, was pleased to note that the deterioration of U.S.-Soviet relations during the Berlin blockade later in the year had "not been without advantage to USA[,] as it has been factor in evoking public support for necessary defense and aid measures." Even so, however, there was—as always—a "danger . . . that this strong public feeling may recoil in opposite direction if it becomes apparent war is not an immediate prospect."[21]

Keeping U.S.-Soviet relations on an antagonistic basis, moreover, was as useful to the administration in crushing dissident Democrats as it was in overpowering Republican resistance. The Truman–Clark Clifford strategy for defeating the challenge from the left of the Wallace campaign consisted in tarring the candidate with the brush of guilt by association. "Prominent liberals and progressives," Clifford advised Truman, "must point out that the core of the Wallace backing is made up of Communists and the fellow-travelers." Truman followed exactly this path, both in his speech in New York on the evening of March 17, 1948 ("I do not want and I will not accept the political support of Henry Wallace and his Communists"), and in a second address at the end of the month, on which occasion he once more "bitterly denounced Henry Wallace, and by obvious allusion asserted that if the third-party leader wished to see the United States subverted he ought to go to Russia and fight against his own country." Hence any hint of a reconciliation between the United State and the U.S.S.R. would have deprived the administration of its means not only of manipulating congressional Republicans, but of beating back the attack from the Wallace forces as well. Regardless of whether Stalin and his associates were eager for an agreement with the Truman administration, the Soviet threat abroad and the Red Menace at home were just too good to give up.[22]

Metaphorically or otherwise, however, the trouble with walking a tightrope is that one risks falling off. In May 1948, the administration did just that. The idea behind the note that the State Department dispatched to Moscow early that month was to return tensions with the U.S.S.R. to the less dangerous levels that prevailed before the war scare—not to end them altogether. Yet this was not a thought that the administration could even begin to formulate, still less transmit, in an open, honest fashion. Simply doing nothing was equally out of the question. As a result, the administration was forced to gamble that it could compose a letter capable of mollifying the Soviets sufficiently to improve relations while still leaving intact the basic framework of Cold War antagonism into which those relations had settled. This was a calculated wager, and the administration lost. Its note to Stalin of necessity had to be ambiguous; and the Soviets, we have seen, elected to exploit that ambiguity by treating it as though it were an invitation to undertake negotiations for a general settlement. Truman, Marshall and the other proponents of the war scare had no one but themselves to blame for their predicament when this occurred. If in March the administration had worked to mislead domestic opinion about the prospects for war, in May it sought to beguile the Soviets about the prospects for peace, appearing to offer something that, as James Reston remarked at the time, it in fact had no intention of delivering. The Soviets, perhaps skeptical or perhaps just puzzled by the mixed messages they were receiving, lost no time in putting U.S. intentions to the test. Thus, the peace scare.

If the foregoing helps us understand both the reasoning behind Smith's note and Washington's instantaneous repudiation of the idea that it comprised a genuine overture to the U.S.S.R., it does little to solve the mystery of why the Soviets elected to bypass the traditional diplomatic channels by making the Smith-Molotov exchange public. This was a topic that gave rise to a considerable amount of contemporary conjecture in the government and the press alike. George Kennan, for one, told the British ambassador "that in his opinion they [the Soviets] had done it for the effect on their own population and the other populations of the satellite countries," and the secretary of state added that he "agreed with this analysis." So, too, did the chargé in Moscow, initially, at any rate; though subsequently he argued that the Soviet response was "primarily designed to confuse America, lend the appearance of substance to the vacuity of Wallace's declarations on foreign affairs and thus emasculate American policy."[23] Journalists had their own ideas. One day headlines postulated that the Soviets were being driven to buy time by their "economic needs"; the next, that the "Soviet move" was "strongly motivated by the failure of her plans for her own rehabilitation through 'reparations' from Eastern Germany." Still a third account stated that the Soviet response was "an indication of the Russians' eagerness to open discussions that might lead to an at least temporary settlement of differences."[24] Overall, from this welter of speculation no consensus emerged—except, of course, that those dastardly "Russians" (that is, Soviets) were, as usual, up to no good.

To this cornucopia of uncertainty, later historians have added little enlightenment. For the most part, they have chosen either to ignore this episode entirely or else to echo Walter Millis's simpleminded judgment that "Moscow had seized an opportunity for a 'peace offensive.'"[25]

Perhaps so. But then again, perhaps not. In the absence of Soviet sources, there is no sure way for the scholar to know. The conventional approach, illustrated by the words of Walter Millis above, has been to impute the worst possible intentions to the Soviets and leave the matter at that. Advocates of this interpretation, however, must then contend with the comments of Under Secretary of State Robert Lovett that James Forrestal inscribed in his diary on April 23. Many of the Soviets's actions, Lovett thought, were "a reflection of their own fear of a preventive or aggressive war on our part," and "overexcitable statements, some by military people, on a preventive war" were "contributing to their motivations" in this regard. So conceivably the peace offensive that Millis insisted on placing in sarcastic quotation marks was just that—an effort to achieve peace with the United States. Even George Kennan, after reconsidering his original opinion, came to this conclusion. "The USSR is anxious for a relaxation of tension in the 'Cold War,'" he stated early in June in an address to the U.S.-Canadian Permanent Joint Board on Defense. "Soviet reaction to the Smith-Molotov exchange, her support of the Wallace candidacy and other indications point to the fact that Russia is extremely anxious for a relaxation of tension."[26]

A closer examination of their rejoinder to the Smith note of May 4 does indeed suggest that the Soviets were attempting to reach an accord with the United States. As printed in the State Department compilation *Foreign Relations of the United States,* this document takes up almost four pages, with roughly one-half of it given over to a defense of the policies of the U.S.S.R. Except for three closing paragraphs, the remaining portion is devoted to complaints about U.S. policies that, from the Soviet perspective, were responsible for the "creation of such a tense situation." Significantly enough, the bulk of these complaints concern issues related to the physical security of the U.S.S.R.: "the increasing development of a network of naval and air bases in all parts of the world, including territories adjacent to the USSR, about which the press and a series of official representatives of the USA frankly declare that the establishment of these bases has the aim of the encirclement of the USSR"; "war-like threats of all kinds directed against the USSR, issuing from certain circles closely connected with the Government of the USA"; "[the] recently formed . . . military union of western countries, including England, France, Belgium, Holland and Luxembourg. . . . In all the English, French and American press it is openly said that this union is directed against the USSR. . . . The formation of the stated military union was possible only thanks to the patronage of the USA. It is clear that the military treaty of the five western states can in no way be regarded as a treaty of self defense."[27]

The most plausible reading of these remarks, I maintain, is in light of the war scare of the previous two months. Having been caught off-guard by the German invasion of 1941, it was unlikely that the Soviet leadership would simply ignore the increasingly hostile pronouncements emanating from Washington during March and April, especially in view of the fact that they were coming not from obscure bureaucrats in lowly positions, but from the highest-ranked officials in the administration: the president (who on March 17 "named" the U.S.S.R. as the "one nation" that was the primary cause of all the turmoil in the world), the secretary of state (who repeatedly likened the situation in 1948 to that existing in 1940) and the secretary of defense (who was no less free with analogies equating the Soviets with the Nazis). It would have been truly remarkable, therefore, if it did not appear to the Soviets that, in addition to their continuing preoccupation with a renewed threat from Germany, they would now also have to be prepared to defend themselves from U.S. aircraft and atomic weapons. The Cold War, in short, was rapidly being transformed into an arms race.

This argument finds additional support in an incident that took place less than a month after the peace scare had come and gone. On June 6, 1948, the Soviet Embassy in Washington lodged a protest with the State Department over an article that appeared in the May 17 issue of *Newsweek* magazine. The article opened with a brief account of a speech by General George C. Kenney, commander of the Strategic Air Command (and resolute opponent of accepting "morons" and "halfwits" into the air force), who informed his audience that the current peace was "little more than a superficial armistice," and that it was "no longer necessary to ask if we think there is a danger of war," but rather, "When will the Communist crowd start 'Operation America'?" From that promising beginning, the article proceeded to describe a detailed scheme for the destruction of the Soviet Union from the air with atomic weapons, predicated on the assumption that "the Russians suddenly went berserk and swept into Western Europe."[28]

The Soviet ambassador objected to the *Newsweek* article because, he claimed, its publication was "an example of unbridled propaganda for a new war against the Soviet Union," and thus "a rude violation of the resolution of the Second Session of the General Assembly" of the United Nations. The latter both condemned "all forms of propaganda . . . designed or likely to provoke or encourage any threat to the peace, breach of the peace, or act of aggression" and urged member states "to promote . . . friendly relations among nations." The Soviet note waxed especially indignant over the fact that the article "set forth a plan to use American air forces, air bases and atomic bombs against the Soviet Union, particularly for the destruction of Soviet cities such as Moscow, Leningrad, Kiev, Kharkov, Odessa, and others. . . . It is further stated in the article that American strategists are thinking in terms of 'closing the circle of air bases around Russia' in order to 'make it smaller and smaller, tighter and tighter, until the Russians are throttled.'"[29]

In his reply, the secretary of state simply dismissed the Soviet protest out of hand, denying that his government was in any way answerable for the publication of the *Newsweek* article. This response was, of course, wholly disingenuous, for it was evident even on a cursory reading that the article could not have been written without access to Pentagon plans for strategic warfare against the U.S.S.R. Robert Lovett, the under secretary of state, tacitly conceded the government's responsibility in a letter sent to James Forrestal on the same day the secretary dispatched an answer to the Soviet ambassador. "I have read the text of General Kenney's address. I am sure you will agree with me that speeches of this character are ill-advised in view of the international situation." Lovett concluded by expressing his relief that "the necessary steps have been taken . . . to safeguard against statements on the part of members of the armed services which would be embarrassing to this Government in its conduct of foreign affairs." The Soviet complaint, it seems, was not quite so groundless as the State Department's response had pretended.[30]

Regardless of the administration's actual intentions, both the reply of the U.S.S.R. to Smith's note of May 4 and its protest over the *Newsweek* article of May 17 indicate that the Soviets believed they had good cause to be disturbed by the U.S. military buildup and the development of a North Atlantic alliance patently directed against them. Precisely this point is made by a distinguished student of Soviet military thinking. In his analysis entitled *Military Objectives in Soviet Foreign Policy,* Michael McGwire calls attention to a shift in Soviet military strategy that took place at this time in reaction to the "overexcitable statements . . . on preventive war" that had perturbed Robert Lovett:

> Drawing together this evidence, it was not hard for the Soviets to envision the scenario they might be faced with in the not too distant future, even if President Truman could resist internal pressures for a preventive strike. . . . The Soviets believed that in the same way that Germany had justified aggressive incursions in 1938–41, some pretext, opportunistic or contrived, would be found to justify a capitalist-imperialist intervention in the name of freedom. . . . The Soviets would have to plan for the worst case, which would involve a combination of land assaults across the German plain and through the Balkans; major amphibious landings on the Baltic and Black Sea coasts . . . ; and massive air attacks by conventional and atomic bombers throughout the Soviet Union.[31]

What is more, at the same time as the Truman administration was accelerating the conventional arms race, it was also inaugurating a new project to create a thermonuclear "superbomb," something that further alarmed the Soviets when they learned of it.* "Soviet work on the thermonuclear bomb began in 1948," notes David Holloway, "after reports of a superbomb had been received from the West." In his book, *The Soviet Union and the Arms Race,* Holloway writes that "Soviet accounts (such as they are)" suggest that "early thermonuclear studies were initiated in response to reports of American work" reaching the U.S.S.R. in 1948. "It is possible to identify important points at which American policy seems to have been crucial for Soviet decisions," Holloway contends, and he cites Soviet "decisions about the development of thermonuclear weapons in the late 1940s and early 1950s" as a case in point.[32]

Additional evidence for these interpretations comes from an unexpected quarter—analysts from the Central Intelligence Agency and the other members of "a joint ad hoc committee representing . . . the intelligence agencies of the Departments of State, the Army, the Navy and the Air Force." The conclusions

---

* One aspect of the change in military thinking described by MccGwire involved the use of the Soviet air force in warfare. In World War II, that use had been largely confined to the "tactical" one of providing support for ground troops, as opposed to the "strategic" one of bombing the enemy's homeland. "Nonetheless," Raymond L. Garthoff has written, "it is clear that by 1949 strategic air power was being allotted a higher role than previously": see Garthoff, *Soviet Strategy in the Nuclear Age* (New York: Praeger, 1958), p. 178. There is little reason to doubt that the U.S. military buildup of 1948, with its emphasis on achieving the ability to destroy the Soviet Union with long-range bombers carrying atomic (or, later, thermonuclear) weapons, accelerated the change.

of this committee's report on the "Possibility of Direct Soviet Military Action During 1948–49" could not be in closer agreement with those of the two scholars whose views I have cited above:

> In ORE 22-48, we stated that "Soviet leaders may have become convinced that US actually has intentions of military aggression in the near future." Recent events may have somewhat strengthened Soviet conviction in this respect. The passage of a peacetime Draft Act, the continued development of atomic weapons, the general acceptance of increased military appropriations, the establishment of US bases within range of targets in the USSR, the activities of US naval forces in the Mediterranean, and the movement to Europe of US strategic airforce [*sic*] units are instances in point. We think it unlikely, however, that these events have actually led Soviet leaders to the conclusion that positive US aggression must be *soon* expected. It is considered that they are more probably taken to mean that the ultimate conflict with the capitalist system will be resolved by force rather than by the methods of "cold war" [emphasis added].

Although the authors of this document acknowledged that "the danger of an *early* Soviet military move, made in calculated anticipation of this ultimate conflict[,] may be slightly increased by these circumstances" (emphasis added), they did "not estimate that such a move has become a probability." What the members of this committee utterly failed—or refused—to take into account, however, were the inevitable *long-term* implications of their own report: if the Soviets truly expected "the ultimate conflict with the capitalist system [to] be resolved by force rather than by the methods of 'cold war,'" surely they would begin preparing themselves for that final confrontation. The Truman administration had just propelled the world an enormous step further down the path of an open-ended and unremitting arms race. I will have a great deal more to say on this subject in the next chapter.[33]

The findings of Michael MccGwire, David Holloway and the CIA's ad hoc committee provide us with the germ of an explanation for the Soviets' decision to publicize the Smith-Molotov exchange, rather than pursuing the matter through conventional diplomatic channels. Desperate situations breed desperate expedients, the saying has it—and the Soviets were close to desperation ("extremely anxious" was the phrase George Kennan used) for an agreement with the United States that would halt the movement towards a separate West German state, slow the pace of the arms race and prevent or retard the development of an anti-Soviet North Atlantic military alliance. So much is unmistakable from the fact that little more than a month after the peace scare, Moscow resorted to a much more dramatic measure in pursuit of the same ends. On June 24, 1948, the Soviets blocked the roads and railroad tracks leading into Berlin from the west.

One need not posit the existence of Soviet "hawks" and "doves" to suppose that the U.S. note of May 4 must have given rise to the most intense discussions in Moscow. After all, throughout 1948, as Ambassador Smith and his subordinates frequently reported, the Soviet leadership had been engaged in a "long-continuing economic controversy" over the prospects for capitalism in the United States. It would be quite startling if Stalin and his principal advisers were in any less of a quandary regarding the best way to deal with the new military and diplomatic measures being put into place by the Truman administration. Indeed, we can detect signs of just such confusion and vacillation at the head of the Soviet state—what Smith described as "fundamental uncertainty in the highest levels of the Soviet regime." At the end of March 1948, Soviet authorities in Germany announced that, as of April 1, they would search all vehicles and trains entering and leaving the sector of the country they controlled—in effect, the first step toward the isolation of West Berlin. Within two days, however, these new restrictions were quietly dropped. In retrospect, it is evident that the Soviets were careening erratically—now this way, now that—in a frantic search for some way of involving the administration in negotiations on the questions they regarded as most pressing.[34]

Hence, once Stalin had had a chance to digest the U.S. note of May 4, he may have thought that by releasing both it and his reply to the public, the near-universal yearning for peace left in the wake of World War II would create irresistible pressures on the United States to enter into "a discussion and settlement of differences" with the U.S.S.R. Granted that this was an unorthodox approach whose chances of success were uncertain at best, it was obvious that traditional methods had failed before and would most likely fail again. Besides, such a move was no more of a gamble than the one the Truman administration had taken in sending the note in the first place. Unlike the case with imposing a blockade on West Berlin, publicizing the Smith-Molotov exchange did not pose any danger of outright hostilities. The worst that could happen would be that the administration would reject the Soviet response; and if this occurred, Washington could be made to look insincere for backing away from an initiative it had itself undertaken, in which case the Soviets would emerge with a propaganda victory of sorts by way of consolation.

All well and good, except for one minor fact: with such an outcome, Moscow still would not have obtained the negotiations it was seeking. Would the Soviets be content to mutter to themselves, "Oh, well—maybe next time," as they trooped stoically from the field? Or, having witnessed their relatively low-key tactics fall short, would they now choose to employ the more risky and confrontational ones they had eschewed during the peace scare?

It is unfortunate that scholars have paid so little attention to the peace scare of May 1948, for closer scrutiny might suggest an answer to the question of why, during the following month, the Soviets attempted to seal off Berlin from the West. If it is true that their response to Smith's note of May 4 sprang from a desire for an accommodation with the United States, the results must have been a sore disappointment to them. When their attempt to obtain this accommodation was rejected by the Truman administration, it is a reasonable surmise that the Soviets concluded they had exhausted every measure short of war save one. What I am proposing, in other words, is that the peace scare supplies the missing link between the war scare and the Berlin blockade: the U.S. military buildup begun in March and April, in conjunction with Washington's campaign for a West German state and its promotion of the North Atlantic Treaty Organization, impelled the Soviets in May to intensify their efforts at reaching an accord with the Truman administration; the failure of those efforts then led directly to the Berlin blockade in June. By the end of the blockade, contrary to Soviet hopes that Cold War tensions might be relaxed, bitterness and enmity between the two nations had become so great that it would take more than four decades before the notion of a permanent resolution of differences could appear to be anything other than a utopian fantasy, a political pipe dream. Should there be any merit in this interpretation, then the period from March 1948 to the beginning of the Berlin blockade in June must rank among the most significant turning points in the history of U.S.-Soviet relations.

8.

Conclusions: Of Presidents and Precedents

For the past eighteen months we have been bombarded with crises. President Truman has demanded $6 billion to $7 billion for a foreign aid program, a return to the wartime draft and now a new $3 billion armament program—all to meet this crisis. Yet we have not been told precisely what this crisis is, what form of danger we are to prepare against. Nevertheless, we are told, it is a tremendous crisis and Congress ought to do all the things the President asks without stopping to debate them. Indeed, the Congress has been severely criticized by the Administration for wanting to discuss the matter awhile before commiting [*sic*] itself. . . .

One day it is a modernized lend-lease program. The next it is universal military training. Another day U.M.T. is too slow; we must have an immediate draft. On still another day it is a long range re-armament program. . . .

To get these programs approved Congress is bombarded with alarums and excursions: It must act immediately. There are submarines close in the Pacific. The foreign situation is rapidly

> deteriorating. Time is pressing; Congress must not quibble about details. . . . We have had too many "crises," too many promises that this or that action if performed immediately would save the day. . . . We have a right to expect more than that from our leaders.
>
> —"The Crisis," an editorial in the *Wall Street Journal,* April 2, 1948[1]

THE TRANSFORMATION OF THE COLD WAR

It is in no sense an exaggeration to assert that 1948 was a crucial juncture in the nation's history, for the events set in motion by the Truman administration that year were fateful in the extreme. Although it would take some time before their full impact was felt, cumulatively they would shape this country's course into the 1990s—and conceivably even beyond. In virtually every case, moreover, their effect was pernicious, setting sinister precedents and creating malign arrangements that subsequent generations would find almost impossible to overturn.

One of the most obvious of the new developments was the Truman administration's penchant for governing by what Richard Freeland has aptly called "crisis politics."[2] Rather than encouraging a rational discussion of the issues by an informed electorate, the president and his chief lieutenants found it more convenient to proceed by deceit and manipulation, using, as we have seen, baseless claims of an impending Soviet military offensive to stampede Congress and the citizenry. Anyone who has lived through the years of the U.S. war in Southeast Asia or, to take a more recent example, the 1991 war against Iraq, will not have to be told how readily later presidents have emulated the kind of chicanery practiced by the Truman administration in 1948.

Because of the administration's unprincipled readiness to resort to crisis politics, alternatives to its policies that should have been weighed by the public were barely mentioned, much less debated. Nowhere is this more true than in the realm of relations with the Soviet Union. Nineteen forty-eight was the last year in which it might have been possible to devise an escape from the iron grip of the Cold War. By following the path charted by Clark Clifford and like-minded political henchmen, however, Harry Truman ensured that such a result would not come to pass. Taking advantage of the power to mold the nation's perceptions that an incumbent president enjoys, Truman was able to discredit Henry Wallace, the foremost advocate of a rapprochement with the

Soviets, as the naive tool of Communists in the United States and the Kremlin. Not only did this tactic write an ignominious ending to a heretofore distinguished career, not only did it pave the way for later and even less scrupulous demagogues such as Joseph McCarthy, but—most reprehensible of all—it foreclosed for decades any chance of reaching an accord with the U.S.S.R. After 1948, the very idea of negotiating an end to hostilities with the Soviets was guaranteed to call down charges of "Appeasement!" on the head of anyone so naive or foolhardy as to advance it. This fouling of the political environment is one of the most lasting bequests that, already by the end of his first term, Harry Truman had willed the nation.

The administration in fact made doubly certain that there would be no amelioration of the Cold War: besides fomenting anti-Soviet hysteria on the domestic front, it also drove a deeper wedge between this country and the U.S.S.R. I demonstrated in the previous chapter that the war scare of March and April 1948 led directly to the peace scare of May; and I further proposed that when the two Soviet proposals for negotiations with the United States—the note given Ambassador Smith by Molotov on May 10 and Stalin's letter to Henry Wallace of May 17—met with rejection, the Soviets next sought to force the issue by blockading Berlin. Should this latter interpretation be correct, rarely in the history of international affairs has a tactic backfired so badly. By shutting off access to Berlin from the West, Moscow played straight into the hands of the Truman administration and, especially, the Pentagon, both of whose representatives could now proclaim that, in light of subsequent events, their alarmist rhetoric in March and April had been entirely justified. In discussing the peace scare of May 1948, I also suggested that Stalin and his advisers were driven to this dire step in a desperate effort to resolve differences with the United States on matters they regarded as crucial. Such reasoning, however, was far too subtle to be grasped by a public whose interest in issues of foreign policy has historically been episodic and casual. So far as that public was concerned, the blockade was evidence that the "Russians" were malevolent, aggressive, untrustworthy—just as the administration had maintained all along.

Were the Soviets truly expecting that the Berlin blockade would eventually bring about improved relations with the United States, they must have been cruelly disappointed, for its outcome was just the opposite—an embittered estrangement that, with only minor fluctuations, lasted from that day forward. Although it was, of course, the Soviets themselves who chose to initiate the blockade, the United States, for its blunt rejection of all attempts at negotiation, deserves an equal share of the blame. In its dealings with the U.S.S.R., Truman and his principal assistants were guided by the precept that it was better to seem overly rigid than to look too conciliatory. The administration may not have begun the blockade, in other words, but by the same token it refused to offer the slightest hope that less extreme measures would yield any of the goals Moscow sought. Once the blockade was in place, moreover, Washington actually appeared to welcome it. Its existence made it that much the easier to convince audiences at home and abroad of the reality of the Red Menace. Here indeed was confirmation of Clark Clifford's dictum that "there is considerable political advantage to the Administration in its battle with the Kremlin," that "the worse matters get" with the Soviets, the better they became for the President.

Nothing conveys more vividly the sharp deterioration in U.S.-Soviet relations produced by the Berlin blockade and the U.S. airlift than the change in tone between Moscow's notes of May 10 and May 17 and the next major Soviet pronouncement, an address at the United Nations by the Soviet ambassador, Andrei Y. Vyshinky, at the end of September 1948. Where the Soviet notes in May had been polite, restrained and cast in general rather than personal terms, Vyshinky's speech in September was truculent, scathing and directed at specific administration officials. His remarks left no room for doubt that the Soviets were profoundly troubled by the new turn of events.

In the course of introducing a motion calling for substantial arms reductions on the part of the world's five greatest powers, Vyshinky was outspokenly critical of both the press and the government of the United States. The former, he charged, was "discussing in the insolent tone of the frantic instigators of war against the U.S.S.R. . . . various plans for attack" from bases on the periphery of the Soviet Union. One article in a U.S. magazine, for example, "boast[s] of the military power of the United States and in particular . . . the power of bombing aviation carrying atomic bombs." Another "openly confirms that the air forces of the United States are being reorganized for the event of possible military operations in Europe." And a third, after "expressing regret to the effect that the United States of America do not have really satisfactory maps for most of Russia's interiors, . . . with cynical frankness lists military air bases from which Soviet cities would be attacked, giving their respective distance."[3]

Vyshinky next turned his fire specifically on "persons holding high official posts," including Secretary of Defense James Forrestal, Secretary of the Army Kenneth Royall, General George C. Kenney of the Strategic Air Command and other unnamed "representatives of the Supreme Military Command of the United States [who] come forward with flashy colored plans for utilizing military aviation and the atomic bomb for the destruction of such Soviet cities as Moscow, Leningrad, Kiev, Kharkov, Odessa." Forrestal's testimony before the Senate Armed Forces Committee in particular had "overstepped all limits" by "insisting on the increasement of the Army and the additional assignment of $3,000,000,000 for war against the U.S.S.R., calling for the creation of powerful air forces capable of inflicting incessant blows far beyond the outer bases existing at present." Then the ambassador came to the heart of his address—a vehement protest against "a furious armament race under way." Accusing the United States of occupying "first place in this armament race," he proceeded to tick off the items in his indictment:

> The United States Army, as it is known, was in 1947, two years after the end of the war, three and one-half times larger than in the prewar years.
>
> Its Air Force grew even faster, their number by 1947 having increased seventeen times as compared with 1937. During the same period of time the United States Navy increased three and one-half times as regards tonnage, operating naval units and personnel of the Navy has [*sic*] even grown five times.
>
> The United States budget approved for 1948-1949 shows an increase in expenditures for war purposes which amounts to nearly $4,000,000,000 as compared with last year.
>
> Not only has [*sic*] the United States themselves carried on intense preparations for aggressive steps against the U. S. S. R. and the new democracies, but they also are helping a number of Western European countries prepare for war, supplying their armies with American armaments.

"Such is the situation in the field of international relations at present," was Vyshinky's mournful summation.[4]

I have quoted this speech at length both because of its contents and because I believe it marks a new departure in the Cold War. From it, one takes away the sense that the Soviets were palpably shaken by the administration's intention to deploy a new generation of long-range bombers whose express mission would be to wage atomic warfare against the U.S.S.R. For if, as the ad hoc committee of intelligence analysts who compiled the report "Possibility of Direct Soviet Military Action during 1948–49" put it, recent U.S. actions had convinced "Soviet leaders . . . that the ultimate conflict with the capitalist system will be resolved by force rather than the methods of 'cold war,' " it was clear that the U.S.S.R. would have no choice but to gird itself for the showdown. As a result, according to the findings of Michael MccGwire and David Holloway presented in the last chapter, the Soviets themselves now began planning for the possibility of war with the United States; and those plans would soon enough include the development of weapons—first bombers, then missiles—that could pose a direct threat to the territory of the United States. By September 1948, then, the die had been cast. The Cold War would henceforth be an arms race as well. It would remain one even after the economic collapse of the Soviet Union became too obvious to be denied.[5]

IDEOLOGY VERSUS REALITY IN THE COLD WAR

Referring to the draft memorandum on Item 1 of the agenda, Mr. Bohlen said that some points were presented in a somewhat different light than that in which the U.S. Government viewed them. For example, the strength of Russia was perhaps overstated. . . . Furthermore, he questioned the statement in the memorandum that Russia's ultimate aim is domination of the entire world. . . . Another point in the memorandum stems from this earlier statement, to the effect that the Kremlin ultimately wishes to dominate the United States. Here again the United States has a somewhat different concept of the problem.

—Summary of Remarks of Charles E. Bohlen, State Department Counsellor, at the Fourth Meeting of the Working Group Participating in the Washington Exploratory Talks on Security, July 20, 1948[6]

What more can the war scare of 1948 tell us about the intensification of the Cold War that took place during Truman's first term?

Granted that the scare comprises but one episode in the early history of the Cold War, it nonetheless offers us an opportunity to sharpen our understanding of how this conflict took root and grew in the years immediately after World War II. This is no minor matter. Impressions formed during the late 1940s about the possibility of peaceful coexistence with the Soviets, as I suggested in the preceding section, have proved to be remarkably durable. So long as the Soviet Union continued to exist, no subsequent president would ever be willing to run the risk of challenging the distorted portrait of the U.S.S.R. that Truman and his accomplices had painted in such bold and garish hues. What is more, even though the U.S.S.R. is now defunct, evil habits engendered by nearly half a century of unabated Cold Warfare have turned out to be difficult to break: without so much as even a halfway plausible foe anywhere in sight, with a thousand and one human needs in this country going unmet, with the global environment deteriorating on every front, this country continues to squander close to $300 billion a year in arming itself against—what? No persuasive answer to that question has been forthcoming, but that minor inconvenience has not been allowed to interfere with the drunken splurge on armaments begun during the 1980s. Enemies come, enemies go—military spending, seemingly invincible, lasts forever.

The war scare of 1948 can provide us with crucial insights into why the Cold War was able to achieve such permanence. The source of these insights lies in two vast discrepancies: first, that between what Truman and his chief lieutenants said in public about Soviet intentions and what they in reality believed to be true; second, the no-less-important gulf between the rationalizations the administration advanced for its actions as opposed to the actual reasons underlying them. Because the administration, as we have witnessed, deviously concealed the existence of these two discrepancies, it was able to take steps that dramatically exacerbated the Cold War and accelerated the arms race, all the while contending that such measures had been forced on it by the need to check Stalin's aggressive designs. In this way, Truman's legions were doubly victorious: not only did they foist upon the nation the military and foreign policies they were determined to impose, but they even managed to saddle "the other side" with responsibility for the unavoidable increase in tensions that these policies caused.

If the tactic of the Truman administration was to contend that its every anti-Soviet move was a reaction to some dastardly Soviet provocation, this argument has remained at the very heart of all officially blessed accounts of U.S.-Soviet relations ever since. Subsequent presidents—indeed, even would-be presidents—knew a good thing when they saw it: Truman had supplied the theme; all they need do was add the occasional embellishment.

The dogma that the Soviets bear the full onus for initiating and perpetuating the Cold War and the arms race is, one supposes, of considerable comfort to those who strive to convince themselves that the powers that be are invariably truthful. A thoroughgoing examination of the war scare of 1948, however, gives that dogma the lie. The scare was in no sense a rejoinder to anything the Soviets had done; on the contrary, it was, as we have seen time and again, an expedient that the Truman administration simply concocted to obtain short-term gains. One can go even further: the administration's willingness to bandy about talk of war so freely was predicated on the firm belief that the Soviets were in no position, and had no wish, to inaugurate hostilities with the West. Had the administration entertained the least thought that the Soviets were actually intent on war, its leading representatives undoubtedly would have been far less reckless in the rhetoric they invoked.

Still, in and of itself, the war scare of 1948 is but a single tile in the complex mosaic of the Cold War. Perhaps, then, it is merely an exception to an otherwise inviolate rule; perhaps U.S. moves in the Cold War were devised to counter a Soviet threat after all.

And perhaps goats will grow wings and fly. The evidence unearthed as part of this investigation, when combined with information that has long been available, leads to a conclusion unlikely to provide ammunition to those who insist on viewing the Cold War in terms of a U.S. "response" to a "Soviet threat." In order to demonstrate why this is so, however, it is first necessary to clarify what we mean by the words "Soviet threat." For just as there were two versions of the war scare of 1948—a crude one, revolving around events in Czechoslovakia, fashioned for public consumption, and a somewhat more polished one, revolving around the Clay telegram, for the delectation of the connoisseurs—the Truman administration has left us two versions of the "Soviet threat." Stated another way, the *nature* of that threat—how it is defined—has varied according to the intended audience. For a mass audience—presumed incapable of comprehending subtleties and requiring graphic imagery "clearer than truth," in Dean Acheson's phrase—the administration developed Version One: the Soviet military threat. This version maintained that the Soviets stood poised to swoop down upon Western Europe as the first step in their assumed drive for world conquest; the U.S. was thus compelled to counter the menace with a series of military measures of its own—a huge leap in Pentagon spending, the enactment of peacetime selective service, the sponsorship of an armed alliance among the North Atlantic powers, et cetera. For audiences considered more knowledgeable—political "insiders," journalists, pundits and academicians—the administration offered Version Two: the Soviet political threat. According to this version, the Soviets hoped to achieve the same goal of world domination, but by political means—"boring from within," as the cliché has it—rather than by naked force of arms.

It is easy enough to dispose of Version One. Suffice it to say that at no time between the end of World War II and the beginning of 1949 was there a significant body of official opinion in the United States holding that the Soviets were planning an attack on Western Europe in the foreseeable future. Such differences of opinion as existed on the question of Soviet military intentions were in the main between those who thought that the Soviets might pursue such a goal at some relatively distant moment—usually placed in the mid-1950s or later—and those who thought that the Soviets would seek to achieve their ends primarily through political, rather than military, methods.

There was, to be sure, no question that the Soviets had the *means* of initiating an attack on the West if they choose to do so. But it was widely recognized, in military and civilian circles alike, that the staggering devastation the U.S.S.R. had endured in World War II made Moscow deeply reluctant to undertake massive military adventures—especially if those adventures promised to embroil it in a war with the United States. Hence there was a general consensus that if the Soviets did strike, it would not be out of any desire to subjugate Western Europe, but because Stalin and his subordinates feared that an invasion from the West was imminent and chose to defend their country by taking the offensive before it could be launched.

Evidence to support this interpretation is not far to seek. The intelligence analyses of Soviet intentions excerpted at length in chapter 4 substantiate it for the interval from January to June 1948. Appendix A, "Estimating Soviet Intentions and Capabilities, 1947–1948," contains an extensive and representative sample of additional such documents for both an earlier and a later period, the year and one-half from mid-1946 to the end of 1947 and the last six months of 1948, respectively. Originally, I had planned to extend my scrutiny of such estimates back to the end of World War II. It soon became apparent, however, that those written in 1947 did not differ in any significant respect from those that had been compiled in late 1945 or the first half of 1946; in some cases, the later documents were hardly more than slightly reworked versions of their predecessors from the previous 11 months. I can assert with complete confidence, therefore, that he who searches the archives expecting to find voluminous evidence that leading figures in the first Truman administration feared that the Soviets were intent on embarking on an immediate military confrontation with the Western powers will search in vain.

Version Two, which asserts that the Cold War resulted from the clash between Soviet efforts to topple the governments of Western Europe by subversion and U.S. measures aimed at frustrating them, does not fare much better. Already by 1945, it was obvious that Stalin had no intention of sponsoring revolutions, whether in Western Europe or in East Asia. In China, France, Greece, Italy and Yugoslavia, Communist-led organizations derived immense popularity from spearheading guerrilla armies seeking to expel the occupying troops of an Axis invader. Not only did each of these Communist parties enjoy great prestige in its respective country, but each also comprised a highly disciplined and well-armed force. Had Stalin given the signal to rise, such parties stood an excellent chance of being able to take—and hold—state power.

But Stalin gave no such signal. Far from it. In every case, he directed European and Asian Communist parties to renounce their revolutionary aspirations, put aside all attempts to establish socialism and content themselves with the position of junior partner in coalition governments controlled by bourgeois parties.

All of this is well known. In his book *Conversations with Stalin,* Milovan Djilas, for one, long ago made clear the fundamentally antirevolutionary stance of the Soviet leadership. In the case of Yugoslavia, Stalin's instructions to Josip Broz

Tito—carried from Moscow by Djilas himself—were to "do nothing to 'frighten' the English, by which he [Stalin] meant that we ought to avoid anything that might alarm them into thinking that a revolution was going on in Yugoslavia or an attempt at Communist control." Stalin's view of "the uprising in Greece" was that it would "have to fold up. . . . The uprising in Greece must be stopped, and as quickly as possible. . . . We should not hesitate, but let us put an end to the Greek uprising." As for China, Stalin admitted to Djilas that the Chinese Communists had come to power *despite* the marching orders he had issued: "When the war with Japan ended, we invited [!] the Chinese comrades to agree on a means of reaching a modus vivendi with Chiang Kai-shek [who was supported by the U.S.]. They agreed with us in word, but in deed they did it their own way when they got home: they mustered their forces and struck."[7]

Poor Djilas! To the best of my knowledge, no one has ever claimed that his account is anything less than accurate. Yet his words have suffered a curious fate. Virtually every historian who writes about the early years of the Cold War makes reference to them—only to disregard their plain meaning when it comes time to formulate conclusions. The inescapable truth remains, however, that Stalin's attitude toward revolution had been unalterably hostile at least since the late 1930s and the civil war in Spain, where the "prime motive" behind the policies he had thrust upon the Spanish Communist Party was "to avoid antagonizing the British and the French Governments." In the interval since then, all that had changed was that the name of the United States had to be added to the list of those powers not to be affronted by the specter of revolution in the West.[8]

Nor were Stalin's intentions on the subject of social revolution in Europe or Asia at all obscure to Washington. Isaac Deutscher's treatment of Stalin's psychology and politics is in many respects still unrivaled. "Soon after the liberation of France" in 1944, Deutscher has written, the Soviet premier used his influence with the European Communist parties

> in a manner calculated to satisfy Conservative opinion and to set at rest any fears or suspicions that [Winston] Churchill and [Franklin D.] Roosevelt may have had. It was undoubtedly under his inspiration that the French and Italian Communist parties behaved with extraordinary . . . moderation. For the first time in their history, disregarding their own programmes, which forbade them to take part in bourgeois administrations, they joined in governments based on broad national coalitions. Although they were then the strongest parties in their countries, they contented themselves with minor positions in those governments, from which they could not hope to seize power either now or later. . . . The army and the police

> remained in the hands of Conservative or, at any rate, anti-Communist groups.

As a result, Deutscher concluded, Western Europe would "remain the domain of Liberal capitalism."[9]

Because the Truman administration attached enormous importance to their outcome, the Italian elections of April 18, 1948, furnish an excellent case in point. One of the administration's chief motives for staging the war scare of 1948, we recall from chapter 5, was to coerce Congress into passing the European Recovery Program (ERP) by April 1, a deadline that reflected the determination of Truman, Marshall and the State Department to have ERP funds in hand in time to employ them in the Italian elections. Washington's plan was to dangle the prospect of ERP assistance before the Italian electorate—and then threaten to withhold it unless the voters fell into line by excluding Communists from the national government. Although both the State Department and the U.S. ambassador in Italy, James Clement Dunn, were obsessed with the notion that a Communist-led insurrection might derail this tidy little scheme before it could be put into effect, neither, to their seeming dismay, could turn up even the smallest sign that any such uprising was in the works.

Thus, the ambassador reported on January 3, 1948, that "Communist policy" was "to stick to quasi legal parliamentary methods and rely on the elections in order to reenter the government and ultimately to control it" (as if there were some other reason for a political party to exist!). Although Dunn was forced to admit that "at the present time" there was no "substantial indication of a Communist-armed coup d'état despite countless unfounded rumors," nonetheless, he advised, "this possibility should not be completely discarded." Two months came and went with no change. On March 6, the CIA reported that "the Communists could not at this time carry out a . . . coup in either Italy or France, as they do not have control of the police or the armed forces";[10] two days later, the National Security Council agreed that the Italian Communist Party was still "foregoing armed insurrection"—but only "for the time being," of course. Another two months after that, with the elections now well past, the Italian ambassador held a conversation with the secretary of state. Notwithstanding the fact that the vote had delivered a stunning setback to the largest Communist party in Western Europe, "it appeared," according to the ambassador, "that the Soviets had decided against direct action by the Italian Communists." Even before the end of March, however, it had become evident that the Communists and their Left Socialist allies would go down to defeat. As early as March 22, Dunn noted an "undefinable but certain optimism in non-Communist political circles"; and on April 7 he told the State Department there was "unanimity" on the part of all his sources "throughout Italy that government oriented parties are gaining ground and an adverse trend is setting in against the Front [the coalition headed by the Communists]." Although the Communist party leadership must have suspected what the election results would be, there was no insurrection, no "direct action," no attempt at "a Communist-armed coup d'état" either before, during or after the elections. Or ever.[11]

Even in the Balkans and Eastern Europe, over much of which the Soviets already held sway, Stalin displayed only the greatest distaste for social upheaval. Greece, like Italy, has special significance in this regard: the argument that Soviet subversion threatened to engulf Greece was the foundation upon which the administration in March of 1947 erected its annual foreign policy "crisis" for that year; in the supercharged atmosphere that ensued, administration stalwarts were able to extort support for the Truman Doctrine from a reluctant Congress and an indifferent public—a dress rehearsal, as it were, for the war scare of 1948.

As usual, however, the facts were other than the Truman administration portrayed them. Late in 1946, notwithstanding Stalin's best efforts, civil warfare broke out in Greece between a left-wing guerrilla movement under Communist leadership and a brutal right-wing government propped up by Great Britain and the United States. (Later, in 1947, the British would allow Washington to shoulder the entire counterrevolutionary burden on its own.) The Soviets greeted this development by simply turning their backs on the rebels. "It might also be noted," states Lawrence Wittner in his definitive account, *American Intervention in Greece,* "that unlike [U.S.] aid to the Athens government—which dwarfed external assistance [almost all from Yugoslavia] to the rebels—Soviet aid was non-existent, *a point not contested by U.S. officials"* (emphasis added).

Besides refusing to provide either arms or money, the Soviets would not even concede that the cause of their ostensible Greek "comrades" was legitimate. Wittner relates that when, during the fall of 1947, Moscow created a new international organization, the Communist Information Bureau (Cominform), in order to tighten its control over other European Communist parties,

> delegates from the KKE [Greek Communist Party] were conspicuously absent. . . . Nor was this the only snub the Russians gave the KKE. . . . "Soviet leaders did not allow the resolution of the first meeting of the Cominform to include a single sentence which might aid the people's revolutionary fight in Greece." "Not a word" appeared in the Cominform paper about Greek events, . . . and the Soviet Union failed to "organise any care for the refugees from Greece, or Greek children, or other aid."[12]

Similarly, when the Greek insurrectionaries proclaimed "the first provisional democratic government of free Greece," no country, "Communist or otherwise, recognized the rebel government." Soviet hostility to the Greek revolution was too pronounced to escape notice, even by the ideologues of the Truman administration; no less than the secretary of state himself remarked on "the present Soviet and satellite attitude in withholding a firm commitment" from the KKE. Not that such grudging admissions for a moment prevented anyone in the administration from continuing to announce that the Greek civil war was one element in the Kremlin's master plan for enslaving the world. On the contrary, administration representatives, with sublime indifference to something so mundane as mere factual evidence, never wavered on this score.

Soviet opposition to revolution in Greece was not an isolated instance; elsewhere, too, the U.S.S.R. showed no desire to overturn capitalist society or embark upon the construction of socialism. Isaac Deutscher has reminded us of Soviet policies in the Balkans and Eastern Europe during the last days of World War II:

> King Michael of Rumania was left on his throne; and he was even awarded one of the highest Russian military orders. . . . The Soviet generals and the local Communist leaders did honour to the Greek Orthodox clergy in the Balkan countries. In Poland they courted the Roman Catholic clergy. There was no talk yet of socialization of industry. Only long overdue land reforms were initiated.[13]

The Soviets were also willing to encourage the trappings of democracy, Western style, in the countries the Red Army had occupied. In 1945, they sponsored free elections in Hungary, Bulgaria, Czechoslovakia and the Soviet zone of occupation in Austria. Although Communist candidates were "routed" in the first and "swamped" in the last, Moscow accepted these results without protest. Only later, after relations between the United States and the U.S.S.R. had soured drastically, did Stalin order a crackdown in Hungary and Czechoslovakia and the imposition from above of state-controlled "socialism" in those countries where his word was law.[14]

Yet in the final analysis, it is perhaps the war scare of 1948 itself that supplies the decisive refutation of the argument that U.S. actions in the Cold War were conceived in order to defend the West from Moscow's subversive maneuvers. Let us, for the sake of discussion, suppose that this argument is correct—that is, that U.S. policies were devised to thwart the menace of Soviet-inspired sabotage, subversion, insurrection and general all-around mischief. What then cries out for explanation is how the measures the Truman administration proposed during the war scare of 1948 were in any sense related to the alleged nature of the threat. It strains one's credulity to believe that Italian Communists hell-bent on a coup, say, or Greek rebels fighting for their life against right-wing totalitarianism would, like Paul on the road to Damascus, undergo instantaneous conversion and repent their sinful ways upon receiving the news that the U.S. Congress had passed a peacetime selective service act. Nor is it any more clear how Truman's decision to rescue the airplane makers with a 57-percent increase in the budget for aircraft procurement could serve to block an uprising in Italy or annihilate antigovernment guerrillas in Greece. The very notions are so fantastic, so utterly farfetched, that one blushes to put them on paper. By process of elimination, we are compelled to conclude that, more often than not, there was no real connection between the military and foreign policy programs the Truman administration urged on Congress on the one hand and the dangers to which the administration claimed to be responding on the other. Instead, expediency and improvisation ruled the day: the administration first decided what it wished to extract from Congress and the electorate, and then, as events during the spring of 1948 illustrate, reached for the nearest available pretexts to justify its demands.

We can quickly dispel any vestigal doubts on this score by noting the breathtaking lack of scruple with which Truman and his most prominent subordinates manipulated the *domestic* version of the "Communist threat" during these years, again for the purpose of pummeling Congress into approving the programs on which the administration placed the highest premium. When the journalist Carl Bernstein interviewed Clark Clifford in 1978 regarding the Truman administration's handling of "internal security" matters in the late 1940s, Clifford was quite unequivocal in declaring that both he and Truman "felt the whole thing [issue] was being manufactured." Although Clifford met with the President every day, he told Bernstein, the two men

> never had a serious discussion about real loyalty problems. . . . I have the sensation that the President didn't attach fundamental importance to the so-called Communist scare. He thought it was a lot of baloney. . . . There was no substantive problem. . . . It was a political problem. We did not believe there was a real problem. A problem was being manufactured. There was a certain element of hysteria. I don't believe any of us ever felt really threatened, Carl. I don't believe anything there constituted a genuine threat.[15]

The "internal security" issue was "a lot of baloney," there was "no substantive problem" and no "genuine threat"; rather, "a problem was being manufactured" in an atmosphere permeated by "a certain element of hysteria." Such a noble stance! The only thing Clifford neglects to mention in this moving recital is the responsibility he shared with Truman for the developments that, three decades later, he so piously deplored. For it was the Truman administration, acting on ideas proposed by Clifford and a handful of other notables, that inflicted the federal loyalty-oath program (Executive Order 9835), the Attorney General's list of subversive organizations, and several other no less odious measures upon a too-credulous nation. Interesting as it may be to contemplate Clifford's moral culpability, however, that is not our primary concern. More germane is this: we have absolutely no reason to believe that those prominent members of the Truman administration who so eagerly indulged in shameless lying about a domestic "Communist threat" they actually regarded as "a lot of baloney" were in any way less eager to engage in similar lying about the nature of the "Communist threat" abroad. Quite the reverse, in fact. Lying with relative impunity about the supposed danger posed by Communism at home—promoting what Clifford now describes as "the so-called Communist scare"—merely encouraged similar lying about the situation overseas; and, naturally, vice versa. In this way, one deceit fed upon and reinforced another, while the truth itself became suspect. But people routinely denied access to the truth will ultimately find it difficult, if not impossible, to make critical choices with any degree of clarity and rationality. Here, too, as in so many other areas, Truman's rash tactics dealt a vicious blow to the body politic, one from which it has yet to recover fully.

What began as a series of opportunistic fictions the Truman administration quickly nurtured into a full-blown ideology, as durable as it was potent. The myth that the survival of the West was imperiled by an insidious Soviet campaign to undermine it from within could be pressed into service in so many different ways that it became an article of faith, the basis of a new secular religion to which every right-thinking person was expected to subscribe ("If there were no Devil, it would be necessary to invent him"). Henry Wallace discovered this fact the hard way in 1948. It took an unprincipled political operator such as Clark Clifford no time at all to realize that the myth could be used to discredit the kind of criticism of Truman administration foreign policy that Wallace advanced: repeat often enough that the former vice president and his followers were either unwitting dupes or conscious agents of the Soviet Union and the job was as good as done. Once the myth won acceptance in the realm of foreign policy—once dissent from the Truman administration's version of the gospel became equated with giving aid and comfort to the enemy—it was easy to extend it. In very short order, voicing dissatisfaction with *any* aspect of the social order—signing this petition or attending that lecture, being seen reading a suspect publication, associating with an individual whose "loyalty" had been questioned—came to mean risking one's career, reputation, friendships, even family ties. This ideology, which the Truman administration embraced as none of its predecessors had, was tailor-made to preserve the status quo—and that is exactly how it was deployed, until the demise of the U.S.S.R. began to render it obsolete.

The ideology had additional virtues that recommended it to those waging Cold War from the front lines. Politics, it is said, makes strange bedfellows; rarely have the bedfellows been more strange than with the politics of anticommunism abroad. The Truman administration, to cite one example, considered it an intolerable imposition that in Western Europe certain powerful and politically influential unions, such as those of the French and Italian dock workers, were led by Communists. Convinced that this source of potential opposition to its programs had to be destroyed, the administration dispatched representatives of the CIA to conclude a deal: if the Italian Mafia and the Corsican gangster syndicates of France would beat and kill members of the dock-workers' unions until the strength of these unions were broken, the CIA would see to it that the law enforcement agencies in Western Europe and the United States did not interfere with the trade in narcotics conducted by the two criminal organizations. Hence in the 1947 strike of 80,000 French dock workers in the city of Marseille,

> the CIA . . . sent agents and a psychological warfare team to Marseille, where they dealt directly with Corsican syndicate leaders through the Guerini brothers. The CIA's operatives supplied arms and money to Corsican gangs for assaults on Communist picket lines and harassment of important union officials. During the month-long strike the CIA's gangsters . . . murdered a number of striking workers and mauled the picket lines. . . .
>
> The Guerinis gained enough power and status from their role in smashing the 1947 strike to emerge as the new leaders of the Corsican underworld. . . . The CIA was instrumental in restoring the Corsican underworld's political influence, [although] it was not until the 1950 dock strike that the Guerinis gained enough power to take control of the Marseille waterfront. This combination of political influence and control of the docks created the ideal environment for the growth of Marseille's heroin laboratories.[16]

Almost at once, the nation began to reap the crops that the Truman administration and the CIA had sowed. During the Korean war, army authorities grew concerned when they discovered that U.S. soldiers, "particularly . . . troops on rest and recreation leaves in Japan," were falling prey to heroin addiction in increasing numbers. When the army complained to the Japanese police, however, the latter

> pointed out that responsibility for much of the drug traffic rested with the Americans. A great deal of the heroin entering Japan was landed by an American airline, Civil Air Transport [CAT], at US bases not open to Japanese customs inspection. . . . CAT was a CIA proprietary airline which was hauling drugs for its Chinese nationalist "assets," who occupied the opium-growing golden triangle in Burma and were supported [by the United States] as a possible guerrilla threat to the Chinese communists. Whatever ideology might suggest, therefore, it turned out to be "our" Chinese and not "theirs" who were helping to subvert [addict] American boys.[17]

The chickens were quick in coming home to roost.

Nor was this yet the worst of it. The Truman Administration even went so far as to ally itself with both high-ranking Nazis known to have committed genocidal crimes against humanity and Japanese war criminals guilty of murdering thousands. Whereas it conspired with narcotics gangsters to eradicate Communist influence in the working-class movements of Western Europe, the administration's purpose in protecting Nazi fugitives from justice was to assemble a force it could sneak into Eastern Europe to carry out assassinations and sabotage. Likewise, in order to learn the results of exposing human subjects to lethal doses of medical and biological-warfare substances, the administration granted immunity from prosecution to the officers and "scientists" of Japan's notorious Unit 731, whose diabolical "research" on prisoners of war in Manchuria had claimed the lives of some 3,000 victims. (Subsequently, the Truman administration would use and even extend these ghoulish techniques in performing similar "experiments" on unsuspecting U.S. citizens.) Once again, considerations of ordinary decency were brutally thrust aside in pursuit of the all-encompassing goal of striking at anything and anyone remotely connected to the Soviet Union.[18]

Cozying up to the Mafia, shielding prominent Nazis from the prosecution that was their due—one would like to believe that these actions caused at least a sporadic twinge of conscience in those who performed them. Should such twinges have occurred, however, a soothing remedy, an exculpation in advance, was near at hand. Here, the ideology so beloved of the Truman administration—that every one of its deeds, no matter how rank, was simply a defense against some more abominable bit of Soviet malevolence—proved its utility. How could one afford the luxury of adhering to conventional ethical practice when pitted against a foe of such ruthless fanaticism? In short order, this line of reasoning produced the self-serving Fundamental Theorem of the first generation of Cold Warriors: in consorting with criminals and conspiring with Nazis, "we" were merely beating "them" at their own game. Thus was the strangling of scruple and principle redefined as a victory for Yankee ingenuity. To protect the legacy of Western Civilization, it turned out, required the destruction of its most precious moral values. The ultimate implication of this kind of thinking was never better expressed than by those soldiers who, taking the Fundamental Theorem to its logical conclusion, explained during the U.S. war in Southeast Asia that they were burning a Vietnamese village in order to save it.

The point on which it is essential to be absolutely clear, however, is this: the foreign policies of the Soviet Union as depicted by the top officials of the Truman administration were one thing; those policies as they existed in reality were quite another. It was only rarely and by happenstance that the two coincided. It necessarily follows that programs the administration presented as a means of repulsing current or impending Soviet offensives—such as the 57-percent increase in aircraft procurement it proposed during the spring of 1948—were typically those that Truman and his assistants wanted for entirely unrelated reasons. Although Truman administration strategists were quite aware that many of these measures, if adopted, promised to exacerbate tensions with the U.S.S.R., that was not, in their eyes, anything like a sufficient reason to abstain from them. In this respect, I will argue immediately below, the outcome of the events of 1948 and 1949, culminating in the Berlin blockade and airlift, decisively affirmed a conclusion toward which the administration had already started to move: no matter how fervent their protests, the Soviets lacked both the means and the will to prevent the United States from doing essentially what it wished. If the Soviets didn't like the administration's policies, then so much the worse for them. Indeed, as we have witnessed, prominent political advisers such as Clark Clifford went so far as to argue that a deterioration in relations with Moscow might even be turned to good advantage, so long as it stopped short of outright war. Thus, the administration seldom displayed much compunction about driving the Cold War to new heights whenever the anticipated rewards made it seem desirable to do so. That is one of the many things that the war scare of 1948 can teach us, and—assuming that we are sufficiently open-minded to learn—it is surely far from the least.

THE ORIGINS OF THE PERMANENT WAR ECONOMY AND THE SEEDS OF DECLINE[19]

Your letter raises as its principle [sic] *question whether our future is encouraging or discouraging. Personally I feel it is encouraging, but I must point out that much of this depends on the kind of peace we achieve. If we have a true and lasting peace, obviously the demand for military airplanes will be limited. On the other hand, if we have an armed truce, and it begins to look as though this may be the case, the demand for military airplanes might be very considerable.*

—Robert E. Gross, President, Lockheed Aircraft Corporation, to William H. Stone, January 16, 1945[20]

It occurs to me that permanent alliances between the A.A.F. [Army Air Force] and representatives of the various industries such as automotive, steel, rubber, etc., which contributed to the war-time aircraft program, should be cemented.

—General Motors executive Harold R. Boyer to W. Stuart Symington, Assistant Secretary of War for Air, June 24, 1946[21]

As a graphic indication of the fact that military procurement does not mean aircraft industry business alone but rather a flow of business into a wide segment of U.S. industry, the following are participating in the huge Boeing B-50 program: Convair (fuselage nose sections), Swallow Airplane Co. (top fuselage center sections), Douglas (rear fuselage sections), Boeing-Wichita (outer wing panels and tail assemblies), Rohr Aircraft Corp. (aft fuselage sections), Northrop (flap assemblies), Goodyear (drop tanks and nose enclosures), Vard Co. (nose gear actuators), Foote Bros. Gear and Machine Corp. (land gear actuators), Cleveland Pneumatic Tool Co. (main landing gear), Iron Fireman Mfg. Co. (miscellaneous machine work), and General Mills, Inc. (miscellaneous gear and machine work).

—"1949 in the Aircraft Industry," *Automotive Industries,* January 1949[22]

However one may view the outlook [for business], . . . increased armament will be mainly a positive business factor simply by introducing new demands on top of those already existing . . . [It will produce an] anticipation eventually of sufficient armament stimulus to keep the economy geared at high levels, with business profits large, prices firm, and recession prospects once more deferred.

—"The Effect on Our Economy—Under Defense Mobilization . . . ," *The Magazine of Wall Street,* April 24, 1948[23]

In the early 1930's it cost about $20 per pound of airframe weight to develop an airplane; today, for the new transports, the development cost is more like $250 per pound. The difference between the two figures reflects not only the rise in wages and materials cost, but the exponential compounding of the complexity of airframe design.

—"Shall We Have Airplanes?" *Fortune,* January 1948[24]

It is no mean feat when an ideology can vanquish all rivals at the outset and reign virtually unchallenged for decades thereafter. The ideology of a "Soviet threat," purveyed by the Truman administration from the middle of the 1940s on, achieved just this supremacy. It could not have conquered with such ease had support for it been restricted to mere politicians and government bureaucrats, however, for to sweep the field so thoroughly, it also had to win the backing of the most powerful economic groups as well: the ruling ideas in any epoch are, in Marx's formulation, the ideas of the ruling class.

For all of its vulgar tendentiousness and distortions, the ideology of the "Soviet threat," especially Version One, which dwelt lovingly on the military nature of the menace, found a predictably warm reception from the armaments industry, with the aircraft corporations marching at the head of the parade. But it was not just the manufacturers of weapons who applauded a large and growing military budget: politically dominant business groups in general were quick to welcome arms spending as a means of warding off both the downturns of the economy and the inception of a welfare state.

To be sure, the increase in arms procurement accomplished by the Truman administration in 1948 was modest in comparison either to that envisioned by the authors of National Security Council Study 68 (NSC-68) in 1950 or to that actually brought about during the Korean War. Yet one can assert that, even without NSC-68 and the Korean War, the administration's actions during 1948 would in themselves have engendered much the same arms race as the one that was in full flower by the late 1950s. Knowing what we do about the time required to design and produce a complex new airplane, it is safe to say that the Soviet long-range bombers that began to appear in quantity during the middle of the 1950s were put on the drawing board late in the previous decade. Although the Soviets may have been led to develop these airplanes for defensive reasons—Washington would not find it so easy to threaten nuclear annihilation if Moscow could counter with corresponding threats of its own—nonetheless, in the prevalent Cold War climate, it was inevitable that their unveiling would provide a perfect pretext for demands that the United States field a new generation of weaponry to overcome the so-called "bomber gap." Similarly, once the U.S.S.R. had launched its first *Sputnik*—also the culmination of efforts dating from the end of the 1940s—ambitious politicians would trample each other in their haste to argue that this nation should spend whatever might be needed to reverse an equally nonexistent "missile gap." Hence even had NSC-68 never been written and the Korean War never been fought, I believe, the state of the arms race between the United States and the Soviet Union by the end of the Eisenhower presidency would not have looked much different.

A second line of reasoning also leads to the conclusion that the events of 1948 marked a significant turn in the growth of the arms race, for their effect was to weaken forces that had until then held such a contest in check. Prior to the war scare of 1948, two considerations restrained the Truman administration from instigating an all-out arms race. One of these, as we have witnessed, was the fear that the inflationary wave sure to be set off by massive military spending would have a devastating effect on the U.S. economy. The other was lingering uncertainty about the nature of the U.S.S.R.'s response: if Soviet leaders felt sufficiently menaced by a U.S. military buildup, might they not decide to preempt the situation by invading Western Europe? And if they did, would that not spell the death of U.S. hopes for maintaining prosperity at home by reconstructing the economies of its principal European trading partners? The first concern persisted right up until the outbreak of the Korean War; but the second was largely dissipated in the aftermath of the war scare of 1948 and the two developments that came directly in its train, the peace scare and the Berlin blockade. I argued in the foregoing chapter that, following their unsuccessful diplomatic attempt at obtaining a general conference with the United States, the Soviets then imposed the blockade as a more drastic means to the same end. Not only did that measure achieve results diametrically opposed to those its authors sought; it also demonstrated that the United States could act with almost complete impunity where the U.S.S.R. was concerned. For regardless of how much they might resent Truman administration policies, regardless of how much vehemence and vitriol they might pour into condemnations of those policies, the conduct of the Soviets during the Berlin blockade revealed their reluctance to cross the line separating peace from war. The blockade was, therefore, a failure on two counts: it produced no agreement with the administration and, ironically, it undermined rather than enhanced the power of the Soviets to intimidate the United States.

Hence by the spring of 1949—one year after the war scare, the peace scare and the onset of the Berlin blockade—there was a new mood in Washington. Dean Acheson had replaced the more cautious George Marshall as secretary of state; the North Atlantic Treaty Organization was in the process of formation; and, perhaps most important, the blockade was coming to a close on what, from the Truman administration's perspective, was a gloriously triumphant note: the Soviets had played their master card—but the United States had been able to trump it! The lesson to be learned from the previous 12 months was thus clear: Moscow was simply impotent to prevent the administration from realizing its principal aims. The reckless intoxication with U.S. power produced by the outcome of the war scare, peace scare and Berlin blockade found its perfect expression a short time later in NSC-68. Only if we take into account the effect of these earlier events, however, will we be able to understand the smug thinking that led Acheson, Paul Nitze and the other champions of NSC-68 to propose a quantum leap in military spending. Those who shared this mentality were utterly confident that although the U.S.S.R. now could boast of its own atomic weapons and point to the Chinese Revolution as a portent of the future, this country's massive military-industrial resources would once again enable it to expose all such Soviet pretensions as hollow—just as had been the case in Berlin.

In this mindless manner, in addition to fostering a repressive political and intellectual atmosphere in 1948, the Truman administration also fashioned the poisonous legacy of a fast-burgeoning competition in armaments with the U.S.S.R.—one from which neither side would feel free to withdraw, and one guaranteed to accelerate each time Pentagon planners could argue that their Soviet counterparts *might* have the capability to introduce a new weapon.* Whether this deadly development, once begun, can ever be halted remains an open question. Already the astronomical costs of military spending have helped

* "The 'threat analysis' used by the Pentagon to establish requirements for new weapons systems . . . assumes that: If the Soviets could deploy a better bomber, missile or submarine, it is therefore valid to assume they will deploy it. This equation has driven the military to set 'requirements' to build new weapons to meet future threats so defined. This is the system that produced the Air Force plan to spend $75 billion for a fleet of Stealth bombers based on CIA and DIA [Defense Intelligence Agency] projections . . . . The same threat analysis is driving the Navy's bid to build a $30 billion fleet of nuclear attack submarines that will be 30 times quieter than the current Los Angeles–class attack boats . . . . [Likewise] Army Secretary Michael P. W. Stone has postulated a new and improved Soviet tank by the end of the century. There is no evidence that the Soviets can afford to build a new generation tank, but the Army believes such a tank might be on the drawing board." Patrick E. Tyler, "Pentagon's Search for New Role," *San Francisco Chronicle,* August 8, 1990, Briefing section, p. 1. In retrospect, it is clear just how accurate was Tyler's judgment that the Soviets would be unable to pay for the production of new weaponry—not, of course, that this fact ever counted for much in Washington.

bring about the destruction of the former Soviet Union. The process is only relatively less advanced in the United States, where, as we shall observe, the production of weapons of apocalyptic warfare has served to forestall programs of social welfare. Thus have the largest corporations been successful in perpetuating what amounts to a national health system for themselves even as the standard of living of the population as a whole has systematically eroded.[25] For such a state of affairs, we can be grateful to the Truman administration for the sequence of events it orchestrated so skillfully in March and April of 1948.

These remarks are particularly relevant to the situation of the aircraft industry. It was, in 1948, admittedly on the brink of failure; yet it does not follow that the only recourse left to the administration was to provide it with a subsidy under the guise of protecting the United States against the threat of a Soviet attack. Had it been truly necessary for the defense of the nation to construct a new fleet of military airplanes boasting the most advanced technology—and, given the extent of the devastation of all the industrial powers during World War II, one must strenuously doubt that such was the case—there were other ways of going about it. One of these, as Henry Wallace proposed, was through nationalization of the industry. "During the six years from 1940 to 1945 inclusive," he wrote in April 1948, "the aircraft companies made, after taxes, an average of 100 percent a year on their prewar invested capital"; and what is more, "90 percent of the wartime capital expansion for these concerns" was, as I showed in chapter 2, "furnished by the government." It was this "wartime experience of easy profits" that had "spoiled these big concerns," Wallace believed. "Their profits now depend on large-scale construction of military planes. Irresistibly, therefore, they push for large-scale appropriations for military airplanes." From which it followed that "the only way to protect peace and the public interest is for the government to take over all companies making military aircraft"—and for good measure, to compensate their owners "on the basis of what has been spent for actual private investment, not on the basis of what the government has poured in."[26]

Wallace's idea merited more consideration than it received. Already the Vinson-Trammel Act of 1934 required at least 10 percent of the navy's planes to be constructed in government-owned shipyards. There is no reason why a similar arrangement could not have been devised for all military aircraft. Precisely such a decision was made by the French, and few would be so benighted as to argue that French-built military airplanes are inferior as a consequence. In the late 1940s, moreover, the option of nationalizing the industry remained a feasible one, for the federal government still owned "five large aircraft plants that have been retained in a stand-by status, along with essential equipment," as well as more than 40 percent of the floor space then used by the 15 largest aircraft manufacturing firms. And for some companies, the figure was much greater. In the case of Republic Aircraft, for example, as its president told the President's Air Policy Commission, "about 10 percent is company owned, and the balance is leased from the Government with an option to purchase."[27]

There were other, less sweeping alternatives as well. The administration could have merely stood aside and allowed the operation of the marketplace to take its toll. In this case, certain of the aircraft firms undoubtedly would have perished. But what of it? Even some aircraft executives, such as Robert E. Gross, the president of Lockheed, held that in the long run the only way the industry could stabilize itself was by shedding excess capacity. Either through mergers or outright failure, he believed, companies lacking "the tremendous amounts of capital that are now required for development . . . will eventually be forced out of business." Gross's notion was that once the aircraft corporations were "grouped into, say, ten strong units, these strong units will be enabled to compete with one another and the healthy free enterprise competition that is so desirable will be fostered rather than destroyed." Although, to be sure, there were those who argued that any shrinking of the industry would endanger "national security," it is most relevant to note that Secretary of the Air Force W. Stuart Symington explicitly rejected that reasoning. Conceding to the members of the President's Air Policy Commission that this was "a delicate question for us," he nonetheless asserted, "We feel that a happy medium must be struck. If we had to guess as to the number of plants we would guess that six to eight would be essential[,] stable manufacturing companies with engineering departments and so forth to go on with the business." Symington's next sentence, however, shot directly to the heart of the matter: "I don't think that the Aircraft Industries Association would quite agree on that."[28]

And that was just the point. Both nationalization and unsubsidized, unfettered competition were anathema to the aircraft manufacturers, as well as to those ruling-class banks (such as the Chase National and National City), giant corporations (such as General Motors), families (such as the Du Ponts and Rockefellers) and individuals (such as Laurance Rockefeller) with investments in the industry;[29] and in any event, the Truman administration—with representatives of big business and banking of the likes of James Forrestal, Averell Harriman, Robert Lovett, Will Clayton, Stuart Symington, John Snyder and William Draper dominating its upper ranks—had not the slightest desire to impose either alternative. Rather than engaging in a debate on the issues, therefore, the administration chose to resort to war-scare tactics, thus fastening upon this country a kind of industrial policy on the sly. Hence another deadly precedent arising out of the events of 1948 is that of using an imaginary Soviet threat to ensure that the arms-making business would never again be forced so near the edge of bankruptcy. More than four decades later, we are just beginning to get an inkling how difficult it will be to reverse this policy. Since 1948, the largest manufacturers of war machines have come to look upon their sustenance by the federal government as a birthright; and, now as then, it appears that government officials, from the president on down, fully share this point of view.

Equally serious, at the same time that companies producing for the military market were coming to expect that Washington would guarantee their well-being, the country's largest corporations were starting to discover new virtues in persistently high levels of arms spending. I do not wish to be thought guilty of exaggeration here. I assuredly am *not* proposing that the events of 1948 immediately galvanized the Fortune 500 into demanding, say, a quadrupling of the Pentagon budget. Still, 1948 did see a significant change in the attitude of big business in this regard—a first step, as it were, on the road to full-blown reliance on military procurement as a means of holding depressions at bay without the necessity for ambitious social programs that would rearrange society to the detriment of the rich. Prior to that year, the foremost business magazines were ambivalent with respect to increased military spending. While some of them carried articles favoring the expansion of arms procurement programs, others—fearful of inflation, higher taxes, diminished consumer spending, shortages of raw materials and/or government controls—were strongly opposed. But after business had come face to face with the first postwar recession that summer, such ambivalence quietly expired. By year's end, the business press not only had come to accept a bigger military budget as a permanent part of the economic landscape, but even began crowing enthusiastically over the deluge of blessings that it would allegedly unloose.

The quotation from the January 1949 issue of *Automotive Industries* at the head of this section illustrates one reason why corporations of all sizes, shapes and forms were increasingly coming to discern advantages in greater military expenditures: although the arms makers might be the primary recipients of such largesse, eventually the benefits would spread themselves more broadly. An article in *Steel* magazine with the revealing title "Aviation Revival Aids General Industry" described this spreading process at work. Thanks to the federal government, which had "prescribed potent medicine" for the aircraft industry, the "general metalworking field is feeling direct benefits now through subcontracting work awarded by airframe producers and federal contracts for the government-supplied equipment on military aircraft." But in addition to these predictable gains, such firms also found that they were "beginning to benefit indirectly, too. Mounting aircraft sales volumes will aid raw material suppliers, tool and die shops, machine tool builders and other segments of industry that deal with aircraft company suppliers, not with the plane makers directly."[30]

Further consolidating a business consensus in favor of military spending was the evident readiness of some of the nation's largest industrial corporations to join the aircraft manufacturers at the table and participate in the procurement feast—a trend that would become only more marked in years to come. "Allison [a division of General Motors], General Electric and Westinghouse now have substantial military contracts that will run through 1950," *Automotive Industries* reported in its annual survey of the aircraft industry in January 1949; and several business journals noted that the $1 million contract for spark plugs awarded General Motors' A/C Sparkplug Division was "a record peacetime order for aircraft spark plugs." In point of fact, as of June 30, 1948, General Electric, with $177 million in aircraft-procurement contracts, led all other companies in this regard, while General Motors, with $128 million, was fifth, and Westinghouse Electric, with $79 million, was eighth.[31]

The Truman administration's arms buildup also offered other opportunities for profitable investments outside the aircraft industry per se, as *The Magazine of Wall Street* observed in April of 1948.

> Producers of lightweight metals like aluminum and magnesium are bound to experience heavier demands from the aircraft industry, and among concerns in this group, Aluminum Company of America and Dow Chemical should be beneficiaries. . . . Since new uniforms have been designed . . . some of the woolen mills should soon be entering some substantial new orders on their books for woolen cloth. Assuredly this would be an element of satisfaction to American Woolen Company. . . . Pacific Mills, too, should benefit. . . . It is possible that the high quality oil products essential to aviation may permit wider profit margins than on normal industrial and civilian products. . . . Oil shares accordingly look more inviting than ever. In like manner, another secondary beneficiary would be the country's numerous transportation systems. . . . Along the same lines, it can be rationally assumed that capacity volume of the steel industry will be fully assured as a result of the preparedness program.[32]

More noteworthy than specific details about which industries would gain most from new military expenditure, though, were the generalized conclusions that the author of this article drew: "In a broad manner, the enlarged Government spending will inject new strength into the entire economy, stimulating a wide range of enterprises from retail stores to movies and liquor." In supporting bigger armaments budgets, business journals repeatedly returned to the idea that military procurement could prevent or overcome recessions by keeping overall levels of spending high. Even as early as the spring of 1948, *The Magazine of Wall Street* was beginning to cast the matter in exactly those terms: "In fact, the contemplated scale of spending . . . may be just enough, together with tax reduction and other outlays such as foreign aid, to act as a cushion against a business decline." Tracing the effects of Truman's military policies on the current economic slowdown, this author asserted that, "purely from a business standpoint," the administration's 30-percent boost in expenditures by the Pentagon had been "salutary"; the increase in spending by the armed services "undoubtedly has prevented a good deal of inventory liquidation that we otherwise might now witness." Hence Wall Street found much to like in Truman's stimulation of the arms race. "The greater confidence displayed by securities markets since proposal of the new armament program rests of course in the hope that the selective business recession that developed in recent weeks will be cushioned and perhaps reversed by the defense program." Later in the year, *Business Week* gave this idea its official imprimatur when it noted that "the economy is already feeling the full impact of last spring's decisions on cold-war spending. . . . It has been strong enough to maintain a generally upward tone in the face of such downward factors as huge farm production and the exhaustion of backlog demand in lines like radios and textiles."[33]

It took very little time for such reasoning to prevail, as big-business circles showed ever-greater willingness to channel taxpayers' money to the military as an antidote to depression. "Industrialists generally are in accord with the military's program of preparedness," *Steel* noted as early as April of 1948, specifically citing "C. E. Wilson, president of General Electric Co.," as a case in point. Similarly, in calling attention to the new "magic formula for almost endless good times," *U.S. News & World Report,* several weeks *before* the onset of the Korean War, reduced the question of business backing for Pentagon spending to its bare essentials: "Cold war is the catalyst. Cold war is an automatic pump primer."[34]

Of all the business magazines and trade journals that sought to follow this issue, however, it was *Business Week* that offered the clearest understanding of the implications of the new state of affairs for the ruling class. "The country is now geared to a $13-billion military budget," the magazine noted in March 1950, and although "that means you can't expect the program for 1951 to give the U.S. economy much additional kick," by the same token "it also means that $13-billion is a big—and reliable—prop under business. For the country as a whole," a Pentagon budget of this size guaranteed "a high level of federal spending," while for "individual suppliers, it means a solid backlog of orders." The following month, the editors again drew the connection between fueling the arms race and maintaining a stable capitalist order: "Pressure for more government spending is mounting. And the prospect is that Congress will give in. . . . The reason is a combination of concern over tense Russian relations, and growing fear of a rising level of unemployment here at home."[35]

But for *Business Week*'s most incisive treatment of why the economic elite should look upon lavish Pentagon budgets with enthusiasm, we must turn to an analysis published the previous year. Seeking to distill the meaning for big business of the war scare of 1948, this February 1949 article lost no time in getting directly to the point: "Today the prospect of ever-rising military spending acts: (1) as a sort of guarantee against any drastic deflation of the economy; (2) as a ceiling on . . . ambitious social-welfare projects." To understand why this was so, it was necessary to distinguish between the consequences of military and social spending. "Military spending doesn't really alter the structure of the economy. It goes through the regular channels. As far as a businessman is concerned, a munitions order from the government is much like an order from a private customer." An expansive program of "welfare and public-works spending," in contrast, "does alter the economy." In the course of achieving its goals, such a program "makes new channels of its own," it "creates new institutions" and, worst of all, it "redistributes income." Hence government spending of this nature "changes the whole economic pattern. That's its object."[36]

One could hardly hope for a more pithy summation, from the standpoint of the corporate rich, of the case for a never-ending military buildup. First of all, such a buildup supposedly would be a bulwark against future depressions. Second and no less significant, it would avoid a redistribution of income—and a corresponding redistribution of political power—that favored the majority. The moral of the sermon was obvious: for the ruling class to be secure in the enjoyment of its wealth and dominance, Pentagon expenditures would have to remain high.

We have now arrived at the point where the main themes of these concluding comments intersect. The year 1948 witnessed three momentous developments: the onset of a decades-long deterioration in U.S.-Soviet relations; the transformation of the Cold War into an arms race; and the inception of a permanent war economy. Each of these was both cause and effect of the others. Inevitably, the outcome of the Truman administration's maneuvers during the war scare of March and April and the subsequent peace scare of May was an upward leap in Cold War tensions. Given that Washington spoke so stridently and repeatedly of war while simultaneously initiating a 30-percent increase in military spending within the space of a few weeks, it is understandable that the Soviets would respond by preparing themselves for an atomic (or thermonuclear) offensive launched by the United States. In this fashion, the measures initiated by Truman and his top advisers in the spring of 1948 provoked a qualitative shift in the Cold War, moving it away from a battle of manifestoes and polemics toward a malignant military competition: in no other peacetime year since 1948 has a president ever been able to equal Harry Truman's record of boosting the Pentagon budget by 30 percent. Even Ronald Reagan, for all his intoxication with arms spending during the 1980s, came nowhere near matching this performance.[37]

The key feature of any arms race, however, is that it is self-fueling (which is why, although any fool can start one, bringing an arms race to a close invariably requires great patience, skill, intelligence—and, above all, commitment). Once such a contest is under way, introduction of a new generation of weaponry by either side is certain to be used by the other as irrefutable "proof" of its foe's implacably hostile intentions. Thus, an arms race not only arises out of a specific situation and fuels its own expansion thereafter; it also continuously regenerates the rancor, mistrust and ill feelings that gave birth to it in the first place. If its creation is predicated upon the existence of an irredeemably evil enemy, an arms race guarantees that this enemy will continue to exist. To these generalizations the armed rivalry with the Soviet Union inherited from the Truman administration has certainly been no exception.

Out of this enduring race a permanent war economy soon evolved, as giant corporations came to recognize the advantages of membership in an industry whose good health was defined as essential to the nation's security, and one that was immune to the vagaries of the consumer marketplace and the rigors of competition in the bargain. Indeed, that the federal government would henceforth ensure the survival of the armaments industry was one of the principal lessons of the events of 1948. As more firms—and bigger and more powerful ones, at that—digested this point and joined the rush for military contracts, the number of giant corporations heavily dependent on Pentagon procurement steadily increased; and so, accordingly, did the political influence they were able to wield. They rapidly learned how to use this influence to perpetuate a political climate in which resolving the conflicts that sustained the arms race and the permanent war economy became unthinkable. For executives in this industry were not *naïfs*; the *Magazine of Wall Street*'s observation that "anything approaching an amicable understanding" with the U.S.S.R. "would bring concerted demands for retrenchment in arms appropriations" was too obvious to require further elaboration; and from this proposition, they drew the appropriate corollary. (Here, too, as I showed in chapter 3, the aircraft companies pointed the way, harnessing the forces of the American Legion and the Veterans of Foreign Wars to browbeat the public into believing that the threat from a hostile, belligerent Soviet Union demanded an increase in procurement of military airplanes.)[38]

If these destructive but foreseeable effects of commencing an arms race occasioned many misgivings within the Truman administration, its leading figures have left little evidence of it behind. And after all, why should they have entertained second thoughts? Had they not discovered that, in *U.S. News & World Report*'s phrase, the "Cold War is an automatic pump primer"? Had this discovery not bestowed upon them "the magic formula for almost endless good times"? Yet not quite everyone was willing to sing the new refrain. There were still some who, even as they admitted that an expanded budget for the Pentagon "does serve as a shot in the arm for business," continued to have reservations. Yes, they conceded, military spending "will be a sustaining force for business," it "will make orders for heavy stuff, the machines of war, which take steel and expert workmanship of thousands of factories, employing many men and women." For all of that, however, as late as May 1949 it remained the view of so influential a business journal as *Changing Times: The Kiplinger Magazine* that "such spending is artificial and non-productive."[39]

No doubt it was easy to dismiss such naysayers as economic sticks in the mud, stodgy traditionalists who continued to adhere to the outmoded concept that military expenditures are always detrimental to the level of consumer spending a capitalist economy needs in order to flourish. If any of these naysayers are still alive in the 1990s, they may be enjoying—or at any rate, experiencing—the last laugh: their skepticism about the economic efficacy of military spending was better founded than their opponents realized.

Nor is this simply a matter of hindsight. Even in the late 1940s there was unmistakable evidence—for those who cared to heed it—that a celebration of the arrival of the millennium might still be a trifle premature. At the root of the matter lay a simple but inescapable reality: with each successive innovation in military technology, such technology becomes more expensive to produce. At the top of the air force hierarchy, officers and civilians alike were only too aware of this fact. Thus, at the fifth meeting of the Air Board in June 1947—where, as we observed in chapter 3, Oliver Echols, the president of the Aircraft Industries Association, so moved his former colleagues that they could scarcely contain their eagerness to enlist in his crusade for a presidential aviation commission—the rapid rise in the price of airplanes came under scrutiny. "Not only has the cost of an airplane gone up," moaned Major General Follett Bradley, "but the cost of equipment has gone up. . . . There is a certain piece of equipment, which a company is making—I happen to know something about it—the equipment that goes into that thing is going to cost more than the airplane itself." Bradley's lament led Lieutenant General Nathan F. Twining to note the corollary:

> When we estimated for the airplanes in this program, last September, based on September prices, we could buy 932 airplanes. Now the increase in cost alone, including the cost of this auxilliary [*sic*]

> equipment, between then and now, has reduced us to 749 airplanes without a dollar being taken away from us. That stems from the increase in cost of labor, cost of material which maybe runs 20 percent, but the big thing is the increase in the cost of equipment. It is more complicated—radar, and all that sort of thing—and the stuff is getting awfully damn expensive.

To which General Bradley offered a rejoinder as accurate as it was laconic: "That is what you pay for high performance."[40]

This was a subject on which Stuart Symington, who had manufactured gun turrets for the army air force prior to becoming a member of the Truman administration, could also hold forth with some authority. "It was not so many years ago that the total amount of research for propellers that was allowed Wright Field was $4500," he testified at a meeting of the President's Air Policy Commission. "Today the cost of the six propellers . . . on the B-36 is $168,000. Gun turrets for the B-24, which was a good airplane, all told, were less than $15,000 a plane. Gun turrets for the B-29 were $180,000 a plane. . . . Unquestionably the type and character of your equipment is going to be more expensive."[41]

Business circles likewise recognized the inexorable tendency for the price of weaponry to rise. In the first installment of its two-part treatment of the aircraft industry in 1948, for instance, *Fortune* remarked that, "In the early 1930's it cost about $20 per pound of airframe weight to develop an airplane; today, for the new transports, the development cost is more like $250 per pound. The difference between the two figures reflects not only the rise in wages and materials cost, but the exponential compounding of the complexity of airframe design." *Automotive Industries,* in calling attention to this phenomenon, even coined a name for it—"technological inflation"—and then supplied a representative case in point. The air force originally had planned to order 88 F-87 fighters from the Curtiss-Wright Corporation, but the "initial $1,500,000 tooling order had barely gotten under way when the performance of the new fighter had already been surpassed by the still newer Northrup [*sic*] FX-89 jet fighter. Superior though the newer plane was, however, it is interesting to note that whereas the Air Force was to have received 88 planes for some $80 million, it is now going to receive only 48 of the new type!"[42]

"Interesting" is scarcely the word for it. Although *Automotive Industries* acutely commented that the "technological inflation" found in the aircraft industry has "no counterpart in our civilian economy," it did not take time to ponder the long-term consequences of this fact—a luxury succeeding generations can no longer afford, however. Far and away the best analytical treatment of "technological inflation" is that of Mary Kaldor in *The Baroque Arsenal,* a work that lays bare the mechanisms ensuring that each new weapon will be more expensive than its predecessor.[43] To begin with, the armed services possess an insatiable hunger for *improved performance*—for airplanes, to take a specific example, that will go further, move faster, fly higher, transport larger loads, sport more deadly armaments, execute more demanding missions, and so on. Such improvements, however, come at a high price, as the foregoing discussion has suggested and as Mary Kaldor well documents. Materials must be strengthened to withstand stress under extreme conditions; engines must be made more powerful to lift heavier loads; new electronic equipment must be developed to control the airplane and the various weapons that it carries; air-conditioning must then be installed to keep the new electronic devices from overheating. And this merely scratches the surface. "The characteristics of an airplane as you approach the supersonic," Stuart Symington told the President's Air Policy Commission in November 1947, "and the tremendous performance of the new bombers, with all the equipment involved—. . . an airplane has been aptly described as an aluminum cage to hang instruments in—means costs are going up."[44] Not only that, but each new enhancement in one aspect of an airplane increases the cost of the finished product even as it demands complementary enhancements elsewhere: expanding an airplane's capabilities means more instruments and a system for cooling them, which means greater weight to lift, which means engines must have more horsepower and airframes must be made lighter, which means new alloys must be synthesized and techniques for working them perfected—all in an endless quest to advance the state of the art of destruction.

What is more, if a complicated weapon such as an airplane is to perform at its optimum, its components must be fabricated to exacting specifications, which almost always dictates that the device in question cannot be manufactured by assembly-line techniques, but instead must be hand-crafted in part or whole. "Republic [Aviation Corporation] today has to have a swarm of 1,100 aeronautical engineers to worry over the countless complexities involved in building its racing fighters and transports," *Fortune* reported in February 1947. "Designed for speed and range, equipped and built to customer [air force] specifications, the XF-12 and the Rainbow are as handmade as a house by Frank Lloyd Wright." Significantly enough, this company's "philosophy," according to *Fortune,* was to turn out "the fastest and most painstakingly clean aircraft [chief engineer Alexander] Kartveli can devise—and to hell with the costs."[45]*

* "In the competitive private-aircraft market," the magazine added, "Kartveli's talents are obviously uneconomic." In that simple statement lies a tacit recognition that an economy reserving its greatest rewards for the development of

Finally, because all of the factors that operate to inflate the cost of an advanced (or, in Mary Kaldor's terminology, a "baroque") weapon interact dialectically, the tendency for this cost to rise is *self-reinforcing*. The emphasis on achieving ever-better performance demands both increasingly exotic technology and a growing reliance on human labor (as opposed to automated machinery) in the process of production. The effect of each of these tendencies, obviously, is to drive up the price of weapons. But if spending on weaponry fails to grow as fast as the costs of production, the trend over time, as we have already observed, will be for newer weapons to be manufactured in *smaller quantities* than those they replace. Thus, an appropriation that would have bought the air force 932 airplanes in September 1946 purchased only 749 by the time General Twining related his tale of woe to the Air Board in June 1947—a decrease of some 20 percent in a mere nine months. But this is not yet the end of the matter, *for the very act of cutting back on production of a given weapon fosters an additional rise in that weapon's unit cost.* This is true because the smaller a weapon's production run, the less able will the manufacturer

---

baroque armaments technology will ultimately render itself unable to compete with one that concentrates on production of goods for the consumer marketplace. Granted that new technology is initially expensive regardless of whether it appears first in the civilian sector or the military, the crucial difference lies in what takes place next. After a new technology makes its debut in the civilian economy, its cost falls rapidly, as companies race each other to develop, and then to dominate, a market based upon it. For the price of the 60-megabyte hard-disk drive in 1987, for instance, in 1992 one could buy a drive capable of storing 1,000 megabytes of data—a sixteen-fold increase in capacity. By virtue of this drastic drop in the cost of hard-disk technology during the late 1980s, the market for these drives expanded phenomenally and an entirely new industry blossomed. In armaments production, in contrast, a different set of incentives prevails. There, success hinges not on lowering the price of existing technology, but on designing a still newer technology that will (on paper, at least) enable a device to outperform its rivals and render them obsolete. That this is so stems from the fact that, given the choice between larger numbers of cheaper weapons with fewer capabilities on the one hand versus smaller numbers of more expensive weapons with enhanced capabilities on the other, the armed services will opt to pay the higher price every time. The inevitable outcome is truly the worst of all possible worlds: "technological inflation" in the military sphere combined with the inability to compete in the commercial one. The reader should consult Kaldor, *Baroque Arsenal*, and the works of Seymour Melman, especially *The Permament War Economy: American Capitalism in Decline* (New York: Simon and Schuster, 1974).

be to invest in the kind of high-volume assembly-line techniques that could cut his costs per unit, and, conversely, the more will he be compelled to resort to production by hand. Hence in the same way that every increase in cost works to decrease the size of the production run of a weapon, each decrease in the size of that run then acts reciprocally to boost the cost of production still further. "It's been an immutable law of physics [sic] in our industry," acknowledges one Lockheed vice president, "that as production [of a particular weapon] declines, your costs go up." As a result, the propensity for the price of modern "baroque" armaments to spiral ever higher is one from which there is no escape. The persistently rising cost of contemporary weaponry leads to reduced production runs; reduced production runs in turn lead to still higher costs; and so the cycle repeats itself *ad infinitum.**

It is imperative that we now examine the implications of the foregoing analysis with respect to employment, for if it is true that, as *U.S. News & World Report* maintained in 1950, Cold War arms spending comprises a "magic formula for almost endless good times," it can only be by virtue of its power to create and maintain high employment. Here, a graphic analogy may be useful: just as an addict

---

* The above reasoning is anything but merely theoretical, as the following item demonstrates: "The Pentagon routinely insists that once in production, the per-unit cost [of a weapon] will drop as contractors learn production-line efficiencies. Consistently, the opposite has happened. On average, weapons programs finish up 23 percent above original cost, according to a recent General Accounting Office study. . . . The rise in weapons costs above budget allocations has forced the Pentagon to stretch out production, spreading its purchase of tanks, planes and ships over a longer period. This saves money the first year, but *inefficient production rates cause per-unit costs to go through the roof. Often, budget shortages force the military to cut back the total purchases as well. This also raises the long-term cost.* The Navy planned in 1988 to build 29 Seawolf nuclear submarines at $1.5 billion each. After delays and cost overruns, the purchase was cut back to two submarines at a cost of almost $3 billion each. To accommodate these rising future costs, Pentagon budgeteers each year simply pencil into their budget plans huge future increases in the defense budget, constantly postponing the day of reckoning" (all emphasis added). For all intents and purposes, this article might have been written in 1948: 45 years have passed, but the political economy of armaments production remains essentially unchanged. See David Wood, "Defense Budget is offensive: Outside experts may be called in to straighten it out," *San Francisco Examiner,* February 7, 1993, p. A-12. For the quotation from Lockheed vice president Dwain Mayfield, see John Diamond, "Lockheed Offers to Cut Price of Fighter," *San Francisco Chronicle,* July 7, 1994, p. D7.

over time requires steadily larger doses of a narcotic to produce a given psychological effect, military spending over time requires steadily larger does of cash to produce a given level of employment. That is to say, because each successive version of a weapon such as an airplane or a tank is more "baroque" than its predecessor, and thus correspondingly more expensive to manufacture, it is by the same token less efficient at generating jobs. Consider again, by way of illustration, the example cited by *Automotive Industries*: for the same funds that would have purchased 88 F-87s, the air force received only 48 FX-89s. It is a reasonable deduction that building the 88 F-87s would have employed nearly twice as many people as building the 48 FX-89s (88 ÷ 48 = 1.833). As these figures once more make clear, a new weapon both costs more and—unless the budget for its procurement is increased proportionally—will be produced in smaller numbers than the weapon it replaces, hence fewer workers will be needed to manufacture it. The FX-89 may well have outperformed the F-87 in the skies; from the standpoint of keeping workers on the job, however, it was the latter that took the prize.

Is it, though, somehow possible to overcome the tendency toward diminishing employment in the armaments industry caused by "technological inflation"? An instant's reflection should show that it is not. Because a single F-87 is roughly twice as expensive as a single FX-89, in order to prevent employment from decreasing when the newer model goes into production, its appropriation would have to be almost double that for the older one. From which it appears that the thesis propounded by *U.S. News & World Report* encounters a bit of an obstacle: the supply of money that can be devoted to the purchase of weaponry is, alas, merely finite; whereas the amount by which the price of such weaponry can increase is quite unbounded. If, in order to procure the same number of fighter airplanes after the FX-89 has made the F-87 obsolete, the appropriation for that purpose must be doubled, what, then, will happen when the same fate befalls the FX-89? How many times can the budget for a given type of weapon be doubled before all available funds are exhausted? Theoretically, of course, in the interest of preserving employment in the armaments industry, the citizenry could agree to forego such amenities as Social Security payments, Medicaid, efforts to improve air and water quality, aid to education, research into the causes of and cures for disease, construction and repair of federal highways, support of rapid transit, enforcement of occupational safety regulations, and so on. This would, to be sure, postpone the day of reckoning; it could not avert it permanently. Only a military budget of infinite proportions could accomplish that. "The magic formula for almost endless good times" turns out to be something less than magical after all.

There is, in other words, no way to repeal what may be called, with a bow in the direction of Mary Kaldor, the iron law of baroque-armaments technology: because a more advanced weapon always tends to be more expensive than the less advanced one it replaces, it will, all other things being equal, always tend to employ fewer workers in its production (and in addition, this tendency will also cause secondary "ripples" throughout the remainder of the economy). But nations as well as individuals, it seems, can be reluctant learners. At this point, our earlier analogy is apropos. Unable to ignore the fact that the customary dosage no longer gives the desired effect, the narcotics addict responds with an attempt to increase the size of the dose. Like that addict, the United States, confronted with the iron law of baroque armaments, has sought to accomplish with larger military budgets what smaller ones have been unable to do. A decade of profligate military spending during the 1980s has confirmed only too fully the futility of this approach. What we have to show for this staggering investment in weaponry are overcrowded schools staffed by underpaid teachers, record numbers of people without homes, levels of air and water pollution little changed from those of 20 years ago, nuclear and toxic waste sites befouling the environment at an out-of-control rate, a stagnant economy that combines a decline in the material standard of living of working-class families with a shrinking of the size of the middle class, a medical system that denies care to tens of millions, a network of highways and bridges that is crumbling into decrepitude for lack of maintenance, an inability to compete in the global marketplace—and that by no means exhausts the list. In what may be the supreme irony, moreover, although the Soviet and Eastern European versions of communism have collapsed, wanton military spending has so impoverished the United States that at the very moment when calls for a second European Recovery Program are loud and growing, this country cannot even *consider* financing one.[46] "The long years we spent plunged in the Cold War made losers of us all," Mikhail Gorbachev has written. Future generations are unlikely to take issue with this conclusion.[47]

Yet if we are now reaping a bitter harvest in the 1990s, it was the Truman administration that in 1948 sowed the seeds. The simple truth is that for over 40 years the nation has been burdened with policies inaugurated by Harry Truman and his chief advisers, the primary consequence of which has been to mire the United States inextricably in a perpetual arms race and a permanent war economy. To succeed in having these policies adopted, the Truman administration deceived Congress and the public about the intentions of the Soviet Union and the likelihood of war; rebuffed all efforts by the Soviets to reach an accommodation with the United States; escalated the nuclear arms race; and, not least, rescued a failing aircraft industry under the guise of enhancing the nation's defenses. At the time these steps were taken, it was the aircraft industry that was near bankruptcy and the country that was prosperous; now, almost 45 years later, by virtue of the measures initiated by the Truman administration, the situation more closely resembles the reverse. As well as any single item can, that unhappy fact encapsulates the legacy bequeathed us by the Truman presidency.

APPENDICES

Appendix A: Estimating Soviet Intentions and Capabilities, 1947-1948

I then referred to the atomic bomb, the fact that I thought the fear of it made somewhat improbable Soviet resort to military action.

—Memorandum of Conversation [with Pope Pius XII], by the Secretary of State, October 19, 1948[1]

Because the Russians have assembled a formidable fighting force in Germany, they will require a tremendous logistical effort in order to launch any large-scale and sustained offensive. Lines of communication to the Eastward are essential to its success. I was told at the G-2 [intelligence] briefing that the Russians have dismantled hundreds of miles of railroads in Germany and sent the rails and ties back to Russia. There remains, at the present time, so I was told, only a single track railroad running Eastward out of the Berlin area and upon which the Russians must largely depend for their logistical support. This same railroad line changes from a standard gage, going Eastward, to a Russian wide

gage in Poland, which further complicates the problem of moving supplies and equipment forward.

—Memorandum for the President from Colonel Robert B. Landry, September 28, 1948[2]

APPROACHING THE WAR SCARE OF 1948

One of the questions I wanted to investigate when I embarked on the research for this book was the extent to which estimates of Soviet military capabilities and intentions changed as a result of the war scare of March 1948. If there were any basis for the Truman administration's claims that the U.S.S.R. was on the verge of invading Western Europe—or for that matter, Manchuria or Iran—surely intelligence reports to that effect would begin to show up with increasing frequency as the war scare approached. And, by the same token, were the scare anything more than a fiction thrown together for expediency's sake by the administration, one would expect U.S. appraisals of Soviet intentions after the scare had waned to be much more cautious and pessimistic than those written months before its onset.

There is no evidence whatsoever that any such developments took place. So far as intelligence estimates are concerned, the war scare was a nonevent; to borrow an analogy from physics, it did not produce enough of an effect to stand out from the background. If, in other words, one did not already know about the war scare from other sources, one would have been unable to infer its existence from the intelligence reports alone. The *only* exceptions to this generalization that I have discovered are the telegram dispatched from Berlin on March 4-5, 1948, by General Lucius D. Clay and the subsequent report, "Estimate of the World Situation," composed by the director of army intelligence, General Stephen J. Chamberlin; and both of these items were, as we saw in chapter 4, completely spurious—political artifacts masquerading as intelligence analyses. It was, after all, Chamberlin who had solicited Clay to send his well-known message, just as it was Chamberlin who then used that message to justify his own "Estimate." Had the Army and the Pentagon not been desperate for a means of bullying a Republican-controlled Congress into voting for an unpopular peacetime draft, it is *extremely* improbable that either document would ever have seen the light of day. And it is certainly significant that in no case could any intelligence agency, military or civilian, be induced to support the dire contentions of the Clay telegram or Chamberlin's "Estimate."

A survey of both formal and informal estimates of Soviet capabilities and intentions makes clear just how little these changed as a result of the war scare of 1948. The documents I introduce below—a representative sample—are a diverse lot: some contain little more than an offhand sentence or two; others are long and elaborate studies of Soviet military strength and strategy. What they have in common is one feature: without exception, they assert that the Soviets will not deliberately go to war with the West, much less attack the United States, at any time in the near future. The key word, of course, is *deliberately*. No bureaucrat—and for the most part it is bureaucrats, whether in uniform or out, whose prose we shall be reading—would be so rash as to argue that the Soviets would never, under any circumstance, resort to force of arms. Consequently, these estimates, especially the formal intelligence reports, often include a ritualistic disclaimer of one sort or another. Sometimes this disclaimer is couched as a statement to the effect that the Soviets might strike first if they judged that they were about to be invaded, or if they came to feel that such-and-such an event—which might be anything from Yugoslavia's break with the U.S.S.R. to the passage of the European Recovery Program (Marshall Plan)—jeopardized their own security. Other reports mention the possibility of a war arising inadvertently because of miscalculations on both sides. I propose, however, that such pro forma statements must be taken with a large grain of salt, for I suspect that their purpose was as much to shield their authors from reprisals in the most unlikely event that war did break out as it was to inform their readers. Anyone who has ever spent much time in one knows well that the first principle of self-preservation in a bureaucracy is to protect one's posterior. Intelligence-gathering agencies are no more immune from the operation of that principle than any other bureaucratic organization.

In general, intelligence estimates dealing with the U.S.S.R. focused on that nation's military *capabilities* and/or its *intentions*. Both civilian and military analysts insisted on the distinction. In discussing the Soviet Union, one naval analyst explained, "Too often it is assumed that her capabilities and intentions are one and the same thing." "In this connection," echoed a second, "it is important to differentiate between Soviet capabilities and intentions."[3] With respect to the former, there was broad agreement that the Soviet Union, still reeling from the massive devastation it had suffered during World War II, came nowhere near being able to attack the United States from either the sea or the air. Even the air force did not dissent from this proposition—although, as the British air vice-marshal for intelligence tactfully hinted to our old friend, Director of Air Force Intelligence George C. McDonald, representatives of that service did systematically inflate their estimates of Soviet capabilities:

> For instance, you put [Soviet] first-line strength at 14,000 [airplanes]; I put it at 10,000. You say they could have 1,000 B-29's by

> January; I am saying that they could not reach 1,000 until May and only then if their factories are as efficient as yours were in 1943, which I doubt. You are inclined to think that they have a bomb [i.e., atomic bomb] now; I don't collate that sort of Intelligence, but I am advised by Directorate which does, that they haven't. . . .
>
> I refer, of course, to the state of Russia's industrial recovery, including precision engineering, training of technicians, communications, availability of raw materials and the time and facilities for basic research. I believe, generally speaking, that we in London are inclined to consider that Russia is more backward in these respects than you consider her to be. Frequently we cut our figures because of these intangible factors.
>
> Incidentally a source which has recently become available to us (and to you through London CIA) has somewhat confirmed our views on this backwardness.[4]

There was greater diversity of opinion on the subject of the U.S.S.R.'s capabilities on land. Although no one doubted that the Soviets had the wherewithal to overrun Western Europe or the Middle East or parts of East Asia, several authors pointed out the obstacles the Red Army would encounter thereafter. Because of the rudimentary and decrepit state of their transportation system, especially railroads, it was questionable whether the Soviets would be able to maintain the supply lines and provide the reinforcements that would be needed to establish firm control over Western Europe. Others observed that the Red Army might have severe problems of morale in launching such an aggressive attack. The Winter War of 1939–1940 between the U.S.S.R. and Finland suggested that although Soviet troops would fight valiantly to defend their homeland, they might be far less formidable when it came to invading other nations that had offered them no provocation.

Compared to estimating capabilities, evaluating intentions is much less straightforward. In the former case, one makes use of all available sources to learn as much as one can about the current order of battle of "the other side," weaponry under development, levels of production, transportation network and the like. Granted that some uncertainty is necessarily involved, still, such information is largely of the objective, or "hard," variety: numbers of troops, disposition of aircraft, location of railroads and refineries—fill in the blanks with the most nearly correct numbers and that, in essence, is that. Estimates of intentions, in contrast, are inherently "softer," their subjective component much larger. How do those in command on "the other side" think? What are their goals? What risks are they willing to run in order to achieve them? What risks dare *we* run in pursuit of ours? Nor can one simply infer intentions from capabilities—this is exactly the fallacy that the two naval analysts cited above warned against. A nation may undertake the deployment of a new weapon—a bomber with longer range, say, or a missile with increased accuracy or a more powerful bomb—not because its leaders plan on using it to conquer another, but in order to minimize the possibility that they themselves will be the victims of an attempted conquest.

In view of the difficulties involved in formulating these estimates, it is particularly impressive that there was so little difference of opinion on the immediate intentions of the U.S.S.R. Some thought the Soviets bent on world revolution; others saw them preparing for an armed confrontation with the United States at a distant date; still others viewed them as masking traditional Russian aims under a veneer of Bolshevik ideology. Regardless of the existence of such diverse points of view, however, estimates of Soviet intentions were virtually unanimous in concluding that the Soviets currently had no wish to initiate hostilities with the West. What is even more striking is that in those rare instances in which an individual expressed some doubt about this thesis at one moment, he reasserted it with redoubled fervor the very next (see, for example, the letter of December 10, 1948, from Rear Admiral L. C. Stevens to Secretary of Defense James Forrestal below). It is also worth mentioning that once the war scare had passed, a number of analysts—perhaps in reaction to the overblown language of Secretary of State Marshall the previous March—took pains to distinguish the foreign policy of the Soviet Union under Stalin from that of Nazi Germany under Adolf Hitler.

Two further notes before commencing our survey. First, in addition to examining the estimates excerpted here, the reader also should look again at the comments of Secretary of Commerce W. Averell Harriman, Chief of Naval Operations Admiral Chester W. Nimitz and retiring Army Chief of Staff General Dwight D. Eisenhower on the question of Soviet intentions; their remarks, made between September 1947 and February 1948, appear at the beginning of chapter 4. Second, many of these estimates were written in outline form; in quoting from them, I have generally chosen to omit topic-level indicators, except where I felt their presence was necessary to preserve the sense of the quotation.

Army Intelligence Estimate, "Soviet Intentions in Scandinavian Countries," July 1, 1946.

This report completely contradicts the Truman administration's depiction of the Soviet policy as aiming at the immediate subjugation of Finland and, by extension, the remainder of Scandinavia:

> *General:* In line with present Soviet policy to appease international opinion, it is not considered that any active military aggression will be initiated by 1 July 1946 nor in the near future, but that the general trend of Soviet aims toward Scandinavia will not be altered. The U.S.S.R. will continue to exert indirect efforts to achieve its aims through political and economic means. Certainly Scandinavia offers no immediate threat to Soviet security now or in the immediate future, so there is no need to hurry the realization of aims in that direction at the expense of international good will. . . .
>
> *Military:* The most significant indication of Soviet intentions towards the Scandinavian countries from the military aspect is the withdrawal of Soviet forces from Norway and Denmark. Despite previous pessimistic reports, the Red Army completely evacuated Bornholm early in April 1946. Soviet troops were withdrawn from Northern Norway and the military mission was replaced by a military attaché at Oslo in the fall and early winter of 1945. Since the presence of those forces would have been of material assistance to any offensive plans against Denmark, Norway, and Sweden their withdrawal constitutes an important negative indication from the military point of view.[5]

U.S. Army, "Intelligence Estimate of the World Situation for the Next Five Years," August 23, 1946:

> Despite much prestige, the largest single army on earth, and considerable gains in both population and territory, the U.S.S.R. has the following weaknesses which will limit global capabilities: war losses in manpower and industry; lack of economic self-sufficiency, particularly in the Far East; poor rail and road nets; vulnerability of oil, rail net and vital industrial centers to long range bombers; lack of a navy, a strategic air force and the atomic bomb; and resistance in occupied areas.
>
> These weaknesses must be eliminated completely, or nearly so, before the U.S.S.R. can mount a successful attack against the United States, during [the period] 1946–51. . . .
>
> The U.S.S.R. does not possess the capability of major bombing operations against the U.S. within the next five years (1946–51), nor is it currently capable of mounting an airborne invasion of the U.S., even with advanced staging areas in Greenland and northern Canada.

> ... The U.S.S.R. [*sic*] development of an atomic bomb by 1949 is possible, *but it is not likely that such bombs could be produced in significant numbers within the next five years.*
>
> Soviet intentions are: ... to avoid war in the next few years in order to build up their industry while simultaneously expanding their political and economic control wherever they can by any means short of war [emphasis added].[6]

War Department Intelligence Staff Study, "Basic Assumptions for Civil Defense Board," December 23, 1946.

Several "factors, principally ... the economic and physical debilitation resulting from World War II," combined to make the Soviets "incapable of waging a long-term, global war, or of waging a war outside the Eastern Hemisphere." Another of these "factors" was the U.S.S.R.'s "lack of a long-range bomber force, large-scale amphibious means, and a deep-sea navy." And even if the Soviets "could produce their first atomic bomb between 1950 and 1953," they still would "not have stockpiled significant quantities [of this weapon] before 1956." As a result, "Prior to 1956 continental United States will not be subject to large-scale invasion or attack. ... It is unlikely that there will be any aggressive military action against continental United States prior to 1956."[7]

Army Intelligence Estimate, "Intentions and Capabilities of Potential Enemies Against the U.S. During the Next Ten Years," July 11, 1947.

Although two of the three guiding assumptions of this study were that the U.S.S.R. was the "one power ... sufficiently powerful to challenge the United States" and that the "ultimate goal of the Soviets is world domination," the authors nevertheless concluded that

> 1. The Soviet economy will not be capable until about 1956 of furnishing the equipment and supplies necessary for such an offensive [attack against the U.S.].
>
> 2. The Soviet Union may be expected to avoid any serious risk of war with the United States for some years to come. Perhaps by about 1956 the war potential of the Soviets will have developed sufficiently to give them powerful offensive capabilities against the United

> States. Then, if other conditions were favorable, they *might* launch an all-out war for the fulfillment of their policies [emphasis added].

Thus, for the period "1949 through 1955," even though the U.S.S.R. might have a "strategic Air Force as early as 1949; [the] atomic bomb between 1950-1953; [and] a stock of these bombs by 1955," the report maintained that "these weapons cannot be employed on a sufficient scale to reduce seriously the United States' war potential or will to resist."[8]

Air Force Intelligence Estimate, "Air Capabilities of the USSR in the Far East," undated, but sometime after August 8, 1947.

The posturing of Air Force civilian and military functionaries during the war scare to the contrary notwithstanding, the chief assumption guiding "Strategic Planning for the Organization and Disposition of the U.S. Air Force" was that "the U.S.S.R. will not take action which *may* precipitate war with the U.S. at this time" (emphasis in the original). A second and related assumption was that "the U.S.S.R. Ground Forces and Air Forces, despite their capabilities for land action, are not presently capable of any inter-hemisphere action of real threat to the continental U.S."—a statement also at variance with air force pronouncements during the war scare. "The U.S.S.R. will not precipitate a shooting war with the U.S.," the estimate continued, "until such time as the Kremlin decides:

> 1. That the economic position of the U.S.S.R. is such as to insure a reasonable chance of supporting a successful war against the U.S.
>
> 2. That the U.S.S.R. is capable of implementing an Inter-Hemisphere Air War.
>
> 3. That the U.S.S.R. has the capability to utilize atomic weapons.
>
> 4. That the U.S.S.R. has advanced sufficiently in the phase of political, economic, and organized subversive action to assist materially in the final armed assault.[9]

Walter Bedell Smith, the Ambassador to the Soviet Union, to the Secretary of State, September 30, 1947:

"We add our convictions USSR is not prepared for and does not want active war in presently foreseeable future."[10]

Notes on Appearance of Donald M. Nelson before the President's Air Policy Commission (PAPC), October 23, 1947.

Nelson had been the director of the War Production Board in World War II and, presumably because of his expertise in such matters and because he had visited Soviet aircraft plants in 1944, was asked to testify before the PAPC; H. E. Weihmiller, a member of the commission's staff, took notes. Nelson, according to these notes,

> Was impressed with Russian production in that it was above his expectancy, but was also very far below our own in magnitude and efficiency.
>
> Stated that in 1944 Russians produced aluminum enough for only 5,000 planes, so he does not see how they could have produced 40,000 or 50,000 planes in 1945 as has been said by others. . . .
>
> Overall, believes the Russians lack technical skill to change their production capabilities very rapidly, and that the few Germans inducted into the Russian economy are not enough to materially alter this situation . . .
>
> Believes Russians will acquire industrial know-how fast, but that it will still be 10 years more before they are in a technical and production position to support a war. . . .

In Nelson's view, the "limiting factors in Russian aircraft production" were shortages of electric power, aluminum and petroleum; in addition, the "Russian economy" was "currently such that if they did make enough planes, for example, for full war needs, they would have to be short on tanks, ordnance, etc. They do not possess sufficient facilities to supply sufficient quantities across the board for a balanced war machine."[11]

Ambassador Walter Bedell Smith to the Secretary of State, "Evaluation of Present Kremlin International Policies," November 5, 1947:

> It seems clear for many reasons, particularly the apathy and lack of ideological enthusiasm on the part of certain Soviet people, coupled with the need of the Kremlin to rebuild its economic-industrial potential, that it neither desires or will force the issue to such a point

> as to become involved in a major war. The possibility cannot be overlooked, however, that these aggressive tactics [of the U.S.S.R.] may cause a serious incident to take place which, of course, might bring about an undesired war.[12]

Navy Captain Thomas J. Kelly, Report on Senate Appropriations Committee Fact Finding Trip to Europe and the Middle East, December 1, 1947:

> Ambassador Smith stated that he did not believe war would come unless the USSR or some one of its satellites worked itself into an impossible position and could not retreat with dignity. He also stated that the USSR, as a matter of policy, keeps pushing on all fronts as long and as much as possible. When the opposition becomes too strong it usually pulls back and awaits a more opportune time or else attempts another and different approach.

Written on the first page of this memorandum, in what appears to be James Forrestal's hand, are the following words: "Tell Kelly I found his report interesting and useful. JF."[13]

Army Intelligence Comments on "Immediate Security Risk Involved in Aid to European Recovery," December 1, 1947:

> It is believed that Moscow wants to avoid war at this time and would not take a calculated risk of precipitating it. However, there is no doubt that the chances of war being precipitated by an incident will be much increased by the effect of the Marshall Plan to heighten tension in international relations.
>
> . . . The Soviets, however, probably believe that since time is in their favor it would be a mistake to risk a conclusive test of military strength with the United States before the USSR has an adequate supply of atomic weapons and has substantially increased its economic capabilities to sustain its armed forces under the conditions of modern scientific warfare. Moreover, "the cold war" which the Soviets have precipitated is probably regarded by them as a long- and not a short-term conflict. Naturally, they want to win this "cold war," if they can, as quickly as possible, but they are undoubtedly

> prepared to lose many battles, such as the one over the Marshall Plan, without losing the war. To risk losing everything in premature armed conflict would, from the Soviet point of view, amount to throwing away their chances of ultimately winning everything in a prolonged cold war. It must be remembered that the Soviets believe, apparently with considerable confidence, that a severe economic depression in the U.S. will tremendously assist their own efforts to obstruct a capitalist recovery in Western Europe.[14]

Memorandum on the Likelihood of Soviet Military Intervention in East Asia from John Paton Davies to George F. Kennan, December 5, 1947.

Davies was a member of the State Department Policy Planning Staff; Kennan was its director.

> The Soviet reluctance to use its army in Asia, I think, is an integral and deep-seated part of their policy in that area. As long as their principal attack on us in Asia is that of imperialism and subjugation of colonial and semi-colonial (i.e., Chinese) people, they will be most loath to put themselves in the same position by armed intervention of white complected Soviet troops. I should guess that this was one of the determining considerations in the Soviet submission to humiliation at the hands of the Iranians during the Azerbaijan fiasco. One Soviet brigade could have redressed the situation. It was not used, I suspect, not only because it might have precipitated American retaliation within the U.N. framework but also because it would have been a clear-cut instance of imperialism. The early withdrawal of Soviet troops from Manchuria, while we had forces still in North China and they could not be sure that we would not put troops in Manchuria, would seem to be another indication of the importance which the U.S.S.R. attaches to keeping its hands militarily clean in Asia. Therefore, I feel that the U.S.S.R. has no idea of action involving Soviet military intervention in the Far East not only because there is no need for such action but also because to do so would run counter to a basic tenet of Soviet policy in Asia. My guess is the U.S.S.R. would permit the Chinese communists to suffer critical losses and still not intervene with the Soviet army. The only action which might precipitate Soviet armed intervention, I think, would be a direct challenge in the form of offensive action by American troops in North Manchuria threaten-

> ing the survival of a Chinese or Mongolian force subservient to the U.S.S.R. As such action is not likely, in the foreseeable future, I think it is possible to rule out for some time to come that bugaboo of our military thinkers—open Soviet intervention in Manchuria or Inner Mongolia.[15]

THE WAR SCARE RECEDES . . .

Air Force Daily Activities Reports, December 29, 1947, to October 1, 1948.

There are among these daily intelligence reports no items suggesting any kind of Soviet military buildup in preparation for launching an immediate war against the West.[16]

The U.S. Ambassador to Poland, Stanton Griffis, on Soviet Intentions, May 25, 1948.

As we observed in chapter 5, Secretary of Defense James Forrestal and Stanton Griffis—two former investment bankers turned bureaucrats—on this date held a luncheon conversation about Soviet intentions. Afterward, Forrestal noted in his diary the observations of "Griffis on war": "Doesn't believe the Russians want one. Saw no sign on his motor trip to Czechoslovakia of any great concentrations of troops. Believes domestic problems of Russia are so serious that they would think hard before starting a fight."[17]

Final Report, Third European Intelligence Conference, Frankfurt, Germany, June 2–7, 1948.

> In war potential, USSR assets are:
>
> 1. An abundance of manpower.
>
> 2. A highly centralized dictatorship government in absolute control of the masses through an efficient police system.
>
> 3. Sufficiency in weapons of World War II models to equip their ground forces.

4. Air forces capable of supporting the Army on the Eurasian Continent.
5. Sufficient food to maintain war on the Eurasian Continent.
6. Vast areas for dispersion to lessen the effect of hostile air attacks.
7. Fifth column representatives in all countries.

Its war liabilities are:

1. Heavy industry will not yet meet the maintenance needs of a world war.
2. An effective strategic bombing force has not yet been produced.
3. The transportation system is still weak.
4. There is no ocean-going navy.
5. There is no atomic bomb in production.
6. There is present weakness in the control of satellite populations through minority governments.

"Balancing" these "liabilities" and "assets," the authors concluded, "It would appear that although the Soviet Union can overrun Europe, the Middle East, and key areas of Asia in a matter of months, she should not expect to be able to provide the equipment required to support successfully an all-out war with the West."[18]

Address by George F. Kennan to the Permanent Joint Board of Defense, Canada-U.S., June 8, 1948.

These remarks were for the most part identical to the report by the State Department Policy Planning Staff, "Factors Affecting the Nature of the U.S. Defense Arrangements in the Light of Soviet Policies," discussed in chapter 5. Kennan did, however, add two new observations:

> The USSR is anxious for a relaxation of tension in the "Cold War." Soviet reaction to the Smith-Molotov exchange [described in chapter 7], her support of the Wallace candidacy and other indications point to the fact that Russia is extremely anxious for a relaxation of tension. . . .
>
> History has shown that Russia is unable to wage a long campaign with long lines of communication. For example, it is not believed

> that she can wage a campaign in the Iberian Peninsular. The Soviets fight well within their own country but poorly outside.[19]

. . . THE BLOCKADE ARRIVES

On June 24, 1948, the Soviets instituted a blockade that prevented entry into West Berlin via railroad and highway. It is highly significant that even such a drastic step did not alter the consensus that the U.S.S.R. was not planning to attack the West. In fact, as we shall shortly witness, less than one month after the blockade began, Charles E. Bohlen, the State Department Counselor, would assert that "the U.S. Government considers that our position vis-à-vis the Soviet Union is better now than at any time since the end of the war"! In any case, the most pessimistic intelligence report that I discovered for the period from June 24 through the end of the year was one entitled "Study of the Impact on National Security of Military Assistance to the Western Union Nations," prepared by the Joint Strategic Survey Committee of the Joint Chiefs of Staff and dated August 5, 1948. The question the study sought to answer was whether "war with the Soviets" was "so imminent that no United States military assistance could be provided in time to improve the Western Union military situation." Even though they held that "war must be considered imminent at this time and the imminence of war may continue for an indefinite period," the authors nevertheless maintained—consistent with their use "of the word imminent . . . in the sense of threatening to occur"—that "war is not inevitable." There were, moreover, even some grounds for a very guarded optimism: "Neither the USSR nor the Western Democracies desire[s] war at this time"; the problem, however, was that "each side can be expected to take action and counteraction on such close calculations as to the reaction of the other that war may be precipitated at any time by an unfortunate incident." But this judgment was a far cry from contending that the Soviet Union was determined to go to war; accordingly, the report reiterated that although "war must be considered imminent at the present time," it was "not inevitable," and there was thus "a possibility that military aid to Western Union nations can be provided in time to improve their military situation." For all its ambivalence, even this assessment steadfastly rejected the argument that the Soviets were contemplating a deliberate armed attack on the West.[20]

Remarks of George F. Kennan at the Third Meeting of the Washington Exploratory Talks on Security, July 7, 1948.

These talks would culminate in the formation of the North Atlantic Treaty Organization in 1949.

> Mr. Kennan discussed Soviet intentions. He expressed disbelief that the Soviet leaders contemplated launching world conflict by armed force. They had not yet repaired the devastated areas of Russia. The people were war weary. In view of the lessons of the two World Wars the Kremlin could not be sure of overcoming Europe without first knocking out North American industrial potential. It believed it could win ideologically more easily than militarily. It was not operating on any fixed timetable and parallels between Stalinism and Hitlerism were dangerous.[21]

The United States Military Governor for Germany, Lucius D. Clay, to the Department of the Army, July 10, 1948.

Given both the central role that his telegram of March 5 played in the Truman administration's war scare and the fact that he was witnessing Soviet actions firsthand in Berlin, Lucius Clay's views are of particular importance. Despite the fact that by the time this urgent top-secret telegram was sent the Berlin blockade had been in place for two and one-half weeks, Clay was "*still* convinced that the Soviets do not want war" (emphasis added).[22]

Memorandum for the Secretary of Defense from the Director of Army Intelligence, July 14, 1948.

This memorandum, written in response to a request from Secretary of Defense Forrestal, supplied empirical confirmation of Clay's estimate that the Soviets, in imposing the Berlin blockade, did not regard this measure as a first step toward war:

> A review of reports from all sources fails to reveal any acceptable evidence of significant Soviet troop movements during the past month. Such movements as have occurred appear to have been connected either with annual maneuvers or with the transfer of personnel.

> Large-scale movements aimed at reinforcing the Soviet armies in Germany for offensive operations or at building up concentrations in Hungary and Rumania for a possible attack on Yugoslavia would be subject to detection by our observers in Poland, Hungary and Rumania. Reports from these areas indicate that there had been no build-up in Hungary or Rumania as recently as 7 July. There have been several recent reports which indicate a thinning out of Soviet troops in Poland. The assumption is that these troops have moved into Germany. There is inadequate information upon which to base an estimate of the number of troops involved. On the other hand there have been no new units identified in Germany. It is our estimate that this probably means that some Soviet cadre units in Germany have received additional personnel.[23]

Summary of Remarks of Charles E. Bohlen, State Department Counselor, at the Third Meeting of the Working Group Participating in the Washington Exploratory Talks on Security, July 15, 1948.

Again, note that even the Berlin blockade failed to dispel the consensus that the Soviets had no plans to undertake a new world war.

> Mr. Bohlen said that as an aftermath of the war Europe had been left in a dangerous state of unbalance. . . . He had concluded, moreover, that the most dangerous period had been in the immediate postwar years, 1945–1947, when the U.S. military establishment was rapidly disintegrating and the American public had not yet been alerted to the Russian peril; yet it was significant that the Soviet Army did not move during this period. Furthermore, it should be remembered that the Russian Army had not moved beyond the line which we now refer to as the "iron curtain." . . . Noting that historically the Kremlin has usually exercised great caution in the risks it has taken to achieve its objectives . . . Mr. Bohlen interpreted the Soviet's [*sic*] anxieties about the eventual success of the Marshall plan as one indication that they perhaps had no positive, specific plans for military aggression in the near future. . . . The Soviet troops in Germany, while numerous, were not generally regarded as being capable of a sustained move westward through Europe; considerable reinforcement of personnel and strengthening would first be necessary, and presumably we would have some indication of this development if and when it occurred. . . . Mr.

> Bohlen agreed . . . that Russia was not in a good position economically to wage a long war, pointing out that the Soviet leaders were extremely dubious of the attitudes and affections of their own people, exemplified in their savage pursuit of displaced persons in Europe.[24]

Summary of Remarks of Charles E. Bohlen at the Fourth Meeting of the Working Group Participating in the Washington Exploratory Talks on Security, July 20, 1948.

Here, Bohlen made some profoundly revealing statements of how the Truman administration actually evaluated Soviet intentions:

> Referring to the draft memorandum on Item 1 of the agenda, Mr. Bohlen said that some points were presented in a somewhat different light than that in which the U.S. Government viewed them. For example, the strength of Russia was perhaps overstated; *the U.S. Government considers that our position vis-à-vis the Soviet Union is better now than at any time since the end of the war.* Furthermore, he questioned the statement in the memorandum that Russia's ultimate aim is domination of the entire world, since he felt that Stalin . . . would seek to achieve only the maximum, feasible extension of the power of the Kremlin. Russia perhaps might endeavor to be the strongest power in the world, in order to make herself and the satellites invincible to attack by other states or groups of states. Another point in the memorandum stems from this earlier statement, to the effect that the Kremlin ultimately wishes to dominate the United States. Here again the United States has a somewhat different concept of the problem [emphasis added].[25]

Report by the Joint Strategic Plans Committee of the Joint Chiefs of Staff on Civil Defense Planning, August 18, 1948.

This is an important document. In it, the Joint Strategic Plans Committee analyzed at length both current and future Soviet capabilities to attack the United States. As of 1948,

> Soviet air attacks against the continental United States, except for attacks on Alaska, and the Northwestern part of continental United States would be limited to one-way missions carrying conventional weapons. These attacks would have very little chance of penetrating

> an adequate air defense. The extent of the anticipated material damage would be light. . . . However, the psychological effects would be serious and far-reaching.

Soviet naval capabilities in 1948 were even less impressive:

> The USSR has a comparatively weak Navy. The main mission of the fleet at present is to act as a seaward anchor for the Soviet Army and to conduct both surface and subsurface raids against enemy commerce from near bases. Soviet naval forces at present and the developments during the problem period (1948–1955) will offer no serious threat to the security of the Continental United States, its territories and possessions. . . .
>
> Considering that there would be other more important demands on the Soviet summarine [*sic*] fleet, the effect of harassing attacks on coastal and harbor installations, by submarines employing naval gunfire or rockets, would be very limited and for morale effect only. The actual damage inflicted would be negligible. . . .
>
> With respect to naval aircraft the USSR has no carrier task force or naval aircraft offensive capabilities against the United States at this time.
>
> Considering that the USSR has a comparatively weak Navy, she has no amphibious capabilities against the United States during the 1948 period.

How would matters stand in later years? Although by 1952 the Soviets might "have the capability of delivering atomic bombs anywhere in the United States plus the capability of delivering a substantial amount of conventional tonnage by air," it would continue to be true that "virtually all attacks against the United States proper would be one-way missions." For that matter, even as late as 1955, this report "estimated that . . . most missions would still be one-way." From the sea, the Soviets would remain unable to harm the continental United States in 1952; in 1955, they might have the capacity "to inflict damage to our vital sea communications by submarine operations" and could be "capable of launching amphibious operations against United States outlying bases, . . . but not against the continental United States." Overall, it was clear that even in the worst of cases, the U.S.S.R. would not be able to pose a substantial, direct and material threat to the population and the territory of this country for the better part of a decade. What this meant was that, in light of the U.S.S.R.'s great weakness in the air and on the seas, even if Soviet leaders took it into their heads to defy all rationality by launching such an attack on the United States, there would be more than ample time to prepare for it.[26]

State Department Policy Planning Staff, "Factors Affecting the Nature of the U.S. Defense Arrangements in the Light of Soviet Policies," June 23, 1948; circulated to the members of the National Security Council, August 25, 1948.

I considered this report in some detail in chapter 5. Its most notable judgment was that "the evidence points to the conclusion that the Soviet Government is not now planning any deliberate armed action . . . and is still seeking to achieve its aims predominantly by political means."[27]

Memorandum Adopted at the Seventh Meeting of the Washington Exploratory Talks on Security, September 9, 1948:

> While there is no evidence to suggest that the Soviet Government is planning armed aggression as an act of policy, there is always the danger that, in the tense situation existing at the present time, some incident might occur which would lead to war. War might also come about by a miscalculation of western intentions on the part of the Soviet Government. Alternatively, a sudden decision by the Kremlin leaders to precipitate war might result from fear: (1) that their own personal power was being undermined, or (2) that Soviet strength in relation to that of the western nations was declining, or (3) that these nations had aggressive intentions toward the Soviet Union.

Commenting on the treatment of the U.S.S.R.'s intentions in this memorandum, Under Secretary of State Robert A. Lovett drew a crucial distinction: "Hitler was a fanatic with a mission, unable to bide his time, but the Marxists [i.e., Soviets] were under no such dictates of urgency, since their very ideology required them to refrain at a given time from taking any action which might prejudice the eventual overthrow of capitalism." The Soviet leadership, in short, could afford to wait.[28]

CIA Report, "Possibility of Direct Soviet Military Action During 1948-49," September 16, 1948.

As part of the argument I formulated in chapter 7, I quoted this document's statement that "recent events"—including the enactment of a peacetime military draft, an arms buildup, further development of atomic weaponry and increasing U.S. emphasis on long-range bombing capabilities—"may have strengthened [the] Soviet conviction . . . that the US actually has intentions of military aggression in the near future." In that chapter I also pointed out the implication of this report's assertion that in Moscow "these events . . . [were] probably taken to mean that the ultimate conflict with the capitalist system will be resolved by force rather than the methods of 'cold war'"—namely, an inevitable intensification of the arms race. In the context of this appendix, however, I wish to focus on the treatment of the short-range military intentions of the U.S.S.R. In the view of the authors, either "events within the Soviet orbit" or "events in the United States" might "induce" the Soviets to "resort to early military action." In the first category,

> the defection of Tito and the Yugoslav Communist Party is our most striking evidence for the existence of an unstable situation. There is no doubt that this situation has caused concern in the Kremlin. While the USSR might consider the use of force to correct this situation, and general war might result, we think such a decision unlikely unless the Soviet leaders believe that the issue has reached a point where it seriously threatens their control of the Soviet orbit. . . . There is no reliable evidence, however, that this point has been reached.

With respect to "events in the United States," the estimate suggested that, after studying the Truman administration's actions during 1948,

> Soviet analysts . . . might conclude that they can no longer assume the early disintegration of the capitalist world, and that US military potential, now low, will steadily improve and will ultimately be accompanied by an improvement in the military potential of Western Europe. This might, in turn, suggest looking to military action for the achievement of their aims. However, since the usefulness of non-military methods has not yet been exhausted in Europe, and since there are other regions open to significant exploitation, we do not estimate that a USSR resort to deliberate military action has become a probability.

Attempting to take both sets of events into account, the authors summarized their findings in these terms:

> We do not believe that the events of the past six months have made deliberate Soviet military action a probability during 1948–49.

> They have, however, added some weight to the factors that might induce the USSR to resort to such action. It is considered, therefore, that the possibility of a resort to deliberate military action has been *slightly* increased [emphasis added].[29]

Naval Intelligence Analysis, "Stalinism: Historical Russian Aspirations and Soviet Dynamic Materialism," September 16, 1948 (circulated September 27, 1948).

Although the author, Lieutenant P. H. Healey, a senior political analyst in the Office of Naval Intelligence (ONI), paid the perhaps unavoidable lip service to the dogma that "the Soviet Union, as the base of expanding Marxist Socialism, has accepted the obligation to use all possible means to overthrow capitalism and its epitome, imperialism, everywhere," his essay was considerably more reflective, more cognizant of the overall historical situation, than the run-of-the-mill intelligence estimate. Healey began by reviewing previous analyses by the Office of Naval Intelligence. According to him, the ONI "party line" had crystallized in January 1946, at which time "available intelligence . . . showed" that the Soviet Union "was exhausted, that she was having trouble with internal morale, and that manifold problems of reconstruction faced her. It was agreed . . . that the Soviet [*sic*] would not in the foreseeable future embark on military adventures unless some miscalculation . . . should lead to an uncontrollable situation. *This original estimate is still held by ONI* with the exception that the field of miscalculation is more fertile than before, largely because of the odd nature of the Berlin crisis" (emphasis added).

The author followed this general introduction with a long disquisition on the present-day intentions of the Soviets. The U.S.S.R., he explained,

> has never in the past and gives no reasonable assurance now that this program [of overthrowing capitalism] is to be carried out by military aggression at the risk of disaster to Russia. It is a reasonable assumption, in the light of available historical and current intelligence, that the leaders of the Soviet Union will limit themselves to "all means short of war," at least until they are confident that their strength has far surpassed that of the U.S. or that the U.S. intends to make an imminent military attack on their orbit.
>
> We believe that Soviet leaders today have the immediate aim of defending the Soviet Union from encirclement and invasion. For this reason they have planned carefully to eliminate sovereign buffer states between Russia and Central or Western Europe. . . . The

U.S.S.R. is now attempting to weld these countries to her to form a protective belt or shock-absorber.

As we have seen, the long-term Soviet aim is the domination of a Communist world, but this is not allowed to jeopardize the Soviet State, which still gives every indication of being defensive in its military strategy, or what is sometimes termed offensive-defensive, i.e., in the event of a pending military conflict to advance to a certain perimeter and plan to retreat slowly if necessary. . . .

In the flood tide of the war, and following the offensive-defensive strategy mentioned before, she mastered Finland, Latvia, Estonia, Lithuania and part of Poland, all of which had been under Russian hegemony previously. In the ebb tide of the war, her influence was permanently felt wherever she was, by our standards, in legitimate occupation. Thus all of Poland, Eastern Germany, Czechoslovakia, Hungary, Eastern Austria, Rumania and Bulgaria fell under her influence. Yugoslavia and Albania were forfeited to her influence, and interests in Manchuria as well as possession of lower Sakhalin, the Kuriles and the occupation of North Korea were, in effect, handed to her on a silver platter. We thus see that her gains have been the fruits of a defensive war . . . and of her native opportunism in the midst of chaos. However, despite her designs on Greece, her demands on Turkey and her wartime occupation of Northern Iran, she has not deliberately in peace-time employed military aggression in the strict sense of the word.

One reason for her not over-running Europe and the Middle East, as is so often predicted, is simply the fact that we under-estimate her troubles at home and within her newly acquired shock-absorber area. Too often it is assumed that her capabilities and intentions are one and the same thing. This is a fallacy built more often than not on the supposition that a dictator reaches a certain point of expansion after which a deterministic immutable law forces him into an abandon of restraint over which he has no control. I believe that an examination of our latter-day dictators will show that they are not as alike as pins.

One wonders how Secretary Marshall would have received this last proposition during the previous March, when he was moving might and main to convince the nation that Hitler and Stalin were fundamentally identical.[30]

Remarks of Walter Bedell Smith, Ambassador to the Soviet Union, to the Members of the Policy Planning Staff of the State Department, September 28, 1948.

On this occasion, Smith reemphasized his oft-stated conviction that the U.S.S.R. did not desire war with the West, and also advanced some insightful ideas about the status of Soviet efforts to develop atomic weapons. With respect to the latter, the reader should pay careful attention to the qualifying phrase that the ambassador twice invoked: "in quantity." The following are notes made at Smith's talk; the source does not identify the rapporteur.

> Regarding our ability to stay in Berlin, we could in fact stay there. The Russian pressure against us would continue persistently. They would not move in with troops to put us forcibly out of Berlin, but they could and would take indirect measures of many kinds to make it difficult for us to stay. . . . I do not expect the Russians to take any direct military action which would precipitate a conflict. They will harass the airlift; we may occasionally lose a pilot or a plane. Summing up I should say, therefore, that we can, if we wish to, stay in Berlin, at great cost, at some hazard, and with diminishing effectiveness except for the business of supplying ourselves, mainly to maintain our symbolic presence there.
>
> As to the likelihood of war, there is a real possibility of it in the Berlin situation. If we had no exposed salients like that, but instead a firm continuous line around our own zone—a line which the Russians could not cross without the onus of direct aggression, there would be relatively less likelihood of war because I believe that the Russians do not themselves wish now to face war deliberately, although this question is of course under constant review by them. They are unable to appreciate the violent reaction of our people to any loss of American life, so that there is of course the possibility of a miscalculation on their part of the probable consequences of harassing actions that they might take; *but I feel so confident they would not now undertake a deliberate military attack on, say, one of our concentrations of aircraft at Wiesbaden, that I would not hesitate to go there and sit on the field myself. . . .*
>
> I think that, especially with our present plans in development, we are gaining strength much faster than the Soviet Union. The Soviet Union's recovery from the war is progressing slowly. It does not compare with recovery in Western Europe, even in Moscow

> which itself is the show-case of the Soviet Union. I think that industrial potential is developing slowly there, and that military potential is likewise developing slowly. Without any evidence whatever to go on, I feel, simply from my "woman's intuition," that the Russians have not got the "A"-bomb and will not have it in quantity five years from now. They simply have not got the degree of technological precision for large-scale mass production required for atomic bomb processes. Their scientists' notebooks are no doubt complete with all the necessary scientific data required but the Soviet Union simply does not have the degree of technological precision for mass production that it would take to make atomic bombs in quantity. I have no doubt they have been working as best they can at it and may even have already developed some simple types of atomic weapons, but I do not think they would be in a position to use atomic bombs during the next five years. Speaking as a soldier, if I were told to choose, I would rather fight the Soviet Union five years from now than at present, because our potential is progressing at a much faster rate than theirs, and will last longer [emphasis added].[31]

Memorandum for the President from Colonel Robert B. Landry, Air Aide to the President, September 28, 1948.

As clearly as any single document can, this memorandum establishes that the Soviet Union had taken not even the most elementary steps that would have been necessary had its government been preparing an invasion of Western Europe.

> During my recent visit to Germany between September 21 and 23, I noted several very interesting and significant points which I discussed, upon my return, with Admiral [William D.] Leahy [Chief of Staff to the Commander-in-Chief] and which, at his suggestion, I have prepared in memorandum form for your information. . . .
>
> Because the Russians have assembled a formidable fighting force in Germany, they will require a tremendous logistical effort in order to launch any large-scale and sustained offensive. Lines of communication to the Eastward are essential to its success. I was told at the G-2 [intelligence] briefing that the Russians have dismantled hundreds of miles of railroads in Germany and sent the rails and ties

> back to Russia. There remains, at the present time, so I was told, only a single track railroad running Eastward out of the Berlin area and upon which the Russians must largely depend for their logistical support. This same railroad line changes from a standard gage, going Eastward, to a Russian wide gage in Poland, which further complicates the problem of moving supplies and equipment forward.[32]

Memorandum for the Chief, Plans and Policy Group, "The Military Situation in Germany," October 16, 1948.

According to Lieutenant James I. Muir, Jr., the author of this document, his superior and the commanding officer of the army's Plans and Operations Division, General Albert C. Wedemeyer, had "expressed additional thoughts on this subject . . . which should be incorporated into the study" then in preparation. One of these "thoughts" was the following: "The Soviets will continue to wage a cold war rather than a hot one; they are more adept than the allies at this type of a warfare, and their concept does not require the military occupation of a country, but only a change in that country's government to the point where Communist precepts can be adopted."[33]

Memorandum of Conversation, by the Secretary of State, November 20, 1948.

Marshall in this memorandum summarized a discussion he had with the Norwegian foreign minister, Halvard M. Lange, in which he had explained why, in his view, a Soviet attack on the West was unlikely: "I mentioned that in my judgment the main deterrent to Soviet aggression has been the possession by the United States of the atomic bomb." Note also Marshall's similar remark to the Pope, quoted at the beginning of this appendix, when, one month earlier, the two had conversed about the Berlin blockade and the U.S. airlift: "I then referred directly to the atomic bomb, the fact that I thought the fear of it made somewhat improbable Soviet resort to military action."[34]

Central Intelligence Agency Memorandum Number 76, "Economic Trends in the USSR," November 19, 1948.

This study contains a very detailed examination of the Soviet economy, upon which the authors drew in formulating their estimate of Moscow's military intentions. In general, although the economy of the U.S.S.R. had "improved rapidly since 1945," at the end of 1948 Soviet production was "still slightly below the 1940 level," as the following statistics illustrated:

> By the end of 1948 it is estimated that Soviet raw steel production will have reached no more than 17.8 million metric tons. In comparison, production in 1940 stood at 18.3 metric tons. . . .
>
> Rail transportation, which accounts for about 85 percent of all freight traffic, remains one of the chief bottlenecks in the Soviet economy. Freight haulage, as reflected in average daily carloadings, is expected to approach the 1940 level by July 1949. Judging by reports of progress under the current Five-Year Plan, however, both construction and rehabilitation of railways are behind planned production levels. . . .
>
> Per capita production of the main foodstuffs in the USSR and Satellite countries for the 1948–49 consumption year is estimated at between 80 and 85 percent of prewar. . . . Because of expected increase in the population of Eastern Europe, per capita production of foodstuffs cannot be expected to reach the prewar level before about 1956–57. If, however, collectivization of agriculture in certain Satellite countries should take place during the five–year period 1950–55, a decrease in production might result, thereby delaying recovery to the prewar level until sometime after 1960. . . .
>
> It is estimated that 1948 production of machine tools will not reach the average prewar annual output of approximately 22,000 units. The Soviet stock of machine tools, however, will probably attain the goal of 1,300,000 units by 1950, largely as a result of rehabilitation of recovered machine tools, postwar imports, and the immense plant-dismantling program in Germany, Manchuria, Hungary, and Austria. . . .
>
> Soviet crude-oil production is expected to reach the 1940 level of 31.2 million metric tons by the end of 1948. . . .
>
> The industrial efficiency of the USSR will remain at a comparatively low level through 1949 because of the shortage of skilled labor, low productivity of labor, backward technology, bureaucratic methods of management, industrial waste, insufficient transport capacity, and continued dislocation of industry and population.
>
> The Satellite countries will not have regained their prewar level of industrial efficiency by July 1949 because of wartime losses of skilled labor and engineers; inept Soviet interference; the natural

antagonism of many workers to Communist control, and shortages of certain machinery and materials.

On the basis of this and similar information, only one verdict was possible: "Economic recovery to the 1940 levels, then, is not as complete as the Soviets imply." From this finding, an extremely significant conclusion automatically flowed:

> While economic considerations alone do not determine Soviet foreign policy, the state of the Soviet economy currently acts as a deterrent on the implementation of Soviet aggressive designs. The above analysis of [the] Soviet economy, therefore, tends to substantiate the belief that Soviet efforts will continue to be concentrated upon (1) consolidation of control over the Eastern European Satellites and over occupied Germany and Austria; and (2) furthering of Moscow-dominated Communist expansion through the activities of native Communist parties. The current rate of improvement in the Soviet economy will not in itself warrant substantial changes in the timetable of Soviet policy implementation.[35]

State Department Policy Planning Staff Paper PPS 43, November 23, 1948.

A footnote in volume 3 of *Foreign Relations of the United States: 1948* states that "the following words in an unidentified handwriting appear on the master copy of the cover page: '"Secretary indicated orally his agreement to the second part of this paper. On the first part there was no disagreement anywhere . . ." GFK'." "GFK," of course, was George Frost Kennan, the director of the Policy Planning Staff. In the first part of this study—on which "there was no disagreement anywhere"—we read that

> basic Russian intent still runs to the conquest of western Europe by political means. In this program, military force plays a major role only as a means of intimidation.
>
> The danger of political conquest is still greater than the military danger. If a war comes in the foreseeable future, it will probably be one which Moscow did not desire but did not know how to avoid.[36]

Letter from Rear Admiral L. C. Stevens, U.S. Naval Attaché in the Soviet Union, to James Forrestal, Secretary of Defense, December 10, 1948.

"I have long been uneasy about the basis for our predictions on the fundamental subject of war or peace," Stevens wrote,

> to the effect that Soviets were not contemplating an early planned war deliberately brought about by themselves, but were making every effort to be ready for eventual war of their own choosing or to face an earlier one brought about by other factors than their own current planning. The recent Soviet policy on travel of foreigners in Russia has removed much of that uneasiness. Although it restricts us worse than before in some respects, particularly in the vicinity of Moscow, it has made it possible for us to see large parts of the country which were previously effectively closed to us. Even with their well-known capability for stagecraft and deceit, it was far simpler for them to dress up Moscow for our benefit than to remove all traces of activity and excitement bordering the tens of thousands of miles of railroad which we are now able to cover.

As a result of the "broader opportunities for personal observation" the new policy allowed, Stevens had been "strengthened . . . in the belief that they are not seeking immediate war," and was, therefore, now "firmer than ever in the opinion that their leaders, the core of the Bolshevik Party, are sincere in their belief in their own teachings." Thus, in contrast to what Secretary of State Marshall had so stridently proclaimed the previous March, the attaché was willing to state for the record, "I do not believe that the top men are cynically out for adventure and personal power and advantage as were those who surrounded Hitler."[37]

Ambassador Walter Bedell Smith to the Secretary of State, December 23, 1948.

It seems appropriate to bring this survey of U.S. estimates of Soviet intentions to an end with a final entry from the ambassador to the Soviet Union. "Looking backward as year draws to [a] close," Smith believed that "several phenomena difficult to interpret currently are beginning to form a pattern indicating some revision of our basic estimate of Soviet intentions." Did this sentence mean that Smith had at last abandoned his frequently proclaimed view that the U.S.S.R. had no immediate plans to go to war? Quite the contrary:

> Soviet Union not only "will not deliberately resort to military action in the immediate future" (Embassy despatch 315, April 1 ["Soviet Intentions," discussed in chapter 5]) but seems to be basing its policies and actions on expectation of peace for the near future, probably several years.
>
> Believing itself safe from attack, Soviet Government is in fact deliberately choosing to weaken itself to a certain extent during next few years vis-à-vis West in order to gain greater strength for later inevitable conflict in which it continues believe.[38]

One of the reasons the ambassador gave in defense of these judgments was that the "growing independence" of Marshal Josip Broz Tito of Yugoslavia "would surely have been handled with carrot instead of club if Kremlin had either expected or intended to precipitate serious international conflict in near future." Similarly, even though "ousting Western powers from strong points within Soviet European orbit, notably Berlin" was, in Smith's opinion, an "essential element of Soviet policy," the U.S.S.R.'s "desire [to] avoid hostilities even for this vital position" remained paramount. Finally, in addition to the "foregoing . . . main considerations," Smith found "other factors . . . to support the thesis or fit the pattern," of which the most noteworthy was that "recent successes in Far and Near East, particularly Communist advances in China and deteriorating Western position in Palestine and Arab East[,] must encourage Kremlin to follow policy of seeking objectives by means short of war."[39]

The cumulative effect of the foregoing intelligence estimates is, to my mind, overwhelming and conclusive. It is impossible to pretend that the combined weight of these documents does not call into question what has been, ever since the days of the Truman administration itself, the prevailing mythology regarding the responsibility for beginning, intensifying and prolonging this contest: that the arms buildup undertaken by the United States during the second half of the 1940s was a necessary response to a belligerent Soviet Union intent on subjugating the world by crude military force. If nothing else, perhaps the evidence in this appendix, together with that in the preceding chapters, will help provoke a reexamination of this bit of sacred dogma. The arms race in particular has exacted a heavy price on all sides, scarcely less from those who supposedly "won" than from those who "lost." If, as I strongly suspect, this race was unnecessary all along, the sooner we can establish that fact, the better our future prospects.

Appendix B: On "Conspiracy Theories" in Fact and Fancy

ACCUSATIONS IN BAD FAITH

Anyone with the gall or naiveté to suggest, in a work about U.S. history, politics or society, that those who enjoy great wealth or high rank act in concert to achieve their ends can expect to be accused of espousing a "conspiracy theory of history." In what follows, I will explain why I think such charges are completely unjustified in the case of this book and try to distinguish what I have written from a "conspiracy theory of history."

Not that I expect this effort to do much good. Typically, when a work that depicts people of wealth and power collaborating to attain a given outcome is attacked for offering a "conspiracy theory of history," the assault is led by those who wish to discredit the author's thesis but—and this point is absolutely crucial—*have been unable to find factual evidence to refute the interpretation they detest.* Consequently, these charges, more often than not, reek of bad faith and, even, intellectual dishonesty. There is no argument that a scholar can make, no evidence he can supply, that will provide him with immunity from denunciations arising out of such motives.

To see why, in these circumstances, charges of "conspiracy theorizing" are likely to be bogus, we need to bring into the open exactly what they imply. Such accusations contain within them several hidden propositions that are never made explicit, because to do so would expose their authors to ridicule. Which of the following, pray tell, would those who are so ready to cry "Conspiracy theory!" have us believe? That people with enormous fortunes and/or high political positions do not have greater ability than the ordinary citizen to get what they want? That men and women who spend most of their adult lives seeking to obtain or retain money and influence do so only in order to abstain from employing the advantages these confer? That those with wealth and power are inhibited by some mysterious force from making use of either to accomplish their purposes? That the rich and well placed not only practice such extraordinary self-denial as individuals, but that they also steadfastly refuse to cooperate with their peers in the pursuit of common political-economic goals?

All of these notions are, of course, absurd on their face. People strive for wealth and power precisely because the more of either one possesses, the more readily one can have his way in every realm—professional, political, personal. Moreover, the idea that the rich and powerful shrink from uniting with others of the same station is even more laughable. If, in fact, there is one thing that characterizes those at the top of the heap, it is their readiness to organize amongst themselves to secure their desires. No other group in society even comes close in this regard.

Having exposed the hidden baggage that charges of "conspiracy theorizing" carry with them, let us move from the general to the specific. In the preceding chapters, I have discussed two sets of events: (1) the campaign of the airplane builders for a presidentially appointed aviation commission that would create pressure for more spending on aircraft procurement and (2) the attempt by the Truman administration during March 1948 to convince Congress and the country that the Soviet Union could be stopped from invading Western Europe only by immediate enactment of the administration's military and foreign policy programs. To dispel any doubts about the matter, I would like to review my handling of these two themes in order to establish that I have not expounded a "conspiracy theory of history."

With respect to the first, the aircraft industry's crusade for a presidential aviation commission and a bigger budget for airplane procurement, there is nothing in my treatment of the subject that even hints, much less claims, the existence of a conspiracy. Just the opposite, actually. In chapter 3, for example, I quote from the speeches in 1945 of Eugene E. Wilson and Robert E. Gross, the president of the Aircraft Industries Association and Lockheed Aircraft, respectively, urging the creation of "another Morrow board." To argue that the manufacturers' efforts to have such a panel appointed or to have the federal government increase expenditures on military airplanes amounted to a conspiracy would require misreading the evidence so monumentally as to inspire questions about the sanity of the author who did so. My dictionary tells me that the nouns *conspiracy, plot, machination, collusion, intrigue* all "denote secret plans or schemes." Although industry executives did on occasion seek to manipulate public opinion by working covertly through such groups as the Veterans of Foreign Wars, on the whole nothing could have been *less* secret than their desire for a presidential aviation board and larger appropriations for aircraft procurement; zealots that they were, they could barely be restrained from babbling about these matters at the drop of a hat. We may, therefore, regard this aspect of the case as closed.[1]

The second sequence of events, the Truman administration's war scare, is more complex. On March 2, Secretary of Defense James V. Forrestal, Secretary of State George C. Marshall and Under Secretary of State Robert A. Lovett agreed that they would cooperate in fomenting such a scare; also present at this luncheon meeting were John J. McCloy, president of the International Bank for Reconstruction and Development, and Sidney W. Souers, executive secretary of the National Security Council and a person in whom the president had confidence. Thus, these five individuals were in on the plan from the very outset. Two days later, on March 4, Forrestal broached the idea to another eight people, including Secretary of Commerce W. Averell Harriman, Secretary of the Interior Julius Krug, House Minority Whip John McCormack of Massachusetts, and Democratic Senator Lister Hill of Alabama. The entry in Forrestal's diary about this so-called "Cabinet Lunch" ends with the observation that "everyone present agreed that the public needed information and guidance on the deterioration of our relations with Russia." It was, in other words, time to set up the propaganda machine and start turning the crank—a decision reached, please note, one day *before* the arrival in Washington of Lucius D. Clay's telegram of March 5, 1948.[2]

It is most unlikely that Marshall, Lovett and Forrestal would have proceeded this far without first having secured permission from the president. Truman's assent would have been necessary if for no other reason than because he had an essential role to play—without him, the show could not be staged. In the course of working out his own ideas about how the scare could best be managed, it would have been natural for the president to have discussed it with his closest associates and advisers, such as Secretary of the Treasury John Snyder and Clark M. Clifford. At a conservative estimate, therefore, it would appear that at least 20 people, and quite possibly more, shared knowledge that the administration was planning to fabricate tales of an imminent Soviet offensive.

It strains our sense of the word's meaning to think of a scheme involving such a loose-knit collection of souls as a *conspiracy,* if for no other reason than the difficulty a group of this size and composition would have keeping information secret.

For all of that, it would be quite misleading to deny that certain aspects of the war scare were completely conspiratorial in nature. Here I have in mind especially the Clay telegram of March 5 and the circumstances surrounding its origins. If the behavior that produced the telegram was not conspiratorial, then we are in need of a new definition for that term. There was, in reality, no other choice for those who sought to make use of the telegram except to conspire. Clay would not have sent such a cable had there not been a request for it from Washington; yet were it to become widely known that this notorious message was actually conceived in the labyrinths of the Pentagon, the document would have been rendered worthless on the spot. In order for it to perform the task for which it was intended, it was necessary that Clay, General Stephen J. Chamberlin, James Forrestal, Secretary of the Army Kenneth Royall or whoever was privy to the plot resolutely conceal the way in which the telegram had come into being.

How, therefore, do we go about reckoning the balance? Was the war scare the result of a conspiracy or was it not? The answer, it seems to me, cannot be a simple matter of yes or no, because the scare itself was not entirely of a piece. On the one hand, the administration did not go to great lengths to disguise the fact that it was preparing to inflict such a scare on the Congress and the public. In that sense, the effort that produced the war scare was a *collaborative,* but not necessarily a conspiratorial, one. On the other hand, however, certain elements of the scare—the Clay telegram most notably—were highly conspiratorial in nature. I do not see how any other judgment is possible, given what we know both about why Clay chose to send the cable in the first place and the way it was put to use by Forrestal and the army thereafter. Like it or not, Clay's message has to be seen as the product of a cabal devised expressly for the purpose of eliciting and exploiting it. Just because most conspiracy hypotheses are far-fetched does not mean that real conspiracies never exist.

It would have been quite in character for Forrestal to engage in clandestine activities, moreover, if we can credit the following account in the *New York Times* of November 25, 1950:

> The American Mercury magazine says James V. Forrestal, late Defense Secretary, quietly spent at least $150,000 in private funds in Europe in a passionate fight against Communism, The Associated Press reported yesterday.

> The magazine said some of the money went to defeat the Communists in Italy's 1948 election, and some to a "prominent Communist leader" to end a French transportation strike in 1947.
>
> The article, by William Bradford Huie, Mercury editor, said that Mr. Forrestal recognized the dangers of Communism and struggled to arm the United States. . . .
>
> Concerning his financial intervention in Europe, the magazine article said:
>
> "In December, 1947, when France was paralyzed by a general transportation strike, Secretary Forrestal summoned his most trusted friends to Washington. He told them that necessity demanded the use of dollars in Europe for bribes.
>
> "He explained that he had spent all the Defense Department's 'non-voucherable funds,' as well as much of his own money, and that more was needed.
>
> "His friends produced $50,000 immediately; the money was carried that night to Paris by an American intelligence officer and paid next day to a prominent Communist leader. The strike ended within twelve hours."
>
> The magazine said Mr. Forrestal also spent private funds on his own responsibility in the Italian elections.
>
> "When the Italian campaign was hottest, he again summoned his friends. He warned that the election would be lost unless dollars were used to overmatch Red payments to Italian propagandists.
>
> "His friends produced, in one lot, upward of $100,000 in cash, and this was carried by a New York attorney and paid out in the most effective manner."[3]

As this article suggests, it was not at all unusual for certain high-level figures in the Truman administration to behave in a conspiratorial fashion; some, in fact, appear to have done so routinely. Again, I wish to be completely clear on this point: I did not set forth in search of material that would "prove" that the war scare of 1948—or anything else—resulted from a conspiracy. But anyone who has ever done much research will be my witness that what one expects to find in the archives is often not what is there; and, conversely, what is there is not always what one expected to find. So it is in this case with documents manifesting a conspiratorial mentality. I think the existence of these documents struck both my wife, Bonnie, and myself at about the same time. At first, they were merely a curiosity, something that we would pass back and forth to amuse ourselves as a way of relieving the tedium. After a while, though, as we continued to encounter them, it occurred to us that so ubiquitous, so thoroughly *idiomatic,* were these items that we would have been remiss had we failed to note them.

Among the most dramatic examples of the genre are the two letters that Secretary of the Air Force W. Stuart Symington sent to Winthrop Aldrich, the president of the Chase National Bank, early in April 1948:

> Dear Winthrop:
>
> I am very sorry, but things you have seen in the papers make it impossible for me to be in New York tomorrow; and therefore I am taking the liberty of sending Colonel Forbes and Colonel Wertenbaker with a memorandum for Mr. Forrestal from the Air Force. Colonel Wertenbaker represents me and Colonel Forbes knows the subject as thoroughly as anybody in the Pentagon.
>
> As you will note, the problem is how to get the money to get what we want; and any advice you could give us to that end would be very much appreciated.
>
> Inasmuch as all this is top secret, I am asking these officers to deliver this memorandum to you, to be prepared to discuss it with you, and to await your written advice, this in that it cannot be discussed over the telephone.

> Dear Winthrop:
>
> Thank you very much for seeing my friends. The client they discussed is getting in touch with you shortly. With appreciation and every good wish.[4]

It is somewhat clear from the situation why Symington's words were guarded in these letters. More often than not, though, the reasons for the use of deliberately opaque language are—probably not accidentally—anything but obvious. Such was the case in this instance, excerpted from a message from Symington to Air Force Chief of Staff General Hoyt S. Vandenberg: "This is the only copy of this memorandum which I would preserve for the record in your own files. We are not keeping one here." And, finally, this sentence from the secretary's two-sentence letter to Frederick B. Rentschler, the president of United Aircraft: "With further reference to the subject you brought up with me, how about a memorandum, unsigned."[5]

Secretary of Defense James V. Forrestal, as we have witnessed, was strongly drawn to the covert and conspiratorial. Here are some typical samples from his correspondence and telephone conversations, commencing, appropriately enough, with a letter in what we might call the implicitly conspiratorial style to the selfsame Winthrop Aldrich: "With reference to our talk the other evening, I think we better let this matter rest for the time being. I have talked about it with Bob Lovett and that is his feeling also."[6] A second letter on the same day, October 9, 1947, found the secretary in a much more explicitly conspiratorial mode. William J. Donovan, the former director of the Office of Strategic Services (forerunner to the Central Intelligence Agency), had written three days before, enclosing "a memorandum suggesting certain moves that might be made, and I assume that CIA is equipped to carry on unorthodox activities." In his reply, Forrestal followed an apparently innocuous paragraph with an abrupt injunction.

> Dear Bill:
>
> I have yours of the 6th. Curiously enough I had a meeting on the same day you wrote your letter. However, it takes more than meetings. It will require plenty of brains, persistent follow-up, and above all, money.
>
> Please destroy this letter.
>
> Sincerely yours,[7]

Putting together the date and the contents of Donovan's memorandum—its title was "Memorandum to Secretary of Defense, James V. Forrestal, on Subversive Warfare from William J. Donovan"—with the foregoing article from the *New York Times,* it is highly probable that the meeting of October 6th to which Forrestal referred was for the purpose of raising money to finance illicit activities against the Communist parties of France and Italy, such as the CIA alliances with the Mafia and the Corsican heroin syndicates that I discussed in chapter 8. Indeed, given the cryptic nature of Forrestal's letter to Winthrop Aldrich, the fact that it was written on the same day as the letter to Donovan and the additional fact that Aldrich would certainly have been a likely person for the secretary to have approached in this regard, my guess is that it, too, pertained to the same topic.

Some other examples: Forrestal, like Symington, refused to discuss a variety of subjects over the telephone, as illustrated in this excerpt from a telephone conversation on January 22, 1948, with an otherwise unidentified Mr. Jackson:

> *Mr. Jackson*: Is there anything you could tell me about over the telephone?
>
> *Mr. Forrestal*: No, I think I'd better not.

Writing Edward Weeks, editor of the *Atlantic Monthly,* in May 1948, Forrestal again fell into the implicitly conspiratorial vein:

> Why don't you get Allen Dulles to do a piece for you? He is extremely well informed and will reflect many of the views of Bill Donovan and others who were in the O.S.S. *When I see you* I will tell you why I am making this suggestion [emphasis added].

Occasionally—but only occasionally—it was someone else who supplied the conspiratorial overtones, as when Hamilton Fish told Forrestal, "I don't want to talk to you on the telephone about it." As was usual in such cases, "it" was nowhere further specified.[8]

From the documents we have just examined, we can see that one need not have an overexcitable imagination to discover conspiratorial elements in the words and deeds of such notables as the secretary of the air force, the secretary of defense, the former director of the Office of Strategic Services and the president of the Chase National Bank. Regardless of how outlandish or nonsensical most "conspiracy theories" may be, the fact of the matter is that members of the ruling class and the power elite in the late 1940s showed themselves ready to resort to conspiratorial machinations whenever they deemed it necessary. There are those who may profess their displeasure at this statement; but that, I dare say, will not alter its truthfulness one whit. My purpose in emphasizing this point is not in the least frivolous. One of the things we most need to understand—and one of the things historians most often fail to discuss—are the precise means by which the dominant class and those who serve it go about accomplishing their goals in politics. In this appendix, I have tried to broaden our perspective by calling attention to an aspect of power wielding that usually is tucked demurely out of sight. By no means do I think that what I have written here is the last word on this subject, nor was that in any way my intent. Far from seeking to bring the discourse to a close, what I wish to do instead is suggest how it might begin.

NOTES

Notes to Chapter 1.

1. Stenographic Report of Proceedings, President's Air Policy Commission (hereafter PAPC), p. 909, National Archives Record Group 340 (Secretary of the Air Force), Entry 53, Air Coordinating Committee (hereafter ACC), General File, 1945–1950, box 60, folder ACC Papers No. 125, vol. 2.
2. "Aviation RFC?" *Business Week,* January 31, 1948, p. 28; the initials "RFC" stood for Reconstruction Finance Corporation.
3. William E. Pemberton, Professor of History, University of Wisconsin-La Crosse, letter to the author, August 16, 1992.
4. Department of State, *Foreign Relations of the United States: 1948,* vol. 2, *Germany and Austria* (Washington, D.C.: U.S. Government Printing Office, 1973), pp. 1195–97; as Smith in 1950 became the director of the Central Intelligence Agency, his estimates demand to be taken seriously.
5. Townsend Hoopes and Douglas Brinkley, *Driven Patriot: The Life and Times of James Forrestal* (New York: Alfred A. Knopf, 1992). On U.S. collusion with the Mafia and the Corsican gangster syndicates of France, see Alfred W. McCoy, *The Politics of Heroin: CIA Complicity in the Global Drug Trade* (Brooklyn, N.Y.: Lawrence Hill Books, 1991); on the alliance with Nazi war criminals evading prosecution, Christopher Simpson, *Blowback: America's Recruitment of Nazis and Its Effect on the Cold War* (New York: Weidenfeld & Nicolson, 1988). See chapter 8, "Conclusions," for further discussion of these alliances.
6. Jeffery M. Dorwart, *Eberstadt and Forrestal: A National Security Partnership, 1909-1949* (College Station, Tex.: Texas A & M University Press, 1991), p. 180.

Notes to Chapter 2.

1. Papers of Robert E. Gross, Manuscript Division, Library of Congress, Business Correspondence File.
2. Ibid.

3. Ibid.
4. Papers of W. Stuart Symington, box 8, Harry S. Truman Library (hereafter HSTL).
5. Gross Papers, Business Correspondence File.
6. Symington Papers, box 12.
7. "Finance: War Baby in a Peace Economy," *Business Week,* June 7, 1947, pp. 58, 63.
8. Phillip Dobbs, "Position and Prospects of the Aircrafts," *The Magazine of Wall Street,* May 26, 1945, p. 194; "Wing Tips," *Steel,* January 1, 1945, p. 238.
9. See Stenographic Report of Proceedings, President's Air Policy Commission (hereafter PAPC), Statement of Ralph V. Hunt, Vice President-Comptroller, Douglas Aircraft Co., Inc., September 30, 1947, p. 1021, and Statement of Mundy I. Peale, President, Republic Aircraft Corporation, September 29, 1947, p. 837, both in National Archives Record Group (hereafter RG) 340 (Secretary of the Air Force), Entry 53, Air Coordinating Committee (hereafter ACC), General File 1945–1950, ACC Papers Folder No. 125, vol. 2; "Happy Days at Grumman," *Fortune,* June 1948, p. 185; and Memorandum to the Commissioners from H. E. Weihmiller, Industry Replies to Questionnaires—Resume, undated (but after October 7, 1947), Addendum (unpaginated), Records of the PAPC, box 40, HSTL. The President's Air Policy Commission (PAPC) is often referred to as the Finletter Commission, after its chairman, Thomas K. Finletter. The 15 companies on which Weihmiller based his findings included "the aircraft engine and propeller divisions of Curtiss-Wright and of United Aircraft."
10. Memorandum for Mr. [Arthur S.] Barrows [under secretary of the air force] from G. B. Woods, March 25, 1948, p. 1, RG 340 (Secretary of the Air Force), Entry 46, Office of the Administrative Assistant, Correspondence Control Division, General File by Organization and Subject, 1947-January 1953, Special Assistant for R & D, 1948–1951, William A. Burden, Bell Aircraft Corporation to Lockheed Aircraft Corporation.
11. William M. Allen letter to Honorable A. S. Barrows, June 4, 1948, p. 2, RG 340 (Secretary of the Air Force).
12. Memorandum for Mr. Barrows from G. B. Woods, March 25, 1948, pp. 1–2; and A. S. Barrows letter to William M. Allen, April 26, 1948, p. 2, RG 340 (Secretary of the Air Force); Table 3, Military and Commercial Aircraft Manufacturers Net Worth and Change in Net Worth, 1940 and 1944–1947, attached to Memorandum for Mr. Larkin from W. H. Mautz, July 8, 1948, Department of Defense records (copy made for the author at the Department of Defense).
13. "Shall We Have Airplanes?" *Fortune,* January 1948, p. 80; Dobbs, "Position and Prospects," p. 194; "Wing Tips," p. 238.

14. Robert E. Gross letters to Mrs. A. H. Flower, July 3, 1946, p. 1, Gross Papers, Personal Correspondence File, and to William H. Stone, January 16, 1945, Gross Papers, Business Correspondence File.
15. Gross to Mrs. A. H. Flower, July 3, 1946, Gross Papers, Personal Correspondence File.
16. *Aviation Week,* July 28, 1947, p. 18.
17. Alan Passen, Summary of Report to the Congressional Aviation Policy Board (hereafter CAPB) on "Financial Condition of the Airline Industry," December 31, 1947, RG 340 (Secretary of the Air Force), Entry 53, Air Coordinating Committee, General File 1945–1950, Radio Technical Commission to Rowe Report. The CAPB, as I will discuss in more detail in the next chapter, was established to conduct much the same kind of inquiry into federal policies with respect to the aircraft and airline companies as the President's Air Policy Commission; for the most part, though, the deliberations of the congressional panel were of much less significance than those of the presidential board.
18. "The Airline Squeeze," *Fortune,* May 1947, pp. 117–18; Stenographic Report of Proceedings, PAPC, Statement of Donald Douglas, President, Douglas Aircraft Company, October 29, 1947, p. 2126, RG 340 (Secretary of the Air Force), Entry 53, Air Coordinating Committee, General File 1945–1950, ACC Papers Folder No. 125, vols. 5–6.
19. Stenographic Report of Proceedings, PAPC, Statement of Ralph V. Hunt, September 30, 1947, pp. 1022–23; see note 9 above for the full citation for this document.
20. Statement by Mr. Glenn L. Martin before Senate Banking and Currency Committee—RFC Inquiry, January 15, 1948, pp. 4–7, Papers of Glenn L. Martin, Subject File, Glenn L. Martin Company, Manuscript Division, Library of Congress; "Shall We Have Airplanes?" p. 159; Selig Altschul, "Manufacturers Report Huge Losses," *Aviation Week,* April 19, 1948, p. 35.
21. "Shall We Have Airplanes?" pp. 78, 159, and Altschul, "Huge Losses," p. 35; Robert Gross to Captain James Addams, February 26, 1946, p. 2, Gross Papers, Business Correspondence File; Lockheed, December 31, 1946, an unsigned memorandum in the Symington Papers.
22. Robert E. Gross to General Carl A. Spaatz, Commanding General, Army Air Forces, September 17, 1947, p. 2, Symington Papers; Altschul, "Huge Losses," p. 35; Notes for Annual Meeting of Shareholders, May 4, 1948, pp. 1–2, Gross Papers, Business Correspondence File; Gross to Mrs. A. H. Flower, July 3, 1946, Gross Papers, Personal Correspondence File; Gross to ·Edward R. Stettinius, Jr., March 14, 1947, Gross Papers., Business Correspondence File.
23. *Aviation Week,* July 28, 1947, p. 18; Altschul, "Huge Losses," p. 35.

24. "Lightplane [*sic*] Production Reached $88,000,000 Peak During 1946," *Aviation News,* January 27, 1947, p. 12; Industrial Plans Section, Air Matériel Command, Industrial Preparedness in the Aircraft Industry, May 1, 1947, p. 6, RG 107 (Office of the Secretary of War), Entry 260, Office of the Under Secretary of War, Security-Classified Correspondence, 400.17 to 461, Folder 461 Pamphlets; George S. Kent, "Realistic Survey of the Aircrafts," *The Magazine of Wall Street,* March 15, 1947, pp. 672–74; H. F. Travis, "New Life in the Aircrafts," *The Magazine of Wall Street,* February 14, 1948, pp. 528, 530; "Light-Plane Market Slumps," *Business Week,* June 7, 1947, pp. 36, 38.
25. "Shall We Have Airplanes?" p. 158.
26. "Experiment at Republic," *Fortune,* February 1947, p. 172; "Shall We Have Airplanes?" pp. 123, 158.
27. Stenographic Report of Proceedings, PAPC, Statement of Mundy I. Peale, President, Republic Aircraft Corporation, September 29, 1947, p. 839, RG 340 (Secretary of the Air Force), Entry 53, Air Coordinating Committee, General File 1945–1950, ACC Papers Folder No. 125, vol. 2; "Experiment at Republic," pp. 170, 172; Travis, "New Life in the Aircrafts," February 14, 1948, p. 530; "Light-Plane Market Slumps," p. 38.
28. Selig Altschul, "Overgrown Aircraft Industry Pining for Procurement Boost," *Aviation Week,* March 15, 1948, p. 36; "War Baby in a Peace Economy," *Business Week,* June 7, 1947, p. 64; "Shall We Have Airplanes?" p. 80.
29. "Shall We Have Airplanes?" p. 80; Stenographic Report of Proceedings, PAPC, Statement of J. Carlton Ward, President, Fairchild Engine and Airplane Corporation, September 29, 1947, pp. 867–68, RG 340 (Secretary of the Air Force), Entry 53, Air Coordinating Committee, General File 1945–1950, ACC Papers Folder No. 125, vol. 2; "Fairchild Reports Largest Peace Profit in Company History," *Aviation Week,* October 20, 1947, p. 20; "Northrop Shows Profit of $240,573 For Year," *Aviation Week,* October 20, 1947, p. 14.
30. Selig Altschul, "Results Vary for Plane Makers with Non-aviation Subsidiaries," *Aviation Week,* November 10, 1947, p. 57; Stenographic Report of Proceedings, PAPC, Statement of Leon A. Swirbul, President, Grumman Aircraft Engineering Corporation, October 1, 1947, p. 1190, RG 340 (Secretary of the Air Force), Entry 53, Air Coordinating Committee, General File 1945–1950, ACC Papers Folder No. 125, vol. 3.
31. Statement of J. Carlton Ward, President, Fairchild Engine and Airplane Corporation, September 29, 1947, p. 868, RG 340 (Secretary of the Air Force), Entry 53, Air Coordinating Committee, General Fiie 1945–1950, ACC Papers Folder No. 125, vol. 2.
32. "Experiment at Republic," p. 125.

33. Although I have made use of Mary Kaldor's argument both here and in the concluding chapter, in neither place does my account of it come close to doing justice to its subtleties; for that, one must have recourse to the original: see *The Baroque Arsenal* (New York: Hill and Wang, 1981). The information about the Rainbow transport is in "Experiment at Republic," p. 125.
34. William A. Anders, "Rationalizing America's Defense Industry: Renewing Investor Support for the Defense Industrial Base and Safeguarding National Security," *Defense Week* annual conference, St. Louis, Missouri, October 30, 1991, p. 13; copy provided to the author by General Dynamics Corporation at taxpayers' expense. For good measure, Anders reiterates his argument later in the same speech: "I see some diversifying out of defense. Good luck! This may create the appearance of growth, but the odds are against profitable returns. At General Dynamics, after studying diversification and its risks, our conclusion was that our management, as a group, didn't bring a clear competitive edge to investment outside defense" (p. 15).
35. Industrial Plans Section, Air Matériel Command, Industrial Preparedness in the Aircraft Industry, May 1, 1947, p. 7, RG 107 (Office of the Secretary of War), Entry 260, Office of the Under Secretary of War, Security-Classified Correspondence, 400.17 to 461, Folder 461 pamphlets; Rudolf Modley, Industrial Planning Service, Aircraft Industries Association of America, Financial Situation of the Airframe Manufacturing Industry, 1937–1946, October 1, 1947, pp. 1–2, PAPC Records, box 39; Ralph V. Hunt, "Aircraft Industry Finances," *Automotive Industries,* December 1, 1947, p. 42.
36. H. E. W[eihmiller], First Draft, Current Status of the Aircraft Manufacturing Industry, November 21, 1947, pp. 3–4, PAPC Records, box 40.
37. "Shall We Have Airplanes?" p. 77; Travis, "New Life in the Aircrafts," p. 528; Robert McLarren, "Record Postwar Year for Aircraft Industry in 1950," *Automotive Industries,* January 15, 1950, p. 36; "Happy Days at Grumman," *Fortune,* June 1948, pp. 112, 114–15.
38. "Aviation RFC?" *Business Week,* January 31, 1948, p. 28; "Aircraft," *Steel,* January 1, 1948, p. 142; Travis, "New Life in the Aircrafts," p. 530; Robert McLarren, "The Aircraft Industry," *Automotive Industries,* December 1, 1947; "Shall We Have Airplanes?" p. 77.
39. "Aircraft Industry Shows Production Gains," *Aviation Week,* February 27, 1950, p. 25; Stenographic Report of Proceedings, PAPC, Statement of Ralph V. Hunt, Vice President Comptroller, Douglas Aircraft Co., September 30, 1947, pp. 1013–14, RG 340 (Secretary of the Air Force), Entry 53, Air Coordinating Committee, General File 1945–1950, ACC Papers Folder No. 125, vol. 2.
40. Verbatim Report, Fifth Meeting of the Air Board, June 5–6, 1947, pp. 36-38, RG 340 (Secretary of the Air Force), Air Board Minutes of Meetings. In April

1948, a group of stockholders in Curtiss-Wright actually did attempt to force a partial liquidation of the company's assets, the returns from which would have been used either to pay a dividend of $7 per share or to purchase outstanding shares at $14 each. See Excerpts from Telephone Conversation Between Honorable James Forrestal, secretary of defense, and Mr. Guy Vaughn [*sic*; Vaughan], April 15, 1948; J. M. Scanlan letter to Honorable James V. Forrestal, April 15, 1948, and attached letter to stockholders from G. W. Vaughan, President, Curtiss-Wright, both in Papers of James V. Forrestal, box 81, Seeley G. Mudd Manuscript Library (hereafter SGMML), Princeton University. Echols's testimony before the PAPC was in the same vein as his remarks to the Air Board: "[T]he companies that are in business now are operating at a rate of loss to the extent that they cannot continue in business"; Stenographic Report of Proceedings, PAPC, Statement of Major General Oliver P. Echols, U.S.A. (Ret.), President, Aircraft Industries Association of America, October 14, 1947, p. 1294, RG 340 (Secretary of the Air Force), Entry 53, Air Coordinating Committee, General File 1945–1950, ACC Papers Folder No. 125, vol. 3.

41. George S. Kent, "Realistic Survey of the Aircrafts," *The Magazine of Wall Street,* March 15, 1947, p. 674; Travis, "New Life in the Aircrafts," p. 530; "Airplanes Now," *Factory Management and Maintenance,* May 1948, p. 90.
42. Aircraft Coordinating Committee Report 22/7.1, Demobilization of the Aircraft Industry—Interim Report of the Ad Hoc Committee on the Aircraft Industry, March 24, 1947, pp. 5–6, RG 340 (Secretary of the Air Force), Entry 53, Air Coordinating Committee, General File, 1945–1950, ACC Papers 97 to 101, untitled folder; "Aircraft Industry Facing Lean Years on Research Diet," *Aviation News,* April 7, 1947, p. 7; Richard P. Cooke, "Aircraft Manufacturers Find Red Ink Tide Ebbing," *Barron's,* December 29, 1947, p. 25; Travis, "New Life in the Aircrafts," p. 530.
43. Glenn L. Martin, "The Problems of Aircraft Development," in *The Aircraft Year Book* (Washington, D.C.: Aircraft Industries Association of America, 1948), p. 146.
44. "Shall We Have Airplanes?" p. 159; Selig Altschul, "Aircraft Makers Finishing Postwar Readjustment," *Barron's,* March 17, 1947, p. 27; "Finance: War Baby," p. 66; "Manufacturing Status Improving in Face of Deficit Reports," *Aviation Week,* July 28, 1947, p. 18; H. F. Travis, "Outlook for Aircrafts Under Unified Military Forces," *The Magazine of Wall Street,* August 30, 1947, p. 593.
45. Rudolf Modley, Industrial Planning Service, Aircraft Industries Association of America, Financial Situation of the Airframe Manufacturing Industry, 1937–1946, October 1, 1947, p. 1, PAPC Records, box 39; "Aircraft Industry's

Biggest Peacetime Year—1946," *Automotive and Aviation Industries,* December 15, 1946, p. 29; Kent, "Realistic Survey of the Aircrafts," p. 672; "Aircraft Industry Equities Suffered Sharpest Declines in 1946," *Aviation News,* January 20, 1947, p. 16; "Aircraft Share Prices Decline Sharply in New Market Break," *Aviation News,* May 16, 1947, p. 26; "Finance: War Baby," p. 58.

46. "Aircraft Manufacturers' Dividends Decline Despite Strong Finances," *Aviation News,* January 6, 1947, p. 21; Travis, "Outlook for Aircrafts," p. 621; The Glenn L. Martin Company Book Value of Land and Buildings, November 30, 1947, unpaginated, Martin Papers, Subject File, Glenn L. Martin Company; R. F. Murray letter to Weldon B. Gibson, Stanford Research Institute, August 15, 1947, p. 3, PAPC, Records, box 18; Ralph Hunt quoted in "Shall We Have Airplanes?" p. 80.

47. "Experiment at Republic," p. 172; Statement by Mr. Glenn L. Martin before Senate Banking and Currency Committee—RFC Inquiry, January 15, 1948, pp. 5–7, Papers of Glenn L. Martin, Subject File, Glenn L. Martin Company; Altschul, "Huge Losses," p. 35; "Shall We Have Airplanes?" p. 79; W. Stuart Symington, Assistant Secretary of War for Air, letter to Reconstruction Finance Corporation, February 11, 1947, Papers of Carl A. Spaatz, Chief of Staff, Secretary of the Air Force folder, Manuscript Division, Library of Congress.

48. Eugene E. Wilson quotes these words of Forrestal in *Slipstream: The Autobiography of an Air Craftsman* (2nd ed.; New York: Science Press, 1965), p. 260; I recount the incident that led up to them in the next chapter.

49. Robert Gross to Randolph C. Walker, August 13, 1946, p. 1, Gross Papers, Business Correspondence File; Gross to Lynn L. Bollinger, October 10, 1946, p. 2, Gross Papers, Aerospace Industry File; Foreman's Mtg, July 1946, Gross Papers, Business Correspondence File; Lynn Bollinger was in charge of aviation research at the Harvard Business School. For information on Gross's background, see "Aviation: Sales at Work," *Time,* January 14, 1946, pp. 77ff.

50. Robert Gross to George McManus, September 17, 1946, p. 2, Gross Papers, Business Correspondence File; Gross to Lynn L. Bollinger, October 22, 1946, pp. 1-2, Gross Papers, Aerospace Industry File; Altschul, "Overgrown Aircraft Industry," p. 36.

51. "Aviation RFC?" p. 28; "Shall We Have Airplanes?" p. 157; Robert Gross to E. E. Wilson, May 3, 1945, Gross Papers, Aerospace Industry File. In his reply of May 9, 1945 (also in the Gross Papers), Wilson stated that he had taken "advantage of [Representative] Claire Luce's announcement upon her return from France to bring the whole matter to her attention and she has promised to see that it gets into the Military Affairs Committee [of the House]. We are laying some other plans in the same direction. To me this is our number one priority project." So much for alleged hopes for "strong commercial markets"!

52. Memorandum for Major General E. M. Powers, from William J. Keary, October 1, 1945, pp. 1-2, Gross Papers, Aerospace Industry File; Gross to Mrs. A. H. Flower, July 3, 1946, p. 2, Gross Papers, Personal Correspondence File. Apparently, the army air force interviewed several of the leading aircraft manufacturers in this fashion; see, e.g., the Memorandum for the Record of Colonel Francis D. Butler, August 1, 1945, describing his meeting with Donald Douglas, RG 340 (Secretary of the Air Force), Entry 53, Air Coordinating Committee, General File, 1945–1950, ACC Papers 22-63-1 to 28-50-1, 28-1-1 U.S. Air Policy folder.
53. "Shall We Have Airplanes?" p. 162.
54. "Step Toward Socialization?" an editorial in *Aviation Week*, August 16, 1948, p. 58; "The Wildest Blue Yonder Yet," *Fortune*, March 1948, p. 96. So great was the dread of nationalization in aircraft circles that *Aviation Week* even extended the prohibition on subsidies to include federal loans, for "to fall back on continued government loans would be to invite eventual socialization of the industry"; "Manufacturers' Capital Reserves Depleted," *Aviation Week*, February 23, 1948, p. 26. Note also another of *Fortune's* remarks about nationalization—again made in the context of subsidies—in the first installment of its two-part series on the aircraft industry: "Presumably the commission [President's Air Policy Commission] will consider, and presumably reject, the solution that goes by the name of 'nationalization'"; "Shall We Have Airplanes?" p. 162.
55. Stenographic Report of Proceedings, PAPC, Statement of Donald Douglas, President, Douglas Aircraft Company, Inc., October 29, 1947, p. 2126, RG 340 (Secretary of the Air Force), Entry 53, Air Coordinating Committee, General File 1945–1950, ACC Papers Folder No. 125, vol. 5–6.
56. "Shall We Have Airplanes?" p. 162; "Aviation RFC?" pp. 28, 30; "Aviation Industry Eyes Congress for Stable Policy and More Funds," *Aviation Week*, January 5, 1948, p. 12.
57. William Kroger, "Need for Military Production Contracts Shown by Industry Losses," *Aviation News*, March 10, 1947, p. 12; "Manufacturing Status Improving in Face of Deficit Reports," *Aviation Week*, July 28, 1947, p. 18.
58. "Finance: War Baby," p. 64; McLarren, "Record Postwar Year," p. 36; Selig Altschul, "Aircraft Makers Finishing Postwar Readjustment," *Barron's*, March 17, 1947, p. 27; "Light-Plane Market Slumps," p. 38; "Northrop Shows Profit of $240,573 for Year," *Aviation Week*, October 20, 1947, p. 14; Robert E. Gross to General Carl A. Spaatz, Commanding General, Army Air Forces, September 17, 1947, p. 2, Symington Papers; Notes for Annual Meeting of Shareholders, May 4, 1948, pp. 1–2, Gross Papers, Business Correspondence File; "Aviation Revival Aids General Industry," *Steel*, May 23, 1949, p. 65.

59. "Experiment at Republic," p. 172; "Happy Days at Grumman," *Fortune,* June 1948, pp. 112, 114, 186.
60. Stenographic Report of Proceedings, PAPC, Statement of Mundy I. Peale, President, Republic Aircraft Corporation, September 29, 1947, p. 840, RG 340 (Secretary of the Air Force), Entry 53, Air Coordinating Committee, General File 1945–1950, ACC Papers Folder No. 125, vol. 2; and Statement of Leon A. Swirbul, President, Grumman Aircraft Engineering Corporation, October 1, 1947, p. 1197, RG 340 (Secretary of the Air Force), Entry 53, Air Coordinating Committee, General File 1945–1950, ACC Papers Folder No. 125, vol. 3.
61. Stenographic Report of Proceedings, PAPC, Statement of Major General Oliver P. Echols, U.S.A. (Ret.), President, Aircraft Industries Association of America, October 14, 1947, pp. 1321–22, RG 340 (Secretary of the Air Force), Entry 53, Air Coordinating Committee, General File 1945–1950, ACC Papers Folder No. 125, vol. 3.
62. More specifically, the attributes of a ruling class are: a disproportionately great amount of wealth, property and income "as compared to other social classes"; "control over the major social and economic institutions of the [national] state"; and "domination over the governmental processes of the country." See G. William Domhoff, *The Powers That Be: Processes of Ruling Class Domination in America* (New York: Vintage Books, 1979), p. 12.
63. Richard P. Cooke, "Aircraft Manufacturers Find Red Ink Tide Ebbing," *Barron's,* December 29, 1947, p. 25; "Shall We Have Airplanes?" p. 77.
64. "Airplanes Now for Security," *Factory Management and Maintenance,* May 1948, p. 89; "Intensified Tool Selling Urged," *Steel,* April 18, 1949, p. 58; "How Much Aid for Aircraft?" *Steel,* November 17, 1947, p. 74.
65. "1949 in the Aircraft Industry," *Automotive Industries,* January 15, 1949, p. 35; Obligations Under "Supplemental National Defense Appropriation Act 1948," as of June 30, 1948, p. 1, attached to Memorandum for Mr. Forrestal from W. H. Mautz, July 22, 1948, Department of Defense records (copy made for the author at the Department of Defense).
66. "Military Plane Program Pushed: Air Force and Navy given green light on 4262 new aircraft, 2201 now being under order by Air Force and 1165 by the Navy," *Steel,* August 16, 1949, p. 62; Peter Collier and David Horowitz, *The Rockefellers: An American Dynasty* (New York: New American Library, 1977), pp. 216, 293–96.
67. Frederick J. Simonelli, "Chase National Bank and the Arsenal of Democracy: Financial Interests, Military Appropriations and Political Influence, 1945–1948," graduate research paper at the California State University, Sacramento, December 1990, pp. 6–9, 12. Chase's foremost rival, the National City Bank (subsequently

Citibank), had also dived deeply into all aspects of the aviation field and was intimately connected with United Aircraft in particular; the president of the bank, Gordon S. Rentschler, was the brother of the president of United Aircraft, Frederick B. Rentschler. See Elsbeth E. Freudenthal, "The Aviation Business in the 1930s," in T*he History of the American Aircraft Industry: An Anthology,* Gene Roger Simonson, ed. (Cambridge, Mass.: MIT Press, 1968), pp. 80–81, 90–91.

68. Simonelli, "Chase National Bank," pp. 12–14; John Donald Wilson, *The Chase: The Chase Manhattan Bank, N.A., 1945–1985* (Boston: Harvard Business School Press, 1986), p. 29, Table 3, and p. 46.
69. Memorandum to Mr. W. W. Aldrich from H. J. MacTavish, October 15, 1947, pp. 1–4, and Barton P. Turnbull, et al., letter to the Board of Directors, Chase National Bank, November 12, 1947, pp. 1, 5–6, Exhibits A and B (unpaginated), both in Papers of Winthrop W. Aldrich, box 46, The Chase Bank—1947, Baker Library, Harvard Business School; the quotation is on p. 6 of the letter of November 12.
70. Telephone conversation between Winthrop Aldrich and Secretary Forrestal, December 15, 1948, Forrestal Papers, box 78.
71. See, for example, the press release announcing Aldrich's appointment as chairman of the President's Committee on Foreign Trade, July 9, 1946, Papers of Harry S. Truman, Official File, HSTL (copy made for author at Harry S. Truman Library); John Donald Wilson, *The Chase,* pp. 51-52.
72. See James Forrestal letter to Winthrop W. Aldrich, December 17, 1948, Forrestal Papers, box 95.
73. W. Stuart Symington letter to Winthrop Aldrich, April 1, 1948, Symington papers, box 1; Symington to Aldrich, April 5, 1948, Aldrich Papers, Correspondence File 2.

Notes to Chapter 3.

1. Papers of W. Stuart Symington, Harry S. Truman Library (hereafter HSTL); Carl A. Spaatz was then the commanding general of the army air force.
2. Ibid., box 14. When Symington took office as secretary of the air force later in the year, Eugene Zuckert became one of the assistant secretaries.
3. ACC Minutes of Meeting of February 27, 1947, p. 9, National Archives Record Group (hereafter RG) 340 (Secretary of the Air Force), Entry 53, Air Coordinating Committee, General File, 1945–1950, ACC Papers, Minutes of Meeting of the ACC notebook.
4. Col. Martin, Informal Minutes of Air Coordinating Committee Meeting of April 3, 1947, p. 2, RG 340 (Secretary of the Air Force), Entry 53, Air

Coordinating Committee, General File, 1945–1950, ACC Papers 91-92, PICAO Panel folder.

5. This letter is in the Records of the President's Air Policy Commission (hereafter PAPC), HSTL. For an example of the aircraft industry's opposition to subsidies *explicitly labelled as such,* see *Aviation Week,* August 16, 1948, p. 58. I explained in the preceding chapter that industry executives feared that proposals to subsidize the aircraft firms would inevitably lead to counterproposals to nationalize them.
6. "The Wildest Blue Yonder Yet," *Fortune,* March 1948, p. 96.
7. Discussion following Air Force Presentation to the Combat Aviation Subcommittee, Congressional Aviation Policy Board, . . . January 21, 1948, p. 32, RG 341 (Headquarters, U.S. Air Force), Entry 337, Deputy Chief of Staff, Operations, Director of Plans, Executive Office, Records Branch, General File, 1944–1953, TS No. 38 to No. 44, untitled folder.
8. Eugene E. Wilson, *Kitty Hawk to Sputnik to Polaris: A Contemporary Account of the Struggle over Military and Commercial Air Policy in the United States* (Barre, Mass.: Barre Gazette, 1960), pp. 2–4; and *Slipstream: The Autobiography of an Air Craftsman* (2nd ed.; New York: Science Press, 1965), pp. 260–63, 347–48; in the above I have drawn on both of Wilson's versions of this meeting. Significantly, he dedicated the second edition of the latter book to Forrestal, whom he credited, in a letter of June 10, 1946, with having "put the aircraft industry's survival in our lap" and thereby "touched off the spark" leading to the industry's postwar prosperity; E. E. Wilson letter to the Honorable James V. Forrestal, Papers of James V. Forrestal (hereafter Forrestal Papers), box 75, Seeley G. Mudd Manuscript Library (hereafter SGMML), Princeton University. Wilson's narrative gains credibility from the fact that when Forrestal himself founded the Navy Industrial Association (later, the Armed Services Industrial Association, then the National Security Industrial Association) the following year, he asked Wilson to become its first president; see *Kitty Hawk,* p. 74. Further corroborative evidence comes from a pair of sources. In a letter of October 7, 1947, to Secretary of the Air Force W. Stuart Symington, Oliver P. Echols, the president of the Aircraft Industries Association of America, Inc., stated that "the Navy Industrial Association was organized by Mr. Eugene Wilson at the request of Mr. Forrestal" (Symington Papers). Only a few days earlier, on October 1, 1947, Frederick Rentschler had written to James Forrestal with respect to the manufacturer's efforts to impel the federal government to sustain the aircraft industry: "Since 1943, I have felt this would be necessary in the postwar era"; RG 330 (Secretary of Defense), Entry 199, Office of the Administrative Secretary, Correspondence Control Section, Numerical File, September 1947–June 1950, CD 3-1-40 to

CD 3-1-21, CD 3-1-22 folder. This said, it must be added for completeness that Wilson's chronology is sometimes confused; on three occasions, for example, he places the start of the Berlin blockade of 1948-1949 in 1947; see *Kitty Hawk,* pp. 75, 83, 85.

9. James Forrestal letters to Paul E. Fitzpatrick, Esq., December 12, 1947, and Robert T. Stevens, Esq., president, J. P. Stevens & Co., December 13, 1947, both in Forrestal Papers, box 93.
10. Elsbeth E. Freudenthal, "The Aviation Business in the 1930s," in *The History of the American Aircraft Industry: An Anthology,* Gene Roger Simonson, ed. (Cambridge, Mass.: MIT Press, 1968), p. 100; *Aircraft Yearbook* of 1936 quoted in Freudenthal, "The Aviation Business"; Rentschler to James Forrestal, October 1, 1947, RG 330 (Secretary of Defense), Entry 199, CD 3-1-22 folder.
11. Wilson, *Kitty Hawk,* p. 42; Wilson, *Slipstream,* pp. 232, 328; see also *Kitty Hawk,* pp. 6, 41–44, and *Slipstream,* chapter 29 and pp. 347–48, for more evidence that both Wilson and Forrestal feared that depressed conditions in the aircraft industry might lead to irresistible demands for its nationalization in the postwar period.
12. Eugene E. Wilson letter to Robert Gross, May 9, 1945, Papers of Robert E. Gross, Aerospace Industry File, Manuscript Division, Library of Congress.
13. Memorandum for General [H. H.] Arnold from Col. Francis D. Butler, June 28, 1945, p. 2, RG 340 (Secretary of the Air Force), Entry 63, Air Coordinating Committee, General File, 1945–1950, ACC Papers 22-63-1 to 28-50-1, 28-1-1 U.S. Air Policy folder.
14. Column by Manchester Boddy, *Los Angeles Daily News,* June 14, 1945, p. 20; "Airplane Industry Reconversion Going to Be Tough, United Aircraft Officer Warns; Maps Program," *National Petroleum News,* May 23, 1945; see also Wilson, *Kitty Hawk,* pp. 42, 54–55, 56, for more on the industry's clamor "for the appointment of a new Presidential advisory commission such as the Morrow Board" (p. 54). For a more jaundiced view of the effectiveness of the Morrow Board by a former federal bureaucrat intimately involved in aviation, see Stenographic Report of Proceedings, President's Air Policy Commission (hereafter PAPC), Statement of F. Trubee Davison, President, National Air Council, December 1, 1947, pp. 2644–47, RG 340 (Secretary of the Air Force), Entry 53, Air Coordinating Committee, General File, 1945–1950, ACC Papers, Folder No. 125, vols. 5 and 6, vol. 6 folder; Davison had been assistant secretary of war for air in the administrations of Warren Harding and Calvin Coolidge. Although Donald Douglas in 1945 was opposed to the idea of a second Morrow Board, I know of no other major figure in the industry who shared that sentiment, and Douglas himself had long since abandoned it by the time the PAPC was appointed in July 1947; for his views as of August

1945, see Memorandum for the Record by Francis D. Butler, August 1, 1945, RG 340 (Secretary of the Air Force), Entry 53, Air Coordinating Committee, General File, 1945–1950, ACC Papers 22-63-1 to 28-50-1, 28-1-1 U.S. Air Policy folder. At the time of the creation of the Morrow Board, its chairman was a leading power in the House of Morgan investment banking firm; subsequently, he would become U.S. ambassador to Mexico, a U.S. senator and, indicative of his close ties to the world of aviation, father-in-law of Charles Lindbergh.

15. For Lovett's position and air force suspicions, see Memorandum for General Arnold from Col. Francis D. Butler, June 28, 1948, pp. 2–4, RG 340, Entry 53, 28-1-1 U.S. Air Policy folder. According to Oliver Echols, speaking of the proposal for a presidential aviation board, "the Army turned it down last year [1946] . . . on the grounds that it might get mixed up with unification"; Verbatim Report, Fifth Meeting of the Air Board, June 56, 1947, p. 49, RG 340 (Secretary of the Air Force), Entry 53, Air Board Minutes of Meetings.
16. Interdepartmental Memorandum Regarding Organization of Air Coordinating Committee, March 27, 1945, and press release, The Air Coordinating Committee and What It Does, November 1, 1945, in RG 340 (Secretary of the Air Force), Entry 53, Air Coordinating Committee, General File, 1945–1950, ACC Papers 97 to 101, untitled folder. For Lovett's initiative in the establishment of the ACC, see Staff Study, approximately April 27, 1948, RG 340, Entry 53, Air Coordinating Committee, General File, 1945–1950, Pan Air do Brazil to Radio Technical Commission, PAPC folder, and George A. Brownell, "The Air Coordinating Committee: A Problem in Federal Staff Work, *Journal of Air Law and Commerce* 14:4 (Autumn 1947), pp. 414–16. I could find no record of opposition to industry representation in any of the minutes of the ACC for 1946; see RG 340, Entry 53, Air Coordinating Committee, General File, 1945–1950, Minutes of Meeting of the ACC.
17. Press release of September 19, 1946, RG 340 (Secretary of the Air Force), Entry 53, Air Coordinating Committee, General File, 1945–1950, ACC Papers 86 to 88, Folder No. 86, ACC Membership; see Stenographic Report of Proceedings, PAPC, Statement of Honorable Garrison Norton, assistant secretary of state and chairman, Air Coordinating Committee, September 8, 1947, pp. 28–30, PAPC Records, box 17, HSTL.
18. Wilson, *Kitty Hawk,* p. 74; Wilson, *Slipstream,* p. 286; letter of W. Stuart Symington, assistant secretary of war for air, December 13, 1946, and clipping, "General Echols' New Job," stamped January 14, 1947, from unidentified newspaper, both in Symington Papers.
19. Brownell, "The Air Coordinating Committee," p. 422; James M. Landis [ACC co-chairman] letter to T. J. Hargrave, Chairman, Munitions Board,

November 12, 1947, p. 1, RG 340 (Secretary of the Air Force), Entry 55, Air Coordinating Committee, Program File, 1948–1951, ACC Working Committee, November 1947–March 1948 folder. See also Garrison Norton's testimony before the PAPC, pp. 32–33, PAPC Records, box 17.

20. Oliver P. Echols letter to the Honorable William L. Clayton, January 24, 1947, RG 340 (Secretary of the Air Force), Entry 53, Air Coordinating Committee, General File, 1945–1950, ACC Papers 97 to 101, untitled folder.
21. Air Coordinating Committee Aviation, Industry Advisory Panel, Minutes of Meeting of February 6, 1947, p. 4, and ACC 72.2, Recommendations of the Industry Advisory Panel—Policy re Selection of Personnel for Key Aviation Positions in the Government—Letter dated March 26, 1947[,] from the President, both in RG 341 (Headquarters, U.S. Air Force), Entry 340, Deputy Chief of Staff, Operations, Director of Plans, Policy Division, Civil Air Branch, ACC Documents 1945–1955, Folders Nos. 110 and 111, Folder No. 111, DO-8D-2A; ACC Meeting of February 27, 1947, pp. 2–4, RG 340 (Secretary of the Air Force), Entry 53, Air Coordinating Committee, General File, 1945–1950, Minutes of Meeting of the ACC.
22. ACC Meeting of February 27, 1947, pp. 4–5, RG 340 (Secretary of the Air Force), Entry 53, Air Coordinating Committee, General File, 1945–1950, Minutes of Meeting of the ACC.
23. Ibid., pp. 5–9 *passim.*
24. Col[onel] [Carlton J.] Martin, Informal Minutes of ACC Meeting of 3 April 1947, p. 2, RG 340 (Secretary of the Air Force), Entry 53, Air Coordinating Committee, General File, 1945–1950, ACC Papers 91-92, PICAO Panel folder.
25. ACC Minutes of April 3, 1947, pp. 2–5, RG 340 (Secretary of the Air Force), Entry 53, Air Coordinating Committee, General File, 1945–1950, ACC Papers, Minutes of Meeting of the ACC Notebook.
26. ACC Minutes of May 1, 1947, pp. 2–5, RG 340 (Secretary of the Air Force), Entry 53.
27. ACC Minutes of June 13, 1947, pp. 48, RG 340 (Secretary of the Air Force), Entry 53.
28. The ad hoc committee's draft of a letter to the president is attached to Memorandum for the Under Secretary of War from Brackley Shaw, Special Assistant to the Assistant Secretary for Air, June 16, 1947, RG 107 (Office of the Secretary of War), Entry 260, Security-Classified Correspondence, November 1945–September 1947, 400.17 to 461; Garrison Norton, letter to the president, June 17, 1947, p. 2, RG 341 (Headquarters, U.S. Air Force), Entry 340, Deputy Chief of Staff, Operations, Division of Plans, Policy Division, Civil Air Branch, ACC Documents 1945–1955, Folder Nos. 110 to 111, Folder No. 110, DO-8D-3A.

29. Nathan F. Twining letter to Hugh J. Knerr, May 19, 1947, p. 1, RG 340 (Secretary of the Air Force), Entry 47, Air Board, General File, 1945-1948, Transportation to Weekly Activity Reports, Letter from General Twining folder.
30. Lieutenant Colonel Galson, U.S. Air Policy, June 28, 1945, p. 3, RG 340 (Secretary of the Air Force), Entry 53, Air Coordinating Committee, General File, 1945–1950, ACC Papers 22-63-1 to 28-50-1, 28-1-1, U.S. Air Policy folder; Memorandum for General [H. H.] Arnold from Major General Lauris Norstad, September 28, 1945, p. 2, RG 340 (Secretary of the Air Force), Entry 53, 23-200-2, Miscellaneous-Special Correspondence folder.
31. Letter from Lieutenant General Nathan F. Twining to General Carl Spaatz, undated [but in response to Spaatz letter to Twining of May 27, 1947], RG 18, Army Air Force, Air Adjutant General, Mail and Records Division, Unclassified Records Section, Decimal File, 1947, 004, Material 23 Resources, 1 June 004 47 folder; Memorandum for the Haislip Board from Major General Hugh J. Knerr, March 25, 1947, p. 2, RG 340 (Secretary of the Air Force), Entry 47, Air Board, General File, 1945–1948, Haislip Board to International Standardization, Haislip Board to Review War Department Policies and Programs folder, Office File; Memorandum for Mr. Symington from Hugh J. Knerr, December 17, 1947, RG 340 (Secretary of the Air Force), Entry 47, Army Air Force Aid Society to Appointments of Theater Commanders, Air Logistics folder.
32. Verbatim Report, Fifth Meeting of the Air Board, June 5–6, 1947, p. 45–46, RG 340 (Secretary of the Air Force), Air Board Minutes of Meetings; see also pp. 70–72 for more of the same from the general. The Williamsburg Conference to which Kenney referred was a once-a-year meeting of the Aircraft Industries Association in Williamsburg, Virginia.
33. Ibid., pp. 58, 70, 278–82; the material I have quoted is on p. 282. The Verbatim Report of the next meeting of the Air Board in September 9–10, 1947, lists Echols as a member. Echols himself wrote to Stuart Symington on October 3, 1947, "At General Spaatz' request I . . . accepted an *assignment* [emphasis added] as a member of the Air Board" (Symington Papers).
34. Verbatim Report, Fifth Meeting of the Air Board, pp. 292, 295.
35. Memorandum for General Spaatz, February 12, 1947, box 14; Symington letter to Oliver P. Echols, May 30, 1947; Symington letter to Major General K. B. Wolfe, June 10, 1947, p. 3, box 14; all in Symington Papers.
36. Notes for Remarks Before the Presidential Air Policy Commission, attached to Memorandum for Mr. Symington from J. B. M., September 5, 1947, and Symington letter to General Oliver P. Echols, September 25, 1947, both in Symington Papers; Memorandum for Secretary Forrestal from W. Stuart

Symington, December 15, 1947, Papers of Carl A. Spaatz, Chief of Staff files, Secretary of Air Force folder, Manuscript Division, Library of Congress.

37. Letter of Robert P. Patterson to Honorable James E. Webb, Director, Bureau of the Budget, July 16, 1947, Papers of James E. Webb, box 11, HSTL.

38. Robert E. Gross letter to Frederick M. Warburg, June 5, 1947, Personal Correspondence File, Gross Papers; Address by Honorable Kenneth C. Royall, under secretary of war, May 16, 1947, Williamsburg AIA Conference, pp. 2–3, Papers of Hoyt S. Vandenberg, Aircraft Industries Association of America folder.

39. Address by Kenneth C. Royall, pp. 4–6.

40. Press Release of July 18, 1947, Official File, box 863, HSTL; "Letter Appointing Members to the Air Policy Commission," *Public Papers of the Presidents of the United States: Harry S. Truman, 1947* (Washington, D.C.: U.S. Government Printing Office, 1963), pp. 148–49 (hereafter cited as *Public Papers of Harry S. Truman*); "Letter to the Chairman of the Air Coordinating Committee," *Public Papers of Harry S. Truman,* p. 149; Robert Gross letter to Frederick M. Warburg, July 30, 1947, p. 2, Personal Correspondence File, Gross Papers.

41. See "Air Council Bill," *Aviation News,* March 10, 1947, p. 30; "Brewster Backs New Aviation Policy Bill," *Aviation News,* May 19, 1947, p. 10; "Manufacturers, AAF Renew Drive for Long-Range Plane Program" and "Latest Moves on National Air Policy," both in *Aviation News,* June 2, 1947, p. 7; Robert Gross letters to Frederick M. Warburg of July 17, 1947, Personal Correspondence File, Gross Papers.

42. "Aviation: Plane Makers Sing the Blues," *Business Week,* April 12, 1947, pp. 34, 36; "Brewster Urges Stronger Air Force," *Aviation News,* March 24, 1947, p. 10; "The Aviation Week," *Aviation Week,* September 1, 1947, p. 7.

43. Excerpts from Telephone Conversation between Honorable James Forrestal, Secretary of the Navy[,] and Senator Owen Brewster, July 17, 1947, p. 1, Forrestal Papers, box 92.

44. Gross to Frederick Warburg, July 30, 1947, pp. 1–2, Personal Correspondence File, Gross Papers.

45. Telephone Conversation between James Forrestal and Owen Brewster, July 17, 1947, p. 1, Forrestal Papers, box 92.

46. *Survival in the Air Age: A Report by the Presidents Air Policy Commission* (Washington, D.C.: U.S. Government Printing Office, 1948), pp. 24–27, 43–70 *passim*; "Statement by the President Upon Making Public the Report of the Air Policy Commission," January 13, 1948, *Public Papers of Harry S. Truman, 1947,* p. 63; Robert H. Wood, "The Betrayal of Air Power II," *Aviation Week,* April 12, 1948, p. 54.

47. Memorandum for Mr. Symington, Secretary of the Air Force, [and] General Spaatz, Chief of Staff, U.S. Air Force, October 3, 1947, attached to Memo-

randum for General Spaatz of same date from Brigadier General B. L. Boatner, Secretary of the Air Staff, Papers of Carl Spaatz, Chief of Staff File, Manuscript Division, Library of Congress. This latter document states, "The attached memorandum for Mr. Symington and General Spaatz, dated 3 October 1947, was dictated by Mr. John A. McCone [a member of the PAPC] this date, after a long distance telephone conversation with Mr. Finletter in New York."

48. "Wanted: Air Power," *Business Week,* April 10, 1948, p. 120; "The Wildest Blue Yonder Yet," *Fortune,* March 1948, p. 151; "A National Air Policy," *Wall Street Journal,* January 10, 1948, p. 4.
49. Biographical Material, p. 2, undated, PAPC Records, box 1.
50. Stenographic Report of Proceedings, PAPC, Statement of Leon A. Swirbul, President, Grumman Aircraft Engineering Corporation, October 1, 1947, p. 1197, RG 340 (Secretary of the Air Force), Entry 53, Air Coordinating Committee, General File 1945–1950, ACC Papers, Folder No. 125, vol. 3; and Statement of George A. Brownell, brigadier general, U.S.A. (Ret.), RG 340 (Secretary of the Air Force), Entry 53, ACC Papers folder No. 125, vols. 5 and 6; James E. Webb letter to Honorable James M. Landis, Chairman, Civil Aeronautics Board, March 3, 1947, Webb Papers, box 11; Biographical Material, p. 2, PAPC Records, box 1; "Aviation," *The Iron Age,* January 3, 1946, p. 116; Lynn L. Bollinger letters to Robert E. Gross, February 14, 1946, and February 3, 1948, and Gross letter to Mr. Phil Hofer, Assistant Dean, February 16, 1946, all in Aerospace Industry File, Gross Papers.
51. Memorandum for the Record by Brigadier General B. L. Boatner, August 12, 1947, RG 340 (Secretary of the Air Force), Entry 53, Air Coordinating Committee, General File, 1945–1950, ACC Papers, Folder No. 122 to 124, Folder No. 122; Statement to the Press to be Released by the White House, September 27, 1947, Official File, HSTL, box 863; Laton McCartney, *Friends in High Places: The Bechtel Story: The Most Secret Corporation and How It Engineered the World* (Simon and Schuster: New York, 1988), pp. 66–70, 97–98; Biographical Material, p. 3, PAPC Records, box 1; John A. McCone letter to The Honorable W. Stuart Symington, January 23, 1948, and enclosure, Symington Papers.
52. Memorandum for Mr. John Brown, Asst. SecNav for Air, from James Forrestal, July 11, 1947, box 92, and Excerpts from Telephone Conversation between the Secretary of the Navy and Mr. Palmer Hoyt, November 1, 1945, Forrestal Papers, box 42; "Truman Board, Congress Group Will Probe Aviation Industry," *Aviation Week,* July 28, 1947, p. 12; Biographical Material, p. 2, PAPC Records, box 1.
53. Congressional Aviation Policy Board, *National Aviation Policy* (Washington, D.C.: U.S. Government Printing Office, 1948); Members of the Advisory

Council, attached to Memorandum for Assistant Chief of Staff-1, et al., from John K. Gerhart, Brigadier General, U.S. Army, October 2, 1947, RG 340 (Secretary of the Air Force), Entry 47, Air Board, General File, 1945–1948, Basic Plan to Current Army Air Force Plans and Programs, Congressional Aviation Policy Board folder; CAPB, press release of October 5, 1947, p. 3, RG 340 (Secretary of the Air Force), Entry 47; Memorandum for Mr. Zuckert from John A. Brooks, Lt. Colonel, U.S. Air Force, April 12, 1948, p. 1, Symington Papers, box 14; Forrestal Papers, box 79.

54. AAF [Army Air Force] Procurement Planning: Summary of testimony given September 18, 1947, p. 2, box 18; AAF Procurement Planning: Summary of testimony given September 25, 1947, p. 1, box 18; Air Force Conference—Pentagon, September 18, 1947, box 40; all documents in PAPC Records. According to the first of these documents, four firms were scheduled to receive 81 percent of the air forces aircraft expenditures in the 1949 fiscal year, with Lockheed, Douglas and Consolidated-Vultee again excluded.

55. Stenographic Report of Proceedings [unrevised], PAPC, Statement of William M. Allen, September 30, 1947, pp. 1036–37; Statement of Mundy I. Peale, September 29, 1947, pp. 838–39; Statement of Lawrence D. Bell, September 29, 1947, pp. 908, 911; Statement of Ralph V. Hunt, September 30, 1947, p. 1019; all in RG 340 (Secretary of the Air Force), Entry 53, Air Coordinating Committee, General File 1945–1950, ACC Papers, Folder No. 125, vol. 2.

56. [Revised] Statement of Major General Oliver P. Echols, U.S.A. (Ret.), president, Aircraft Industries Association of America, October 14, 1947, p. 1304, PAPC Records; Statement Submitted to the PAPC by Major General Oliver P. Echols, October 14, 1947, RG 340 (Secretary of the Air Force), Entry 53, Air Coordinating Committee, General File 1945–1950, ACC Papers, Folder Nos. 116 to 121, Folder No. 120.

57. Memorandum for Mr. Secretary from Marx Leva, August 25, 1947, Forrestal Papers, box 73; Forrestal's dinner with Donald Douglas noted in Diaries of James V. Forrestal (hereafter, Forrestal Diaries), entry for August 29, 1947, p. 1790, box 4, SGMML, Princeton University; Memorandum for Mr. Symington from James Forrestal, August 30, 1947, Symington Papers. Leon Swirbul was the president of Grumman Aircraft; J. H. ("Dutch") Kindleberger, of North American Aviation; Frederick B. Rentschler, chairman of the board of United Aircraft, we met at the outset of this chapter. During World War II, as I have noted, Echols administered aircraft procurement for the army; Towers was his naval counterpart. Forrestal told Rentschler he had also recommended to Thomas Finletter that the last "get your views," which "coincided with my own." James Forrestal letter to Frederick B. Rentschler, October 18, 1947, Forrestal Papers, box 76.

58. Memorandum for Secretary Forrestal from W. Stuart Symington, September 2, 1947, Symington Papers, box 5; Carl Spaatz was the current air force chief of staff, and Hoyt Vandenberg would succeed him during 1948. W. Stuart Symington letter to Honorable John Snyder, September 2, 1947, Webb Papers. Snyder had been Symington's banker prior to joining the Truman administration and was also the person who introduced Symington to then-Senator Truman; see Symington oral history interview, p. 15 and *passim,* HSTL.
59. Statement of Honorable W. Stuart Symington [unrevised] to the PAPC, September 9, 1947, p. 279, Papers of Harry S. Truman, Files of Clark M. Clifford, HSTL. In a later appearance before the same body, Symington was again quizzed about this "constructive way of distributing the aircraft business." "Would the industry take to that?" Thomas Finletter inquired. "The suggestion was made by perhaps their leading representative," Symington replied. Statement of Honorable W. Stuart Symington [unrevised] before the PAPC, November 26, 1947, p. 12, RG 340 (Secretary of the Air Force), Entry 53, General File, 1945–1950, Air Coordinating Committee papers, No. 125, vols. 5 and 6, folder, vol. 6.
60. See the Memorandum for Dr. Leach from Brant Woods, July 11, 1949, attachments on Distribution of Airframe Backlogs, A.F. & Navy, and Backlog of Military Airframe Orders, Symington Papers, box 6.
61. *Aviation Week,* December 29, 1947, p. 12, and January 5, 1948, p. 11.
62. *Aviation Week,* March 22, 1948, p. 33.
63. Memorandum for Secretary Forrestal from W. Stuart Symington, December 16, 1947, Papers of Harry S. Truman, Files of Clark M. Clifford, box 11; W. Stuart Symington to Honorable James E. Webb, December 16, 1947, pp. 13, RG 340 (Secretary of the Air Force), Entry Air Board, General File, 1945–1948, Investigation to Minutes of Meetings, Air Coordinating Committee, Minutes of Meeting folder; W. Stuart Symington to Mr. Clark Clifford, December 16, 1947, Truman Papers, Clifford Files, box 11; Clark Clifford with Richard Holbrooke, *Counsel to the President: A Memoir* (New York: Random House, 1991), p. 38. Despite the evidence here and in chapter 5 of his interest in the subject, Clifford has nonetheless maintained that he "was not involved in any way in the procurement of military aircraft in the Truman Administration, nor do I have any information with reference to it"; Clark Clifford letter to the author, October 24, 1986.
64. Memorandum for the Secretary from Felix Larkin, December 11, 1947, RG 330 (Secretary of Defense), Entry 200, Office of the Administrative Secretary, Correspondence Control Section, Central Numerical File, September 1947 to December 1949, G to G1, Folder G1, Legislation, October 17, 1947, to June 30, 1948, vol. 1.

65. "Russian Scare," *Wall Street Journal,* September 12, 1947, p. 1.

Notes to Chapter 4.

1. Stenographic Report of Proceedings, President's Air Policy Commission (hereafter PAPC), Statement of Honorable W. Averell Harriman [unrevised], Secretary of Commerce, September 8, 1947, p. 18, Records of the PAPC, Harry S. Truman Library (hereafter HSTL), box 17.
2. Stenographic Report of Proceedings [unrevised], PAPC, Statement of Admiral Chester W. Nimitz, Chief of Naval Operations, U.S. Navy, to the PAPC, November 12, 1947, p. 2293, National Archive Record Group (hereafter RG) 340 (Secretary of the Air Force), Entry 53, Air Coordinating Committee, General File, 1945–1950, ACC Papers, Folder No. 125, vols. 5–6.
3. Harold B. Hinton, "Eisenhower Scoffs at Fears of a War Started By Russia," *New York Times* (hereafter *NYT*), February 6, 1948, p. 1.
4. Papers of James V. Forrestal (hereafter Forrestal Papers), box 93, Seeley G. Mudd Manuscript Library (hereafter SGMML), Princeton University. For similar sentiments on Forrestal's part, see his letter to Honorable Chan Gurney, Chairman, Senate Committee on the Armed Services, December 8, 1947, p. 2, Forrestal Papers, box 93. Significantly, Forrestal added the following words by hand below the typed body of this letter: "The above, of course, for your own information and guidance only."
5. U.S. Department of State, *Foreign Relations of the United States* (hereafter *FRUS*): *1948,* vol. 4, *Eastern Europe; The Soviet Union* (Washington, D.C.: U.S. Government Printing Office, 1974), pp. 766–67.
6. Thus Truman wrote on March 25, 1948, to Edwin G. Nourse, Chairman of the Council of Economic Advisers, "We must be very careful that the military does not overstep the bounds from an economic standpoint domestically. Most of them would like to go back to a war footing—that is not what we want." President's Secretary's Files, Subject File, Agencies, box 143, HSTL.
7. See, for example, Charles Hurd, "Army, Navy Reject Supremacy of Air," *NYT,* December 3, 1947, p. 59.
8. "I am all too familiar with the process myself," Thomson explains, "from my years at the State Department and on the National Security Council staff in the Kennedy–Johnson era." Review of *Friends and Enemies: The United States, China and the Soviet Union, 1948–1972,* by Gordon H. Chang, *New York Times Book Review,* July 29, 1990, p. 25. The editors of the *Book Review* identify Thomson as "an East Asia specialist in the State Department and White House from 1960 to 1966."

9. Walter Millis and E. S. Duffield, eds., *The Forrestal Diaries* (New York: Viking, 1951), p. 385 (hereafter *Forrestal Diaries*). It is possible that the March 1 cable from Smith to Marshall was actually a response by the ambassador to an earlier message from the secretary of state on the topic of a war scare. In reaching the decision to promote such a scare, Marshall also may have been influenced by what some members of the influential Senate Armed Services Committee had told him on March 2 prior to his meeting with Forrestal—namely, "that it would be impossible for the Senate committee to make any progress unless he, Marshall, made it clear to the country through either a speech or statement, which would have wide circulation and receive broad attention, of the relation of universal military training to his conduct of foreign policy" (*Forrestal Diaries*, p. 384).
10. Ibid., p. 385.
11. Excerpts from telephone conversation between Honorable James Forrestal, Secretary of Defense, and Representative Walter Andrews, March 3, 1948, p. 1, Forrestal Papers, box 48. There is a discrepancy in dating between the Forrestal Papers, which places the Marshall-Forrestal meeting on March 3, and Forrestal's diary (in both its published and unpublished forms), which indicates that it took place on March 2. Marshall's appointment book lists the meeting on March 2, however, so that is undoubtedly the correct date. See Papers of George C. Marshall, box 159, folder 10, George C. Marshall Library (hereafter GCML), Virginia Military Institute, Lexington, Virginia.
12. Excerpts from telephone conversation between Honorable James Forrestal, Secretary of Defense, and Representative Walter Andrews, March 3, 1948, p. 2, Forrestal Papers, box 48.
13. John G. Norris, "Military to Seek More Funds For Planes, Forrestal Says," *Washington Post*, December 4, 1947.
14. Memorandum for the President from James Forrestal, February 6, 1948, RG 330 (Secretary of Defense), Entry 199, Office of the Administrative Secretary, Correspondence Control Section, Numerical File, September 1947–June 1950, CD 3-1-40 to CD 3-1-21, CD 3-1-39 folder; this document bears the handwritten note, "Shown to the Pres. by the Sec., but not signed or dispatched—per Mr. Ohly" (John Ohly was one of Forrestal's three principal assistants). Also from the same source: Letter from James Forrestal to the President, February 17, 1948, CD 9-2-5 folder; Report to the President from the Secretary of Defense, attached to cover letter of February 29, 1948, CD 25-1-11 folder; Memorandum for the Secretary from Felix Larkin, December 11, 1947, Entry 200, Office of the Administrative Secretary, Correspondence Control Section, Central Numerical File, September 1947 to December 1949, G to G1, folder G1, Legislation, October 17, 1947, to June 30, 1948, vol. 1.
15. "Russian Scare," *Wall Street Journal*, September 12, 1947, p. 1.

16. Diaries of James Vincent Forrestal (hereafter Forrestal Diaries), entry for March 4, 1948, p. 2115, box 4, SGMML, Princeton University.
17. Memorandum for General Spaatz from Stephen F. Leo, [Air Force] Director of Public Relations, March 3, 1948, Papers of Carl A. Spaatz, Chief of Staff file, box 252, general correspondence, folder 3/1–3/6/48, Manuscript Division, Library of Congress. Presumably, similar letters were sent to representatives of the other two services as well.
18. Memorandum for Brigadier General Ralph F. Stearley from Felix E. Larkin, March 9, 1948, RG 300, Entry 200, Office of the Administrative Secretary, Correspondence Control Section, Central Numerical File, September 1947–December 1949, G to G1, folder G1 Legislation, October 17, 1947–June 30, 1948, vol. 1.
19. Memorandum by the Chief of Naval Operations, March 9, 1948, pp. 1, 2, RG 341 (Headquarters U.S. Air Force), Entry 337, Deputy Chief of Staff, Operations, Division of Plans, Executive Office, Records Branch, General File, 1944–1953, TS #29 to TS #32.
20. James F. Byrnes, *All in One Lifetime* (New York: Harper and Brothers, 1958), pp. 396–97; Walter Millis, quoting Forrestal, *Forrestal Diaries,* p. 386.
21. Press Releases[,] Statements & Speeches[,] Secretary George C[.] Marshall While Secretary of State, box 157, folder 1, Marshall Papers.
22. Thus, he can be observed working himself into the proper frame of mind for the war scare in his March 3, 1948, letter to his daughter Margaret—written, be it noted, two full days before the arrival of the Clay telegram of March 5; see Margaret Truman, *Harry S. Truman* (New York: William Morrow, 1973), pp. 359-60. My guess is that this letter reflects the effects of his conversation with Forrestal on February 29.
23. American Institute of Public Opinion, *Public Opinion: 1935-1971,* vol. 1, *1935–1948* (New York: Random House, 1972), pp. 650, 727.
24. See Memorandum for the President from Clark M. Clifford, November 19, 1947, p. 15, Papers of Clark M. Clifford, Harry S. Truman Library. Clifford's memorandum was essentially a copy with minor modifications of a memorandum sent by James H. Rowe, a Washington lawyer, to the director of the Bureau of the Budget, James E. Webb, on September 18, 1947; see Document No. 576, miscellaneous historical document file, HSTL.
25. See Clifford, Memorandum for the President, November 19, 1947, pp. 29, 31.
26. *Forrestal Diaries,* pp. 381-82.
27. Telegram to the Secretary of State, July 15, 1947, *FRUS: 1947,* vol. 4, *Eastern Europe; The Soviet Union* (Washington, D.C.: U.S. Government Printing Office, 1972), pp. 221–22.

28. Telegrams of September 29 and 30, 1947, *FRUS: 1947,* vol. 4, *Eastern Europe; The Soviet Union,* pp. 232–35.
29. Hanson W. Baldwin, "Case for Arming: Forrestal's Argument Called Reasonable but More Facts on the Peril Are Sought," *NYT,* March 29, 1948, p. 4; Lilienthal Journals, May 25, 1948, Papers of David E. Lilienthal, box 197, SGMML, Princeton University. In addition to his work as a journalist, Baldwin was an influential member of the Council on Foreign Relations, the ruling-class organization that specialized in the determination of foreign policy. It was under the Council's aegis, for example, that his book on military policy, *The Price of Power* (New York: Harper and Brothers, 1947), was published.
30. Letter to the Secretary of State, April 30, 1948, *FRUS: 1948,* vol. 4, *Eastern Europe; The Soviet Union* (Washington, D.C.: U.S. Government Printing Office, 1973–1974), pp. 747, 750–51.
31. Memorandum for the Chief of Staff from the Army Intelligence Division, Daily Briefing for February 24, 1948, RG 330 (Secretary of Defense), Entry 199, Office of the Administrative Secretary, Correspondence Control Section, Numerical File, September 1947–June 1950, CD 2-1-20; a copy of this memorandum went to the Secretary of the Army, who forwarded it with a cover memorandum on February 27.
32. Memorandum for the President from R. H. Hillenkoetter, Director of Central Intelligence, March 2, 1948, p. 1, RG 218 (United States Joint Chiefs of Staff), Chairman's File, Admiral Leahy, 1942–1948, Memos to and from the President, 1948–1949 folder.
33. Central Intelligence Agency Review of the World Situation as it Relates to the Security of the United States, CIA 3-48, March 10, 1948, pp. 2–3, RG 319 (Army Staff), Entry 153, Plans and Operations Divisions, Decimal File, 1946–1948, 350.5, case 266 to 305.
34. See, respectively, Memorandum for the Secretaries of the Army, Navy, Air Force, Chiefs of Staff of the Army, Navy, Air Force, March 2, 1948, RG 341 (Headquarters U.S. Air Force), Entry 337, Deputy Chief of Staff, Operations, Divisions of Plans, Executive Office, Records Branch, General File, 1944–1953; Tentative Agenda for the Meeting of the Committee of Four Secretaries, March 5, 1948, Spaatz Papers, Chief of Staff File, box 252, General Correspondence folder, 3/1-3/6/48; National Security Council Tentative Agenda for the Meeting to be held March 11, March 8, 1948, and Memorandum for the Service Secretaries and Chiefs of Staff, March 10, 1948, both in RG 341 (Headquarters U.S. Air Force), Entry 337, Deputy Chief of Staff, Operations, Divisions of Plans, Executive Office, Records Branch, General File, 1944-1953, TS #29 to TS #32.

35. George F. Kennan, *Memoirs: 1925-1950* (Boston, Toronto: Little, Brown and Company, 1967), pp. 378–79; Kennan reiterates these points on pp. 401–03.
36. *Memoirs,* p. 403.
37. George Marshall to George F. Kennan, January 6, 1948, Marshall Papers, box 133, folder 21, Kennan, George F. file.
38. Quoted in Daniel Yergin, *Shattered Peace: The Origins of the Cold War and the National Security State* (Boston: Houghton Mifflin, 1977), pp. 346–47.
39. Telegram, Marshall to Jefferson Caffery, U.S. Ambassador in France, February 24, 2948, 7 p.m., *FRUS: 1948,* vol. 4, *Eastern Europe; The Soviet Union,* pp. 735–36.
40. See Memorandum to Mr. Lovett from James Forrestal, July 18, 1947, Forrestal Papers, box 92.
41. The telegrams for the secretary of state from U.S. embassies in Moscow and Helsinki are in *FRUS: 1948,* vol. 4, *Eastern Europe; The Soviet Union,* pp. 766, 769, respectively; see also Memorandum for the President from R. H. Hillenkoetter, March 2, 1948, pp. 1–2, RG 218, Chairman's File, Admiral Leahy 1942–1948, folder 122, Memos to and from President 1948–1949; Top Secret Summary for the Secretary, March 8, 1948, p. 1, Marshall Papers, National Archives Collection, Xerox 2055.
42. Central Intelligence Agency Review of the World Situation as it Relates to the Security of the United States, CIA 3-48, March 10, 1948, p. 2, RG 319 (Army Staff), Entry 153, Plans and Operations Divisions, Decimal File, 1946–1948, 350.5, case 266 to 305.
43. *FRUS: 1948,* vol. 4, *Eastern Europe; The Soviet Union,* pp. 773–77, *passim.*
44. Ibid., pp. 777–79, 781–82.
45. The Chargé in the Soviet Union to the Secretary of State, July 9, 1948, *FRUS: 1948,* vol. 4, *Eastern Europe; The Soviet Union,* p. 784; Smith to the Secretary of State, August 5, 1948, *FRUS: 1948,* vol. 4, *Eastern Europe; The Soviet Union,* p. 786.
46. *Forrestal Diaries,* p. 387.
47. Ibid., p. 387.
48. See oral history interview with Wilfred J. McNeil, pp. 62–63, HSTL. McNeil was a special assistant to the secretary of defense at the time of the Key West conference, and he and "Forrestal . . . were the only civilians" in attendance at it.
49. Yergin, for example, writes that the "Clay message certainly galvanized official opinion; policymakers took it as a most serious warning"; Yergin, *Shattered Peace,* p. 351; see also: Yergin, *Shattered Peace,* pp. 350–360, *passim*; Walter LaFeber, *America, Russia, and the Cold War, 1945–1984,* 5th ed. (New York:

Alfred A. Knopf, 1984), pp. 71–73; and Thomas G. Paterson, *On Every Front: The Making of the Cold War* (New York: W. W. Norton, 1979), pp. 63–64.

50. Jean Edward Smith, *Lucius D. Clay: An American Life* (New York: Henry Holt and Company, 1990), pp. 466–67. Clay is quoted on p. 467; the first two insertions in the quotation are by Smith; the last insertion and the ellipses are mine.
51. Ibid., p. 760 (second note for page 467).
52. David E. Lilienthal, *The Journals of David E. Lilienthal,* vol. 2: *The Atomic Energy Years 1945–1950* (New York: Harper and Row, 1964), p. 302.
53. Letter from Forrestal to MacArthur, rough copy dated February 13, 1948, handwritten entry, "3/17/48," RG 330 (Secretary of Defense), Entry 199, Office of the Administrative Secretary, Correspondence Control Section, Numerical File, September 1947–June 1950, CD 100-1-8 folder. As Forrestal was well aware, the likelihood of U.S. military intervention in Italy, at least, was next to none. On December 9, as a case in point, he had attended "a luncheon discussion" with the director of Central Intelligence, the executive secretary of the National Security Council, and others. The "general feeling," Forrestal recorded in his diary, was that "the French crisis had reached a peak and the worst [was] past," and the director of the CIA in particular "felt confident" that the Italian Communist Party would not be successful in taking power. *Forrestal Diaries,* p. 349.
54. Entry for Monday, February 2, 1948, p. 2855, Forrestal's calendar for Tuesday, March 16, 1948, p. 2436, both in Forrestal Diaries, box 4.
55. Extract from Eberstadt Report, vol. 1, p. 17, attached to Memo. for the Secretary [of Defense] from Robert J. Wood, December 20, 1948, RG 330 (Secretary of Defense), Entry 199, Office of the Administrative Secretary, Correspondence Control Section, Numerical File, September 1947–June 1950, CD 12-1-26 folder.
56. A transcript of this portion of portion of Pearson's broadcast is in Ferdinand Eberstadt's files on the Eberstadt Committee and the Hoover Commission, Papers of Ferdinand Eberstadt, box 63, SGMML, Princeton University.
57. See Eberstadt Papers, box 79, for a truly awe-inspiring collection of newspaper stories about the "mistaken estimate."
58. *Forrestal Diaries,* p. 395.
59. Ibid.
60. Memo. for the Secretary [of Defense] from Robert J. Wood, December 20, 1948, RG 330 (Secretary of Defense), Entry 199, Office of the Administrative Secretary, Correspondence Control Section, Numerical File September 1947–June 1950, CD 12-1-26 folder.

61. Memorandum for the Secretary [of Defense] from Robert Blum, December 23, 1948, p. 1, RG 330 (Secretary of Defense), Entry 199, Office of the Administrative Secretary, Correspondence Control Section, Numerical File September 1947–June 1950, CD 12-1-26 folder.
62. Ibid., pp. 2–3.
63. See, for example, Memorandum for the Secretary from Robert J. Wood, January 10, 1949, RG 330 (Secretary of Defense), Entry 199, Office of the Administrative Secretary, Correspondence Control Section, Numerical File September 1947–June 1950, CD 12-1-26 folder.
64. Memorandum to the Chief of Staff from S. LeRoy Irwin, January 4, 1949, p. 1, RG 330 (Secretary of Defense), Entry 199. Chamberlin's transfer out of Washington could have been merely a routine reassignment. Equally well, it might have been a way of singling him out for punishment or a way of protecting him and/or the secretary of the army, the chief of staff and General Clay by making certain that Chamberlin was not available to talk to investigators from the Eberstadt Committee. Chamberlin's papers offer no help in deciding among the alternatives.
65. Ibid.
66. See Forrestal's calendar for Saturday, March 6, 1948, Forrestal Diaries, box 4.
67. Memorandum to the Chief of Staff from S. LeRoy Irwin, pp. 1–2.
68. John A. Giles, "Forrestal Convinced Air Force Didn't Make Intelligence Error," *Washington Star,* December 23, 1948.
69. I show in appendix A that even McDonald's British counterpart was critical of the general's habit of overestimating the rate of Soviet aircraft production.
70. Memorandum for the Secretary [of Defense] from Robert Blum, December 23, 1948, p. 2, RG 330 (Secretary of Defense), Entry 199, Office of the Administrative Secretary, Correspondence Control Section, Numerical File September 1947–June 1950, CD 12-1-26 folder.
71. Excerpts from Telephone Conversation Between Colonel Wood and Mr. F. Eberstadt, December 22, 1948, pp. 1, 3, RG 330 (Secretary of Defense), Entry 199, Office of the Administrative Secretary, Correspondence Control Section, Numerical File, September 1947–June 1950, CD 12-1-26 folder.
72. Comments by the Director of Intelligence, USAF[,] and the Director of Naval Intelligence, undated, p. 1, RG 330 (Secretary of Defense), Entry 199, Office of the Administrative Secretary, Correspondence Control Section, Numerical File September 1947–June 1950, CD 12-1-26 folder.
73. Arnold L. Punaro, Staff Director, United States Senate Committee on Armed Services, letter to the author, May 28, 1991.

74. It would have been an unmitigated disaster for both Forrestal and the administration had the press gotten wind of the Clay telegram early in March and sought to determine the true views of its author. Could Forrestal's desire to head off such an outcome have been connected to his proposal, released at just this moment, to establish a system of censorship over journalists who wrote about military affairs? In any event, Forrestal's scheme, which would have required reports to "consult" with a Defense Department "information board" before "publishing information in areas he would designate [as] vital to the national security," was immediately shouted down by the news media. See Richard M. Freeland, *The Truman Doctrine and the Origins of McCarthyism: Foreign Policy, Domestic Politics and Internal Security, 1946–1948* (New York: Schocken Books, 1974), pp. 221–22.
75. "Peace: War Fears Grip Capital and Nation," *Newsweek,* March 22, 1948, p. 23; Forrestal is quoted in *Forrestal Diaries,* p. 389; Minutes of Press Conference Held by Secretary Forrestal, March 10, 1948, 10:30 A.M., Forrestal Papers, box 8; Marquis Childs, "Washington Calling," *Washington Post,* April 6, 1948, p. 8.
76. Secretary of the Army Royall forwarded his copy of the Estimate to James Forrestal with the comment, "It is my only copy and I would like it returned." Memorandum to the Secretary of Defense, March 17, 1948, RG 330 (Secretary of Defense), Entry 199, Office of the Administrative Secretary, Correspondence Control Section, Numerical File, CD 2-1-26 folder.
77. Memorandum to the Chief of Staff from Lieutenant General Stephen J. Chamberlin, Director of Intelligence, Subject: Estimate of World Situation, March 14, 1948, p. 5, RG 319 (Army Staff), Entry 154, Plans and Operations Division, Decimal File 1946–1948, 092. Section 6-D to Section 7 (TS).
78. Ibid., pp. 1–2.
79. Ibid., pp. 2–5. See the discussion in note 53, above, on the improbability that the United States would commit troops in Italy.
80. Ibid., pp. 5–6.
81. Ibid., pp. 6–8.
82. Stenographic transcript of hearings on Universal Military Training before the Committee on Armed Services, United States Senate, April 21, 1948, pp. 291–92, RG 330 (Secretary of Defense), Entry 199, Office of the Administrative Secretary, Correspondence Control Section, Numerical Files, September 1947–June 1950, CD 9-2-4 folder. See also Forrestal's testimony on pp. 318–19 of the same source; and Robert F. Whitney, "Bradley 'Not Sure' No War Is at Hand: In UMT Plea to Senators He Says Chances Are Greater Than Three Months Ago," *NYT,* April 26, 1948, pp. 1, 6, which is based on an

edited version of the transcript from this session of the committee that was released on April 25.

Notes to Chapter 5.

1. Remarks delivered before the Armed Services Committee of the House of Representatives at the National Defense Building, January 8, 1948, p. 16, National Archives Record Group (hereafter RG) 330 (Secretary of Defense), Entry 199, Office of the Administrative Secretary, Correspondence Control Section, Numerical File, September 1947–June 1950, CD 3-1-36 folder.
2. This letter is in the Papers of James V. Forrestal (hereafter Forrestal Papers), box 80, Seeley G. Mudd Manuscript Library (hereafter SGMML), Princeton University.
3. U.S. Department of State, *Foreign Relations of the United States* (hereafter *FRUS*): *1948,* vol. 3, *Western Europe* (Washington, D.C.: U.S. Government Printing Office, 1974), p. 157. Robert A. Lovett was Under Secretary of State; the Washington Exploratory Talks were to culminate in the formation of the North Atlantic Treaty Organization (NATO).
4. Felix Belair, Jr., "ERP Critics Force Senate Vote Delay Beyond Next Week," *New York Times* (hereafter *NYT*), March 6, 1948, pp. 1, 4.
5. Jay Walz, "Senate Slated to Back ERP But Delay Is Likely in House," *NYT,* March 8, 1948, p. 1.
6. Bertram D. Hulen, "'Reign of Terror' Seen by Marshall," *NYT,* March 11, 1948, pp. 1, 6.
7. James Reston, "Marshall's Press Statement Seen as Increasing Alarm: Reference to 'Reign of Terror' Is Considered Disquieting, Not Truly Representative," *NYT,* March 12, 1948, p. 12; State Department press release No. 188, March 10, 1948, Papers of George C. Marshall, box 158, folder 6, George C. Marshall Library (hereafter GCML), Virginia Military Institute, Lexington, Virginia.
8. Quoted in Walter Millis and E. S. Duffield, eds., *The Forrestal Diaries* (New York: Viking, 1951), p. 389.
9. Telegram, Marshall to Jefferson Caffery, U.S. Ambassador in France, February 24, 1948, 7 p.m., *FRUS: 1948,* vol. 4, *Eastern Europe; The Soviet Union* (Washington, D.C.: U.S. Government Printing Office, 1974), pp. 735-36.; Central Intelligence Agency Review of the World Situation as it Relates to the Security of the United States, CIA 3-48, March 10, 1948, pp. 2–3, RG 319 (Army Staff), Entry 153, Plans and Operations Divisions, Decimal File, 1946–1948, 350.5, case 266 to 305.

10. See the stories in the *NYT* and the *Washington Post* for March 12, 1948.
11. *Public Papers of the Presidents of the United States: Harry S. Truman, 1948* (Washington, D.C.: U.S. Government Printing Office, 1963), p. 178; hereafter cited as *Public Papers of Harry S. Truman.* The lead headline on page one of the *Washington Post* (hereafter *WP*) for March 12, 1948, read, "Truman's Confidence in Peace Shaken by European Events; House Plans Single Aid Bill."
12. State Department press release No. 194, March 11, 1948, Marshall Papers, box 158, folder 7; see also the *NYT* and *WP* for March 12, 1948.
13. "Byrnes Advocates 'Action" on Russia," *NYT,* March 14, 1948, p. 1; the last quotation is from "Byrnes Asks Action on Russia," *WP,* March 14, 1948, p. 8.
14. John G. Norris, "Military to Seek More Funds For Planes, Forrestal Says," *WP,* December 4, 1947.
15. See, by way of illustration, Talking Points for Conference with the President and Memorandum for the President ("Shown to the Pres. by the Sec., but not signed or dispatched"), both February 6, 1948, RG 330 (Secretary of Defense), Entry 199, Office of the Administrative Secretary, Correspondence Control File, Numerical File, September 1947–June 1950, CD 3-1-39 folder; Forrestal's letter to the President, February 17, 1948, RG 330 (Secretary of Defense), Entry 199, CD 9-2-5 folder; For Discussion with the President (memorandum), March 14, 1948, Forrestal Papers, box 127.
16. Report to the President from the Secretary of Defense, attached to cover letter of February 29, 1948, RG 330 (Secretary of Defense), Entry 199, Office of the of the Administrative Secretary, Correspondence Control File, Numerical File, September 1947–June 1950, CD 25-1-11 folder.
17. "Byrnes Asks Action on Russia." Byrnes recounts Forrestal's covert role in arranging for this speech in *All in One Lifetime* (New York: Harper and Brothers, 1958), pp. 396-97.
18. James Reston, "Basic Decision Facing U.S. in Foreign Policy . . . ," *NYT,* March 14, 1948, p. E2.
19. John H. Fenton, "Russian War Aims Doubted by Taft," *NYT,* March 15, 1948, p. 1; "Taft Doubts Early Crisis With Russia," *WP,* March 15, 1948.
20. "World News Summarized," *NYT,* March 16, 1948, p. 1; see also C. P. Trussell, "Truman to Tell Congress Tomorrow of World Status; Leaders Expect New Policy," p. 1 in the same issue.
21. *Forrestal Diaries,* p. 394.
22. Ibid.
23. Statement before Senate Foreign Relations Committee, March 12 [*sic*; actually, March 15], 1948, p. 8, Marshall Papers, box 158, folder 9; see also the *NYT* and *WP* for March 16, 1948.
24. Trussell, "Truman to Tell Congress," p. 1.

25. Felix Belair, Jr., "Martin's Warning," *NYT,* March 17, 1948, p. 1.
26. Ibid., p. 2.
27. Appendix to Joint Strategic Plans Group, General Guidance on Strategic Concepts, J.S.P.G. 502/1, March 15, 1948, pp. 3, 4, 5, RG 218 (U.S. Joint Chiefs of Staff), Central Decimal File, Security Classified, 1948–1950, CC8 381 (2-18-46) Section 1 folder.
28. Memorandum for the President from R. H. Hillenkoetter, Director of Central Intelligence, March 16, 1948, RG 300 (Secretary of Defense), Entry 199, Office of the Administrative Secretary, Correspondence Control Section, Numerical File, September 1947–June 1950, CD 12-1-26 folder.
29. See also the collection of headlines for the days leading up to the St. Patrick's Day speech cited in Richard M. Freeland, *The Truman Doctrine and the Origins of McCarthyism: Foreign Policy, Domestic Politics and Internal Security, 1946–1948* (New York: Schocken Books, 1974), p. 271.
30. James Forrestal Letter to Kenneth G. Reynolds, Esq., March 17, 1948, Forrestal Papers, box 81. The full text of the letter reads: "Dear Ken: I was sorry to be away when you came through Washington. I feel better about the world situation than I have for 2½ years. My love to Lydia. Sincerely yours, [signed] Jim."
31. Memorandum for Secretary Forrestal (Dictated over the telephone by Mr. Clifford), March 15, 1948, Forrestal Papers, box 127. Note Clifford's unequivocal assertion, this memorandum notwithstanding, that he "was not involved in any way in the procurement of military aircraft in the Truman Administration, nor do I have any information with reference to it." Clark Clifford letter to the author, October 24, 1986.
32. Memorandum for the President from Clark M. Clifford, November 19, 1947, p. 15, Papers of Clark M. Clifford, Harry S. Truman Library (hereafter HSTL). Clifford's memorandum was essentially a copy with minor modifications of a memorandum sent by James H. Rowe to the director of the Bureau of the Budget, James E. Webb, on September 18, 1947; see Document no. 576, miscellaneous historical document file, HSTL. See also Daniel Yergin, *Shattered Peace: The Origins of the Cold War and the National Security State* (Boston: Houghton Mifflin, 1977), p. 353. Clifford's own account of his years at the Truman White House, *Counsel to the President: A Memoir* (New York: Random House, 1991), written with Richard Holbrooke, predictably fails to discuss the entire war scare, much less his role in fomenting it.
33. *Public Papers of Harry S. Truman,* pp. 182–186 *passim.*
34. "Secretary Marshall's Plea for Universal Military Training," *NYT,* March 18, 1948, p. 6; Hanson W. Baldwin, "Case for Arming," *NYT,* March 29, 1948, p. 4.

35. *Public Papers of Harry S. Truman,* pp. 186–90; Memorandum for the President from Clark M. Clifford, November 19, 1947, pp. 22-23; James Forrestal letter to Clark M. Clifford, Esq., March 18, 1948, Forrestal Papers, box 94. Clifford's own discussion of the advice he gave Truman with respect to Wallace in the November 1947 memorandum is typically tendentious and misleading; see *Counsel to the President,* p. 193.
36. See the *NYT* for March 18, 1948.
37. William S. White, "Congress Hesitant on Draft, Training . . . ," *NYT,* March 18, 1948, pp. 1, 2; Memorandum for the President from the Secretary of Defense, February 27, 1948, President's Secretary's File: Cabinet, box 157, HSTL.
38. C. P. Trussell, "Military Leaders Call UMT, Draft Vital for Safety . . . ," *NYT,* March 19, 1948, pp. 1, 3; "More Data Sought in Congress on UMT," *NYT,* March 20, 1948.
39. "Senate Uncertain Over Draft, UMT," *NYT,* March 21, 1948.
40. Department of State press releases No. 218 and No. 221, both March 19, 1948, Marshall Papers, box 158, folder 15.
41. See the article with that headline by Lawrence E. Davies, *NYT,* March 20, 1948, p. 1
42. The Ambassador in Belgium (Alexander C. Kirk) to the Secretary of State, March 19, 1948, *FRUS: 1948,* vol. 3, *Western Europe,* p. 57. Marshall wrote Bevin on May 11 that he was "in general agreement with Mr. Bevin's clear and comprehensive analysis of the situation. The information available to the United States Government confirms the indications cited by Mr. Bevin in support of his estimate that the Soviet Government does not want war at this time" (Memorandum, The Department of State to the British Embassy, May 11, 1948, *FRUS: 1948,* vol. 4, *Eastern Europe; The Soviet Union,* p. 858). The principal difference between Marshall and his British counterpart was that the latter's public and private positions were consistent.
43. C. P. Trussell, "Senate Committee Reported Backing Draft and the UMT," *NYT,* March 23, 1948; Felix Belair, Jr., "Hoover Supports $5,300,000,000 ERP; Opposition Fading," *NYT,* March 24, 1948.
44. Jay Walz, "House Vote Looms This Week on Aid; Revisions Doubted," *NYT,* March 29, 1948.
45. Harold R. Hinton, "Marshall's 6-Week Stay in Bogota Viewed as Sign of Easier Tension," *NYT,* March 23, 1948, p. 1. This conference was the founding meeting of the Organization of American States.
46. John D. Morse, "3 Billion to Rearm Asked by Truman; Tax Cut Veto Set," *NYT,* April 2, 1948, p. 19.
47. .See the Memorandum for the Secretary of Defense from Fleet Admiral William D. Leahy, Chief of Staff to the Commander in Chief of the Armed

Forces, for the Joint Chiefs of Staff, March 10, 1948, *FRUS: 1948,* vol. 3, *Western Europe,* pp. 782–83.

48. *Forrestal Diaries,* p. 393.
49. Memorandum for the President from Clark M. Clifford, November 19, 1947, p. 31, Clifford Papers, HSTL.
50. Thus, Assistant White House Press Secretary Eben A. Ayers, part of the small group of aides who met with Truman on an almost daily basis, wrote in his diary on April 21 that the latter had "directed his comment at Forrestal in talking this morning and he showed considerable feeling. . . . He said he was 'getting damn sore.' Forrestal, he said, had been working with Republicans in Congress as though they were in control and that if he does not stop he can go with the Republicans and 'I'll get someone else.' " Ayers Diary, Papers of Eben A. Ayers, HSTL.
51. Memorandum from James Forrestal for the Secretary of the Army, Navy, Air Force, March 18, 1948, Papers of James E. Webb, Bureau of the Budget, box 1593, HSTL.
52. Meeting Called by the Secretary of Defense, 1300 Hours, Saturday, 20 March 1948, pp. 1–2, RG 330 (Secretary of Defense), Entry 199, Office of the Administrative Secretary, Correspondence Control Section, Numerical Files, September 1947–June 1950, folder CD 101-1 1950; see also Memorandum for the Secretary from Felix Larkin, March 17, 1948, RG 330 (Secretary of Defense), Entry 199, folder CD 5-1-12, summarizing two meetings between Larkin and Wilfred J. McNeil, a special assistant to Forrestal, and representatives of the Bureau of the Budget. In an oral history interview, McNeil recalled the opposition of the Bureau of the Budget to Forrestal's proposed program: "Webb was quite vociferous in arguing that . . . he needed a balanced budget and we can't afford it," while Secretary of the Treasury "Snyder was worried about trying to keep the force level up because it cost money." See oral history interview with Wilfred J. McNeil, p. 68, HSTL.
53. "The Text of Forrestal's Plea for the Draft and UMT as Vital Moves for Averting War," *NYT,* March 26, 1948, p. 3. Although Truman gave Forrestal written permission to ask Congress for a supplemental appropriation of $3 billion for the Pentagon only on March 26, he must have conveyed his oral assent earlier; see Truman to the Secretary of Defense, March 26, 1948, and James E. Webb, Director, Bureau of the Budget, Memorandum to the President, March 25, 1948, both in Papers of Harry S. Truman, Official File, box 1593, HSTL.
54. "Administration Boosts Its Military Budget Request $3 Billion, Asks Congress for $14 Billion in 1948–49," *Wall Street Journal,* March 26, 1948, p. 3; see also C. P. Trussell, "Top Military Men Urge that U.S. Arm . . . ," *NYT,* March

26, 1948, pp. 1–2. Sullivan's testimony, we shall see, was not only designed to alarm his audience, but also to preempt the other armed services by defining the "Soviet threat" as preeminently a naval one.

55. Hanson W. Baldwin, "Case for Arming," *NYT,* March 29, 1948, p. 4.
56. "They Fight the Cold War Under Cover," *Saturday Evening Post,* November 1948, p. 194.
57. Memorandum by the Chief of Staff, U.S. Army, to the Joint Chiefs of Staff on Necessity for Seacoast Armament, March 20, 1948, pp. 31, 34, RG 319 (Plans and Operations Division), Entry 154 (Army Staff), Decimal File, 1946–1948, 602. to 660.3 (TS), P & O 660.2TS (cases 1 through [?]) folder.
58. George Gallup, "Public Favors Arms Build-up, Poll Indicates," *Los Angeles Times,* March 19, 1948. More than likely, these views rested on two beliefs, each vigorously encouraged by the air force: that only that branch of the military was capable of protecting the United States itself from atomic bombing raids; and that by making use of atomic bombs and long-range bombers, the United States could fight another world war without incurring massive casualties on the ground or at sea.
59. The Air Information Division of the air force, for example, circulated An Analysis of Press Opinion at two-week intervals; RG 340 (Secretary of the Air Force), Entry 53, Air Coordinating Committee, General File, 1945–1950, ACC Papers Folder, Memoranda and Minutes of Meetings.
60. Council of Economic Advisers to the President, March 24, 1948, and Truman letter to Dr. Nourse, March 25, 1948, both in President's Secretary's File (hereafter PSF), Subject File, Agencies, box 143, HSTL.
61. "Inquiry Into Russian Trade Set; Soviet Using 87 Lend-Lease Ships," *NYT,* March 24, 1948, p.1.
62. Telegram from the Secretary of State to the Embassy in France, *FRUS: 1948,* vol. 4, *Eastern Europe; The Soviet Union,* p. 565; also see on this issue pp. 489–592 *passim*; Freeland, *Truman Doctrine.*
63. Control of Exports to the Soviet Bloc, Diaries of James V. Forrestal (hereafter Forrestal Diaries), March 26, 1948, p. 2158, box 4, SGMML.
64. "Warplane Engines Shipped to Russia; Truman Ban Near," *NYT,* March 25, 1948, p. 1.
65. H. Walton Cloke, "State, Justice Agencies Let Plane Engines Go to Russia," *NYT,* March 26, pp. 1, 8.
66. *Public Papers of Harry S. Truman,* p. 193.
67. Cloke, "State, Justice Agencies Let Plane Engines Go to Russia."
68. *NYT,* March 31, 1948; although Millis includes accounts of many of Forrestal's most important meetings in the *Forrestal Diaries,* he makes no mention of this one.

69. Marquis Childs, "Washington Calling," *WP*, April 6, 1948.
70. Memorandum for Mr. Forrestal from W. Stuart Symington, March 31, 1948, p. 2, Papers of W. Stuart Symington, box 4, HSTL; Stenographic Transcript of Hearings before the Committee on Armed Services, April 7, 1948, pp. 50–51, RG 46, Senate, Committee on Armed Services, Unprinted Hearings, Executive Session, January 27, 1947–May 19, 1948.
71. "Air Secretary Blasts U.S. Peace Position," *Sacramento Bee*, April 9, 1948, p. 31.
72. W. Stuart Symington, Secretary of the Air Force, "We've scuttled our [*sic*] Air Defenses," *American Magazine*, February 1948, p. 50.
73. For accounts of an earlier enunciation of the line, see John G. Norris, "U.S. in 'Insecure Position'[:] Russians Have 14,000 Planes, 3 Times Ours, Spaatz Says," *WP*, November 17, 1947; Charles Hurd, "Russian Air Gain Noted by Spaatz: Says Soviet [*sic*] . . . Is Believed to Have 14,000 Military Planes," *NYT*, November 18, 1947. The "Spaatz" in question was General Carl A. Spaatz, Air Force Chief of Staff.
74. Transcript of Symington Testimony, April 13, 1948, pp. 2–3, Symington Papers, box 3; "Warns Soviets Outstrip U.S. In New Planes," *New York Daily News*, April 24, 1948.
75. Committee on Armed Services, Unprinted Hearings, RG 46, Records of the U.S. Senate, 80th Cong., Executive Session, April 7, 1948, pp. 38–40.
76. "The original contract estimate of speed for the B-29 was 377 miles per hour. The speed of the B-29's that we are building now, that is the B-50, is 410 miles per hour. . . . The first B-29 had a bombload of 2,000 pounds. The present bombload of the B-29 in production is 10,000 pounds. . . . The range of the original B-29 was . . . 4,529 [statute miles] and the present theoretical range of the plane that we are building now is 4,800 statute miles." Symington's testimony, Committee on Armed Services, Unprinted Hearings, RG 46, Records of the U.S. Senate, pp. 24–5.
77. Ibid., p. 41.
78. Forrestal to John Ohly, April 24, 1948, Symington Papers, box 4; Excerpts from telephone conversation between Honorable James Forrestal, Secretary of Defense, and Representative Clarence Cannon, April 9, 1948, p. 1, Forrestal Papers, box 94.
79. McDonald to Symington, April 26, 1948, Symington Papers, box 4; McDonald claimed—erroneously—that "[t]he production figure of approximately 1,000 all-type aircraft per month for 1947 must be recognized as a decidedly conservative figure—a minimum." In fact, the generally accepted minimum was half that; see, e.g., Hanson W. Baldwin, "Soviet Power—III," *NYT*, March 23, 1948. As I bring out in appendix A, even his British counterpart

chided McDonald for his irrepressible tendency to inflate Soviet aircraft production figures.

80. W. B. Smith to the Secretary of State, April 1, 1948, RG 330 (Secretary of Defense), Entry 199, Office of the Administrative Secretary, Correspondence Control Section, Numerical File, September 1947–June 1950, CD 2-2-2 folder; *Forrestal Diaries,* p. 409; Forrestal Diaries, October 21, 1948, p. 2475, box 4.
81. Soviet Intentions, pp. 7, 13, 18.
82. Ibid., p. 17.
83. Ibid., pp. 10, 11, 18, 19, 22–23, 26.
84. Ibid., pp. 8-9.
85. *Executives' Club News,* 25:13, December 17, 1948, p. 8; Symington Papers, box 5.
86. Stenographic transcript of hearings on Universal Military Training before the Committee on Armed Services, United States Senate, April 21, 1948, pp. 291–92, RG 330 (Secretary of Defense), Entry 199, Office of the Administrative Secretary, Correspondence Control Section, Numerical File, September 1947–June 1950, CD 9-2-4 folder. See also Robert F. Whitney, "Bradley 'Not Sure' No War Is at Hand: In UMT Plea to Senators He Says Chances Are Greater Than Three Months Ago," *NYT,* April 26, 1948, pp. 1, 6, which is based on an edited version of the transcript from this session of the committee that was released on April 25. My suspicion, just as in the case of Marquis Childs's column on the Clay telegram (cited in full in note 69, above), is that it was Forrestal who saw to the release of Bradley's testimony, both in order to breathe new life into the war scare and to put more pressure on Congress for passage of selective service.
87. U.S. Army Intelligence Staff Study, Project No. 4199, Cumulative Effects . . . , March 26, 1948, p. 1, Appendix A, p. 1, and Appendix B, p. 1, RG 319 (Army Staff), Entry 154, Plans and Operations Division, Decimal File, 1946–1948, 092. Section, P and O TS 29 March 1948 envelope.
88. Ibid., pp. 1, 2, 4, and Appendix B, pp. 2–4.
89. Ibid., p. 5, and Appendix B, pp. 5–6.
90. *Forrestal Diaries,* p. 409.
91. Central Intelligence Agency, Possibility of Direct Soviet Military Action During 1948, April 2, 1948, pp. 2–3, RG 330 (Secretary of Defense), Entry 199, Office of the Administrative Secretary, Correspondence Control Section, Numerical File, September 1947–June 1950, CD 12-1-26 folder. According to the footnote on p. 1, "The date of the estimate is 30 March 1948."
92. Ibid., pp. 1, 4–5.
93. Memorandum of Conversation by the Chief of the Division of Western European Affairs, *FRUS: 1948,* vol. 3, *Western Europe,* p. 76.

94. Rear Admiral Thomas B. Inglis, Russian Capabilities in Undersea Warfare, April 5, 1948, pp. 2–5, RG 218 (U.S. Joint Chiefs of Staff), Chairman's File, Admiral Leahy, 1942–1948, Folders 65-71, box No. 11, folder 70, Russia 1947–1948.
95. Central Intelligence Agency, Review of the World Situation as It Relates to the Security of the United States, April 8, 1948, pp. 1–3, RG 319 (Army Staff), Entry 153, Plans and Operations Division, Decimal File, 1946–1948, 350.05 Case 266 to 305 (booklet).
96. Aide-mémoire, the British Embassy to the Department of State, April 30, 1948, *FRUS: 1948,* vol. 4, *Eastern Europe; The Soviet Union,* pp. 842–44.
97. Memorandum, the Department of State to the British Embassy, April 30, 1948, *FRUS: 1948,* vol. 4, *Eastern Europe; The Soviet Union,* p. 858. The day before the British aide-mémoire arrived, Marshall wrote to Walter Bedell Smith, "We did not have in mind the probability of some Russian counter move in Europe proper since we agree with you that the present indications are that, with the exception of a possible miscalculation in Berlin or Vienna, the Kremlin does not intend to mount any action in Europe proper which would carry the risk of actual hostilities." Telegram, the Secretary of State to the Embassy in the Soviet Union, *FRUS: 1948,* vol. 4, *Eastern Europe; The Soviet Union,* p. 840.
98. State Department Policy Planning Staff, Factors Affecting the Nature of the US Defense Arrangements in the Light of Soviet Policies, June 23, 1948, n.p., RG 330 (Secretary of Defense), Entry 199, box 4, Office of the Administrative Secretary, Correspondence Control Section, Numerical File, September 1947–June 1950, CD 2-2-2 folder; Forrestal Diaries, October 23, 1948, pp. 2598–2600, box 5.
99. Factors Affecting the Nature of the US. Defense Arrangements in the Light of Soviet Policies, RG 330 (Secretary of Defense), Entry 199, pp. 1–8, 11.
100. Entry for May 25, 1948, p. 2271, Forrestal Diaries, box 4. Forrestal and Griffis were well acquainted from prewar days, when the two had been prominent Wall Street investment bankers.
101. Telegram to the Secretary of State, April 22, 1948, *FRUS: 1948,* vol. 4, *Eastern Europe; The Soviet Union,* p. 833.
102. Stenographic transcript of hearings on Universal Military Training before the Committee on Armed Services, United States Senate, Wednesday, April 21, 1948, p. 318, RG 330 (Secretary of Defense), Entry 199, Office of the Administrative Secretary, Correspondence Control Section, Numerical Files, September 1947–June 1950, CD 9-2-4 folder.
103. *Forrestal Diaries,* pp. 444, 438; both ellipses in the first quotation appear in the original.
104. See *NYT,* March 31, 1948.

105. *Forrestal Diaries,* p. 432; Statement by the President to the Secretary of Defense, the Secretaries of the Three [Armed Service] Departments, and the Three Chiefs of Staff, May 13, 1948, PSF, Subject File, Cabinet, box 157; memorandum of May 13, 1948, p. 2, Papers of Harry S. Truman, Official File, box 1593.
106. Quoted in Robert H. Ferrell, ed., *Off the Record: The Private Papers of Harry S. Truman* (New York: Harper and Row, 1980), p. 134.
107. General Omar Bradley to Lt. General Albert C. Wedemeyer, Director of Plans and Operations Division, May 20, 1948, RG 319 (Army Staff), Entry 153, Plans and Operations Division, Decimal File, 1946–1948, 091 Poland to Sardinia, P & O 091 Russia (Section I) (Cases 1-[1]) folder.

Notes to Chapter 6.

1. "Aviation RFC?" *Business Week,* January 31, 1948, p. 28; the initials "RFC" stood for Reconstruction Finance Corporation, as explained in chapter 2.
2. Selig Altschul, "The Dynamic Aviation Scene," *The Commercial and Financial Chronicle,* March 11, 1948, p. 32; Altschul was a financial consultant to the Congressional Aviation Policy Board (Brewster Board).
3. Stenographic Transcript of Hearings before the Committee on Armed Services, United States Senate, April 7, 1948, pp. 55-56, National Archives Record Group (hereafter RG) 46, Senate, Committee on Armed Services, Unprinted Hearings, Executive Session, January 27, 1947–May 19, 1948.
4. Ibid., p. 63.
5. Stenographic Report of Proceedings, President's Air Policy Commission (hereafter PAPC), p. 909, RG 340 (Secretary of the Air Force), Entry 53, Air Coordinating Committee (hereafter ACC), General File, 1945–1950, box 60, folder ACC Papers No. 125, vol. 2.
6. Jerry Kluttz , "Federal Diary: War Scare Produces Rumors U.S. Agencies Will Leave Capital," *Washington Post* (hereafter *WP*), March 28, 1948.
7. "Autos in the Spring: Detroit Is Deluged by New Car Orders; It's Partly a War Scare," *Wall Street Journal,* April 29, 1948, p. 1; "Auto Demand Firms Up Again," *Business Week,* April 10, 1948, p. 79; "Prices Up Again," *Business Week,* May 8, 1948, p. 42.
8. "Mr. America on War," *Newsweek,* March 22, 1948, pp. 24–5.
9. Ferdinand Kuhn, "$6.2 Billions Aid Bill Voted by House, 329–74," *WP,* April 1, 1948, p. 1.
10. "Aircraft," *Steel,* January 5, 1948, p. 142; "Subcontracting Follows Plane Orders," *Business Week,* August 14, 1948, p. 32; *Steel,* May 23, 1949, p. 64.

11. John G. Norris, "Military to Seek More Funds For Planes, Forrestal Says," *WP*, December 4, 1947.
12. See, for example, Material for the Secretary of Defense Before the Congressional Aviation Policy Board, December 11, 1947, RG 330 (Secretary of Defense), Entry 200, Office of the Administrative Secretary, Correspondence Control Section, Central Numerical File, September 1947 to December 1949, G to G1, folder G1, Legislation, October 17, 1947, to June 30, 1948, vol. 1; and James Forrestal letter to Honorable Owen Brewster, Chairman, Congressional Aviation Policy Board, United States Senate, January 13, 1948, Papers of Hoyt S. Vandenberg, Secretary of Defense (Forrestal) folder, Manuscript Division, Library of Congress.
13. Memorandum for the Secretary of Defense from LeRoy Lutes, Comments on Aircraft Situation, February 3, 1948, RG 300 (Secretary of Defense), Entry 199, Office of the Administrative Secretary, Correspondence Control Section, Numerical File, September 1947–June 1950, CD 19-1-12 to CD 19-1-11, CD 19-1-11 folder.
14. Excerpts from Telephone Conversation between Honorable James Forrestal, Secretary of Defense, and Congressman Carl Hinshaw of California, February 5, 1948, Papers of James V. Forrestal (hereafter Forrestal Papers), box 93, Seeley G. Mudd Manuscript Library (hereafter SGMML), Princeton University; Talking Points for Conference with the President, February 6, 1948, and Memorandum for the President from James Forrestal, February 6, 1948, both RG 330 (Secretary of Defense), Entry 199, Office of the Administrative Secretary, Correspondence Control Section, Numerical File, September 1947–June 1950, CD 3-1-40 to CD 3-1-21, CD 3-1-39 folder. The last document bears the handwritten note, "Shown to the Pres. by the Sec., but not signed or dispatched—per Mr. Ohly." John Ohly was one of Forrestal's three special assistants. There was a broad and general mention of aircraft procurement in Forrestal's earlier Memorandum to the President of February 1, 1948, p. 2, but the secretary did not make a specific request for additional funds at this time; RG 330 (Secretary of Defense), Entry 199, Office of the Administrative Secretary, Correspondence Control Section, Numerical File, September 1947–June 1950, CD 25-1-11 to CD 25-1-7, CD 25-1-11 folder.
15. Memorandum for the Secretary from Marx Leva, January 31, 1948, Forrestal Papers, box 80.
16. See James Forrestal letter to the President, February 17, 1948, RG 330 (Secretary of Defense), Entry 199, Office of the Administrative Secretary, Correspondence Control File, Numerical File, September 1947–June 1950, CD 9-2-5 folder; and Report to the President from the Secretary of Defense,

attached to cover letter of February 29, 1948, RG 330 (Secretary of Defense), Entry 199, CD 25-1-11 folder.

17. Memorandum for the Secretary of the Navy and the Secretary of the Air Force from James Forrestal, February 18, 1948, RG 330 (Secretary of Defense), Entry 199, CD 5-1-25 to CD 5-2-6, CD 5-1-12 folder.
18. Private Memorandum, April 7, 1948, p. 1, Papers of Arthur Krock, box 26, SGMML, Princeton University.
19. Appointment Book, Saturday, March 20, 1948, Forrestal Papers, box 132; President's Engagements for Friday, March 26, 1948, President's Appointments File, box 80, Harry S. Truman Library (hereafter HSTL). Letter from Harry S. Truman to The Honorable James Forrestal, The Secretary of Defense, March 26, 1948, Papers of Harry S. Truman, Official File, box 1593, HSTL.
20. James Forrestal letter to Frederick B. Rentschler, April 6, 1948, in Walter Millis and E. S. Duffield, eds., *The Forrestal Diaries* (New York: Viking, 1951), p. 412, and also in Forrestal Papers for the same date, box 94; Memorandum for Mr. John McCone, a copy of which, with McCone's handwritten explanation of the circumstances behind it, is in the Papers of W. Stuart Symington, undated (but after June 4, 1948), HSTL. See also James Forrestal letter to Donald W. Douglas, Esq., March 5, 1948, Forrestal Papers, box 127; W. Stuart Symington letter to Mr. Donald Douglas, June 16, 1948, Symington Papers; Robert Hotz, "Orders Are Coming for Aircraft Industry," *Aviation Week,* April 19, 1948, p. 11; "Key Advisers," *Aviation Week,* June 28, 1948, p. 7.
21. James Forrestal letter to Major General Oliver P. Echols, April 6, 1948, box 94; Excerpts from Telephone Conversation between Honorable James Forrestal, Secretary of Defense, and Congressman Carl Hinshaw of California, April 14, 1948, pp. 1-2, box 94; James Forrestal letters to Honorable Owen Brewster, April 11, 1948, box 94, and to Donald W. Douglas, Esq., April 12, 1948, box 127; all in Forrestal Papers. Note from Forrestal's letter to Echols that there obviously had been previous conversations between the two about the latter becoming the adviser of the former. In all probability, these discussions began around the time of Ferdinand Eberstadt's conversation with Marx Leva on January 31, 1948, if not before.
22. Robert Hotz, "USAF, Navy to Order 3300 New Planes," *Aviation Week,* June 7, 1948, p. 11. In its issue of April 19, 1948 ("Changeable Minds," p. 7), the same magazine stated that this proposal had not originated with Forrestal, but rather that, "Two weeks ago [i.e., around the end of March], members of the Senate Armed Services Committee proposed to Defense Secretary James Forrestal that . . . immediate funds should be made available for aircraft procurement to start industry expansion." Forrestal, according to the maga-

zine, replied, "the actual gain in time, in terms of contracts let, would . . . not be sufficient to warrant that additional burden upon you." Although it is possible that this account is correct, it is not corroborated by any other evidence I have seen.

23. James Forrestal letter to Honorable Chan Gurney, April 2, 1948, p. 2, Papers of Carl Spaatz, Chief of Staff section, Secretary of the Air Force (2) folder, Manuscript Division, the Library of Congress; Forrestal letter to Honorable John Taber (with a copy to Honorable Styles Bridges), April 5, 1948, Forrestal Papers, box 94; *Forrestal Diaries,* pp. 411–12. Truman himself gave Forrestal credit for this idea: "Secretary Forrestal suggested, and I concurred, that we propose to the Congress that the aircraft procurement money in the regular 1949 Budget, plus the amounts allocated for such purposes in the supplemental request, be submitted and considered separately in order that Congress could make the total of such funds immediately available in order to get a substantial volume of aircraft production under way." Statement by the President to the Secretary of Defense, the Secretaries of the Three [Armed Service] Departments, and the Three Chiefs of Staff, May 13, 1948, p. 2, President's Secretary's File (hereafter PSF), Subject File, Cabinet, box 157, HSTL.
24. See the Memorandum for Secretary Forrestal from Secretary of the Air Force W. Stuart Symington, March 25, 1948, Symington Papers, box 4.
25. W. Stuart Symington to Winthrop Aldrich, April 1, 1948, Symington Papers, box 1. Four days later (April 5, 1948), Symington sent a second letter to Aldrich, which I quote in its entirety (except for the closing): "Dear Winthrop: Thank you very much for seeing my friends. The client they discussed is getting in touch with you shortly. With appreciation and every good wish." Papers of Winthrop W. Aldrich, Correspondence File 2, Baker Library, Harvard Business School.
26. Testimony Before the Senate Armed Services Committee by W. Stuart Symington, March 25, 1948, Symington Papers, box 3.
27. *Forrestal Diaries,* pp. 400-419, *passim*; the quotation is on p. 417.
28. Ibid., pp. 429–32 (the quotation is on p. 432); Forrestal's Appointment Book for Friday, May 7, 1948, Forrestal Papers, box 132; Statement by the President to the Secretary of Defense, the Secretaries of the Three Departments, and the Three Chiefs of Staff, May 13, 1948, PSF, Subject File, Cabinet, box 157.
29. *Forrestal Diaries,* pp. 434–37 *passim*; statement by the President, May 13, 1948, Subject File, Cabinet, box 157, p. 4; Letter to the Speaker of the House of Representatives from the President, May 13, 1948, Papers of Clark M. Clifford, box 12, HSTL.
30. For Symington's April 7 testimony in the Senate, see C. P. Trussell, "Rise for Air Power Gains in Congress; May Shut Out UMT," *New York Times*

(hereafter *NYT*), April 8, 1948, pp. 1, 20. For Symington's testimony in the House, see Transcript of Testimony before the House Committee on Armed Services, Selective Service, April 13, 1948, p. 1, Symington Papers, box 3. For Spaatz's testimony, see Stenographic Transcript of Hearings, April 7, 1948, p. 58, RG 46, Senate, Committee on Armed Services, Unprinted Hearings, Executive Session, January 27, 1947–May 19, 1948; I have used the unexpurgated version of the General's remarks, rather than the more sedate "corrected" version.

31. Resolution Adopted by the Armed Services Committee to the Secretary of National Defense, April 7, 1948, p. 1, Confidential Files (hereafter CF), box 36, HSTL; C. P. Trussell, "House Overrides Truman to Order Vast Air Armada," *NYT,* April 16, 1948.
32. See the following articles by C. P. Trussell in the *NYT*: "Senators Slow Defense Bill In Fear of Deficit Spending," April 17, 1948, pp. 1, 3; "Forrestal Shifts to 66 Air Groups in Move for Truce, April 22, 1948, pp. 1, 18; "Senate Votes 74–2 to Build Air Force of 70 Full Groups," May 7, 1948, pp. 1, 5; "Conferees Endorse $3,198,100,000 Fund for Top Air Power," May 11, 1948, pp. 1, 20. Also see the Statement by the President Upon Signing Bill Providing Funds for Military Aircraft, May 21, 1948, *Public Papers of the Presidents of the United States: Harry S. Truman, 1948* (Washington, D.C.: U.S. Government Printing Office, 1963), p. 272 (hereafter cited as *Public Papers of Harry S. Truman*).
33. Verbatim Report, Fifth Meeting of the Air Board, June 5–6, 1946, p. 45, RG 340 (Secretary of the Air Force), Air Board Minutes of Meetings, ellipses in original; Statements of Lawrence D. Bell, President, Bell Aircraft Corporation, September 29, 1947, p. 909, and Donald Douglas (replying to question by John McCone), President, Douglas Aircraft Company, October 29, 1947, p. 2102, Stenographic Report of Proceedings, PAPC, RG 340 (Secretary of the Air Force), Entry 53, ACC, General File, 1945–1950, ACC Papers Folder No. 125, vol. 2. James Forrestal letter to Donald W. Douglas, April 12, 1948, Forrestal Papers, box 127.
34. Oliver J. Gingold, "News of the Market," *Wall Street Journal,* June 3, 1948, p. 7.
35. Memorandums for the Secretary from Felix Larkin, Status of studies concerning additional procurement of aircraft, March 17, 1948, pp. 1–2, and March 23, 1948, both in RG 330 (Secretary of Defense), Entry 199, Office of the Administrative Secretary, Correspondence Control Section, Numerical File, September 1947–June 1950, CD 5-1-25 to CD 5-2-6, CD 5-1-12 folder.
36. Telephone conversation with Mr. William Allen, Boeing Aircraft, Monday, June 7, 1948, pp. 3–4, Symington Papers, box 1; I have omitted Allen's portion of the conversation.
37. USAF Airframe Weight, April 5, 1950, Symington Papers, box 2.

38. "House Group Expected to Report Out Bill Today That Will Provide $1,976 Billion for 3,200 Planes" *Wall Street Journal,* April 13, 1948, p. 3. For all the furor over the size of the air force's budget for the 1949 fiscal year, there is some evidence that even the commanding officers of that service were uncomfortable with the kind of huge appropriations for aircraft procurement that Congress favored in the spring of 1948. In July of 1947, for example, Army Air Force Commanding General Carl Spaatz "stated that in his opinion we are not justified in requesting funds [for new airplanes] greater than those necessary to sustain the industry in a sound and healthy condition as recommended by the Air Coordinating Committee"; Minutes of Air Staff Meeting—1 July 1947, p. 4, Vandenberg Papers, Subject File, Air Staff Meeting Minutes.
39. "Report on Procurement," *Aviation Week,* June 21, 1948, p. 7; Memorandum for Mr. [Arthur] Barrows from W. Stuart Symington, May 22, 2948, Symington Papers, box 2; Memorandum for Mr. McCone from W. Stuart Symington, May 22, 1948, Symington Papers, box 2.
40. "Report on Procurement," p. 7; "Industry Regains Health and Productivity," *Aviation Week,* February 28, 1949, p. 23; *Business Week,* June 19, 1948, p. 26.
41. Information Memorandum to the Secretary, Airframe weight production, from Felix Larkin, February 6, 1948, RG 330 (Secretary of Defense), Entry 199, Office of the Administrative Secretary, Correspondence Control Section, Numerical File, September 1947–June 1950, CD 19-1-12 to CD 12-1-11, CD 19-1-11 folder. *Aviation Week* reported in its April 19, 1948, issue (actually published April 12) that "Maj. Gen. Oliver P. Echols, retired Air Force procurement chief, and now president of the Aircraft Industries Association, has been working as a special consultant to Defense Secretary Forrestal" (Robert Hotz, "Orders Are Coming for Aircraft Industry," p. 11). H. E. Weihmiller, Aircraft Industry Minimum Annual Volume of Business, September 30, 1947, PAPC, box 40, HSTL. The original amount allocated for aircraft procurement in the budget for fiscal year 1949 was $1.24 billion; the addition of $725 million brought the total to $1.965 billion, exclusive of contracts for research and development; see "Aviation Expenditures Included in the Budget for Fiscal Year 1949," *Aviation Week,* February 23, 1948, p. 51.
42. "Navy Proposes Change in Procurement Policy, Using Wartime Methods," *Wall Street Journal,* January 16, 1947, p. 3; "1949 in the Aircraft Industry," *Automotive Industries,* January 15, 1949, p. 98; Excerpts from Telephone Conversation between Honorable James Forrestal and Honorable Hume Wrong, Canadian Ambassador, October 25, 1948, Forrestal Papers, box 94. The arrangement to have the F-86A produced in Canada was the first instance of what Thayer has termed *co-production*—the manufacture in another coun-

try of a weapon designed by a U.S. firm, with license fees paid to the latter; see George Thayer, *The War Business: The International Trade in Armaments* (New York: Simon and Schuster, 1969), pp. 180–83 (the quotation is on p. 181). Co-production would soon enough lead to an even more clever mechanism for undermining the power over appropriations granted Congress by the Constitution. *Offshore military procurement*—that is, U.S. payments to other countries to manufacture armaments and even non-military goods—provided funds to these countries under the rubric of "defense" at a time when Congress would not authorize further foreign aid expenditures. The definitive treatment of this topic is William S. Borden, *The Pacific Alliance: United States Foreign Economic Policy and Japanese Trade Recovery, 1947–1955* (Madison, Wis.: University of Wisconsin Press, 1984).

43. Oliver Echols, "Procurement Planning Methods and Procedures," Statement Submitted to the PAPC, October 14, 1947, RG 340 (Secretary of the Air Force), Entry 53, Air Coordinating Committee, General File, 1945–1950, ACC Papers Folder Nos. 116 to 121, Folder 120; "Congress' Work Shows New Air Interest," *Aviation Week,* July 5, 1948, p. 10; Joseph L. Howard, Lieutenant Commander (SC), U.S. Navy, "How Law 413 Streamlines Buying for Military Requirements," *Steel,* April 19, 1948, p. 72.
44. "1949 Military Aircraft Program," *Automotive Industries,* June 15, 1948, pp. 92, 96.
45. Statement of Hon. W. Stuart Symington Before the PAPC, November 26, 1947, p. 12, Spaatz Papers, Chief of Staff section, Secretary of the Air Force folder.
46. Memorandum for Mr. Deale from James Forrestal, September 1, 1947, Forrestal Papers, box 73. Memorandum for the Secretary of the Navy, Aircraft Procurement Program for Fiscal Years 1948–1949, April 2, 1948, RG 330 (Secretary of Defense), Entry 199, Office of the Administrative Secretary, Correspondence Control Section, Numerical File, September 1947–June 1950, CD 19-1-12 to CD 19-1-11, CD 19-1-11 folder; it is unclear whether this memorandum was actually sent or whether Forrestal's wishes were conveyed orally. Memorandum for the Secretary, Sale of 10 Constellations to the Air Force, from Felix E. Larkin, April 6, 1948, RG 330 (Secretary of Defense), Entry 199, CD 5-1-25 to CD 5-2-6, CD 5-1-12 folder; Robert E. Gross to General Carl A. Spaatz, Commanding General, Army Air Forces, September 17, 1947, Symington Papers, box 12.
47. Memorandum for Mr. Larkin from James Forrestal, May 31, 1948, box 94; James Forrestal letter to Mr. Felix Larkin, July 19, 1948, box 127; Memoranda for General Lutes and for Mr. Mautz from James Forrestal, both July 25, 1948, and Memorandum for Mr. McNeil, August 29, 1948, box 94; all in Forrestal Papers. Questions and Answers Relating to 1950 Budget Estimates, p. 27,

attachment to James Forrestal letter to Honorable James E. Webb, December 1, 1948, RG 330 (Secretary of Defense), Entry 199, Office of the Administrative Secretary, Correspondence Control Section, Numerical File, September 1947–June 1950, CD 5-1-25 to CD 5-2-6, CD 5-1-25 folder.

48. Statement of Ralph V. Hunt, Vice President-Controller, Douglas Aircraft Company, September 30, 1947, p. 1020, Stenographic Report of Proceedings, PAPC, RG 340 (Secretary of the Air Force), Entry 53, ACC, General File, 1945–1950, ACC Papers Folder No. 125, vol. 2.

49. Remarks by W. Stuart Symington, Secretary of the Air Force, at Annual Meeting of Board of Directors, Aircraft Industries Association, Williamsburg, Va., May 19, 1948, pp. 4–5, Symington Papers, box 1. For other of Symington's pronouncements along the same lines, see also "Air Force to Boost B-49 Orders," *Aviation Week,* August 2, 1948, p. 11, and Robert Hotz, "12 Companies Share Aircraft Program," *Aviation Week,* June 21, 1948, p. 12.

50. Statement of Mundy I. Peale, President, Republic Aircraft Corporation, September 29, 1947, p. 839, Stenographic Report of Proceedings, PAPC, RG 340 (Secretary of the Air Force), Entry 53, ACC, General File, 1945–1950, ACC Papers Folder No. 125, vol. 2; Statement of Hon. W. Stuart Symington Before the PAPC, November 26, 1947, p. 12, Spaatz Papers, Chief of Staff section, Secretary of the Air Force folder.

51. For these quotations, see, in order: "Industry Regains Health and Prosperity," *Aviation Week,* February 28, 1949, p. 24; "1949 in the Aircraft Industry," *Automotive Industries,* January 15, 1949, p. 96; *Business Week,* August 14, 1948, p. 34. For more on the Northrop-Convair subcontracting arrangement, see "Air Force to Boost B-49 Orders," p. 11. For evidence that the administration's new procurement policy produced a wider distribution of contracts within a matter of weeks, see "Air Force Tells How It Will Spend $1.3 Billion . . . ," *Wall Street Journal,* June 11, 1948, p. 2.

52. "Cash Flow Increases," *Aviation Week,* August 23, 1948, p. 7; "Your Big Customer: Government," *Aviation Week,* September 6, 1948, p. 11; "Profits Seen From Peak Peacetime Sales," *Aviation Week,* December 27, 1948, p. 12.

53. Robert E. Gross to Lawrence C. Ames, April 15, 1948, Papers of Robert E. Gross, Business Correspondence File, box 8, Manuscript Division, Library of Congress; "Plane Industry Sees 5 Years of Stability," *NYT,* May 14, 1948, p. 47.

54. Robert E. Gross to Edward O. McDonnell, August 12, 1948, Business Correspondence File, box 8, Gross Papers; Gross to Air Commodore C. B. Wincott, August 25, 1948, Gross Papers, Personal Correspondence File, box 2; Gross to G. W. Vaughan, August 31, 1948, Gross to Lloyd H. Fales, April 21, 1949, and Gross to J. C. Franklin, United States Atomic Energy Commission, May 4, 1949, Business Correspondence File, box 8, Gross Papers.

55. "1949 in the Aircraft Industry," pp. 34–35; "Big Year Assured for Plane Makers," *Aviation Week,* March 27, 1950, p. 11.
56. "1949 in the Aircraft Industry," pp. 35-36.
57. Financial Condition of Military and Commercial Aircraft Manufacturers 1934–1947, July 8, 1948, p. 2, attached to Memorandum for Mr. Larkin from W. H. Mautz, July 8, 1948, Department of Defense records (copy made for the author at the Department of Defense). Forrestal showed an inordinate interest in the financial status of the aircraft industry and started having periodic reports on it compiled almost from the moment he became secretary of defense.
58. Office of Progress Reports and Statistics, Office of the Secretary of Defense, Financial Condition of the Aircraft Industry at the End of 1948, April 25, 1949, Department of Defense records.
59. David Lilienthal recorded Baldwin's view on May 25, 1948; see *The Journals of David E. Lilienthal,* vol. 2: *The Atomic Energy Years 1945–1950* (New York: Harper and Row, 1964), p. 351.
60. "Occasions of Formal Recommendation to Congress of Universal Training, by the President," August 1, 1950, in the Papers of George Elsey, box 90, HSTL; announcement of the appointment of the Advisory Commission on Universal Military Training, December 19, 1946, Webb Papers, General File, box 20; letter from the President to the Speaker of the House and the President of the Senate pro tempore, June 4, 1947, Elsey Papers, box 89.
61. General of the Army Omar N. Bradley and Clay Blair, *A General's Life: An Autobiography* (New York: Simon and Schuster, 1983), p. 482; William S. White, "Congress Hesitant on Draft, Training . . . ," *NYT,* March 18, 1948, pp. 1, 2; General J. Lawton Collins, U.S.A., *Lightning Joe: An Autobiography* (Baton Rouge: Louisiana State University Press, 1977), p. 346. For the sources of opposition to UMT, see also Clyde E. Jacobs and John F. Gallagher, *The Selective Service Act: A Case Study of the Governmental Process* (New York: Dodd, Mead, 1967), pp. 33, 39, 46; and James M. Gerhardt, *The Draft and Public Policy: Issues in Military Manpower Procurement 1945–1970* (Columbus, Ohio: Ohio State University Press, 1971), chapter 2, "The Return of Selective Service."
62. Clark M. Clifford oral history interview, p. 109, HSTL.
63. Memorandum for the Secretary and Under Secretary of the Navy from Captain Ira H. Nunn, November 18, 1947, p. 2, RG 330 (Secretary of Defense), Entry 199, Office of the Administrative Secretary, Correspondence Control Section, Numerical File, September 1947–June 1950, CD 3-1-24 folder; Memorandum for the Secretary of the Navy, February 17, 1948, p. 1, RG 330 (Secretary of Defense), Entry 199, CD 9-2-4 folder.

64. Excerpts from Telephone Conversation between Honorable James Forrestal and Honorable Chan Gurney, November 18, 1947, Forrestal Papers, box 93; Memorandum to Mr. Marx Leva and Mr. Felix E. Larkin from R. A. Buddeke, February 18, 1947, RG 330 (Secretary of Defense), Entry 200, Office of the Administrative Secretary, Correspondence Control Section, Numerical File, September 1947–December 1949, G to G1, folder G1 Legislation, October 17, 1947–June 30, 1948, vol. 1; Memorandum for the President from the Secretary of Defense, February 27, 1948, PSF, Cabinet, box 157; William S. White, "Congress Hesitant on Draft, Training . . . ," *NYT,* March 18, 1948, pp. 1, 2.
65. Memorandum for the Secretary from Charles E. Bohlen, March 5, 1948, National Archives Collection, Xerox 2061, George C. Marshall Library (hereafter GCML), Virginia Military Institute, Lexington, Virginia; Letter to Mr. Secretary from George E. Butler, March 12, 1948, p. 1, National Archives Collection, Xerox 2063, GCML.
66. John Snyder oral history interview, p. 1497, HSTL.
67. Memorandum to the Secretary of Defense from Kenneth C. Royall, March 15, 1948, p. 2, RG 330 (Secretary of Defense), Entry 199, Office of the Administrative Secretary, Correspondence Control Section, Numerical File, September 1947–June 1950, CD 9-2-4 folder.
68. Stenographic transcript of hearings on Universal Military Training before the Committee on Armed Services, United States Senate, April 21, 1948, p. 287, RG 330 (Secretary of Defense), Entry 199, Office of the Administrative Secretary, Correspondence Control Section, Numerical File, September 1947–June 1950, CD 9-2-4 folder.
69. Memorandum for the Secretary of the Army from Omar N. Bradley, undated (but in response to a memorandum from the Office of the Secretary of Defense dated September 22, 1948), RG 330 (Secretary of Defense), Entry 199.
70. Letter to Mr. Secretary from George E. Butler, March 12, 1948, p. 1, National Archives Collection, Xerox 2063, GCML; Memorandum by the Joint Chiefs of Staff for the Secretary of Defense, March 10, 1948, *Foreign Relations of the United States* (hereafter *FRUS*): *1948,* vol. 4, *Eastern Europe; The Soviet Union* (Washington, D.C.: U.S. Government Printing Office, 1974), p. 783.
71. W. Stuart Symington to Honorable Harry S. Truman, March 29, 1948, Symington Papers, box 13; Compton Report quoted in Memorandum for Secretary Forrestal from W. Stuart Symington, March 7, 1948, Spaatz Papers, Chief of Staff section, Secretary of the Air Force (2) folder. Even after his testimony before the Senate Armed Services Committee on April 7 had given UMT the coup de grace, Symington continued to maintain his innocence. "The Air Force has stood squarely behind UMT in principle," he told Robert

Cutler, a sometimes assistant of James Forrestal; letter of April 12, 1948, to Robert Cutler, Spaatz Papers, Chief of Staff section, Secretary of the Air Force folder.

72. Oral History Interview with Stuart Symington, May 29, 1981, pp. 26–27, HSTL.
73. Verbatim Report, Seventh Meeting of the Air Board, January 6–7, 1948, pp. 14–15, RG 340 (Secretary of the Air Force), Air Board Minutes of Meetings.
74. Ibid., pp. 124–25, 132–33. Note also the remarks of Eugene M. Zuckert, Assistant Secretary of the Air Force from 1947 to 1952, in his oral history interview at the Truman Library: "We . . . didn't want the grade fours (lower intelligence) in the percentages that we would *have* to take if the Army was to be able to man their organization" through UMT. "We wanted a volunteer force . . . and we could get it" (pp. 41–42).
75. Verbatim Report, Seventh Meeting of the Air Board, pp. 122–26 *passim.*
76. See Annual Message to the Congress on the State of the Union, *Public Papers of Harry S. Truman, 1949* (Washington, D.C.: U.S. Government Printing Office, 1964), p. 6; Doris Fleeson, "The Air Force Lobby: Even Truman Co-operates at Big [Air] Show Designed to Prove His Policy Wrong," *Washington Star,* February 16, 1949.
77. The quotations come, respectively, from "Truman Won't Ask Training of Youth," *NYT,* August 12, 1950; "Odd Gyrations on UMT," *WP,* September 1, 1950; "U.M.T. Postponed," *NYT,* September 1, 1950.
78. C. P. Trussell, "Military Leaders Call UMT, Draft Vital for Safety . . . ," *NYT,* March 19, 1948, pp. 1, 3; "Senate Uncertain Over Draft, UMT," *NYT,* March 21, 1948.
79. James Forrestal letter to Bernard M. Baruch, Esq., March 31, 1948, Forrestal Papers, box 94 (the list referred to in this letter is not in Forrestal's papers); John G. Norris, "Full Hearings Voted On UMT, Defense," *WP,* March 9, 1948; James Forrestal letter to Honorable Chan Gurney, Chairman, Armed Services Committee, United States Senate, April 22, 1948, pp. 1–2, Clifford Papers, box 12.
80. C. P. Trussell, "Hearings on UMT to Begin in Senate," *NYT,* March 9, 1948, p. 11.
81. Memorandum for Mr. Leva from James Forrestal, January 31, 1948, Forrestal Papers, box 127.
82. James Forrestal letters to Honorable Henry Cabot Lodge, Jr., November 11, 1947; Honorable Leverett Saltonstall, September 25, 1947; Rear Admiral Wm. Brent Young, (SC) U.S.N. Ret, October 23, 1947; all in Forrestal Papers, box 93. The navy's long-standing dislike of UMT was undoubtedly well known to the president. In selecting James Forrestal, for seven years a top navy

bureaucrat, "to head up the handling of UMT for him," did Truman expect the secretary to rise above the Navy's bias—or succumb to it?

83. James Forrestal letter to Mr. President, November 29, 1948, Tab B, unpaginated, RG 330 (Secretary of Defense), Entry 201, Office of the Administrative Secretary, Correspondence Control Section, Policy Directives, 1947–1949, vol. 1, folder Directives. I argued in chapter 5 that the speech delivered by James Byrnes at The Citadel on March 13, 1948, in response to a request from Secretary of Defense Forrestal and Secretary of the Army Kenneth Royall, was in essence a statement of Forrestal's own thinking. If that is so, then the fact that Byrnes's endorsement of UMT in the Citadel address was lukewarm at best offers further support for my interpretation of Forrestal's actual views on UMT.
84. "House Group Expected to Report Out Bill Today That Will Provide $1,976 Million for 3,200 Planes," *Wall Street Journal,* April 13, 1948, p. 3.
85. Excerpts of Telephone Conversation between Honorable James Forrestal and Senator Chan Gurney, March 19, 1948, pp. 1, 2, Forrestal Papers, box 94; Forrestal letter to Honorable Walter G. Andrews, April 2, 1948, RG 330 (Secretary of Defense), Entry 199, Office of the Administrative Secretary, Correspondence Control Section, Numerical File, September 1947–June 1950, CD 18136 to CD 18-1-8, CD 9-2-4 folder.
86. Excerpts of Telephone Conversation between Honorable James Forrestal and Honorable Chan Gurney, April 12, 1948, Excerpts from Telephone Conversation between Honorable James Forrestal and Honorable Walter G. Andrews, April 29, 1948, pp. 1–2, both in Forrestal Papers, box 94.
87. Stenographic transcript of hearings on Universal Military Training before the Committee on Armed Services, United States Senate, April 21, 1948, pp. 285–86, 289–92, 307–08, RG 330 (Secretary of Defense), Entry 199, Office of the Administrative Secretary, Correspondence Control Section, Numerical File, September 1947–June 1950, CD 9-2-4 folder.
88. Margaret Truman, *Harry S. Truman* (New York: William Morrow, 1973), pp. 11, 350; John Snyder oral history interview, pp. 1702–03.
89. Charles A. Plumley to Honorable W. Stuart Symington, February 15, 1949, Symington Papers, box 10.
90. C. P. Trussell, "Rise for Air Power Gains in Congress; May Shut Out UMT," *NYT,* April 8, 1948, p. 9; Stenographic Transcript of Hearings, Senate Armed Services Committee, April 7, 1948, p. 61, RG 46, Senate Committee on Armed Services, Unprinted Hearings, Executive Session, January 27, 1947–May 19, 1948. If Symington's testimony before the Senate put UMT in its coffin, that before the House Armed Services Committee on April 13 shoveled on the dirt. "If my two boys have to go back again into the Army and the

Marines," he told members of the second panel, "I would rather see them have a minimum air force than I would a group of young boys trained for six months or a year. And, incidentally, I am in complete agreement—and the Air Force is—with the Compton report [*sic* ; the report of the Advisory Commission on Universal Military Training]. The Compton report said that if U.M.T. had to be at the expense of the military services that they not only would not be for it, they would be against it." Transcript of testimony, p. 1, Symington Papers, box 3.

91. Practically from the day he became Assistant Secretary of the Army for Air, Symington had been besieging Truman with such protestations; witness this excerpt from a letter of May 16, 1946: "I am sure you will be astonished at the attached figures. They show (1) that the Navy has been approved for several hundred more planes than has the Air Forces for the Fiscal Year 1947; and (2) that the Navy has been allowed millions of dollars more than the Air Forces to spend on the purchase of airplanes." Symington Papers, box 13. For another instance of the genre, see the five-page lament sent to the Honorable Harry S. Truman by W. Stuart Symington on May 24, 1948, Symington Papers, box 13.
92. Truman to Symington, March 25, 1948, Symington Papers, box 13. It is surely significant that although Truman criticized "the Air contingent" for its lack of discipline, he made no claim that its hostility to UMT imperiled the nation's security. In any case, Symington could not restrain himself from responding to this one-sentence comment—even though it tactfully mentioned no names and aimed no criticism at the secretary personally—and on March 29 he sent Truman a four-paragraph denial, during the course of which he again took the opportunity to instruct the president that "there is some dissatisfaction in the Air Force at being granted less than one-half of the personnel increases allowed the Navy, and less than one-sixth of those allowed the Army; also there is regret that the recommendations of your Air Policy Commission and the Congressional Aviation Policy Board were not approved with respect to aircraft procurement," etc.; Symington Papers, box 13.
93. See C. P. Trussell, "House Overrides Truman To Order Vast Air Armada," *NYT,* April 16, 1948, p. 1; and memorandum from Karl Bendetsen to Clark Clifford on April 8, 1948, Clifford Papers, box 11. Bendetsen's memorandum, written the day after Symington appeared before the Senate Armed Services Committee, requested that Truman issue a statement criticizing the secretary's testimony as "a proposal which relates to only one Service . . . not one which takes into account simultaneously the complementary needs of each Armed Service." So far as I have been able to discover, Truman never issued any such statement.

94. Such indulgence caused Forrestal to wonder aloud to Robert Cutler, who was temporarily assisting at the Pentagon, "Perhaps Stu had the ear of the President?" Robert Cutler, *No Time for Rest* (Boston: Little, Brown, 1965), p. 257.
95. Landry's remarks are in the transcript of an interview conducted by William Hillman and David M. Noyes, January 7, 1954, pp. 7-8, Papers of Harry S Truman, Post-Presidential Memoirs, HSTL.
96. Review of *Friends and Enemies: The United States, China and the Soviet Union, 1948–1972,* by Gordon H. Chang, *New York Times Book Review,* July 29, 1990, p. 25.

Notes to Chapter 7.

1. U.S. Department of State, *Foreign Relations of the United States* (hereafter *FRUS*): *1948,* vol. 4, *Eastern Europe; The Soviet Union* (Washington, D.C.: U.S. Government Printing Office, 1974), p. 833.
2. The Diaries of James V. Forrestal, p. 2589, box 5, Seeley G. Mudd Manuscript Library (hereafter SGMML), Princeton University.
3. J. C. Clifford, "Confused Prospects for Aircrafts," *The Magazine of Wall Street,* July 2, 1949, p. 352.
4. *FRUS: 1948,* vol. 4, *Eastern Europe; The Soviet Union,* p. 946.
5. See Joseph Frayman, "Russians Accept a U.S. Bid to Parley on 'Differences'; Our Note Calls Policy Firm," *New York Times* (hereafter *NYT*), May 11, 1948, pp. 1, 12.
6. George F. Kennan, *Memoirs: 1925–1950* (Boston: Little, Brown, 1967), p. 346; Memorandum, John Davies, Jr., to Mr. Butler, March 19, 1948, National Archives Collection, Xerox 2072-1, folder 1, George C. Marshall Library (hereafter GCML), Virginia Military Institute, Lexington, Virginia. Walter Bedell Smith, the U.S. ambassador to the Soviet Union, claimed that he had also conceived the same idea; see his telegram to the Secretary of State of April 26, 1948, *FRUS: 1948,* vol. 4, *Eastern Europe; The Soviet Union,* pp. 836–37.
7. Entry for April 23, 1948, in Walter Millis and E. S. Duffield, eds., *The Forrestal Diaries* (New York: Viking, 1951), p. 424 (hereafter *Forrestal Diaries*); *FRUS: 1948,* vol. 4, *Eastern Europe; The Soviet Union,* p. 834; James Reston, "Truman Says Note to Russia Means No Change In Policy . . . : Position Clarified," *NYT,* May 12, 1948, pp. 1, 3.
8. *FRUS: 1948,* vol. 4, *Eastern Europe; The Soviet Union,* p. 834.
9. Telegram, the Ambassador in the Soviet Union to the Secretary of State, May 4, 1948, *FRUS: 1948,* vol. 4, *Eastern Europe; The Soviet Union,* pp. 849–50;

note the similarity to the language of the March 19 memorandum of John Paton Davies.

10. The Ambassador in the Soviet Union to the Secretary of State, May 10, 1948, *FRUS: 1948,* vol. 4, *Eastern Europe; The Soviet Union,* pp. 854, 851.
11. Ibid., pp. 854, 851.
12. "The Reply by the Soviet Union," *NYT,* May 11, 1948, p. 12.
13. For the Soviet release see Joseph Frayman, "Russians Accept a U.S. Bid," pp. 1, 12. For the Wallace speech and "Open Letter," see Warren Moscow, "Wallace Presents Peace Bid to Stalin," *NYT,* May 13, 1948, pp. 1, 14; and "Text of Wallace Letter to Stalin Calling for Peace," *NYT,* May 13, 1948, p. 14. Following Wallace's Madison Square Garden address, the State Department did its utmost to discredit him by unearthing evidence that he had received advance notification of, and had coordinated his speech with, the Soviet response to Smith's note. The effort was a failure. See the memoranda in the National Archives Collection, Xerox 2072-1, folder 1, State Department-Policy Planning, GCML.
14. James Reston, "Marshall Asks Soviet Deeds on Peace, not General Talk; Recalls 'Bitter Experience,'" *NYT,* May 13, 1948, p. 4.
15. See the flow of messages to and from Washington, London, Paris and Moscow on this score in *FRUS: 1948,* vol. 4, *Eastern Europe; The Soviet Union,* pp. 860ff.; "French Cautious on Talk Prospect" and Herbert L. Matthews, "British Suspicious, Fear Secret Deal," both in *NYT,* May 12, 1948, p. 11.
16. James Reston, "Marshall Asks Soviet Deeds on Peace," p. 1; Statement by the President Following an Exchange of Views in Moscow Between the U.S. Ambassador and the Foreign Minister, *Public Papers of the Presidents of the United States: Harry S. Truman, 1948* (Washington, D.C.: U.S. Government Printing Office, 1963), p. 95 (hereafter cited as *Public Papers of Harry S. Truman*). See also: James Reston, "Truman Says Note to Russia Means No Change in Policy; Bid for Talks Not Intended," *NYT,* May 12, 1948, pp. 1, 12; the text of Marshall's statement of May 12 and an interview with him, *NYT,* May 13, 1948, p. 4; and "French Fears Quieted on Moscow 'Notes'; Paris Asks for Role in European Settlement," *NYT,* May 13, 1948, p. 3.
17. See "Stalin Declares Wallace Letter Is Basis for Talk," *NYT,* May 18, 1948, pp. 1, 4; "The Text of Stalin's Reply," *NYT,* May 18, 1948, p. 4.
18. Reston, "Marshall Asks Soviet Deeds on Peace," p. 4.
19. Ibid.
20. Memorandum for the President from James Forrestal, May 28, 1948, and Conversation with Senator Taft, May 31, 1948, President's Secretary's Files, Cabinet, box 157, Harry S. Truman Library (hereafter HSTL); James Forrestal letter to Honorable Walter G. Andrews, June 17, 1948, Papers of James V. Forrestal (hereafter Forrestal Papers), box 94, SGMML.

21. Walter Bedell Smith telegrams to the Secretary of State of April 22 and December 23, 1948, *FRUS: 1948,* vol. 4, *Eastern Europe; The Soviet Union,* pp. 833 and 946, respectively.
22. St. Patrick's Day Address, *Public Papers of Harry S. Truman, 1948,* p. 189; Anthony Leviero, "Truman Asks Peace but Bars 'Slavery'; Attacks Wallace," *NYT,* March 30, 1948, p. 1. The two quotations of Clark Clifford are from his Memorandum for the President, November 19, 1947, p. 23, Papers of Clark M. Clifford, HSTL. Clifford's memorandum was a near-verbatim copy of an earlier one sent by James H. Rowe, a Washington lawyer, to the director of the Bureau of the Budget, James E. Webb, on September 18, 1947; see Document no. 576, Miscellaneous Historical Document File, HSTL. As I have pointed out in earlier chapters, Clifford's own discussion of this memorandum contains no reference to any of his words that I have quoted above; see Clark Clifford with Richard Holbrooke, *Counsel to the President: A Memoir* (New York: Random House, 1991), pp. 191–94.
23. Charles Bohlen, Memorandum of Conversation, by the Secretary of State, May 11, 1948, *FRUS: 1948,* vol. 4, *Eastern Europe; The Soviet Union,* p. 861; telegrams, the Chargé in the Soviet Union to the Secretary of State, May 11 and May 18, 1948, *FRUS: 1948, vol. 4, Eastern Europe; The Soviet Union,* pp. 862–63 and 870–71, respectively.
24. Drew Middleton, "Economic Needs of Soviet Regarded as Its Motivation," *NYT,* May 12, 1948, pp. 1, 9; Delbert Clark, "Soviet Move Tied to German Yield," *NYT,* May 13, 1948, p. 3; "Berlin Sees Soviet Eager for Accord," *NYT,* May 12, 1948, p. 12.
25. *Forrestal Diaries,* p. 441. In *Foreign Policy and U.S. Presidential Elections: 1940–1948* (New York: Franklin Watts, 1974), p. 203, for example, Robert A. Divine describes the Soviet overtures as a "Russian ploy."
26. *Forrestal Diaries,* p. 424; Major General Ray T. Maddocks, Memorandum for Record: Address of Mr. George F. Kennan . . . to the Permanent Joint Board on Defense, Canada-U.S., June 8, 1948, p. 2, RG 319 (Army Staff), Entry 153, Plans and Operations Division, Decimal File, 1946–1948, 091 Poland to Sardinia, P & O 091 Russia (Section I) (cases 1-) folder. Even Forrestal himself used the phrase "the semi-hysteria which has developed" in describing the events of March and April; see his May 10, 1948, draft Outline of Subject Matter for the President's Use in a Discussion with the Secretary of Defense, Secretaries of the Three Departments [Armed Services] and the Three Chiefs of Staff, attached to Memorandum to Miss Foley of June 12, 1948, Forrestal Papers, box 42, SGMML.
27. Telegram, the Ambassador in the Soviet Union to the Secretary of State, May 10, 1948, *FRUS: 1948,* vol. 4, *Eastern Europe; The Soviet Union,* pp. 856–57.

28. See "National Affairs: White Star vs. Red: If Moscow Starts 'Operation America' . . . ," *Newsweek,* May 17, 1948, pp. 30–32; ellipsis in original.
29. The Embassy of the Soviet Union to the Department of State, June 9, 1948, *FRUS: 1948,* vol. 4, *Eastern Europe; The Soviet Union,* pp. 886–87.
30. See the letter from the Secretary of State to the Ambassador of the Soviet Union, *FRUS: 1948,* vol. 4, *Eastern Europe; The Soviet Union,* pp. 896–98; n. 2, p. 897, contains an excerpt from Lovett's letter to Forrestal.
31. Michael MccGwire, *Military Objectives in Soviet Foreign Policy* (Washington: D.C.: Brookings Institution, 1987), p. 19.
32. David Holloway, *The Soviet Union and the Arms Race* (New Haven: Yale University Press, 1983), pp. 24–26, 178.
33. Central Intelligence Agency, Possibility of Direct Soviet Military Action During 1948–49, September 16, 1948, p. 3, RG 330 (Secretary of Defense), Entry 199, Office of the Administrative Secretary, Correspondence Control Section, Numerical File, September 1947–June 1950, CD 12-1-29 to CS [*sic*] 12-1-26, CD 12-1-26 folder; the estimate was actually prepared on August 27, 1948 (note 1, p. 1).
34. For reports from the U.S. Embassy during 1948 on the Soviet debate over the future of capitalism in the United States, see the dispatches in *FRUS: 1948,* vol. 4, *Eastern Europe; The Soviet Union,* for the following dates: May 26 (pp. 875–76), December 6 (pp. 940–42), December 23 (pp. 944–45), December 27 (pp. 947–48); the first quotation is on p. 944, the second, on p. 941. For the events at the end of March 1948, see *Forrestal Diaries,* pp. 407–9.

Notes to Chapter 8.

1. *Wall Street Journal,* April 2, 1948, p. 4.
2. Richard M. Freeland, *The Truman Doctrine and the Origins of McCarthyism: Foreign Policy, Domestic Politics and Internal Security, 1946–1948* (New York: Schocken Books, 1974).
3. "Soviet Resolution and Vyshinky Excerpts," *New York Times* (hereafter *NYT*), September 26, 1948, p. 4. The first article cited by Vyshinky was Joseph and Stewart Alsop, "If War Comes," *Saturday Evening Post,* September 11, 1948; the second, an editorial in the April 9, 1948, issue of *U.S. News & World Report*; the last, Hanson W. Baldwin, "What Air Power Can—and Cannot—Do," *New York Times Magazine,* May 30, 1948. Note that although this portion of Vyshinky's speech reiterates the substance of the Soviet note of June 6, 1948, discussed in the preceding chapter, the language of the speech is much more caustic; see the Embassy of the Soviet Union to the Department of State, June

9, 1948, *Foreign Relations of the United States* (hereafter *FRUS*): *1948,* vol. 4, *Eastern Europe; The Soviet Union* (Washington, D.C.: U.S. Government Printing Office, 1974), pp. 886–87.

4. "Soviet Resolution and Vyshinky Excerpts," p. 4. Note that the bulk of Vyshinky's comments about U.S. military plans focused on airplanes and atomic bombs. Thomas J. Hamilton, "Vyshinky Asks 5 Powers to Cut Arms by Third, Says U.S. Aides Plot Attack . . . ," *NYT,* September 26, 1948, p. 1, stated that this speech also "singled out" Secretary of the Air Force W. Stuart Symington for condemnation, but I have not been able to find Symington's name in the excerpts of the speech carried by the *Times.*
5. Central Intelligence Agency, Possibility of Direct Soviet Military Action During 1948–1949, September 16, 1948, p. 3, RG 330 (Secretary of Defense), Entry 199, Office of the Administrative Secretary, Correspondence Control Section, Numerical File, September 1947–June 1950, CD 12-1-29 to CS [*sic*] 12-1-26, CD 12-1-26 folder; the estimate was actually prepared on August 27, 1948 (note 1, p. 1).
6. Memorandum in *FRUS: 1948,* vol. 3, *Western Europe* (Washington, D.C., U.S. Government Printing Office, 1974), p. 193.
7. Milovan Djilas, *Conversations with Stalin* (Harmondsworth, England: Penguin Books, 1967), pp. 61, 140–41.
8. Isaac Deutscher, *Stalin: A Political Biography* (New York: Vintage Books, 1960), p. 425. To Deutscher's interpretation one must also add Djilas's penetrating observation that Stalin "felt instinctively that the creation of revolutionary centers outside Moscow could endanger its supremacy in world Communism, and of course that is what actually happened. . . . At any rate, he knew that every revolution, just because it is new, becomes a new epicenter of revolution and shapes its own government and state, and this was what he feared in China." And, of course, not only there. See Djilas, *Conversations,* pp. 103, 141–42.
9. Deutscher, *Stalin,* p. 518.
10. Central Intelligence Agency Review of the World Situation as it Relates to the Security of the United States, CIA 3-48, March 10, 1948, p. 3, RG 319 (Army Staff), Entry 153, Plans and Operations Divisions, Decimal File, 1946–1948, 350.5, case 266 to 305; The Ambassador in Italy (Dunn) Telegram to the Secretary of State, January 21, 1948, *FRUS: 1948,* vol. 3, *Western Europe,* pp. 820–21.
11. See the following documents in *FRUS: 1948,* vol. 3, *Western Europe:* Report by the National Security Council, March 8, 1948, p. 776; Memorandum of Conversation, by the Secretary of State, May 6, 1948, p. 797; the Ambassador in Italy (Dunn) Telegrams to the Secretary of State, March 22, 1948, p. 858, and April 7, 1948, p. 868.

12. Lawrence S. Wittner, *American Intervention in Greece, 1943–1949* (New York: Columbia University Press, 1982), pp. 255, 259; the material within quotation marks in the indented quotation comes from Svetozar Vukmanovic-Tempo, *How and Why the People's Liberation Struggle of Greece Met With Defeat* (London: Merritt and Hatcher, 1950), pp. 6, 82.
13. Deutscher, *Stalin,* p. 519.
14. See Gar Alperovitz, *Cold War Essays* (New York: Anchor Books, 1970), pp. 45–48.
15. Carl Bernstein, *Loyalties: A Son's Memoir* (New York: Simon and Schuster, 1989), pp. 197–98.
16. Alfred W. McCoy, *The Politics of Heroin: CIA Complicity in the Global Drug Trade* (Brooklyn, N.Y.: Lawrence Hill Books, 1991), pp. 61–62.
17. Callum A. MacDonald, *Korea: The War Before Vietnam* (New York: Free Press, 1987), p. 224.
18. Christopher Simpson, *Blowback: America's Recruitment of Nazis and Its Effect on the Cold War* (New York: Weidenfeld and Nicolson, 1988); John W. Powell, "Japan's Germ Warfare: The U.S. Cover-up of a War Crime," *Bulletin of Concerned Asian Scholars* 12 (October-December 1980), and "Japan's Biological Weapons: 1930–1945," *Bulletin of the Atomic Scientists* 37 (October 1981).
19. To the best of my knowledge, the term "permanent war economy" owes its coinage to Seymour Melman; see his *The Permanent War Economy: American Capitalism in Decline* (New York: Simon and Schuster, 1974).
20. Papers of Robert E. Gross, Business Correspondence File, Manuscript Division, the Library of Congress.
21. Papers of W. Stuart Symington, box 1, Harry S. Truman Library (hereafter HSTL).
22. "1949 in the Aircraft Industry," *Automotive Industries,* January 1949, p. 96.
23. E. A. Krauss, "The Effect on Our Economy—Under Defense Mobilization—Under All-Out Preparedness," *The Magazine of Wall Street,* April 24, 1948, pp. 60, 62.
24. "Shall We Have Airplanes?" *Fortune,* January 1948, p. 159.
25. For an excellent discussion of the interrelationship between military spending and the decline in the living standard of the vast majority, see Richard B. DuBoff, *Accumulation & Power: An Economic History of the United States* (Armonk, N.Y.: M. E. Sharpe, 1989), chapters 6 through 9 especially.
26. Henry A. Wallace, "Terrorism at Evansville," *The New Republic,* April 19, 1948, p. 11.
27. Frederick K. Dodge, "Which Securities under Preparedness?" *The Magazine of Wall Street,* April 24, 1948, p. 64; Memorandum to the Commissioners from H. E. Weihmiller, Industry Replies to Questionnaires—Resume, undated (but after October 7, 1947), Addendum (unpaginated), Records of the

President's Air Policy Commission (hereafter PAPC), box 40, HSTL; Stenographic Report of Proceedings, PAPC, Statement of Mundy I. Peale, President, Republic Aircraft Corporation, September 29, 1947, p. 837, National Archives Record Group (hereafter RG) 340 (Secretary of the Air Force), Entry 53, Air Coordinating Committee (hereafter ACC), General File 1945–1950, ACC Papers Folder No. 125, vol. 2.

28. Robert E. Gross letter to Lynn L. Bollinger, October 22, 1946, p. 2, Gross Papers, Business Correspondence File, Manuscript Division, Library of Congress; PAPC, Statement of Honorable W. Stuart Symington [not revised], Assistant Secretary of War for Air, September 9, 1947, p. 286, Papers of Harry S. Truman, Files of Clark M. Clifford, HSTL. In his notes for a speech to the Lockheed Foremen's Meeting in July 1946, Gross wrote that there was "Not enough biz for 14" (p. 4) and that "It all probably leads to settling down to 3 or 4 big companies (25 yr?)" (p. 5); this document is also in the Business Correspondence File of the Gross Papers.

29. In chapter 2, I called attention to the heavy involvement in the aircraft industry of the Chase National Bank under Winthrop Aldrich's direction. With respect to General Motors, controlled by the Du Pont family, note the following: "For many years, General Motors Corp. was the largest stockholder of North American Aviation, owning 1,000,061 shares or 29 per cent of the capital stock. Remaining stock was held by 28,200 holders . . . "; "Military Plane Program Pushed: Air Force and Navy given green light on 4262 new aircraft, 2201 now being under order by Air Force and 1165 by the Navy," *Steel,* August 16, 1949, p. 62. For Laurance Rockefeller's participation in the aircraft industry, see Peter Collier and David Horowitz, *The Rockefellers: An American Dynasty* (New York: New American Library, 1977), pp. 216, 293–96. For general business opposition to nationalization, see, e.g., "Shall We Have Airplanes?" p. 162.

30. "Aviation Revival Aids General Industry," *Steel,* May 23, 1949, p. 64.

31. "1949 in the Aircraft Industry," *Automotive Industries,* January 15, 1949, p. 35; "More Warplanes," *Business Week,* September 18, 1948; "Additional Military Plane Orders, U.S. Warnings Spur Aircraft Plants," *American Machinist,* October 7, 1948, p. 125; Obligations Under "Supplemental National Defense Appropriation Act 1948," as of June 30, 1948, p. 1, attached to Memorandum for Mr. Forrestal from W. H. Mautz, July 22, 1948, Department of Defense records (copy made for the author at the Department of Defense).

32. Frederick K. Dodge, "Which Securities under Preparedness?" pp. 65, 98.

33. Ibid., p. 98; Krauss, "The Effect on Our Economy," pp. 60, 102; "Where's That War Boom?" *Business Week,* October 30, 1948, p. 23.

34. "Industry Sizing Up New Military Program," *Steel,* April 5, 1948, p. 46; "Newsgram," *U.S. News & World Report,* May 26, 1950, p. 7.

35. "Defense Buying Hits Stride," *Business Week,* March 18, 1950, pp. 19–20; "Washington Outlook," *Business Week,* April 15, 1950, p. 15.
36. "From Cold War to Cold Peace?" *Business Week,* February 12, 1949, pp. 19–20.
37. See Employment Research Associates, *A Shift in Military Spending to America's Cities: What It Means to Four Cities and the Nation* (Washington, D.C.: United States Conference of Mayors, 1988), p. 7, Table 1. The most that Reagan could manage was a 9-percent boost in military spending between 1981 and 1982; it took him almost four full years to accomplish the 30-percent jump that Truman achieved in a matter of weeks during 1948.
38. "Aviation: Plane Makers Sing the Blues," *Business Week,* April 12, 1947, p. 34; "The Aviation Week," *Aviation Week,* September 1, 1947, p. 7; J. C. Clifford, "Confused Prospects for Aircrafts," *The Magazine of Wall Street,* July 2, 1949, p. 352.
39. *Changing Times,* May 1949, p. 2.
40. Verbatim Report, Fifth Meeting of the Air Board, June 5–6, 1947, pp. 29–30, RG 340 (Secretary of the Air Force), Air Board Minutes of Meetings.
41. Statement of Hon. W. Stuart Symington, Secretary of the Air Force, Before the PAPC, November 26, 1947, p. 14, Spaatz Papers, Chief of Staff section, Secretary of the Air Force folder, Manuscript Division, The Library of Congress.
42. "Shall We Have Airplanes?" p. 159; "1949 in the Aircraft Industry," p. 100.
43. The following bald summary does not begin to do justice to the subtleties of Kaldor's argument, which, to be appreciated, must be read in the original; see *The Baroque Arsenal* (New York: Hill and Wang, 1981).
44. Statement of Hon. W. Stuart Symington, Secretary of the Air Force, Before the PAPC, November 26, 1947, p. 14, Spaatz Papers, Chief of Staff section, Secretary of the Air Force folder.
45. "Experiment at Republic," *Fortune,* February 1947, p. 125.
46. With respect to providing aid to the former Soviet Union, "Many European officials . . . say they resent the leadership role being taken by the United States, which some of them argue is an attempt to disguise how little Washington is actually doing. The Europeans say that if the United States wants to lead the coordination effort, it must lead in giving. After all, they say, the United States did not simply 'coordinate' the Marshall Plan for European recovery in 1947, it fully financed it" (Thomas L. Friedman, "Nations to Discuss Aid to Ex-U.S.S.R.," *San Francisco Chronicle,* January 22, 1982, p. A7). And just as the United States is now unable to sponsor a new Marshall Plan, so it is also unable to pay for a new Korean War—whence the spectacle of the Bush administration going hat in hand to Western Europe, the Persian Gulf oil states and Japan during 1990 and 1991 in order to procure financing for its war against Iraq.
47. Mikhail Gorbachev, "Socialism Has a Place in Quest for Democracy," *San Francisco Chronicle,* February 24, 1992, p. A2.

Notes to Appendix A.

1. In U.S. Department of State, *Foreign Relations of the United States* (hereafter *FRUS*): *1948*, vol. 3, *Western Europe* (Washington, D.C.: U.S. Government Printing Office, 1974), p. 888.
2. Landry's memorandum is in the Papers of Hoyt S. Vandenberg, Subject File, White House 1 folder, Manuscript Division, Library of Congress; Landry was the air aide to the President.
3. Navy Lieutenant Lawrence P. H. Healey, Senior Political Analyst in the Office of Naval Intelligence, Stalinism: Russian Historical Aims and Soviet Dynamic Materialism, September 16, 1948, p. 9, attached to Memorandum from Chief of Naval Intelligence to Chief of Naval Operations [Chief of Staff], September 27, 1948, National Archives Record Group (hereafter RG) 330 (Secretary of Defense), Entry 199, Office of the Administrative Secretary, Correspondence Control Section, Numerical File, September 1947–June 1950, CD 25-1-40 to CD 25-1-27, CD 25-1-39 folder; Minutes of Fourth Anti-Submarine Conference, November 28 to December 2, 1948, pp. 18–19, RG 330 (Secretary of Defense), CD 23-1-6 folder.
4. Air Vice-Marshal L. F. Pendred, C.B., M.B.E., D.F.C., letter to Major General George C. McDonald, Director of Intelligence, Department of the Air Force, December 22, 1947, p. 1, RG 18 (Army Air Force), Air Adjutant General, Mail and Records, Classified Records Section, Project Decimal File, January to October 1948, Foreign Miscellaneous, 000-800, January–March 1948 folder.
5. Pages 1, 4, RG 319 (Army Staff), Entry 154, Plans and Operations Division, Decimal File, 1946–1948, P & O 350.05, Section I (cases 1-44) folder.
6. Pages 4, 6, 8, RG 107 (Office of the Secretary of War), Entry 260, Office, Under Secretary of War, Security-Classified Correspondence, November 1945–September 1947, 370.01 to 400.2, 387, Plans for Post War Military Establishment folder.
7. Pages 1–3, RG 319 (Army Staff), Entry 154, Plans and Operations Division, Decimal File, 1946–1948, P & O 350.05, Section I, envelope Project 3560, Basic Assumptions for Civil Defense.
8. Pages 1–3, RG 319 (Army Staff), Entry 154, Plans and Operations Division, Decimal File, 1946–1948, P & O 350.05, Section 2, P & O 350.05 TS (Section II) (Cases 45-70) (except case 49) folder.
9. Pages 11–12, RG 341 (Headquarters U.S. Air Force), Entry 337, Deputy Chief of Staff, Operations, Director of Plans, Executive Office, Records Branch, General File, 1944–1953, TS No. 29 to No. 32, AAG file F-500 through F-749 folder.

10. Telegram in U.S. Department of State, *Foreign Relations of the United States* (hereafter *FRUS*): *1947*, vol. 4, *Eastern Europe; The Soviet Union* (Washington, D.C.: U.S. Government Printing Office, 1972), p. 591.
11. Records of the President's Air Policy Commission (hereafter PAPC), box 40, Harry S. Truman Library (hereafter HSTL).
12. Telegram, *FRUS: 1947,* vol. 4, *Eastern Europe; The Soviet Union,* p. 611.
13. Memorandum from Captain Thomas J. Kelly, U.S. Navy, to Chief of Naval Operations, p. 1, RG 330 (Secretary of Defense), Entry 199, Office of the Administrative Secretary, Correspondence Control Section, Numerical File, September 1947–June 1950, CD 3-1-40 to CD 3-1-21, CD 3-1-33 folder.
14. Memorandum for the Director of Intelligence from the Director of Plans and Operations, RG 319 (Army Staff), Entry 154, Plans and Operations Division, Decimal File, 1946–1948, 092 Section VI-D to Section VII (TS), P & O 092 TS (Section VII) (Class 115-125) (case 118 W/D & filed in Section VII-A) folder.
15. National Archives Collection, Xerox 2072-1, folder 1, George C. Marshall Library (hereafter GCML), Virginia Military Institute, Lexington, Virginia.
16. See the Daily Activities Report folder, RG 341 (Headquarters U.S. Air Force), Deputy Chief of Staff, Operations, Director of Plans, Executive Office, Records Branch, General File, 1944–1953, TS No. 8 to No. 9.
17. Entry for May 25, 1948, p. 2271, Diaries of James V. Forrestal, box 4, Seeley G. Mudd Manuscript Library, Princeton University.
18. Major General R. C. Macon, Military Attaché, USSR, and Brigadier General W. R. Carter, Military Air Attaché, USSR, Significant Military Trends in the Soviet Union During the Past Year, pp. 47–48, pp. 1–3, RG 319 (Army Staff), Entry 153, Plans and Operations Division, Decimal File, 1946–1948, P & O 350.05 Case 266 to 305, booklet.
19. Major General Ray T. Maddocks, Memorandum for Record, pp. 2, 5, RG 319 (Army Staff), Entry 153, Plans and Operations Division, Decimal File, 1946–1948, 091 Poland to Sardinia, P & O 091 Russia (Section I) (cases 1-) folder.
20. J.C.S. 1868/16, August 5, 1948, pp. 106–07, RG 319 (Army Staff), Entry 154, Plans and Operations Division, Decimal File, 1946–1948, 092. Section 7-A, Part 4 to Section 9 (TS), P & O, 092 TS (Section 7-A) (Part 4) (case 118 only) (Sub-Nos. 61-80) folder.
21. Minutes of the Third Meeting of the Washington Exploratory Talks on Security, June 7, 1948, *FRUS: 1948,* vol. 3, *Western Europe,* p. 157.
22. In U.S. Department of State, *Foreign Relations of the United States: 1948,* vol. 2, *Germany and Austria* (Washington, D.C.: U.S. Government Printing Office, 1973), p. 957. "However," Clay's telegram continued, "they know that the Allies also do not want war and they will continue their pressure to the point at which they believe hostilities might occur."

23. RG 330 (Secretary of Defense), Entry 199, Office of the Administrative Secretary, Correspondence Control Section, Numerical File, September 1947–June 1950, CD 18-1-36 to CD 18 1-8, CD 18-1-25 folder.
24. Memorandum in *FRUS: 1948,* vol. 3, *Western Europe,* pp. 185–87.
25. Memorandum in *FRUS: 1948,* vol. 3, *Western Europe,* p. 193.
26. Joint Chiefs of Staff 1723/1, pp. 25–28, 30, 34, 38 and *passim,* RG 165 (Army-CAD), Decimal File, 1948, 250.041 to 381, SG 122 (TS) A 49-175, (Sla (1) (a)), CSCAD 381, 16 Aug 48, Case of "General Guidance for the Office of Civil Defense Planning" folder.
27. State Department Policy Planning Staff, Factors Affecting the Nature of the U.S. Defense Arrangements in the Light of Soviet Policies, June 23, 1948, p. 4, RG 330 (Secretary of Defense), Entry 199, box 4, Office of the Administrative Secretary, Correspondence Control Section, Numerical File, September 1947–June 1950, CD 2-2-2 folder.
28. Lovett's comments are on pp. 1–2 of the meeting minutes, and the quotation is taken from pp. 3–4 of the attached memorandum, RG 218 (U.S. Joint Chiefs of Staff), Entry Leahy, Chairman's File, 1942–1948, Folders 26-32, Folder No. 26, Western European Union 1948.
29. Central Intelligence Agency, Possibility of Direct Soviet Military Action During 1948–49, September 16, 1948, pp. 1–4, RG 330 (Secretary of Defense), Entry 199, Office of the Administrative Secretary, Correspondence Control Section, Numerical File, September 1947–June 1950, CD 12-1-29 to CS [*sic*] 12-1-26, CD 12-1-26 folder.
30. P. H. Healey, Stalinism: Russian Historical Aims and Soviet Dynamic Materialism, September 16, 1948, pp. 1–2, 6–9, attached to Memorandum from Chief of Naval Intelligence to Chief of Naval Operations, September 27, 1948, RG 330 (Secretary of Defense), Entry 199, Office of the Administrative Secretary, Correspondence Control Section, Numerical File, September 1947–June 1950, CD 25-1-40 to CD 25-1-27, CD 25-1-39 folder.
31. In *FRUS: 1948,* vol. 2, *Germany and Austria,* pp. 1195–97. Prior to becoming ambassador to the U.S.S.R., Smith had been a career army officer—he retired with the rank of general—who served as chief of staff to General Dwight D. Eisenhower during World War II. That Smith's intelligence skills were held in high regard is shown by the fact that Truman in 1950 chose him as the new director of the Central Intelligence Agency.
32. Landry's memorandum is in the Papers of Hoyt S. Vandenberg, Subject File, White House 1 folder, Manuscript Division, Library of Congress.
33. RG 319 (Army Staff), Entry 154, Plans and Operations Division, Decimal File, 1946–1948, 381 Section 5-A Part 2 to Section 5-A Part 6 (TS), P & O (Section 5-A) (Case 88 only) (Part 6) (Sub-numbers 131-) folder.

34. See, for accounts of these two discussions, *FRUS: 1948,* vol. 3, *Western Europe,* pp. 281 and 888, respectively.
35. CIA Memorandum No. 76, November 19, 1948, p. 2, and attached Enclosure A, Comments on Selected Fields of the Soviet Economy (same date), pp. 1–3, 5, RG 330 (Secretary of Defense), Entry 199, Office of the Administrative Secretary, Correspondence Control Section, Numerical File, September 1947–June 1950, CD 6-3-45 to CD 6-3-32, CD 6-3-44 folder.
36. *FRUS: 1948,* vol. 3, *Western Europe,* pp. 284–85.
37. L.C. Stevens letter to Forrestal, December 10, 1948, pp. 1–2, RG 330 (Secretary of Defense), Entry 199, Office of the Administrative Secretary, Correspondence Control Section, Numerical File, September 1947–June 1950, CD 6-3-45 to CD 6-3-32, CD 6-3-41 folder.
38. Telegram in *FRUS: 1948,* vol. 4, *Eastern Europe; The Soviet Union* (Washington, D.C. U.S. Government Printing Office, 1974), p. 943.
39. Ibid., pp. 943–46.

Notes To Appendix B.

1. William Morris, ed., *The American Heritage Dictionary of the English Language* (Boston: American Heritage and Houghton Mifflin, 1969), p. 285.
2. Diaries of James V. Forrestal, March 4, 1948, p. 2115, box 4, Seeley G. Mudd Manuscript Library (hereafter SGMML), Princeton University.
3. "Forrestal Fight on Reds Reported," *New York Times,* November 25, 1950, p. 30.
4. W. Stuart Symington letters to Winthrop Aldrich: April 1, 1948, Papers of W. Stuart Symington, box 1, Harry S. Truman Library; April 5, 1948, Papers of Winthrop W. Aldrich, Correspondence File 2, Baker Library, Harvard Business School.
5. W. Stuart Symington Memorandum for General Vandenberg, October 13, 1948, Papers of Hoyt S. Vandenberg, Subject File, Budget-1948 folder, Manuscript Division, Library of Congress; Symington letter to Mr. Fred Rentschler, January 18, 1949, Symington Papers, box 10.
6. James V. Forrestal letter to Winthrop Aldrich, Esq., Aldrich Papers, box 70.
7. William J. Donovan letter, "Personal and Confidential," to Hon. James V. Forrestal, October 6, 1947, and attached memorandum, and Forrestal letter to General William J. Donovan, October 9, 1947, all in the Papers of James V. Forrestal, box 75, SGMML.
8. Excerpts from Telephone Conversation between Honorable James Forrestal, Secretary of Defense, and Mr. Jackson, January 22, 1948, box 93; Forrestal

letter to Mr. Edward Weeks, May 13, 1948, box 82; Excerpts of Telephone Conversation between Honorable James Forrestal and Mr. Hamilton Fish, July 1, 1948, box 79; all in Forrestal Papers.

SELECTED BIBLIOGRAPHY

MANUSCRIPT SOURCES

Harry S. Truman Library, Independence, Missouri

Eben A. Ayers Papers
Clark M. Clifford Papers
George M. Elsey Papers
Thomas K. Finletter Papers
W. Stuart Symington Papers
Harry S. Truman Papers
James E. Webb Papers
Records of the President's Air Policy Commission (Finletter Commission)

Seeley G. Mudd Library, Princeton University, Princeton, New Jersey

Ferdinand Eberstadt Papers
James V. Forrestal Diaries
James V. Forrestal Papers
Arthur Krock Papers
David E. Lilienthal Papers

Manuscript Division, Library of Congress, Washington, D.C.

Robert E. Gross Papers
Glenn L. Martin Papers
Carl A. Spaatz Papers
Hoyt S. Vandenberg Papers

George C. Marshall Library, Virginia Military Institute, Lexington, Virginia

George C. Marshall Papers

National Archives, Washington, D.C., and Suitland, Maryland

Records of the Armed Services, Department of Defense, Department of State, and unprinted hearings of the Senate Armed Services Committee (see footnotes for detailed citations)

ORAL HISTORIES

Harry S. Truman Library, Independence, Missouri

Eban A. Ayers
Karl R. Bendetsen
Lucius D. Clay
Clark M. Clifford
Matthew J. Connelly
William H. Draper, Jr.
George M. Elsey
Gordon Gray
Thomas K. Finletter
Leon H. Keyserling
Felix E. Larkin
Marx Leva
Robert A. Lovett
Wilfred J. McNeil
Charles S. Murphy
Edwin G. Nourse
John H. Ohly
Frank Pace, Jr.
Samuel I. Rosenman
John W. Snyder
John L. Sullivan
W. Stuart Symington
James E. Webb (a joint interview that included Charles Murphy, Richard Neustadt and David Stowe in addition to Webb)
Eugene M. Zuckert

UNITED STATES GOVERNMENT DOCUMENTS

U.S. Congress: General

Congressional Record. 1947–1949.

U.S. Congress: House

Committee on Appropriations. *Hearings on Supplemental National Defense Appropriations Bill for 1948.* 80th Cong., 2nd sess., 1948.

Committee on Armed Services. *Hearings on Universal Military Training.* 80th Cong., 2nd sess., 1948.

Report of the Air Coordinating Committee, 1947. 80th Cong., 2nd sess., 1948. H. Doc. 524.

Report of the Air Coordinating Committee, 1948. 81st Cong., 1st sess., 1949. H. Doc. 59.

Report to the Air Coordinating Committee of the Standing Subcommittee on Demobilization of the Aircraft Industry. 80th Cong., 1st sess., 1947. H. Doc. 148.

U.S. Congress: Senate

Committee on Appropriations. *Hearings on Supplemental National Defense Appropriations Bill for 1948.* 80th Cong., 2nd sess., 1948.

Committee on Military Affairs. *War Plants Disposal–Aircraft Plants. Hearings before the Surplus Property Subcommittee of the Committee on Military Affairs and Industrial Reorganization Subcommittee of the Special Committee on Economic Policy and Planning pursuant to S.R. 46 and S.R. 33.* 79th Cong., 1st sess., 1945.

Special Committee Investigating the National Defense Program. *Investigation of the National Defense Program. Hearings before a special committee investigating the national defense program pursuant to S.R. 55.* 79th Cong., 1st sess., 1945.

U.S. Congress: Joint Committees

Congressional Aviation Policy Board. *National Aviation Policy.* 80th Congress, 2nd session, 1948. S. Rep. 949. Joint Committee Print.

Executive Branch: Documents, Collections, Reports, Histories, Etc.

Gaddis, John Lewis, and Thomas H. Etzold, eds. *Containment: Documents on American Policy and Strategy. 1945–1950.* New York: Columbia University Press, 1978.

Public Papers of the Presidents of the United States. Washington D.C.: Office of the Federal Register, National Archives and Records Service, 1963– . Harry S. Truman, 1947–1950.

Rearden, Steven L. *History of the Office of the Secretary of Defense.* Vol. 1, *The Formative Years. 1947–1950.* Washington, D.C.: Office of the Secretary of Defense, Historical Office, 1984.

U.S. Air Coordinating Committee. *A Statement of Certain Policies of the Executive Branch of the Government in the General Field of Aviation.* Washington, D.C.: U.S. Department of Commerce, 1947.

U.S. Air Coordinating Committee. *First Report of the Air Coordinating Committee for 1946.* Washington, D.C.: U.S. Department of State, 1947.

U.S. Air Coordinating Committee. *Report of the Subcommittee on Demobilization of the Aircraft Industry.* Washington, D.C.: Government Printing Office, 1945.

U.S. Bureau of the Census. *Historical Statistics of the United States, Colonial Times to 1970.* Washington, D.C.: U.S. Department of Commerce, 1975.

U.S. Committee on the National Security Organization. *Task Force Report on the National Security Organization (Appendix G).* Washington, D.C.: Government Printing Office, 1949.

U.S. Department of Defense. *First Report of the Secretary of Defense, 1948.* Washington, D.C.: Government Printing Office, 1949.

U.S. Department of State. *Foreign Relations of the United States: 1947.* Vol. 2, *Council of Foreign Ministers; Germany and Austria.* Vol. 3, *The British Commonwealth; Europe.* Vol. 4, *Eastern Europe; The Soviet Union.* Washington, D.C.: Government Printing Office, 1972.

U.S. Department of State. *Foreign Relations of the United States: 1948.* Vol. 2, *Germany and Austria.* Vol. 3, *Western Europe.* Vol. 4, *Eastern Europe; The Soviet Union.* Washington, D.C.: Government Printing Office, 1973–1974.

U.S. Department of State. *Foreign Relations of the United States: 1949.* Vol. 3, *Council of Foreign Ministers; Germany and Austria.* Vol. 5, *Eastern Europe; The Soviet Union.* Washington, D.C.: Government Printing Office, 1974, 1976.

U.S. President's Air Policy Commission. *Survival in the Air Age.* Washington, D.C.: Government Printing Office, 1948.

BUSINESS JOURNALS AND PERIODICALS

Barron's National Business and Financial Weekly
Business Week
Commercial and Financial Chronicle
Fortune
The Magazine of Wall Street
The Wall Street Journal (San Francisco edition)

TRADE JOURNALS

Aero Digest
American Machinist
Automotive Industries
Automotive and Aviation Industries
Aviation Week (formerly *Aviation News*)
Banking
Factory Management and Maintenance
Mechanical Engineering
National Petroleum News
Product Engineering
Steel
Technology and Culture
The Iron Age
Tool Engineer

MISCELLANEOUS PERIODICALS AND MAGAZINES

Newsweek
Soviet Russia Today
The New Republic
The New York Times
Time
U.S. News & World Report

MEMOIRS, DIARIES AND PERSONAL ACCOUNTS

Anderson, Jack, with James Boyd. *Confessions of a Muckraker: The Inside Story of Life in Washington During the Truman, Eisenhower, Kennedy and Johnson Years.* New York: Random House, 1979.

Bernstein, Carl. *Loyalties: A Son's Memoir.* New York: Simon and Schuster, 1989.

Bradley, Omar N., and Clay Blair. *A General's Life: An Autobiography by General of the Army Omar N. Bradley and Clay Blair.* New York: Simon and Schuster, 1983.

Byrnes, James F. *All In One Lifetime.* New York: Harper and Brothers, 1958.

Clifford, Clark, with Richard Holbrooke. *Counsel to the President: A Memoir.* New York: Random House, 1991.

Collins, Joseph Lawton. *Lightning Joe: An Autobiography.* Baton Rouge: Louisiana State University Press, 1979.

Cutler, Robert. *No Time for Rest.* Boston: Little, Brown, 1965.

Ferrell, Robert H., ed. *The Autobiography of Harry S. Truman.* Boulder: Colorado Associated University Press, 1980.

———, ed. *Dear Bess: The Letters from Harry to Bess Truman, 1910–1959.* New York: W. W. Norton, 1983.

———, ed. *Off the Record: The Private Papers of Harry S. Truman.* New York: Harper and Row, 1980.

Hechler, Ken. *Working with Truman: A Personal Memoir of the White House Years.* New York: Putnam, 1982.

Hillman, William. *Mr. President: The First Publication from the Personal Diaries, Private Letters, Papers, and a Revealing Interview of Harry S. Truman, Thirty-second President of the United States.* New York: Farrar, Straus and Young, 1952.

Jones, Joseph M. *The Fifteen Weeks.* New York: Viking Press, 1955.

Kennan, George F. *Memoirs.* Vol. 1, *1925–1950.* Vol. 2, *1950–1963.* Boston: Little, Brown, 1967, 1972.

Krock, Arthur. *Memoirs: Sixty Years on the Firing Line.* New York: Funk and Wagnalls, 1968.

Lilienthal, David E. *The Journals of David E. Lilienthal.* Vol. 2, *The Atomic Energy Years 1945–1950.* New York: Harper and Row, 1964.

Millis, Walter, ed., with the collaboration of E. S. Duffield. *The Forrestal Diaries.* New York: Viking Press, 1951.

Poen, Monte M., ed. *Letters Home.* New York: Putnam, 1984.

———, ed. *Strictly Personal and Confidential: The Letters Harry Truman Never Mailed.* Boston: Little, Brown, 1982.

Reston, James. *Deadline: A Memoir.* New York: Random House, 1991.

Smith, Jean Edward, ed. *The Papers of General Lucius D. Clay: Germany, 1945–1949.* Vol. 2. Bloomington, Ind.: Indiana University Press, 1974.

Smith, Walter Bedell. *My Three Years in Moscow.* Philadelphia: J. B. Lippincott Company, 1950.

Stimson, Henry L., and McGeorge Bundy. *On Active Service in Peace and War.* New York: Harper and Brothers, 1947.

Sulzberger, C. L. *A Long Row of Candles: Memoirs and Diaries, 1934–1954.* New York: Macmillan, 1969.

Truman, Harry S. *Memoirs.* Vol. 1, *Year of Decisions.* Vol. 2, *Years of Trial and Hope.* Garden City, N.Y.: Doubleday, 1955.

Truman, Margaret. *Letters from Father: The Truman Family's Personal Correspondence.* New York: Arbor House, 1981.

———. *Where the Buck Stops: The Personal and Private Writings of Harry S. Truman.* New York: Warner Books, 1989.

Vandenberg, Arthur H., Jr., ed., with Joe Alex Morris. *The Private Papers of Senator Vandenberg.* Boston: Houghton Mifflin, 1952.

Wilson, Eugene E. *Kitty Hawk to Sputnik to Polaris: A Contemporary Account of the Struggle over Military and Commercial Air Policy in the United States.* Barre, Mass.: Barre Gazette, 1960.

———. *Slipstream: The Autobiography of an Air Craftsman.* 2nd ed. New York: Science Press, 1965.

BOOKS AND PAMPHLETS

Abels, Jules. *The Truman Scandals.* Chicago: H. Regnery, 1956.

Aerospace Industries Association of America. *Aerospace Facts and Figures for 1960.* 8th ed. Washington, D.C.: American Aviation Publications, 1960.

Aircraft Industries Association of America. *The Aircraft Year Book for 1948.* 30th ed. Washington, D.C.: Lincoln Press, 1948.

Aircraft Industries Association of America. *The Aircraft Year Book for 1950.* 32nd ed. Washington, D.C.: Lincoln Press, 1970.

Albion, Robert G., and Robert H. Connery. *Forrestal and the Navy.* New York: Columbia University Press, 1962.

Alperovitz, Gar. *Atomic Diplomacy: Hiroshima and Potsdam: The Use of the Atomic Bomb and the American Confrontation With Soviet Power.* Expanded and updated edition. New York: Penguin Books, 1985.

———. *Cold War Essays.* Garden City, N.Y.: Anchor Books, 1970.

Ambrose, Stephen E. *Eisenhower: Soldier, General of the Army, President-Elect, 1890–1952.* New York: Simon and Schuster, 1983.

Andrews, Marshall. *Disaster Through Air Power.* New York: Rinehart and Co., 1950.

Arnold, General H. H. *Global Mission.* New York: Harper and Brothers, 1949.

Backer, John H. *Winds of History: The German Years of Lucius DuBignon Clay.* New York: Van Nostrand Reinhold, 1983.

Baldwin, David A. *Economic Development and American Foreign Policy, 1943–1962.* Chicago: University of Chicago Press, 1966.

Baldwin, Hanson W. *Power and Politics: The Price of Security in the Atomic Age.* Claremont, Calif.: Claremont College Press, 1950.

———. *The Price of Power.* New York: Harper and Brothers, 1947. Published for the Council on Foreign Relations.

Ballard, Jack Stokes. *The Shock of Peace: Military and Economic Demobilization After World War II.* Washington, D.C.: University Press of America, 1983.

Balogh, Thomas. *The Dollar Crisis: Causes and Cures. A Report of the Fabian Society.* Oxford: Basil Blackwell, 1949; reprint ed., *The Dollar Crisis.* New York; Arno Press, 1979.

Barghoorn, Frederick C. *The Soviet Image of the United States: A Study in Distortion.* New York: Harcourt, Brace and Co., 1950.

Barnet, Richard J. *The Economy of Death.* New York: Atheneum, 1970.

———. *Roots of War: The Men and Institutions.* New York: Atheneum, 1972.

Bell, Coral. *Negotiation from Strength: A Study in the Politics of Power.* New York: Alfred A. Knopf, 1973.

Berman, Larry. *The Office of Management and Budget and the Presidency, 1921–1979.* Princeton: Princeton University Press, 1979.

Bernstein, Barton., ed. *Politics and Policies of the Truman Administration.* Chicago: Quadrangle, 1970.

———. "America in War and Peace: The Test of Liberalism." In *Twentieth Century America: Recent Interpretations,* ed. Barton Bernstein and Allen Matusow. New York: Harcourt, Brace and World, 1969.

Block, Fred L. *The Origins of International Economic Disorder: A Study of United States International Monetary Policy from World War II to the Present.* Berkeley: University of California Press, 1977.

Borden, William S. *The Pacific Alliance: United States Foreign Economic Policy and Japanese Trade Recovery, 1947–1955.* Madison: University of Wisconsin Press, 1984.

Borklund, C. W. *Men of the Pentagon: Forrestal to McNamara.* New York: Praeger, 1966.

———. *The Department of Defense.* New York: Praeger, 1968.

Borowski, Harry R. *A Hollow Threat: Strategic Air Power and Containment Before Korea.* Westport, Conn.: Greenwood Press, 1982.

Boyd, Alexander. *The Soviet Air Force Since 1918.* New York: Stein and Day, 1977.

Bright, Charles D. *The Jet Makers: The Aerospace Industry from 1945 to 1972.* Lawrence, Kans.: The Regents Press of Kansas, 1978.

Burns, Richard Dean, ed. *Guide to American Foreign Relations Since 1700.* Santa Barbara, Calif.: ABC-CLIO, 1983.

Caraley, Demetrios. *The Politics of Military Unification.* New York: Columbia University Press, 1966.

Chernow, Ron. *The House of Morgan: An American Banking Dynasty and the Rise of Modern Finance.* New York: Atlantic Monthly Press, 1990.

Cochran, Bert. *Harry Truman and the Crisis Presidency.* New York: Funk and Wagnalls, 1973.

Cole, Leonard A. *Clouds of Secrecy: The Army's Germ Warfare Tests over Populated Areas.* Totowa, N.J.: Rowman & Littlefield, 1988.

Condit, Kenneth W. *The History of the Joint Chiefs of Staff: The Joint Chiefs of Staff and National Policy.* Vol. 2, *1947–1949.* Wilmington, Del.: Michael Glazier, 1979.

Connery, Robert Hough. *The Navy and the Industrial Mobilization in World War II.* Princeton: Princeton University Press, 1951.

Cray, Ed. *General of the Army: George C. Marshall Soldier and Statesman.* New York: W. W. Norton, 1990.

Cumings, Bruce., ed. *Child of Conflict: The Korean-American Relationship, 1943–1953.* Seattle: University of Washington Press, 1983.

Cunningham, William Glenn. "Postwar Developments and the Location of the Aircraft Industry in 1950." In *The History of the American Aircraft Industry: An Anthology,* edited by G. R. Simonson. Cambridge, Mass.: Massachussetts Institute of Technology Press, 1968.

Daniels, Jonathan. *The Man of Independence.* Philadelphia: Lippincott, 1950.

Davis, Vincent. *Postwar Defense Policy and the U.S. Navy, 1943–1946.* Chapel Hill: University of North Carolina Press, 1966.

Day, John S. *Subcontracting Policy in the Airframe Industry.* Boston: Harvard University Press, 1956.

De Seversky, Alexander P. *Air Power: Key to Survival.* New York: Simon and Schuster, 1950.

Deutscher, Isaac. *Stalin: A Political Biography.* New York: Vintage Books, 1960.

Dinerstein, Herbert S. *War and the Soviet Union: Nuclear Weapons and the Revolution in Soviet Military and Political Thinking.* New York: Praeger, 1959.

Divine, Robert A. *Foreign Policy and U.S. Presidential Elections: 1940–1948.* New York: Franklin Watts, 1974.

———. *Second Chance: The Triumph of Internationalism in America During World War II.* New York: Atheneum, 1967.

Djilas, Milovan. *Conversations with Stalin.* Harmondsworth, England: Penguin Books, 1962.

Doenecke, Justus D. *Not to the Swift: The Old Isolationists in the Cold War Era.* Lewisburg, Pa.: Bucknell University Press, 1979.

Domhoff, G. William. *The Powers That Be: Processes of Ruling Class Domination in America.* New York: Vintage Books, 1979.

Donovan, Robert J. *Conflict and Crisis: The Presidency of Harry S. Truman, 1945–1948.* New York: W. W. Norton, 1977.

———. *Tumultuous Years: The Presidency of Harry S. Truman, 1949–1953.* New York: W. W. Norton, 1982.

Druks, Herbert. *Harry S. Truman and the Russians, 1945–1953.* New York: Robert Speller and Sons, 1966.

DuBoff, Richard B. *Accumulation & Power: An Economic History of the United States.* Armonk, N.Y.: M. E. Sharpe, 1989.

Dunar, Andrew J. *The Truman Scandals and the Politics of Morality.* Columbia, Mo.: University of Missouri Press, 1984.

Eglin, James Meikle. *Air Defense in the Nuclear Age: The Post–War Development of American and Soviet Strategic Defense Systems.* New York: Garland Publishing, 1988.

Employment Research Associations. *A Shift in Military Spending to America's Cities: What It Means to Four Cities and the Nation.* Washington, D.C.: United States Conference of Mayors, 1988.

Ferrell, Robert H. *Harry S. Truman and the Modern Presidency.* Boston: Little, Brown, 1983.

———. *Truman, A Centenary Remembrance.* New York: Viking Press, 1984.

Fitzgerald, A. Ernest. *The High Priests of Waste.* New York: W. W. Norton, 1972.

Fleming, D. F. *The Cold War and Its Origins, 1917–1960.* Vol. 1: *1917–1950.* Garden City, N.Y.: Doubleday, 1961.

Fontaine, André. *History of the Cold War: From the October Revolution to the Korean War, 1917–1968.* Translated by D. D. Paige. New York: Vintage Books, 1968.

Freeland, Richard M. *The Truman Doctrine and the Origins of McCarthyism: Foreign Policy, Domestic Politics and Internal Security, 1946–1948.* New York: Schocken Books, 1974.

Freudenthal, Elsbeth E. "The Aviation Business in the 1930s." In *The History of the American Aircraft Industry: An Anthology,* edited by G. R. Simonson. Cambridge, Mass.: Massachussetts Institute of Technology Press, 1968.

Fulbright, J. W. *The Crippled Giant: American Foreign Policy and Its Domestic Consequences.* New York: Random House, 1972.

Furer, Howard B., ed. *Harry S. Truman 1884– : Chronology, Documents, Bibliographic Aids.* Dobbs Ferry, N.Y.: Oceana, 1970.

Futrell, Robert Frank. *Ideas, Concepts, Doctrine: A History of Basic Thinking in the United States Air Force, 1907–1964.* New York: Arno Press, 1980.

Gaddis, John Lewis. *Strategies of Containment: A Critical Appraisal of Postwar American National Security Policy.* New York: Oxford University Press, 1982.

Gardner, Lloyd C. *Architects of Illusion: Men and Ideas in American Foreign Policy, 1941–1949.* Chicago: Quadrangle, 1970.

———. *A Covenant with Power: America and World Order from Wilson to Reagan.* New York: Oxford University Press, 1984.

Garthoff, Raymond. *Soviet Strategy in the Nuclear Age.* New York: Praeger, 1958.

Gati, Charles, ed. *Caging the Bear: Containment and the Cold War.* Indianapolis: Bobbs-Merrill, 1974.

George, Alexander L., and Richard Smoke. *Deterrence in American Foreign Policy: Theory and Practice.* New York: Columbia University Press, 1974.

Gerhardt, James M. *The Draft and Public Policy: Issues in Military Manpower Procurement 1945–1970.* Columbus, Ohio: Ohio State University Press, 1971.

Goldberg, Alfred, ed. *A History of the United States Air Force, 1907–1957.* Princeton: Van Nostrand, 1957.

Goodwin, Jacob. *Brotherhood of Arms: General Dynamics and the Business of Defending America.* New York: Times Books, 1985.

Gosnell, Harold F. *Truman's Crises: A Political Biography of Harry S. Truman.* Westport, Conn.: Greenwood Press, 1980.

Hamby, Alonzo L. *Beyond the New Deal: Harry S. Truman and American Liberalism.* New York: Columbia University Press, 1973.

Hamilton, Walton. *The Politics of Industry.* New York: Alfred A. Knopf, 1957.

Hammond, Paul Y. *Organizing for Defense: The American Military Establishment in the 20th Century.* Princeton: Princeton University Press, 1961.

Hammond, Paul Y., W. R. Schilling, and G. H. Snyder. *Strategy, Politics and Defense Budgets.* New York: Columbia University Press, 1962.

Harris, Seymour, ed. *Economic Reconstruction.* New York: McGraw-Hill, 1945.

Hartmann, Susan M. *Truman and the 80th Congress.* Columbia, Mo.: University of Missouri Press, 1971.

Haynes, Richard F. *The Awesome Power: Harry S. Truman as Commander in Chief.* Baton Rouge: Louisiana State University Press, 1973.

Heller, Francis H., ed. *Economics and the Truman Administration.* Lawrence, Kans.: Regents Press of Kansas, 1981.

Herken, Gregg. *The Winning Weapon: The Atomic Bomb in the Cold War, 1945–1950.* New York: Alfred A. Knopf, 1980.

Herz, Martin F. *Beginnings of the Cold War.* Bloomington: Indiana University Press, 1966.

Herzog, Arthur. *The War-Peace Establishment.* New York: Harper and Row, 1963.

Hitch, Charles J. and Roland N. McKean. *The Economics of Defense in the Nuclear Age.* Cambridge, Mass.: Harvard University Press, 1967.

Holloway, David. *The Soviet Union and the Arms Race.* New Haven: Yale University Press, 1983.

Horowitz, David, ed. *Containment and Revolution.* Boston: Beacon Press, 1967.

———, ed. *Corporations and the Cold War.* New York: Monthly Review Press, 1967.

Huntington, Samuel P. "Interservice Competition and the Political Roles of the Armed Services." In *Total War and Cold War: Problems in Civilian Control of the Military,* edited by Harry L. Coles. Columbus, Ohio: Ohio State University Press, 1962.

———. *The Common Defense.* New York: Columbia University Press, 1961.

———. *The Soldier and the State.* Cambridge, Mass.: Belknap Press, Harvard University Press, 1964.

Huthmacher, J. Joseph, ed. *The Truman Years: The Reconstruction of Postwar America.* Hinsdale, Ill.: The Dryden Press, 1972.

Huzar, Elias. *The Purse and the Sword: Control of the Army by Congress Through Military Appropriations, 1933–1950.* Ithaca, N.Y.: Cornell University Press, 1950.

Ingham, John N. *Biographical Dictionary of American Business Leaders.* Westport, Conn.: Greenwood Press, 1983.

Isaacson, Walter, and Evan Thomas. *The Wise Men: Six Friends and the World They Made: Acheson, Bohlen, Harriman, Kennan, Lovett, McCloy.* New York: Simon and Schuster, 1986.

Jackson, Robert. *The Red Falcons.* Brighton, Okla.: Clifton Books, 1970.

Jacobs, Clyde E., and John F. Gallagher. *The Selective Service Act: A Case Study of the Governmental Process.* New York: Dodd, Mead, 1967.

Jacobson, C. G. *Soviet Strategy—Soviet Foreign Policy.* Glasgow: R. Maclehose and Co., 1972.

Jourbert, Air Chief Marshal Sir Philip, RAF (Ret.). "Long Range Air Attack." In *The Soviet Air and Rocket Forces,* edited by Asher Lee. New York: Praeger, 1959.

Kaldor, Mary. *The Baroque Arsenal.* New York: Hill and Wang, 1981.

Kaufman, Richard F. *The War Profiteers.* Indianapolis: Bobbs-Merrill, 1970.

Kennedy, Paul. *The Rise and Fall of the Great Powers: Economic Change and Military Conflict from 1500 to 2000.* New York: Random House, 1987.

Kilmarx, Robert A. *A History of Soviet Air Power.* New York: Praeger, 1962.

Kinnard, Douglas. *The Secretary of Defense.* Lexington, Ky.: University of Kentucky Press, 1980.

Kirkendall, Richard S., ed. *The Truman Period as a Research Field.* Columbia, Mo.: University of Missouri Press, 1967.

———, ed. *The Truman Period as a Research Field: A Reappraisal, 1972.* Columbia, Mo.: University of Missouri Press, 1974.

Kolko, Gabriel, and Joyce Kolko. *The Limits of Power: The World and U.S. Foreign Policy, 1945–1954.* New York: Harper and Row, 1972.

Kolodziej, Edward A. *The Uncommon Defense and Congress, 1945–1963.* Columbus: Ohio State University Press, 1966.

Kraft, Joseph. *Profiles in Power: A Washington Insight.* New York: New American Library, 1958.

Krepon, Michael. *Strategic Stalemate: Nuclear Weapons and Arms Control in American Politics.* New York: St. Martin's Press, 1984.

Lacey, Michael J., ed. *The Truman Presidency.* New York: New York University Press, 1989.

LaFeber, Walter. *America, Russia, and the Cold War, 1945–1975.* 5th ed. New York: Alfred A. Knopf, 1985.

Leary, William M., ed. *The Central Intelligence Agency: History and Documents.* Birmingham: University of Alabama Press, 1984.

Lee, Asher. *The Soviet Air Force.* 2nd ed. London: Gerald Duckworth, 1952.

———, ed. *The Soviet Air and Rocket Forces.* New York: Praeger, 1959.

Lippmann, Walter. *The Cold War: A Study in U.S. Foreign Policy.* New York: Harper and Row, 1972.

MacDonald, Callum A. *Korea: The War Before Vietnam.* New York: Free Press, 1987.

Marzani, Carl. *We Can Be Friends.* New York: Topical Book Publishers, 1952.

McCartney, Laton. *Friends in High Places: The Bechtel Story: The Most Secret Corporation and How It Engineered the World.* New York: Simon and Schuster, 1988.

MccGwire, Michael. *Military Objectives in Soviet Foreign Policy.* Washington, D.C.: Brookings Institution, 1987.

McConnell, Grant. *Private Power and American Democracy.* New York: Alfred A. Knopf, 1966.

McCormick, Thomas J. *America's Half-Century: United States Foreign Policy in the Cold War.* Baltimore: Johns Hopkins University Press, 1989.

McCoy, Alfred W. *The Politics of Heroin: CIA Complicity in the Global Drug Trade.* Brooklyn, N.Y.: Lawrence Hill Books, 1991.

McCoy, Donald R. *The Presidency of Harry S. Truman.* Lawrence, Kans.: University Press of Kansas, 1984.

McLellan, David S. *Dean Acheson: The State Department Years.* New York: Dodd, Mead, 1976.

McNaughton, Frank, and Walter Hehmeyer. *Harry Truman, President.* New York: Wittlesey House, 1948.

Messer, Robert L. *The End of an Alliance: James F. Byrnes, Roosevelt, Truman and the Origins of the Cold War.* Chapel Hill: University of North Carolina Press, 1982.

Miles, Carroll F. *The Office of the Secretary of Defense, 1947–1953: A Study in Administrative Theory.* New York: Garland Publishing, 1988.

Miller, Merle. *Plain Speaking: An Oral Biography of Harry S. Truman.* New York: Berkley Books, 1973.

Millis, Walter. *Arms and Men: A Study of American Military History.* New Brunswick, N.J.: Rutgers University Press, 1956.

———, et al. *Arms and the State: Civil-Military Elements in National Policy.* New York: Twentieth-Century Fund, 1958.

Mills, C. Wright. *The Power Elite.* New York: Oxford University Press, 1956.

Morris, Charles R. *Iron Destinies, Lost Opportunities: The Arms Race Between the U.S.A. and the U.S.S.R., 1945–1987.* New York: Harper and Row, 1988.

Nagai, Yonosuke and Akira Iryie, eds. *The Origins of the Cold War in Asia.* New York: Columbia University Press, 1977.

Nash, Henry T. *American Foreign Policy: Changing Perspectives on National Security.* Homewood, Ill.: Dorsey Press, 1978.

Nelson, Donald M. *Arsenal of Democracy: The Story of American War Production.* New York: Harcourt, Brace and Co., 1946.

Neustadt, Richard E. *Presidential Power: The Politics of Leadership from FDR to Carter.* New York: John Wiley and Sons, 1980.

O'Ballance, Edgar. *The Red Army: A Short History.* New York: Praeger, 1964.

Paterson, Thomas Graham, ed. *Cold War Critics: Alternatives to American Foreign Policy in the Truman Years.* Chicago: Quadrangle, 1971.

———. *Meeting the Communist Threat: Truman to Reagan.* New York: Oxford University Press, 1988.

———. *On Every Front: The Making of the Cold War.* New York: W. W. Norton, 1979.

———. *Soviet-American Confrontation: Postwar Reconstruction and the Origins of the Cold War.* Baltimore: Johns Hopkins Press, 1973.

Peltason, Jack W. *The Reconversion Controversy.* The Inter-University Case Program, no. 17. New York: Bobbs-Merrill, 1950.

Pemberton, William E. *Harry S. Truman: Fair Dealer and Cold Warrior.* Boston: Twayne Publishers, 1989.

Phillips, Cabell. *The Truman Presidency: The History of a Triumphant Succession.* New York: Macmillan, 1966.

Pogue, Forrest C. *George C. Marshall.* Vol. 1, *Education of a General, 1880–1939.* New York: Viking Press, 1963.

———. *George C. Marshall.* Vol. 2, *Ordeal and Hope, 1939–1942.* New York: Viking Press, 1965.

———. *George C. Marshall.* Vol. 3, *Organizer of Victory, 1943–1945.* New York: Viking Press, 1973.

Popper, Frank. *The President's Commissions.* New York: Twentieth Century Fund, 1970.

Prados, John. *The Soviet Estimate: U.S. Intelligence Analysis and Russian Military Strength.* New York: Dial Press, 1982.

Rae, John Bell. *Climb to Greatness: The American Aircraft Industry, 1920–1960.* Cambridge, Mass.: The MIT Press, 1968.

RAND Corporation. *The RAND Corporation: The First Fifteen Years.* Santa Monica, Calif.: RAND Corporation, 1963.

Rapoport, Anatol. *The Big Two: Soviet-American Perceptions of Foreign Policy.* New York: Bobbs-Merrill, 1971.

Rearden, Steven L. *The Evolution of American Strategic Doctrine: Paul H. Nitze and the Soviet Challenge.* Boulder, Colo.: Westview Press, 1984.

Riddle, Donald H. *The Truman Committee: A Study in Congressional Responsibility.* New Brunswick, N.J.: Rutgers University Press, 1964.

Rogow, Arnold A. *James Forrestal: A Study of Personality, Politics and Policy.* New York: Macmillan, 1963.

Rose, Lisle A. *Dubious Victory: The United States and the End of W. W. 2.* Kent, Ohio: Kent State University Press, 1973.

Schaffer, Ronald. *Wings of Judgment: American Bombing in World War II.* New York: Oxford University Press, 1985.

Schnabel, James F. *The History of the Joint Chiefs of Staff: The Joint Chiefs of Staff and National Policy.* Vol. 1, *1945–1947.* Wilmington, Del.: Michael Glazier, 1979.

Schoenebaum, Eleanora W., ed. *Political Profiles: The Truman Years.* New York: Facts on File, 1978.

Schriftgiesser, Karl. *Business Comes of Age: The Impact of the Committee for Economic Development, 1942–1960.* New York: Harper and Brothers, 1960.

Schulzinger, Robert D. *The Wise Men of Foreign Affairs: The History of the Council on Foreign Relations.* New York: Columbia University Press, 1984.

Schuman, Frederick L. *Government in the Soviet Union.* New York: Thomas Y. Crowell, 1961.

———. *Russia Since 1917: Four Decades of Soviet Politics.* New York: Alfred A. Knopf, 1957.

Schwartz, Morton. *Soviet Perceptions of the United States.* Berkeley: University of California Press, 1978.

Sherry, Michael S. *Preparing for the Next War: American Plans for Postwar Defense, 1941–1945.* New Haven: Yale University Press, 1977.

Shoup, Laurence H. and William Minter. *Imperial Brain Trust: The Council on Foreign Relations and United States Foreign Policy.* New York: Monthly Review Press, 1977.

Simpson, Christopher. *Blowback: America's Recruitment of Nazis and Its Effect on the Cold War.* New York: Weidenfeld and Nicolson, 1988.

Sivachev, Nikolai V. and Nikolai N. Yakovlev. *Russia and the United States.* Translated by Olga A. Titlebaum. Chicago: University of Chicago Press, 1979.

Skodvin, Magne. *Nordic or North Atlantic Alliance: The Postwar Scandinavian Security Debate.* Oslo: Institutt for Forsvarsstudier, 1990.

Smith, Bruce L. R. *The RAND Corporation: Case Study of a Nonprofit Advisory Corporation.* Cambridge, Mass.: Harvard University Press, 1966.

Smith, Jean Edward. *Lucius D. Clay: An American Life.* New York: Henry Holt, 1990.

———. "The View from USFET: General Clay's and Washington's Interpretation of Soviet Intentions." *Occupation in Europe After World War II: Papers and Reminiscences from the April 23–24, 1976, Conference Held at the George C. Marshall Research Foundation, Lexington, Virginia.* Edited by Hans A. Schmitt. Lawrence, Kans.: University of Kansas Press, 1978.

Smith, Perry McCoy. *The Air Force Plans for Peace, 1943–1945.* Baltimore: Johns Hopkins Press, 1970.

Stapleton, Margaret L. *The Truman and Eisenhower Years, 1945–1960: A Selective Bibliography.* Metuchen, N.J.: Scarecrow Press, 1973.

Stein, Harold, ed. *American Civil-Military Decisions.* Birmingham: University of Alabama Press, 1963.

Steinberg, Alfred. *The Man from Missouri: The Life and Times of Harry S. Truman.* New York: Putnam, 1962.

Stockwell, Richard E. *Soviet Air Power.* New York: Pageant Press, 1956.

Stone, I. F. *The Truman Era.* New York: Monthly Review Press, 1953.

Taubman, William. *Stalin's American Policy: From Entente to Détente to Cold War.* New York: W. W. Norton, 1982.

Thayer, George. *The War Business: The International Trade in Armaments.* New York: Simon and Schuster, 1969.

Theoharis, Athan. *The Truman Presidency: The Origins of the Imperial Presidency and the National Security State.* Stanfordville, N.Y.: Earl M.Coleman Enterprises, 1979.

Truman, Margaret. *Harry S. Truman.* New York: Morrow, 1973.

Tugwell, Rexford G. *Off Course: From Truman to Nixon.* New York: Praeger, 1971.

Turnbull, Archibald D. and Clifford L. Lord. *The History of United States Naval Aviation.* New Haven: Yale University Press, 1949.

Ulam, Adam B. *The Rivals: America and Russia Since World War II.* New York: Viking Press, 1971.

Underhill, Robert. *The Truman Persuasions.* Ames, Iowa: Iowa State University Press, 1981.

Vagts, Alfred. *Defense and Diplomacy: The Soldier and the Conduct of Foreign Relations.* New York: Columbia University Press, 1956.

Van Zandt, J. Parker, ed. *World Aviation Annual for 1948.* Washington, D.C.: Aviation Research Institute, 1948.

Walton, Richard J. *Henry Wallace, Harry Truman and the Cold War.* New York: Viking Press, 1976.

Warburg, James Paul. *Last Call for Common Sense.* New York: Harcourt, Brace and Co., 1949.

Watt, D. Cameron. *Succeeding John Bull: America in Britain's Place, 1900–1975.* Cambridge: Cambridge University Press, 1984.

Weidenbaum, Murray L. "Problems of Adjustment for Defense Industries." In *Disarmament and the Economy,* edited by Emile Benoit and Kenneth E. Boulding. New York: Harper and Row, 1963.

Weigley, Russell F. *The American Way of War: A History of United States Military Strategy and Policy.* New York: Macmillan, 1973.

Wellman, Paul I. *Stuart Symington: Portrait of a Man with a Mission.* New York: Doubleday, 1960.

Wexler, Imanuel. *The Marshall Plan Revisited: The European Recovery Program in Economic Perspective.* Contributions in Economics and Economic History, no. 55. Westport, Conn.: Greenwood Press, 1983.

White, Gerald T. *Billions for Defense: Government Financing by the Defense Plant Corporation During World War II.* Birmingham: University of Alabama Press, 1980.

Whiting, Kenneth R. *Soviet Reactions to Changes in American Military Strategy.* Maxwell Air Force Base, Ala.: Air University Documentary Research Study, 1965.

Wilson, John Donald. *The Chase: The Chase Manhattan Bank, N.A., 1945–1985.* Boston: Harvard Business School Press, 1986.

Wittner, Lawrence S. *American Intervention in Greece, 1943–1949.* New York: Columbia University Press, 1982.

Wolanin, Thomas. *Presidential Advisory Commissions: Truman to Nixon.* Madison: University of Wisconsin, 1975.

Wolfe, Alan. *America's Impasse: The Rise and Fall of the Politics of Growth.* New York: Pantheon, 1981.

Wolfe, Thomas W. *Soviet Power and Europe, 1945–1970.* Baltimore: Johns Hopkins Press, 1970.

Yergin, Daniel. *Shattered Peace: The Origins of the Cold War and the National Security State.* Boston: Houghton Mifflin, 1977.

Zhdanov, Andrei A. *The International Situation.* Moscow: Foreign Languages Publishing House, 1947.

JOURNAL ARTICLES, MAGAZINE ARTICLES AND SPEECHES

Alsop, Joseph, and Stewart Alsop. "If War Comes." *Saturday Evening Post,* September 11, 1948, 15–17, 180, 182–83.

Anders, William A. "Rationalizing America's Defense Industry: Renewing Investor Support for the Defense Industrial Base and Safeguarding National Security." Keynote address by William A. Anders, chairman and chief executive officer, General Dynamics Corporation, *Defense Week* 12th annual conference, St. Louis, Missouri, October 30, 1991.

Baldwin, Hanson W. "The Myth of Security." *Foreign Affairs* 16, no. 2 (January 1948): 253–63.

———. "U.S.A. and U.S.S.R.—An Assay of Strength." *New York Times Magazine,* September 24, 1950, 9, 68–72.

———. "What Air Power Can—and Cannot—Do." *New York Times Magazine,* May 30, 1948, 5–7, 20–21.

Bergson, Abram. "Russian Defense Expenditures." *Foreign Affairs* 16, no. 2 (January 1948): 373–76.

Bernstein, Barton J. "The Automobile Industry and the Coming of the Second World War." *The Southwestern Social Science Quarterly* 47, no. 1 (June 1966): 22–33.

———. "The Debate on Industrial Reconversion: The Protection of Oligopoly and Military Control of the Economy." *American Journal of Economics and Sociology* 26, no. 2 (April 1967): 159–72.

———. "The Removal of War Production Board Controls on Business, 1944–1946." *Business History Review* 39, no. 2 (Summer 1965): 243–60.

Bradley, Omar N. "This Way Lies Peace." *Saturday Evening Post,* October 15, 1949, 33, 168–70.

Cooke, Admiral Charles M., USN (Ret.). "Soldiers Need Wings: The Development of Ground Air Forces." *Foreign Affairs* 27, no. 4 (July 1949): 576–585.

Dulles, John F. "The General Assembly." *Foreign Affairs* 24, no. 1 (October 1945): 1–11.

Evangelista, Matthew A. "Stalin's Postwar Army Reappraised." *International Security* 7, no. 3 (Winter 1982–1983): 110–138.

Friedman, Saul. "The RAND Corporation and Our Policy Makers." *The Atlantic Monthly,* September 1963, 61–68.

Griffith, Robert. "Truman and the Historians: The Reconstruction of Postwar American History. *Wisconsin Magazine of History* 51, no. 1 (Autumn 1975): 20–50.

Hanieski, John F. "The Airplane as an Economic Variable: Aspects of Technological Change in Aeronautics, 1903–1955." *Technology and Culture* 14, no. 4 (October 1973): 535–52.

Irwin, R. Randall. "A Crucial Industry: Aircraft." *Annals of the American Academy of Political and Social Science* 238 (March 1945): 140–45.

Kupinsky, Mannie. "Growth of Aircraft and Parts Industry, 1939–1954." *Monthly Labor Review* 77, no. 12 (December 1954): 1320–26.

Lamont, Corliss. "Incitements to War Against Soviet Russia." *Soviet Russia Today,* November 1948, 12–13, 33.

Leffler, Melvyn P. "The American Conception of National Security and the Beginnings of the Cold War." *American Historical Review* 89 (April 1984): 346–81.

Lo, Clarence Y. H. "Military Spending as Crisis Management: The U.S. Response to the Berlin Blockade and the Korean War." *Berkeley Journal of Sociology* 20 (1975–1976): 147–81.

———."The Conflicting Functions of United States Military Spending After World War II." *Kapitalistate,* no. 3 (1975): 26–44.

———. "Theories of the State and Business Opposition to Increased Military Spending." *Social Problems* 29, no. 4 (April 1982): 424–38.

Messer, Robert L. "New Evidence on Truman's Decision." *Bulletin of the Atomic Scientists* 46, no. 7 (August 1985): 50–56.

———. "Paths Not Taken: The United States Department of State and Alternatives to Containment, 1945–1946." *Diplomatic History* 1, no. 4 (Fall 1977): 297–319.

Middleton, Drew. "Do the Men in the Kremlin Want War?" *New York Times Magazine,* March 28, 1948, 7, 20–23.

Mrozek, Donald J. "The Truman Administration and the Enlistment of the Aviation Industry in Postwar Defense." *Business History Review* 48, no. 1 (Spring 1974): 73–94.

Paterson, Thomas Graham. "Presidential Foreign Policy, Public Opinion, and Congress: The Truman Years." *The Journal of Diplomatic History* 3, no. 1 (Winter 1979): 1–18.

Patterson, David S. "Recent Literature on Cold War Origins: An Essay Review." *Wisconsin Magazine of History* 55, no. 4 (Summer 1972): 320–29.

Powell, John W. "Japan's Biological Weapons: 1930–1945." *Bulletin of the Atomic Scientists* 37 (October 1981): 43–53.

———. "Japan's Germ Warfare: The U.S. Cover-up of a War Crime." *Bulletin of Concerned Asian Scholars* 12 (October–December 1980): 2–17.

Robinson, Donald. "They Fight the Cold War Under Cover." *Saturday Evening Post,* November 20, 1948, 30, 191, 194.

Roose, Diana. "Top Dogs and Top Brass: An Inside Look at a Government Advisory Committee." *Insurgent Sociologist* 5, no. 3 (Spring 1975): 53–63.

Spaatz, General Carl, USAF (Ret.). "If We Should Have to Fight Again." *Life,* July 5, 1948, 35–44.

———. "Strategic Air Power." *Foreign Affairs* 24, no. 3 (April 1946): 385–396.

Stimson, Henry L. "The Challenge to Americans." *Foreign Affairs* 26, no. 1 (October 1947): 5–14.

Wallace, Henry. "Terrorism at Evansville." *The New Republic,* April 19, 1948, p. 11.

Ward, Barbara. "Europe Debates Nationalization." *Foreign Affairs* 15, no. 1 (October 1946), 44–58.

Yergin, Daniel. "The Arms Zealots." *Harper's,* June 1977, 64–76.

UNPUBLISHED DISSERTATIONS AND PAPERS

Baker, Francis J. "The Death of the Flying Wing: The Real Reasons Behind the 1949 Cancellation of Northrop Aircraft's RB-49." Ph.D. dissertation in the Graduate Faculty of Executive Management, Claremont Graduate School, 1984.

Eakins, David W. "The Development of Corporate Liberal Policy Research in the United States, 1885–1965." Ph.D. dissertation, University of Wisconsin, 1966.

Fanton, Jonathan Foster. "Robert A. Lovett: The War Years," Ph.D. dissertation, Yale University, 1978.

Mrozek, Donald John. "Peace Through Strength: Strategic Air Power and the Mobilization of the United States for the Pursuit of Foreign Policy, 1945–1955." Ph.D. dissertation, Rutgers University, 1972.

Paterson, Thomas Graham. "The Economic Cold War: American Business and Economic Foreign Policy, 1945–1950." Ph.D. dissertation, University of California, Berkeley, 1968.

Simonelli, Frederick J. "Chase National Bank and the Arsenal of Democracy: Financial Interests, Military Appropriations and Political Influence, 1945–1948." Graduate research paper, California State University, Sacramento, 1990.

Wilson, Donald Edward. "The History of President Truman's Air Policy Commission, and Its Influence on Air Policy 1947–1949." Ph.D. dissertation, University of Denver, 1978.

Wolff, William Marx, Jr. "Peak Business Associations in National Politics: The Business Council and the Committee for Economic Development." Ph.D. dissertation, Tufts University, 1978.

INDEX